Transforming Communication

Leading-edge professional and personal skills
Third edition

Dr Richard Bolstad

Transformations International Consulting & Training
PO Box 35111, Browns Bay, Auckland 0753, New Zealand
www.transformations.net.nz

Transforming Communication:
Leading-edge professional and personal skills

Publishing history:
Author: Richard Bolstad
Cross-cultural consultants: Robin and Sharron Fabish
Previously published as Communicating Caring by Longman Paul 1992
Reprinted 1994
First edition pubishd by Addison Wesley Longman New Zealand Limited 1997
Reprinted 1999
Reprinted by Pearson Education New Zealand 2000, 2001, 2002, 2003, 2003
Second edition published 2004
Reprinted 2006, 2007, 2008, 2010, 2010, 2011, 2013

ISBN 13: 9781519663719

Transforming Communication: Contents

He Tauparapara

Tini whetu ki te Rangi Ko nga whakaaro hou taka haere Ki Papatuanuku Hei kakano mo nga aitanga Whakatupu, whakarapu Ka werohia Ka whakapoutamahia Ka tu te tangata Mana motuhake.

Just as there are multitudes of stars in Father sky, so there are new thoughts roaming Mother earth: seeds for descendants growing and searching. By challenging; they progress until they are able to stand tall in their own uniqueness.- Te Hata Ohlson

The Author

Richard Bolstad is a father and grandfather. He has taught communication skills to parents, teachers, health professionals, counsellors and business people. Richard has a doctorate in Clinical Hypnotherapy and is a nurse (RCpN), teacher (Dip Tchg Tert), psychotherapist (NZAP), herbalist (Dip Herb) and a certified instructor in Chi Kung (traditional Chinese exercises). He is a master practitioner and trainer (IANLP, INLPA, IN) in Neuro Linguistic Programming (NLP). With his wife Julia Kurusheva, he runs training courses each year in New Zealand, Asia, America, Africa and Europe. The original draft of this book was written with his partner Margot Hamblett, who died in 2001, and with cross-cultural advice from Te Hata Ohlson and Jan Hardie. This current text was written with advice from Robin Fabish (Ngäti Maniapoto) and Sharron Fabish (nee Koopu, Te Whänau a Apanui, Ngäti Kahungunu) Robin and Sharron have three children whom they learn a great deal from, in the application of the Transforming Communication skills! Robin is the principal at Tamatea High School, Napier and has taught the Transforming Communication model to company managers and to primary and secondary teachers. Sharron is a Professional Learning and Development Practitioner with the University of Auckland.

Preface
Communication - a beginning

In a way, your reading this preface is like a meeting between you, the reader, and me, the writer. In that sense it's important that I welcome you to this book.

I'm sure you'll discover that what you have in front of you will not only give you the opportunity to learn how to communicate better when you are working with others; it will also be almost impossible to read without learning how to enjoy your life more, discovering new ways to make your dreams become realities and becoming more fully who you are. I am sure of this because I know how my own life has changed over the last 50 years, as I have discovered the things you'll read about here.

When someone claims to teach "communication skills', or writes a book about how people get on with each other, I'm always curious to know how they themselves get on with others. If they're going to help me, can they do it themselves? And anyway, what do they mean by 'good communication'? Well, the reasons I have written this book are most importantly because I treasure life with my family; because I enjoy my friendships, both professional and personal, and because I so much appreciate the human interaction that my job requires. Each day I wake up looking forward to excitement, relaxation, love and a sense of abundance. To me these are the most important successes I could ask for, and I have a very genuine sense of gratitude, and sometimes even of amazement, as I think of them. Gratitude because I know that it is not luck that has led me to them, but the skills explained in this book.

I have had the opportunity to train as a nurse, a teacher, and a psychotherapist; to be a parent, a marital partner and a business manager. What you are about to read is the heart of what I learned in each of those roles. You too may have chosen to work in a profession involving people, or in a helping role. In that case I know something of your underlying affection for people and your willingness to meet the needs of others as well as needs of your own. You have probably wondered how you can keep that caring and openness alive in the day-to-day realities of the years ahead. In this book we will learn how to ensure it not only stays alive, but flowers.

You won't be learning tricks involving how to manipulate others, or theories that have to be ignored so you can survive in the real world. You will be learning how to make contact with others in their own way; how to see what people mean, and how to present yourself so that they can see what you mean. You will find out how to help both yourself and others set goals and actually achieve the kind of success that really counts; how to stick up for your own rights and explain your opinions without putting others down; even how to help a group function fluently. As we progress, you'll learn to celebrate the diversity of people, based on factors such as culture and gender.

Obviously, all this will help in your job. You could even choose to use this as 'just' a textbook. But why sell yourself short? You deserve to enjoy the fruits of good communication throughout your life. So why not take the time right now to get a sense of what it would be like to have those skills I mentioned above as fully as you want? This is something you can do especially well if you actually create an image in your mind of what your life will look like once you've learned the skills discussed in this book. Imagine yourself with these abilities - picture where you work and what you do, who you live with and how, the way you behave and how others respond to you. Make that picture as big and as bright as you would like, and tell yourself just how worthwhile it is for you to learn to communicate. Now, just for a moment, put this book down and actually take the time to imagine this future you, before you go on to the next sentence.

As you engage in this kind of imaginative process, you begin to feel some of the sense of delight that you can experience when you read this book. Now you'll be able to read playfully, enjoying the journey, but seriously as well, knowing the incredible potential you have. You'll be able to experiment, trying things out, disagreeing with us when it suits you, and still taking out exactly what you need to create that future you've imagined.

I wanted this book to have a personal style and have therefore used the first person('I' and 'me') throughout. Many of the examples are experiences from my own life. However, I am not the only author of this book. Margot Hamblett wrote sections of the original text from which it evolved, including the sections relating to women's issues. Te Hata Ohlson, Jan Hardie, Robin Fabish and Sharron Fabish reviewed the book and provided important insights about cultural difference specific to the New Zealand context. And finally, my wife Julia Kurusheva contributed further important insights to its development. The richness of this book comes from our collective experience.

Leading-edge discoveries and Neuro Linguistic Programming (NLP)

In updating this book two decades after the first edition, I draw on the experience of teaching communication skills to thousands of people around the world. I have made sure to check how the very latest research confirms my original models. I also share with you leading-edge disco\ human relationships, and new skills to help you live the life y many of them from the field of Neuro Linguistic Programming (l of several international communication skills models of which I am ...ier.

NLP is the study of how people do things well. It began in the 1970s when linguistics professor John Grinder and his colleague Richard Bandler began researching the specific communication skills used by excellent communicators. This process of studying success itself, which they called modelling, led them to a series of remarkable discoveries.

At first, I was very sceptical about the claims of NLP. However, research now suggests that NLP techniques can, amongst other things, increase visual memory by 60 per cent, resolve lifelong disorders such as phobias and many allergies in one session, and boost sales in large corporations by 250 per cent*. Small wonder NLP is being used by large businesses, trauma treatment clinics, medical practitioners, teachers and others.

The first models studied by Grinder and Bandler were excellent communicators, and it's here that our attention focuses. One thing that really impressed me in my experience of John Grinder's training, for example, was his ongoing commitment to effective, clear, mutually supportive communication. How do people create close, loving relationships? How do they resolve conflicts and cooperate successfully? How do they assist others to change? No one professional group deserves to 'own' these skills. They belong to all of us.

* *http://nlpwiki.org/wiki*

A note about the activities

To enable you to enjoy learning through experience, and to find out exactly how the processes described work for you, I have included many activities and practice examples throughout the book. Some of these activities are described for you to do individually, some to be done in pairs or groups. If you are using this book individually, I would suggest that you can easily adapt most of these activities for use as individual learning experiences.

Richard Bolstad 2015

Legal owners of this book can download it in PDF form from www.transformations.net.nz/tcbook.html

PART ONE

The Heart of Communication

Chapter 1. Getting in contact

KEY CONCEPTS .

- Developing realistic beliefs about meeting people
- Group warm-up and group contracts
- Effects of culture: Maori, Pakeha, Japanese and Chinese welcomes

Introducing yourself

AIM: to be able to initiate and maintain a two-minute conversation with someone you've just met.

Starting out

Have you ever wondered how some people make such a powerful positive impression at first meetings? In 1964 Nelson Mandela was sent to South Africa's feared Robben Island prison for life. At the age of 46, locked in a six-foot-wide cell, Mandela was hardly in the ideal place to begin friendships. But today, some of his warders say they became both friends and admirers there (Mandela, 1994). Warrant officer Swart, for example, learned English from him, and in return taught Mandela Afrikaans. He later described their friendship as the most important one in his life.

New Zealand's Dame Whina Cooper was the leader of indigenous Maori land protests, and was foundation president of the Maori Women's Welfare League (King, 1991).

But her first public meeting was almost a disaster. A Maori woman stood up and angrily called out, asking just who Cooper thought she was, coming round the country 'telling us what to do'. It was every speaker's nightmare and, as the meeting grew tense, an older delegate offered to field the complaint. However, Whina Cooper responded with energy: *'I am so pleased to hear somebody talk like that, because when I hear something like that I know our Maori women will always be strong, will always be leaders...'. Having thus acknowledged the woman's concern and congratulated her for speaking, Cooper went on to emphasise that her only intention was to serve the women of New Zealand who had chosen her 'to knit the people together'. Immediately the challenger and the meeting swung behind her, and her career as a public speaker had begun.

In 1964, psychologist Carl Rogers agreed to be filmed in a half-hour counselling session with a woman named Gloria (Rogers, 1965). During these 30 minutes he simply sat down and talked to Gloria, whom he had never met before. Despite the brevity of the conversation, Gloria maintained that those minutes had profoundly affected her life, and kept in contact by mail with Dr Rogers for the next eight years.

What was the magic which enabled these three people to have such an impact on people they had just met? It was what communications experts have since come to call rapport - a sense of mutual understanding and "at oneness' which close friends often experience routinely. Can it be learned? Absolutely! You can have that same extraordinary effect in your job, in building friendships and in your family.

Over the next three chapters you'll learn the structure of rapport. We'll begin by collecting some important ideas about how to start a conversation or a relationship with someone. Later in the book we'll revisit these 'choices for talk' and explain them in detail. So for now, you don't have to be an expert in these methods. The aim is merely to have enough ideas to be able to start a conversation or meet someone new.

An introduction is not 'just' an introduction. A great deal of research shows that the first four minutes with someone are crucial. Therefore I encourage you to make sure you've read my Preface - it's your introduction to me.

The need for meeting

Those of you who work with people, in particular, will want to be able to meet them in a way that immediately conveys welcoming and quickly creates rapport. A health professional, for example, is often required to interact with clients at an intimate, private level only minutes after meeting them. He or she needs to build high-quality communication quickly.

A businessperson may be expected to negotiate issues which involve a client's entire economic success in a similarly short time after meeting.

And yet for many people, to achieve any form of communication is difficult. I worked as a counsellor with the phone-in line *Men's-line* in Christchurch. In our first year, we discovered that the most common problem men rang us about was loneliness. Some of these men did not know where to meet people or what to say to begin a conversation with a stranger. Others, however, were married men - having someone in the house is not a guarantee of good communication! If you have ever been at a party where you know only one or two people, you'll be aware that it's quite possible to be lonely in a crowd.

Beliefs about introductions

Everything we study in this book will be useful as you set out to meet people, but for now the following is crucial: what you say to *yourself* before you meet someone, and what you say to *them* when you do meet.

Most people who *don't* often make contact with others have some unpleasant beliefs about what will happen if they do. They quite often tell themselves that:

1. People want to be left alone. They don't want to talk to me.
2. If I approach someone who doesn't want to talk to me, a disaster will happen.
3. Most other people are totally confident and totally in charge in social meeting situations. They will therefore be able to watch me and hear what I say from a critical perspective.
4. If someone is able to notice what I'm doing and mentally criticise it, a disaster will happen.

New beliefs

Sounds familiar? The best one could say about these beliefs is that they make some fairly big assumptions about people we don't even know yet. If you have shared these assumptions, you might like to remind yourself of more realistic beliefs, such as:

1. Although people do *sometimes* want to be left alone, more often they enjoy meeting others.
2. If I approach someone who doesn't want to talk to me, I can easily back off and find someone else to meet, knowing I have given myself an extra opportunity to practise introducing myself.
3. Most people are much more aware of their own needs and of working out what they will say when they meet me, rather than theorising about me.
4. If someone is aware of what I'm doing and even disapproves of it, this can actually be an interesting chance to meet this person at a new level.

You will certainly feel different about meeting people depending on your set of beliefs.

Map and territory

The fact that people can have such widely different beliefs about the same situations reminds us of a very basic principle of communication: what people *believe is* happening in a situation - their internal feelings, images and the way they talk to themselves - is not the same as the actual situation. Put another way, *the map in your head is not the territory.*

People get information about the territory they live in through their eyes, ears, nose, tongue, skin, and so on. Then they filter that information through their own experiences and beliefs and organise it into their own internal map of the world (what we'll later call their 'internal representations').

A person locked in jail may have a physical challenge meeting people. Their territory is limited. The challenge most of us have, though, is that our *map* of the territory is limited. It's not what *happens* that holds us back, but our *beliefs* about what happens. The core challenge in communication is people's belief that they know what others are thinking without having to check it out.

Psychologists Daniel Simons and Daniel Levin conducted an extraordinary study in the 1990s to demonstrate how our brain fools us into seeing what we expect to see. Imagine you are walking down the street and a stranger stops to ask you for directions. While you're talking to him, two men pass between you carrying a large wooden door. After they move on, you finish giving the directions, and the stranger advises you that you've just been the subject of a psychology experiment. He asks you if you noticed anything odd after the men with the door passed between you. He then explains that he is not really the person who asked you for directions! The original person who asked for directions actually walked off behind the door, and was replaced by your current interviewer. The original man now re-appears; he is a different height and build, has different clothes on, and has a different voice. But amazingly, 50% of people approached in this way do not notice the substitution occurring (Simons and Levin, 1998). What they "see" is not just what is in front of their eyes. It is even more a result of what they expect to see.

Research on the brain shows how we filter experiences and take our own meanings out of them (creating our own maps). Consider the case of what people "see" in the experiment above, as an example. When the person being interviewed sees the interviewer, messages from the retina of the eye go back into the brain to an area called the lateral geniculate body, where they are combined with information from a number of other places in the brain. The results are then sent on to the visual cortex, the part of the brain where "seeing" happens. Only 20% of the flow of information into the lateral geniculate body comes from the eyes. Most of the information that will be organised to create what you "see" comes from areas such as the hypothalamus, a mid-brain centre which has a key role in storing memories and creating emotions (Maturana and Varela, 1992, p 162). What we "see" is more a result of the emotional state we are in, and of our expectations based on what we remember happening to us before. These emotions and memories are more powerful than what is actually in front of our eyes.

Activity 1. 1

AIM: To recognize the way beliefs (or maps) change the way we feel about and respond to situations.

Imagine yourself in the following situation: you are waiting in class for your group leader/teacher to appear. She is now half an hour late.

Divide into five groups and number each from one to five. Each group should read the correspondingly numbered belief below (and none of the others).

Assuming that you accept the belief, discuss in your group how *you feel* in this situation.

- Group 1. You've noticed that the teacher seems to be taking a very casual attitude lately, and you suspect she may have not bothered to turn up. Find a word to describe how you feel about her not having arrived.

- Group 2. You saw the teacher earlier in town on her bike, and think she may have had an accident. Find a word to describe how you feel about her not having arrived.
- Group 3. You seem to recall that the teacher gave you this session off. You have turned up unnecessarily. Find a word to describe how you feel in this situation.
- Group 4. You can't quite remember what the arrangements were for this session. Perhaps you were to meet somewhere else today, or perhaps this session was cancelled. You're not sure what you believe about this. Find a word to describe how you feel about the teacher not having arrived.
- Group 5. You've developed the impression that your teacher is rather shy, and finding it difficult to cope with the sessions. Find a word to describe how you feel about her not having arrived.

Now get together in one large group and share your words to describe the feelings you had in that same situation. Were they the same? If not, how would this have affected your actions if the teacher had eventually arrived?

Most people are not aware that every 'situation' they are in is actually an internally generated map of the real world events. In order to understand a situation, we always create our own model or image of what actually exists.

Practice

Giving yourself the opportunity to meet people will enable you to form a whole new map of what that's like, and you can *feel* differently about it as a result. If simply talking is difficult for, you, you can experiment several times over the next week as follows:

Smile and say "Hello' to people you pass in your work or study situation. Phone a library, a citizens' advice bureau, a cinema or a department store to ask for information about their services. Make brief, safe conversational statements in a place where you need to wait with others (for example a bus stop, a supermarket queue, a cinema queue or a waiting room). A comment about the situation is fine (for example in a supermarket: "Seems to take longer and longer doesn't it? Do you know what is the quietest time here?'; in a cinema queue: 'Well, there are plenty of people here. Have you heard what the movie's like?).

In such situations some people may be surprised enough not to respond, but in most cases you will get an encouraging reply.

What to say

What people actually say when beginning a conversation will vary of course. But the most powerful and engaging comments fit into three basic categories. It helps to be able to:

1. Say things about yourself

a. *Introduce yourself:* 'Hello, my name's...'

b. *Ask for what you want:* 'May I sit here?', 'What's happened at the meeting so far?', 'I was trying to find the cafeteria before. Do you know where it is?'

c. *Say something about how you are right now:* ' I've just started my course and don't know anyone here', 'I've been studying all day and really need a break'

2. Say things about the other person

a. *Ask about them:* 'Where are you from?', "What kind of work do you do?', 'How has your day been?'

b. *Offer assistance when needed:* 'I'm just getting a cup of tea. Can I get you anything?', 'Here, let me help you with that'

c. *Acknowledge what the other person has said:* 'Sounds like you had a good day', 'So you're new here too'

d. *Offer genuine compliments* (these may be followed by a question to make them easier to reply to): 'That's a nice jacket, where did you get it?', 'You seem to know your way around here well. Have you been here for a while?'

3. Say things about shared experiences. For example: ' I see you're doing the same course as me.', 'It has been incredibly hot lately hasn't it?', "Did you watch that programme on body language on TV last night?'

The point is not to memorise all these topics, but to read through them now and choose which options you would like to be able to add to your choices. Then you can practise them. Good communication is about giving yourself more effective choices.

Three meetings

In the following example, someone is initiating a conversation in a traditional meeting place (a bar). Notice which of the above skills they use to do that.

Robin: Hello. Id like to join you for a drink if that's OK.
Gina: Ah. Sure.
Robin: *My* name's Robin.
Gina (nods, then points to herself): Gina.
Robin: I've just started a welding course at the Polytech this month. What do you do with yourself, Gina?
Gina: Well, I work as a cleaner in a department store. It"s OK, but it doesn't leave me much time in the evenings.
Robin: I'm glad to have caught you on an evening off then.
Gina (laughing): *You* haven't 'caught me' yet. Anyway, I don't usually bother going out, but tonight just felt like a break.

In the next example a nurse is introducing herself to a client. Once again, check which of the topics the nurse uses to initiate conversation:

Nurse (entering room and pulling back the curtain): Good morning Mrs Upton. I'm Jo Adamson and I'll be looking after you today.

Mrs Upton: Oh, good morning.
Nurse (seeing Mrs Upton attempting to sit up in bed and moving to assist): Can Ihelp you with that pillow?
Mrs Upton: Thank you. I feel so frail having to be moved around like this.
Nurse: It is hard to get used to isnt it? Luckily it's just for a few days until the incision heals. How are you sleeping?
Mrs Upton: Oh, alright I guess. I find the ward very warm you know.
Nurse: Yes, so do 1. Does it mean you don't get to sleep till late, or do you have a sort of restless night?
Mrs Upton: Oh no, I'm getting to sleep. But I still feel tired in the morning when I wake, and I think that"s the heat. So last night I got the nurse to open that window there. I hope that's alright.
Nurse: Certainly. Good for you. It helps me to do my job better when you're able to tell me what you need. Well, I'll be back to take you for your shower after breakfast. OK?

One thing both of these conversations have in common is their simplicity. It's not really necessary to have a lot of fancy lines to start talking to someone - you only need a few basic ideas.

Here is how Dr Carl Rogers began that extraordinary conversation which Gloria felt changed her life. Notice again that same simplicity, as he uses similar comments to those in the three categories we discussed (Rogers 1965) :

Carl Rogers: Good morning.
Gloria: How are you Doctor?
Carl Rogers (overlapping her comment): I'm Doctor Rogers. You must be Gloria.
Gloria: Yes I am.
Carl Rogers: Won't you have this chair? *(They sit down.)* Well now, we have half an hour together, and I really don't know what we'll be able to make of it, but I hope you can make something of it.- I'd be glad to know whatever concerns you.
Gloria: Well, I'm .... right now I'm nervous, but I feel more comfortable the way you're talking in a low voice, and I don't feel like you'll be so harsh on me. But, ah...
Carl Rogers: I hear the tremor in your voice, so I'm aware
Gloria: Ah, well the main thing I want to talk to you about is: I'm just newly divorced…

Even in these first few comments Gloria draws our attention to another important part of meeting people, when she says: 'I feel more comfortable the way you're talking in a low voice'. As you develop your ability to initiate a conversation, you'll want to know more than just: 'What do I say?' - you'll be curious about how you say it. And that's exactly what we go on to deal with in Chapter 2.

Activity 1.2

AIM: To investigate different ways of initiating conversations.

1. Begin with everyone walking around the room, weaving in and out of the others, attempting to walk into any empty spaces you see. Once everyone is moving, greet each person you meet with a smile. After a minute or so, greet each person with "Hello'. After another couple of minutes greet each other by shaking hands or by touching elbow to elbow.

2. Next, find a partner (preferably someone you don't know well) and sit down in pairs. Take 2.5 minutes each to introduce yourself to your partner by talking about 'what I hope to get out of attending this course'.

3. Change partners and pair off again, this time introducing yourself by talking for 2.5 minutes each about 'the most significant, positive experience I have had recently'.

4. Change partners and introduce yourselves by talking about 'who I am as a person'.

5. (Optional) Other topics for pairs could include: 'the person I get on best with'; 'the ways in which you and I are similar or different'; 'the movie I most enjoyed'.

6. Get together in one large group and share:
- which activity or topic was most helpful in getting to know the person you were with?
- what other topics do you need to discuss to get to know someone well?
- how would you need to modify the list of topics if you were thinking about meeting people in your professional situation?

7. (Optional) Choose the most popular topic, and get each person to introduce themselves to the whole group by saying a few sentences about it.

Activity 1.3

AIM: to recognise how beliefs about people we meet affect our meeting

1. Get into pairs and take turns making statements to each other beginning with the words: 'It's obvious to me that..., followed by something you have seen or heard regarding your partner (for example: 'It's obvious to me that you are wearing a red jersey').

2. Next, take turns making statements that begin: 'I guess that.. .', followed by something you can guess about the other person based on what you've seen or heard (for example: "I guess you're feeling tired').

3. Next, make statements beginning: 'I guess you can tell...' followed by something you think the other person knows about you (for example: 'I guess you can tell that I'm aged about 20').

4. Finally, make statements beginning: 'I hope you can tell...', followed by something you would like the other person to know about you (for example: 'I hope you can tell that I'm interested in getting to know you').

5. Discuss, still in your pairs, what this activity was like.

6. Come back to the main group and discuss the following:
- were people's guesses always correct?
- if not, in what ways did their guesses vary from reality?
- how might this affect our meeting people?
- what effect did making these statements have on your feeling of closeness to the other person in your pair?

Warm-up

AIM: to be able to describe the need for warm-up to a group, and suggest at least four specific activities to meet this need.

What is warm-up?

In 1980 1 attended a *Leadership Skills Laboratory* seminar run by counsellor George Sweet and others. I had only met a couple of the course participants before, and had no idea what to expect from the course apart from information provided in the enrolment form.

After only five days, I felt as if each person in the group was dear to me, and there were tears in my eyes as I prepared to leave. Furthermore, I had made a commitment to change almost every relationship in my life, based on the principles that the course taught. I had formed a friendship with George which was to be the basis of a whole career change. And I had learned some of the most central concepts which I now share with you in this book.

It's interesting to ask what makes a group work so well together that people's lives can be changed by it over as brief a time as five days. In fact, how do people who have never met before get to feel like a 'group'? The answer is warm-up. If your job involves working in a group (with clients or with colleagues), if you ever plan to live in a group (such as a family), then the process of warm-up is essential for you to understand.

Two questions

To understand the meaning of the term 'warm-up', let me remind you what it's like at first to be part of a group. Think of a group you've joined (perhaps when you started a new school or a new job). At such a time, people have two sets of questions paramount in their minds. The first is:

Who is here?

Will they like me? and
Will I like them?

The second set is:

What will we do here?
What are the rules? and
What will I get out of it?

People joining any group put a lot of energy into trying to find the answers to these sets of questions. If they find satisfactory answers to the first set (the 'who' questions) they develop a sense of cohesion. The group feels together because people see each other as likeable and trustworthy. If they then find satisfactory answers to the second set (the 'what' questions), they develop a sense of contract. The group knows what results to expect from its time together, and is committed to getting those results.

Answering the two questions

It's not a good idea to leave it to chance whether people get satisfactory answers to these questions. When group members don't feel connected to each other or don't know what to expect from their time together, they often give up. Also, they may keep trying to sound out the situation, make links to others and s e what's going on while the group is trying to do its task.

It makes more sense to set aside time at the start to actually answer both sets of questions. Time to introduce people; time to discuss what will be going on in the group and what its aims are. Once this has been done, the rest of the group's task will be accomplished much quicker.

If you plan to help a group work well, it is most important that you arrange some time to discuss these issues. It may be as simple as having a meal together and discussing it. Or it may involve doing some of the following specific activities.

Activity 1.4

AIM: to learn each others' names and begin creating a sense of group cohesion

Here is choice of group activities:

1. Introducing a friend

Get into pairs (perhaps by finding someone of similar height or by turning to the person beside you), and take four minutes to learn each others' names and reasons for coming on the_course. Then return to sitting in a circle and, in no particular order, take turns to introduce your partner to the group. Partners may correct or add information as they are introduced.

2. Adjective and name
Choose an adjective which begins with the same letter as your name (the adjective does not have to suit your personality). For example: "Able Adam', 'Intelligent Imelda'. One at a time, introduce yourselves to the group by this adjective and name. As you go round the group, each person should recite all the names created so far and then add their own. Examples of adjectives are: adaptable, accepting, bold, boisterous, calm, carefree, dependable, determined, energetic, elegant, friendly, fair, gentle, giving, happy, helpful, imaginative, intelligent, jovial, jaunty, kind, keen, lively, loving, merry, mature, notable, nice, observant, organised, playful, powerful, quick, questioning, relaxed, reliable, satisfied, sociable, trustworthy, thoughtful, understanding, upright, visionary, valuable, warm, wise, xenophilic (liking strangers), youthful, yummy, zestful, zealous.

3. Cushion toss
In this activity, someone begins by tossing a small cushion to someone else in the group, calling out that person's name as they do so. (At first people will choose to toss to those whose names they recall. Later they can try for those they are less certain of. After everyone has had two or three turns, most of the names will be known.) The person catching the cushion says 'Thank you...', giving the name of the person who threw it to them, and then calls out the name of the person they are throwing it to.

4. Imaginary map
Stand on an imaginary map of New Zealand (or whichever country you are in) by placing yourselves either where you come from, or somewhere you feel most connected to. (This requires a large floor space. Distort geography as appropriate, for example by putting other countries nearby if needed.) Each person should then talk about where they are standing and why.

5. Circle activities
If you have at least ten people, there are many introductory group activities that begin by standing in a circle. Some examples:

Hold hands and close your eyes, then attempt to form a square and then a triangle, each time without talking or opening your eyes, until you "sense' you have the right shape.

Everyone turn to the right and give the person in front of you a shoulder massage (if you're not sure how, check what the person behind you is doing).

Still facing the person on your right, move the circle in tighter, and all sit down on the knees of the person behind you (the bigger the group and the tighter the circle, the easier this task).

The circle is a common cultural symbol of togetherness, and these activities emphasise that symbolism.

6. 'Everyone who...'

This is a kind of cooperative musical chairs. Seat everyone on chairs in a circle (facing inward), and remove one chair so that one person is standing in the centre. This person then makes a statement beginning: ‘everyone who...', and describing some quality that at least some group members will have in common (for example: "everyone who is wearing something blue', or 'everyone who had toast for breakfast this morning'). All the people for whom this statement is true must stand up and quickly try and sit down in a different chair. The person in the centre is also aiming to sit in a chair at this time. If they succeed, a new person will be in the centre ready to think up the next 'everyone who...' statement.

7. Many of the other group activities described later in the book (for example the 'trust toss' described in Chapter 2) are good for building cohesion, too.

Activity 1.5

AIM: to create a sense of contract about how the group sessions are run

A group contract can here be seen as a list of agreements about how the group will work together rather than what members will learn. An example of such an agreement could be: having some understanding about confidentiality, so people feel safe discussing how they've used communication skills in their life without having the world told about it.

1. Get into pairs and discuss what you would like included in such a contract.

2. The group leader, or a member of the group, should collect ideas from each pair, writing them up on a whiteboard or sheet of paper. At this time do

not debate or clarify the ideas; simply collect them for later consideration. Finally, the group leader should add his or her own ideas.

3. As a group, go through the list of ideas one by one, checking:

- Do you understand what is meant by each idea? (The person who suggested it can explain.)
- Do you agree with it? Attempt to reach agreement and leave for later any ideas that cannot be agreed on.

4. Decide as a group who will be responsible for ensuring that this list of agreements is being put into practice. Except for a very few matters (for example making sure the class gets through the course outline), the whole group can be encouraged to be collectively responsible for keeping the contract working.

5. Either keep the sheet of paper on which the list was written and bring it to future sessions, or copy out the list and give a photocopy to all group members.

A group warms up

How did this warm-up process work at the *Leadership Skills Laboratory I* mentioned earlier? We began with cups of tea and coffee, and sat in a circle for introductions. The three leaders introduced themselves first, after which the participants did the same. Next, the group divided into three smaller sections, each of which planned a 30-minute introductory event 'to introduce us to one another to commence the life of the group'. Each section then ran its introductory event with the whole group.

After this, we got into pairs to discuss our expectations and goals for the course. When we returned to the main group, we collected these and discussed guidelines or standards for working together. The leaders suggested:

- work in the here and now
- speak for yourself
- make statements not questions
- confidentiality

The group agreed with these and added:

- remain flexible about these guidelines
- respect and support the feelings of others

- be responsible for ourselves
- encourage experimental behaviour.

Two examples

As we look at two other examples of groups' first meetings, check for yourself how these particular groups are meeting their needs for *cohesion* and *contract.*

The playgroup

Sally (a mother of two pre-school-age children) was invited by her friend Annette to come over and discuss setting up a playgroup for local children and their parents. There were five parents at that first get-together, and Annette had made hot drinks and scones.

A woman who helped run another playgroup started the discussion. She began by checking that everyone knew each others' names. There was one person whose name Sally was unsure of, so they reintroduced themselves.

The woman went on to explain how her playgroup was run, and that led to a discussion about the best times to run it. They decided on Mondays, from 1 pm to 2.30 pm, which gave two of the parents time to get back for school-age kids.

Someone asked what they would do about "discipline', and it was agreed that individual parents would try and supervise their own children, at least at first. Because Annette's house had the biggest main room, it was proposed to hold the playgroup there for now. Before leaving, people made a list of the toys they could bring, and Sally offered to bake a cake for the first session.

The IDS Financial Services pilot team

IDS Financial Services is a large-scale American financial corporation. Founded in 1894 in Minneapolis, it decided in the 1990s to change to self-managing teams. (This story is written up in the book *Business Without Bosses* by Charles Manz and Henry Sims.)

The first team to be set up was called the Pilot Team, and it had 27 members. One of the first things the members discovered about working as a team was that they were expected to run their own affairs. Someone who had been a filing clerk all their life was now expected to be able to write a letter or make arrangements over the phone with another team. The team therefore decided to find out who had what skills, so they could plan how to share them. One person was given the job of team facilitator, and part of their job was to help connect people up with those who had the skills they needed.

The next issue was that, although making decisions together sounded great in theory, people had different approaches. One man explained: 'I like to get everything done quickly and get it out of the way. And some people need more time to deliberate. We're working through a lot of style issues.'The group realised, too, that they needed a different attitude to responsibility. One explained: "We don't go to the facilitator and say "Can I have the day off?" and expect them to find somebody to cover for us. We check it out with the people in our group.'

Despite these issues, only one month into its life the Pilot Team members were enthusiastic, saying: 'You feel more important; 'My definition of fun is: interesting. Also, being able to make a difference in what's going on, as opposed to sitting back and observing things'.

Importance of contract

Every group which functions well has a contract of some sort. It may be written down, agreed upon verbally, or merely worked out based on 'what we've always done'. But it exists.

Discussing the 'rules' openly gives people a chance to design the very best agreement for all involved. Without open discussion, each person must *guess* the rules from the reactions they get to their actions. This results in group members 'testing out' a new teacher, for example, to find his or her limits.

In some groups the rules will be developed by one person or subgroup, or even by an outside agency. But research confirms the fairly obvious fact that people are much more committed to rules they participate in making. Remember, for a rule to work it not only has to be written down or announced, it also has to be put into action by each person. We'll discuss this point further in Chapter 8.

Culture and meeting

AIM: to understand differences in procedures for meeting people, using examples from cultures in New Zealand and Asia.

The effects of culture

The word 'culture' describes the total way of life of a people, including all their beliefs, values, ways of behaving, language, and so on. Obviously, then, good communication requires an understanding of culture. No matter how good a communicator I may be, if you move me halfway round the world and put me in a totally different cultural setting, I'll have difficulty. It's like trying to play rugby football with a netball rulebook.

As a counsellor and coach, I have worked with many people who don't feel very good about their communication skills. One such man came to see me because of increasing arguments with the woman he lived with. He sat by me, looking down at the floor and explaining that one of his biggest failings was his inability to make eye contact with people. Also, when he and his partner argued, he was somehow unable to get across to her that he wanted to apologise. No matter how he demonstrated his sadness, sitting close to her and trying to do things for her, she didn't get the message.

Furthermore, the things they argued about really puzzled him. For example, when they went to her parents' place for the weekend, she wanted to ring up beforehand and sort out what food they would take. He felt humiliated by this - it seemed rather petty and rude. Surely they should just take whatever they could, and things would work out.

Different, not bad

Was this man a poor communicator? No - he was an excellent communicator. Then why was he having so much trouble, and why did he believe he was no good at communicating? Because he was playing rugby with the netball rulebook. His way of communicating worked perfectly in the family he grew up in, because that family was Maori. It did not work with his partner because she was from a European-based culture - a culture where people value 'looking you in the eye-' rather than looking down to indicate politeness; where people talk about their feelings rather than expressing them (for example at a funeral his partner might say: 'I'm so sorry' rather than simply weep and hold someone); where people negotiate the arrangements for hospitality rather than giving a gift (koha).

Both ways of life work perfectly, and it's quite possible for people to live together even when they grew up in different cultures - providing they understand the differences and understand each other.

Challenges begin when we assume one culture is better than another, or is more 'normal'. The next step towards difficulties is to pretend that cultures don't exist, and that everyone is 'the same'. It's as if someone said: "There's no difference between netball and rugby. The reason why you're losing the game is because you're no good at sports (or too lazy to try). You'll have to learn our rules better.'

The fact is that there are differences. And in the last 30 years, communications experts have begun to document the details of cultural difference (details that many people from minority cultures knew all along).

As I listened to this man describing each of his communication "failures', I affirmed for him that his responses sounded perfectly sane and skilled and that they were very much as I understood Maori responses to be. After half an hour or so he was glowing with a new sense of understanding, and working out how he could contact a Maori counsellor to explore this further. We spent the last quarter of an hour rehearsing how he would explain this to his partner in a way that would be respectful of her.

Cultures in New Zealand

Every time someone tells me that 'Most so-called Maoris aren't really Maori at all; they don't even speak the language', I remember that man and what he taught me. Indeed, he didn't know all the Maori words to explain what was happening to him - he didnt even think of himself as Maori at first. And why would he, after 12 years in a school system where culture was never even discussed? But none of that changed the fact that, culturally, his responses were most easily understandable from a Maori perspective.

Like most countries, New Zealand has a history of colonialism, and cultural groups here are still in the process of discovering how their ethnic roots affect their maps of the world (figuratively and literally). Cultures that have a place here today include those of the original Maori people; the descendants of the European colonists; Pacific cultures such as Samoan, Nuiean and Tongan plus a variety of other ethnic groups from Asia and elsewhere.

In New Zealand there is a special word for the European-originated culture - Pakeha - so we can discuss it and affirm its worth, just as this man came to affirm his being Maori. What I like about the word Pakeha is that it reminds me that I am a New Zealander, not a European. It was developed at a time of friendship between European explorers and Maori, and used by the British to refer to themselves when they wrote Te Tiriti o Waitangi (the treaty by which Maori agreed to have British colonies). Its most likely origin is the older Maori word Pakehakeha ('imaginary beings resembling people with fair skins', according to A Dictionary of the Maori Language by H.W.

Williams). I'll use this word Pakeha to refer to the European-based New Zealand cultures in the following section.

The welcome

In their book Talking Past Each Other, Joan Metge and Patricia Kinloch discuss the different responses Maori, Samoan, and Pakeha people have to situations of meeting. These points are crucial for us to understand in this chapter, as we think about how we meet people.

Both Maori and Samoans stress the importance of formal welcomes, including speeches of welcome, and they therefore often feel unwelcomed in Pakeha introductions, which tend to emphasise the importance of dispensing with formality. In the Maori setting, a formal welcome involves a succession of steps in which the emotional distance between hosts (tangata whenua) and guests (manuhiri) is reduced. Movement past the gate to the marae (the space in front of the meeting house) is initiated by women from each group giving the call (karanga). This may be followed by a chant to wave the visitors on (the powhiri). Next, there are exchanges of acknowledgements to God, speeches and greetings (karakia, whaikorero and mihi), each of which is embellished by a song (waiata). A gift (koha) is given by the visitors and they are then invited forward to make physical contact and press noses together (hongi) with the local people. The ceremony is concluded with the sharing of food. Each step in this process has a correct protocol related to its deeper spiritual significance.

Informal welcome

After the formal welcome, an informal welcome (mihimihi) will often occur, inside the meeting house (wharenui) or at another appropriate space. Here, people may stand, one at a time, introducing themselves by stating their links to:

- mountain (maunga)
- subtribe (hapu)
- river/ lake /harbour/sea (awa/moana)
- marae (community centre)
- ancestral ocean travelling 'canoe-' (waka)
- tribe (iwi)
- ancestral house (whare tupuna)

and mentioning:

- their own name
- own occupations and interests
- parents' names

- something about the occasion and their expectations.
- children's names

This speech will usually conclude with a song or poem (waiata). From a Maori perspective, important aspects of such meetings are:

1 The physical closeness between speaker and audience, and the use of touch.
2 The open, non-threatening and warm atmosphere with a total acceptance of each person.
3 The generous use of non-verbal language such as nods of the head and eyebrow gestures. (These are discussed more fully in Chapter 3.)

(References in Maori are from Williams, 1985)

Individual meetings

When meeting an individual, say Metge and Kinloch, both Maori and Samoans focus their questions on where the person has come from (immediately and more long-term in ancestry). They avoid asking directly: "Who are you?' (which is tantamount to asking: 'Who do you think you are?'), but instead ask: 'Where are you from?'.

Maori and Samoan meetings or group sessions usually begin with prayers (karakia). Food is eaten after the formal proceedings, not before or during them.When we train in Samoa every day begins and ends with a prayer.

In contrast, Pakeha gatherings often emphasise informality by mixing eating and discussion, and people are expected to make individual contact with others if they want, rather than routinely greeting them. At many Pakeha - meetings, however, the reverse is true once formal discussions have begun. Whereas Maori might debate an issue relatively freely within the meeting house (wharenui), Pakeha meetings often follow a complex protocol of motions, amendments and points of order.

Meetings in Japan and China

When we first began teaching in Japan and China, we learned two other sets of cultural rules about meetings.

Although most Japanese and Chinese are familiar with western etiquette, there are some principles of Japanese etiquette that it is useful for visitors to know. Diana Rowland points out in her book Japanese Business Etiquette that Japanese greetings are often more formal than western ones. Family names or even titles such as Sensei (teacher) are used rather than personal names. The name of anyone other than yourself or your group has the respectful title 'san' placed after it (as in Tanaka-san, Smith-san). Similarly, in China, a title will usually be placed after the family name in an introduction. Titles include Laoshi, which means teacher, Xiansheng meaning Mr. and Xiaojie meaning Miss (Foster, 2000)

People are introduced in order of seniority, from highest level to lowest level. If one person introduces two people to each other, he or she does so by presenting the lower-ranked person to the higher-ranked one: 'Mr Director, may I present Mr Brown?'. In a business setting, the presentation of business cards (called meishi in Japan) is an important process. The business card is an object of respect. It is kept in a jacket pocket, is presented with two hands, ideally while standing, and is to be looked at carefully and not defaced by writing on or sitting on it in a trouser pocket.

The bow (which a typical business person in Japan performs 200-300 times a day) is an important part of Japanese meeting. Japanese do not usually expect foreigners to know how to bow, but if someone (other than a shop assistant) bows to you, this gesture is always returned. Usually a bow is a careful 15-30 ^{0} inclining of the upper body. It indicates, like much of Japanese interaction, a respect bordering on humility. In China a much smaller bow may be performed, but this is not generally expected of westerners.

Basic humanity

As we ask how these differences in meeting rituals came about, we are reminded of the basic unity of humankind. Every culture has formed its own unique answers to such questions as: 'How do people meet and come to feel close to each other?'; 'What can be done about the fact that strangers often see the world through different eyes?' and 'How do we create the conditions which all human beings need for sustenance, such as love?'. These questions are put in English here, but there is a universality to them. Only the answers vary. And with such urgent questions, can we really afford not to welcome that variety of answers?

Summary

Every relationship has a beginning, and in this chapter we have learned how to make those beginnings work for you. We considered the importance of positive internal beliefs when you are getting the confidence to meet people. In several examples you saw how people begin conversations by talking about:

- how they are and what they want,
- how the other person is and what they want, and
- shared experiences.

When people meet as a group, particularly, the appropriate process depends on the cultural setting. Pakeha group introductions often emphasise informality and individual approaches. Maori welcomes often use a sense of increasingly less formal steps, gone through in a group. These steps include acknowledgements to God (karakia), and speeches of greeting (mihi), usually embellished with songs (waiata).

In any group, the successful results of the first meeting are a sense of contract (understanding what will happen in the group) and cohesion (feeling closer to the people who are there). Creating this sense of contract and cohesion is known as warm-up.

Chapter 2. Just a state of mind

KEY CONCEPTS .

- Visualisation, affirmation and physiology
- Changing internal states: relaxation
- Maoritanga, Maori and Pakeha esteem
- Women's and men's issues
- Resolving incongruity

Anchoring yourself to the state of your choice

AIM: to be able to use visualisation, affirmation, postural change and anchoring to produce a desired internal state.

State

Shortly after I began teaching, I noticed something puzzling about marking students' assignments. I discovered that, on certain mornings, I woke up eager to get into the job, realising that it would only take me a few hours and looking forward to the satisfaction of completing it well. My body felt full of energy and I had the same sense of eager curiosity I sometimes get when reading a new novel.

On other mornings I woke up feeling totally different. I'd look across at the mountain of assignments to mark: there they were, and here I was. My body felt tired, and I knew that getting started wasn't going to help, because even after maybe half an hour of work, there'd still be a mountain of assignments to do. I'd think of all the other things I could achieve more easily in that half hour, and start doing one of them, so avoiding the assignments.

How can the same task feel so totally different from one day to the next? The answers are all about how we get ourselves from one state of mind to another. What state of mind you're in is the single most important factor in how well you relate to others.

For example, remember the last time you fell 'in love'? Actually put the book down for a moment and think back to a time when you first realised you were in love with someone. Do you remember how that felt? There may have been a pounding in your chest, or butterflies in your tummy. The chances are you woke up that day charged with energy. Perhaps you were more affectionate with others around you, touching them a little more, smiling more. The whole world probably looked brighter to you, and you may have been particularly aware of the beauty of the flowers, or the way the birds were singing in the trees. You may have taken time out to watch the sunset, or savoured the smells of blossoms or autumn leaves.
If you can't recall a time like this for yourself, I'm sure you can remember noticing the difference when someone else around you was 'in love'.

Research on the 'love' state

Researchers at the Menninger Foundation in Kansas, USA, studied people who reported being 'in love', and found that they had reduced levels of lactic acid in their blood (lactic acid is a byproduct of muscle use: it gives that aching feeling after exercise). They also had higher levels of endorphins (the body's natural painkillers) and immunoglobulins (which help protect against infection). So these people weren't just imagining that they felt good. Their bodies were naturally less tired, more comfortable, and healthier than usual (Siegel, 1988, p 182). They were in a different state.

Defining state

Your state is the total neurophysiological pattern you have at a particular time (that is, all the things going on in your mind and body at that moment). Love is a state, and so are confidence, relaxation, self-esteem, creativity, and most of the other things you've ever wanted to experience.

As you know, people can go through the same events and yet be in totally different states. You and I may listen to the same speaker and find that, while I enter a state of boredom, you enter a state of fascination. What causes one person to experience the state called boredom and another the state called fascination, then, is something going on inside each of them.

Have you ever wished something could feel more interesting and look more exciting, but you don't know how to get out of the state you're in? In this chapter you'll learn three ways to do just that. It won't just be 'positive thinking' - you'll learn how to produce real change. And it won't require a lot of hard work or telling yourself off - it will happen naturally. Too good to be true? The three ways are called internal representations, physiology and anchoring. Read on!

One more thing: if you want to have effective relationships, you need to know how to get into the state of mind where you can actually use all the skills you'll learn in this book. Becoming "Emotionally Flooded" as evidenced by the person being physically over-aroused, with a pulse above 95 beats per minute, is associated with a guaranteed failure of conflict resolution. Relationship researcher John Gottman says that in his study of thousands of couples arguing, he never saw a single couple who could resolve their conflict while one of them had a pulse this high. Couples who resolve conflicts learn to "self nurture" and calm down (Gottman and Silver, 1999, p 25-46).

The causes of state: internal representations

The "in love' people that the Menninger Foundation studied were living in the same world as everyone else in Kansas that year. Their different state of mind was a result of two important changes happening inside them. Firstly, their internal ‚map of the world' (see Chapter 1) was different. In this case their map showed them where to look to see sunsets and spring flowers, where to hear the music of the birds, and how to feel the beating of their own heart. It was their internal representation of the world which enabled them to find these things. Someone with a different internal representation would have found different things. Similarly, what enabled me to feel enthusiastic about marking assignments one morning and overwhelmed another morning, was the different way I represented the situation to myself.

There are basically six different ways in which people represent their world internally.

1. They can make pictures in their mind (either by remembering things they have seen before or by imagining things). These are called visual representations.
2. They can create internal sounds, either remembered or imaginary. These are called auditory representations.
3. They can create body sensations or feelings (called kinesthetic representations).
4. They can talk to themselves. (This is a special category of internal sounds in which the person listens to the words their internal voice says, and pays attention to the meaning of the words rather than listening to the sounds or the music of the voice.) This type of verbal thinking is called auditory digital representation in NLP.
5. They can smell smells (called olfactory representations).
6. They can taste tastes (called gustatory representations).

A tasty experiment

When I write the word 'lemon', you can probably remember the shape of a lemon and its shiny yellow colour (visual). If you pictured a knife slicing into the lemon, you could probably imagine the slight sound the cut would make (auditory). You know how it would smell (olfactory), and if you picked up a slice of the lemon, you would know how the skin would feel (kinesthetic). Now imagine taking a bite of that lemon (gustatory). You have probably heard the saying: 'If life hands you a lemon, make lemonade!'. Say it to yourself now (auditory digital).

Now, what's really interesting is that if you actually thought of each of the things I described in the last paragraph, then your mouth will be salivating. Why? Because you made a series of internal representations of a lemon, and your brain responded as if there was a real lemon there! Since your brain responds to internal representations as if they were real experiences, your internal representations determine what state you're in, and that even affects the chemical balance in your body - instantly. So what you say to yourself and what you imagine inside decides whether you feel up or down, bored or motivated. The quality of your internal representations is the quality of your life!

Visual representations

For me, a very important part of my internal representations is the internal pictures I make about what I'm doing. (For you it may be more important how you talk to yourself, or the sensations you get in your body.) On mornings when I felt ‚overwhelmed' by my work, I created a picture of myself struggling through the assignments. It was a still picture, which didn't give me much feeling of achievement, and I could see all the work still to do beside me. I even saw the picture as rather small, dark and gloomy.

On mornings when I felt 'enthusiastic' about my work, I created a movie of myself doing the assignments, completing them, and smiling as I congratulated myself on getting the job done. The picture was big, bright and fast-moving. I only had to play that movie through a couple of times to start feeling really eager to get started.

Once I understood the difference, I was able to get myself into the state of enthusiasm easily, every time. It didn't take any work, it just meant using the natural way of motivating myself which I had already developed. For most people, imagining themselves doing the thing they want to do, finishing it, and enjoying the results is a powerful motivator. Usually it works even better than imagining all the bad things that could happen if you didn't get the job done. And it certainly works better than just imagining yourself stuck halfway through the job. But don't take my word for it. Watch next time you feel really enthusiastic about doing something, and see what kind of things you picture. When you eagerly bake a cake, for instance, do you see the mixture lying still in the bowl, or do you imagine how it will look finished and then sense how you'll feel as you and others enjoy it?

Your brain has a very specific set of ways of incorporating the information about your emotions into the actual picture you are seeing. The emotional information is “coded” visually (and in the other senses) as a result of some specific detailed distinctions made within the brain. Inside the visual cortex, there are several areas which process "qualities" such as colour, brightness and distance. When you are hungry, food often looks bigger and brighter (television advertisers know this – they makes the food on their adverts bigger and brighter too). In NLP these qualities are known as visual "submodalities" (because they are produced in small sub-sections of the visual modality). The first fourteen visual submodalities listed by Richard Bandler (1985, p 24) were colour, distance, depth, duration, clarity, contrast, scope, movement, speed, hue, transparency, aspect ratio, orientation, and foreground/background.

To give a sense of how these submodalities carry emotional information, consider the following study. In research by Emily Balcetis, an assistant professor in NYU’s Department of Psychology, and David Dunning, a Cornell professor of psychology, volunteers tossed a beanbag towards a gift card (worth either $25 or $0) on the floor. They were told that if the beanbag landed on the card, they would be given the card. Interestingly, the volunteers threw the beanbag much farther if the gift card was worth $0 than if it was worth $25 — that is, they underthrew the beanbag when attempting to win a $25 gift card, because they viewed that gift card as being closer to them. These findings indicate that when we want something, we actually view it as being physically close to us. Moving an object, in our imagination, closer to us makes us see it as more significant.

How visualising works

The reason why these pictures make a difference is that your mind responds to the pictures in your head as if they were real. Therefore, two people with different visual images will have different states of mind, and will behave as if they are in different situations. Making pictures which work for you is called 'visualisation'.

Some people say they can't see things in this way. That's OK. It works if you just pretend to see things. In fact, even people who are very good at imagining don't see things with the same intensity as in real life (if they do, we usually encourage them to get psychiatric help!). Your "unconscious mind' knows how to visualise, and that's all you need.

For example, take the way you found your way home yesterday. Did you need to carry a piece of paper with your address written on it, or did you just recognise which house was yours? To recognise your house amongst all those others means having a really good unconscious picture of what it looks like. If you can visualise yourself achieving tasks even half that clearly, it'll work fine!

Auditory representations

Another important part of how people's internal representations help them to move from one state to another , is how they talk to themselves. (I mentioned in Chapter 1 that different beliefs will make people feel differently as they meet others.) Usually, people find that talking to themselves about how well they're doing, or hearing someone else's voice telling them that they've done well, creates a positive state.

Telling yourself all the things that are wrong with you, and talking to yourself about how things might go badly, is generally not as much fun. Most people get enough of that while they are young to last them a lifetime. Telling yourself you are lovable, intelligent, capable, and in other ways a worthwhile human being, is called self-affirmation or self-validation. If it's not culturally appropriate for you to tell yourself this, then imagine hearing the voice of someone who loves you and wishes you well saying the affirmations to you. This is a way of accepting and valuing their love for you.

There is, however, an art to making affirmations work. Psychologists Joanne V. Wood and John W. Lee from the University of Waterloo, and W.Q. Elaine Perunovic from the University of New Brunswick, first asked 249 research subjects to fill in a short questionnaire designed to analyse their self-esteem and to say how often they said positive things about themselves, on a scale from 1(never) to 8 (almost daily). About 50% gave a rating of 6 or higher. Subjects who already had high self-esteem said they already often said affirming things to themselves, particularly to help themselves cope with exams, prepare for presentations, cope with challenges, or even as part of their everyday routine. On average, they felt that such statements were helpful. Those with low self-esteem also claimed that such statements sometimes helped them, but they said that they more often made them feel worse.

To find out why, the researchers did two follow-up studies. They discovered that everyone has a range of ideas they are prepared to accept. Messages that lie within this boundary are more persuasive than those that fall outside it - those meet the greatest resistance and can even lead to people holding onto their original position more strongly. If a person with low self-esteem says something that's positive about themselves but is well outside the range of what they'll actually believe, their immediate reaction is to dismiss the claim and feel even worse. Statements that contradict a person's current self-image and basic model of the world, no matter how positive in intention, are likely to trigger mismatching thoughts. People are better off saying "I choose good gifts for people" rather than "I'm a generous person". They cautioned that "outlandish, unreasonably positive self-statements, such as 'I accept myself completely,' are often encouraged by self-help books. Our results suggest that such self-statements may harm the very people they are designed for: people low in self-esteem."

To stretch yourself while still saying things are match your current reality, you can create statements that are possibility and capability oriented eg "It is possible for me to be healthy and well," "I have the capabilities to be healthy and well," rather than outcome based "I am healthy and well."

Each thing you say to yourself becomes a suggestion as powerful as any a hypnotist could make. NLP trainer Tony Robbins emphasises that: 'the quality of your communication with yourself is the quality of your life!" (Robbins, 1988). He points out that your unconscious mind is listening to and reacting to every internal comment, even the ones you didn't intend it to hear. For example, if you say to yourself: 'I'm aware of my left foot' several times, you'll find yourself very aware of your left foot. However it's also true that if you say to yourself: 'I'm not aware of my left foot', you'll also become very aware of it. The unconscious mind can only understand the "don't think of your left foot', by thinking of the left foot! Why is to know? Well, it means that if you tell yourself: 'I'm not going to get anxious. I'm not going to worry about this...' over and over, guess what? You'll find your unconscious mind is more and more aware of the worry. Instead, it's more effective to tell yourself: 'I'm relaxing more and more. I'm getting more and more comfortable. I'm more and more aware of the places in my body that are at ease.' And then you will relax more.

Choosing your voice

How you hear the voice saying these things is very important, too. Saying: 'I am lovable and capable', in a high, tense, trembling internal voice is not nearly as convincing as saying it in a warm, calm, relaxed tone. In fact, the tone, speed and loudness of the voice may be more important than the actual words. You'll understand this if you've ever had insomnia. Most people who can't get to sleep lie there talking to themselves about how they need to get to sleep, how they'll be in trouble the next day, and so on. But even worse, they usually shout frantically at themselves. No wonder they don't sleep with all that racket going on inside their head! Say the same thing in a slow, quiet, sleepy voice (with even a yawn occasionally) and you'll be able to tell the difference right away. It's like visualisation. Your mind reacts as if the sounds inside your head are real.

Another example: if you've got a critical voice inside your head telling you off, you could get it to say the same words in Donald Duck's voice, or to the theme music of your favourite comedy TV programme. Again, your mind will respond to the way the words are said as if they were really being said that way. If you're going to have voices telling you off, it's only logical to make them a little light-hearted.

What you're learning to do now is to change the auditory submodalities (fast or slow, loud or quiet, steady or with a musical rhythm, and so on). Counsellor and NLP trainer Lynn Timpany points out that talking to themselves in an aggressive, critical voice, is how most people get to feel less than positive about themselves. Changing that voice to a supportive one is the secret of self-esteem. She calls her technique for doing this the esteem generator'.

An example from Sport

Here's how top New Zealand triathlete Steve Gurney explains his use of this understanding of how to change state.

"I'd like to share with you a small but extremely powerful story of how I used mental attitude through Neuro-Linguistic-Programming (NLP), to boost my performance in this year's Coast to Coast race. It's a story about turning a negative into to a positive - converting "worry" into a "challenge"! Instead of being scared of the competition I wanted to "relish in the challenge" I was worried about the mountain run. Despite being a handy runner and getting plenty of run training under my belt I'm not as fast over Goat Pass as Gelately. Historically, I would emerge from the mountain run with a deficit of 8 to 10 minutes on the leader. It then requires a mammoth effort for me to close this gap before the finish line.,...very stressful! (Of course I could run through the mountains faster than the leaders, but I need to carefully pace myself to race at a speed that I can maintain for the entire 11 hours, not just a 3-hour mountain run)"

"I enlisted the help of my NLP guru, Richard Bolstad. To summarise, the solution lay in blowing apart my belief that I always trail the lead runners by 10 minutes. Bolstad powerfully pointed out to me that reality is whatever I imagined it to be, and in fact, with a little work I could alter my beliefs to be more powerful and positive. I visualised the lead runner to be "just around the corner" ahead of me, possibly even behind me, and not the dreaded 10 minutes that I was imagining. It worked a treat! I emerged from the run 1 minute ahead of Gelately!! My best mountain run to date!! The mechanism is one of positivity, fun and enjoyment. This releases endorphins and other natural "go-fast" chemicals that enhance focus, concentration and more efficient use of muscles and blood glycogen." (Gurney, 2003)

The causes of state: physiology

A second way in which people can change state naturally and easily is by use of body posture and movement. Like visualisation and affirmation, this is something you've probably done before. By learning the pictures, words and body actions that work for you, you can do them well and almost effortlessly whenever you need to.

What do you think would happen if, for the next half hour, you hunched your shoulders, hung your head, breathed slowly with an occasional sigh, and moved very slowly? That's right. You'd probably feel less energetic and, quite possibly, depressed. (You could make sure of it by seeing only vague, gloomy, still images, and by telling yourself off for being so 'hopeless'.) The same thing works for states you'd like to create.

Confidence

You don't need to force yourself to feel different. Simply change your posture with an attitude of 'I might as well be in this posture as the other'. Let's try it with "confidence'. Remember a time when you felt extremely confident. It may have been a time when you were by yourself, or with others who liked you; it may have been when you were doing something you knew you could do well, or when you felt sure you could do something. Whatever it was, take the time to find such a memory now, before you read on.

Now, as you remember that occasion, sit or stand in the exact same position you were in at the time. Be aware of your back, of your arms and legs, and of your breathing. (You can increase the sensation by visualising the things you could see on that occasion, and by talking - either to yourself or aloud - and listening to the subtle change in your tone of voice.) Being in this position will help you to access your own natural ability to be confident.

It's no surprise that the way your body feels affects your state of mind. Have you ever had a warm bath or shower and washed your hair to make yourself feel better? Have you ever done some challenging exercise and felt more awake afterwards? Have you ever laid down after a hard day and begun to feel more relaxed? The physical sensations you give yourself affect your emotions, just as visualisation and affirmation do. Insurance companies have found that people who are kissed goodbye each morning by their spouse have less accidents - even when the kiss was simply a 'routine measure'. The sensation affects the person's state.

Breathing

In his book The Psychobiology of Mind Body Healing, Ernest Lawrence Rossi details many of the ways in which our body has been shown to affect the mind. Even the way you breathe through your nose is related to your state of mind. In an alert and active state, right-handed people breathe more fully through the right nostril. When they do so, EEG recordings of the brainwaves show more activity in the dominant half of the brain.

In a very relaxed state, right-handed people breathe through the left nostril. During relaxation, the brainwaves show more activity in the non-dominant side of the brain. Even more amazing is that simply blocking the left nostril (by pressing the side of the nose) makes right-handed people more alert, and blocking the right nostril relaxes them. (All these findings are reversed for lefthanded people.) The nostril you breathe through changes your brainwave pattern and your state of mind! Give it a five-minute trial now while you this book. You couldn't ask for an easier way to relax at night and wake in the morning.

The causes of state: anchors

Changing your breathing is only one of a number of easy ways to change your state of mind within five minutes. Consider another experience we have all had. You are listening to the radio and a song is played which you haven't heard for several years. As you hear it, the feeling of what it was like all those years ago comes back to you, and you begin to recall details of what was happening then.

Another example: you're going past a dental surgery, and as the door opens you catch a whiff of antiseptic. Even though you're not getting treatment, your heart begins to pound and you feel a twinge of anxiety, checking your mouth and wondering if you need any fillings.

A third situation: there's a place you visited many times when you were younger, where you had many happy experiences. Now you visit it again and just sit there, like you used to, looking around at the scene you recall from those times. As you do so, you're surprised by the feelings of pleasant nostalgia that flood over you. You can almost hear the voices of those who were there, and feel like doing again the things you once did there.

In each of these situations, a dramatic change in state occurred which required no 'effort'. And in each case, there was some 'stimulus'. When you saw, heard, felt, tasted or smelt that stimulus, the whole state began to recur all by itself. The song on the radio was a stimulus first present when you were in a certain state; the smell of the dentist's was a stimulus first present when you were in an anxious state; and the scene of your earlier visits was a stimulus first present when you were in a happy state.

Anchoring

Using a stimulus from an earlier time to recreate a certain state in the present is called anchoring. Anchoring is happening all the time: the only way you can understand these written words is from the way each particular group of letters anchors you to a meaning you have associated it with before.

For example, if I write the word 'anchor', you can hear how those letters are meant to sound and see a picture of what an anchor looks like. You may even have a feeling associated with those letters.

The most famous use of anchoring is in Dr Ivan Pavlov's experiment with hungry dogs. Every time Pavlov fed his dogs, he rang a bell. Soon he found that just ringing the bell caused the dogs to salivate - to go into the state of readiness to eat (Pavlov, 1927).

There's not a great demand for getting people to salivate by ringing a bell. But there is a demand for enabling people to relax, to feel confident, to feel caring towards each other, to be creative and so on. Let's say you would like to feel relaxed while communicating with people. Luckily, you probably have a time each day when you are already relaxed. Choose a time when you are very relaxed (perhaps just before you fall asleep), and try the following: at that time each day, press your left thumb and forefinger together and say to yourself in a calm voice: 'relaxed and confident. (There's nothing magic about pressing your thumb and forefinger together, it just happens to be something you're only likely to do in this state, so it probably doesn't have any contradictory states already anchored to it.) After only two or three days, you'll be able to approach someone, press your thumb and forefinger together in just the same way, say 'relaxed and confident' to yourself in the same calm voice... and you will relax. The more you use this technique, the more powerful it will get.

The process of anchoring was "rediscovered" by Richard Bandler and John Grinder (1979, p 79-136). It can be used to take any emotional state that a person has experienced at some time in their life, and "connect" it to situations they would like to experience that state in. In a controlled research study published in Germany (Reckert, 1994), Horst Reckert describes how in one session he was able to remove students' test anxiety using this simple technique, described below. In another study, John Craldell discusses the use of anchoring to access a "self-caring-state" useful for adult children of alcoholics (Craldell, 1989), and in a third study, Mary Thalgott discusses the use of anchors to support children with learning disabilities (Thalgott, 1986).

Ensuring anchors work

You can expect anchoring to be absolutely effortless and reliable (even a dog can do it!). So if it doesn't 'work, simply check four things:

- you really were fully experiencing the desired state when you 'set' the anchor
- your timing was right, so you set the anchor at exactly the moment when you felt the state strongly
- the anchor you are using is unique and distinctive - it doesn't also occur in other, contradictory situations
- you recreated the anchor exactly the same as it was originally.

After checking these four things, repeat the anchoring process.

When you are communicating with others, especially if you work with people, your state of mind is crucial. Confidence, relaxation, alertness, caring and creativity are amongst the many important states you will be able to create using the techniques outlined in this section. Mary Kay Ash, manager of the multimillion dollar company Mary Kay Cosmetics, used anchoring with her staff. When she met a new staff member, she would greet them with a smile and say "Hi, how are you!" She explained "When a new employee answers, "Uh, pretty good. How are you Mary Kay?" I'll say, "You're not just good, you're great!" This generally gets a faint smile, and the next time I see him or her and ask "How are you?" he or she will say, "I'm great." Each time afterward, the response is, "I'm great!" and the smile gets bigger and bigger. If you act enthusiastic, you become enthusiastic." (Williams and Williams, 2003, p 341-342) This process of anchoring every new employee was so important to Ash that she once declined an invitation from President Ronald Regan because she had to be in Dallas greeting the new employees there, and setting up what we would call in NLP the anchor of "I'm great."

John Gottman's research on relationships shows the importance of anchoring relaxed states for negotiation and conflict resolution. He has demonstrated that no matter what verbal skills someone uses, in any conflict where one person becomes "Emotionally Flooded" as evidenced by the person being physically over-aroused, with a pulse above 95 beats per minute, conflict resolution is guaranteed to fail. Couples who resolve conflicts learn to do what Gottman calls "self nurturing", which basically means to anchor themselves into better states of mind (Gottman and Silver, 1999, p 25-46).

NLP Trainers John Grinder and Anthony Robbins negotiated with the United States Military to run a series of NLP Training programmes. The military were excited by the idea of being able to have their best performing soldiers "modelled" so that new recruits could be taught the strategies that work perfectly; however they had previously expressed concern at the price the NLP Trainers considered fair. They met in a big conference room. At the head of the table was the chair reserved for the General in charge. Even though the General wasn't present, Grinder and Robbins noticed that people unconsciously glanced over to his chair every so often. The two of them moved over to the chair and stood with their hands on it, as they presented the price they wanted. This time, no-one questioned their rate. It had been anchored to the General's chair.

To recap, the techniques for altering state include:

- creating useful internal representations
- visualising in the way you most successfully create the desired state (for example seeing yourself in a bright, life-sized movie showing the success of your endeavour)
- affirming yourself and talking to yourself in a voice appropriate to the desired state.
- Assuming a posture and breathing style (physiology) appropriate to the desired state.
- Using a stimulus associated with the desired state, to anchor yourself into it.

Activity 2.1

AIM: to use postural change to create a state of trust ('trust fall')

This activity can be carried out by groups of between six and twelve people. If you have a group leader, it is easier if he or she demonstrates it first.

1 One person (the 'central person') stands with their arms folded or held by their sides, keeping their legs straight and remaining in the same spot throughout the activity. The rest of the group forms a fairly close circle round the central person. Those in the circle then raise their hands, palms facing the central person, ready to catch them as they fall. (This may be easier if the people in the circle brace themselves by putting one foot back a little.)

2 The central person closes their eyes and, keeping their body straight, falls backwards to be caught by those in the circle. The circle then passes them gently around or across to be caught by others. It is most important not to drop the central person, and to be in close enough to ensure they feel safe (you may start right up close and move back a little as they indicate). The sense of trust which this exercise generates is related to the sense of caring with which people are handled.

3 Discuss how the exercise went, accepting each person's own experience rather than comparing or evaluating it as 'good' or 'bad'.

Activity 2.2

AIM: to use visual representations to create state of raised self-esteem ('visual swish')

1 Think of a situation in which, due to low self-esteem, you often behave in a way you'd like to change. (We might define self-esteem as the ability to like yourself, so 'low self-esteem' means not liking yourself; judging, blaming, or rejecting yourself. The kind of behaviour you might want to change includes smoking, overeating, avoiding others, criticising others, getting nervous, and so on.)

Once you have chosen the behaviour you want to change, think about what you always see just before the behaviour starts. (For example, a smoker might see their hand holding a cigarette; someone who gets nervous might see a group of people waiting for them to speak.) You need to find something your mind can use as a cue that this is the time when this exercise will have its effect. Visualise this cue situation (as you see it in the real situation) as clearly as you can. This is the 'cue picture'.

2 Next, clear your mind and create an imaginary picture of yourself as you look when you are confident, happy with yourself, and full of skills and new ways to act. This picture should be such that, by just looking at your new self, you can tell that you no longer have any need to change the behaviour (just as, for example, you would know from looking at a confident skier that they don't need skiing lessons).

As you look at your new self, check that there is no part of you that objects to becoming the person in the picture. If you are uncertain in any way, ask the 'uncertain' parts of yourself to change the picture slightly, so it 'feels right.

I'll call this picture of the person with all these new choices the 'resourceful picture'.

3 Visualise a big, bright, square image of the cue picture in front of you, with a small, dark, square image of the resourceful picture in its centre. Now visualise these pictures changing over: the small resource picture brightens up and floods out to fill up the whole screen, and at the same time the cue picture shrinks and darkens to insignificance. If this seems complex, be assured that you can do this just as well 'subconsciously' by only pretending to see the changes.

4 Once you can see the big, bright resource picture, clear the screen ready to start again. Repeat this process, starting each time with the cue picture as the big picture, and ending with the resource picture as big and bright, always clearing the screen between times. Continue until you cannot get back the cue picture at all, or you find that it automatically triggers the resourceful picture (usually about two to five times).

5 Get into pairs and re-imagine the situation where the behaviour used to happen. Discuss the changes in how you feel when you go to think of the situation that was a challenge.

Activity 2.3

AIM: to use tone of voice and anchoring to create a state of relaxation

1 Group leader: read out the following series of instructions to help the group to remember times when they have been very relaxed. Begin in your ordinary talking voice, but gradually slow down and lower the tone of your voice so you are talking in a relaxed way. Read words printed in bold just slightly more emphatically.

While you are reading, the group members should follow these suggestions and remember the situations. At certain points in the instructions they will be told to "anchor" their memory. This means, for the purpose of this activity, to press their left thumb and forefinger together (thus anchoring what they are remembering to the sensation of that hand position). Explain this before beginning. Group members should be seated, with their eyes open or closed as it suits them.

Instructions (any ambiguity is Intended)

'I'd like you to choose from your memory a time when you were completely safe and relaxed... a time when you may have been at home in your room... or on holiday somewhere... or in a place that is special to you... and remember what it is like to be relaxed now..." (pause ten seconds)'... And as you recall a time... perhaps even just coming home from work and resting so fully that you drift off... I'd like you to notice what you could see at that time... because often there is something you can see that really reminds you of how easy it is to relax... which may be the deep blue of a sky... or the colour of the walls... or some particular thing that reminds you of how you slow down... even if it's just the way your eyes defocus a little and blur round the edges as you get that sense of ease... when it really doesn't seem important to focus on anything in particular... except to notice what you see that reminds you of being relaxed... and anchor it by pressing your finger and thumb together now... so you can go on to ask yourself what you could hear as you relaxed in that place... which may be just that silence... like the quietness in this room, which any unexpected noises remind you of... or may be the sounds of nature ... or of the things which are so much a part of that place where you relax ... or even just the way that, as you relax, the sounds around you have a slightly different, even echo-like quality... like the sound of my voice now... as you anchor the sounds of relaxation by pressing your finger and thumb together again now... leaving you ready to recall the position you were sitting or lying in then... and how your body feels as it is relaxed now... because you are relaxing now, are you not... ? And often as you begin to relax you may be aware of the discomforts in your body... just like when you put your feet up and feel the tension drain out of your legs... which is part of your blood flowing more easily... like the warmth of your cheeks as the blood flows more easily to the outside of your body... and the gradual slowing down of your breathing... which happens when you are at ease... so that as you are aware of the feeling of being relaxed you can anchor that feeling by pressing your finger and thumb together again now...' (pause four seconds* then begin gradually speeding up your voice again) '...And knowing that you have that sense of relaxation stored with that anchor, begin to remember where you are, here, now, in this group. In your own time, open your eyes fully (you may want to blink them and focus again), stretch your arms, and listen to the normal sounds of the room, as you come back to being fully here and ready to talk.' * If you are using this relaxation process as a prelude to another exercise, move on to the next exercise from this asterisked point, instead of bringing the group back to the room.

2 Discuss how this was, in pairs and then in the group.

3 At a later date, group members should test their anchors by pressing their finger and thumb together. Group leader: as you explain that you want them to do this, use the same tone of voice you used while reading the relaxation exercise.

Activity 2.4

AIM: to create a resource anchor for confidence

Get into pairs and choose one person to be anchored and the other to guide them through the process.

Guide:

I Ask your partner to remember a time when they had the state of confidence. (Tell them to be aware that the easiest way to remember this state may be by remembering times when they were doing something they enjoy, rather than having confidence in a challenging situation.) Once they remember a time when they had that state intensely and purely, get them to 'step into their body in that memory'. In order to assist them into the state:

- experience the state of confidence yourself, as you talk to them

- say: 'step into your own body in that memory, seeing through your own eyes, hearing through your own ears, and feeling fully that feeling of confidence'

- say to them: 'adjust your body now, so that you're sitting the way you sit when you feel that confidence. Notice the kind of voice you use as you feel that confidence.' (Check that they actually look like they're feeling it!)

2 Say: 'when you feel that confidence fully, make a gesture with your hand,
so that the feeling becomes totally associated with that gesture. If the feeling isn't as strong at some time, just release the hand and wait until you can feel it fully again.'

3 Ask your partner to stand up and walk round, feeling that state of confidence and noticing how they stand and walk in that state. Tell them again to make the hand gesture once they know that the state is strong.

4 Tell your partner to release the gesture and sit down again. Now get them to stretch and look out of the window in order to change the state.

5 Now say to them: 'make the gesture again, and feel how that gesture now causes the state of confidence.' Check that this works, watching what it looks like. This is testing the anchor. Afterwards, change the state (for example by getting them to release the anchor, take a breath, and think of something they're looking forward to later). If the anchor is working go to step 6. Otherwise repeat the first five steps.

6 Repeat for other resourceful feelings, if you have time, 'stacking" them on the same anchor (the same hand gesture) to build an even stronger positive state.

7 Say to your partner: 'now, using that anchor and feeling those resourceful feelings [get them to make the hand gesture], think of a future time when you'd like to use that anchor; a time when, in the past, you would have found it a little challenging to feel resourceful. This is not a time to think about really distressing memories or traumatic events. just choose a time when you wish you had felt more confident. Check how much more confident you feel now, when you think of that future time'.

Activity 2.5

AIM: to observe how your state of mind naturally changes

1 Allow half an hour for this exercise. Sit with your back straight and your legs uncrossed (or crossed in such a way as to balance the left/right sensations, for example cross-legged or in a yoga posture). Close your eyes and pay attention to your internal state, including all the images, internal or external sounds and sensations you are aware of. This is not a time to try and change these experiences, but simply to observe, as one might listen to excellent music, watch a beautiful sunset or experience a warm bath. There is no need to choose one thought above another, to search for a particular state, or to theorise about or organise one's mind. This is simply a process of being with whatever state of mind occurs, being aware of it, observing it with fascination. There is no particular aim, and no one sensation, state, or thought is more important than any other. This is an experiment to discover what actually occurs over the 30 minutes.

2 After 30 minutes, open your eyes, return to external reality, and share what happened in pairs. Discussion might include: what states of mind did you enter? were you able to simply be aware, or did you find yourself thinking about and trying to change what occurred, i.e. making yourself an observer separate from the state you were observing? (Notice that this is how internal conflict occurs: one state opposes another state, tries to alter, or stop it.) If you were able to be aware, did you find that your state of mind changed naturally (for example calmed down) without using any technique?

The social roots of self-esteem

AIM: to be able to identify the social processes which create different states of self-esteem for people of different culture or gender.

Self-esteem and society

Self-esteem is a state of mind where a person is able to appreciate or like themselves. Psychologist Carl Rogers (1980) considered it the most important state of all. His research showed that, whatever the challenges people have when they come to a counsellor for help, the one thing they have in common is low self-esteem. Whatever else happens when counselling is successful, the one thing you can be sure about is that the person has more self-esteem.

In the last section you learned some of the ways you can build your own self-esteem (for example through affirmation, visualisation and anchoring). To change your own state of mind gives you the freedom to respond to people in the way you would like to, despite any outside influences.

Of course, there are outside influences on your state of mind. They include your childhood experiences as well as the influence of the world around you today. Below is an example of how the social world around people affects their state of mind.

Unemployment

In their book Poor New Zealand, Charles Waldegrave and Rosalyn Coventry quote research from several countries regarding the social effects of unemployment. This includes the following findings:

• Every time unemployment rises by one per cent, six per cent more people need psychiatric treatment, four per cent more commit suicide, four per cent more end up in prison, and six per cent more commit murder.

• There are more cases of bronchitis, heart disease, skin disease and stomach ulcers amongst unemployed people.

Does unemployment influence people's state of mind? Without a doubt. Does it affect their communication? Yes, drastically! Our main focus in this book is on what the individual can do to improve communication. But in this part of the book I will discuss some of the ways in which society as a whole affects people's self-esteem and their ability to communicate.

Maori in Pakeha society

Another interesting example of the social causes of self-esteem is revealed when we compare Maori New Zealanders with Pakeha (European New Zealanders). In 2010, the Māori youth suicide rate was 35.3 per 100,000 Māori youth population: more than 2.5 times higher than that of non-Māori youth (13.4 per 100,000). It's a story we see reflected in the lives of indigenous people around the world, from Northern Ireland to Australia, from Canada to South Africa. What is happening in New Zealand society to damage Maori esteem like this? (Ministry of Health 2012)

Part of the answer, I believe, is the suspicion and anger which many Pakeha direct at Maori. Once, while I was biking to work, I passed a man with the slogan 'Speak English or Die!' written on his tee-shirt. I myself felt frightened, and I speak English fairly well! What effect was this man having on immigrants to New Zealand who had difficulty with English, or on Maori, whose language will only survive if it can be spoken regularly here in its home country?

Research shows that applicants with a Maori name will be offered 20 per cent less job interviews than similarly trained people with an English name. Real estate agents will offer them less properties to consider in 84 per cent of cases, and they will be accepted as tenants for flats less often than other people (Spoonley, 1988, p 28). While unemployment in September 2013 stood at 6.2% for Pakeha, it was 15.6% for Maori. Police Commissioner Mike Bush acknowledged in interviews on 29 November 2015 that Police research had identified that they used their discretionary ability to divert offenders to non-punitive solutions for minor offenses in a way that was biased against Maori. It was not, he said, conscious racism, but simply an unconscious tendency to assume that Maori would not benefit from the process. Whatever you may think are the reasons for these facts, they are bound to have a major effect on Maori.

Mana Maori (Maori esteem)

In different cultures, people find different ways to feel good about themselves (individually or as a group) and to have a sense of identity (of knowing who they are). In many European-based cultures, one of the first things one person asks another is: 'What do you do for a job? Much of the sense of identity in these cultures comes from work. The following model and explanation of the origin of Maori identity are given by Te Hata Ohlson (Communicating Caring, 1992):

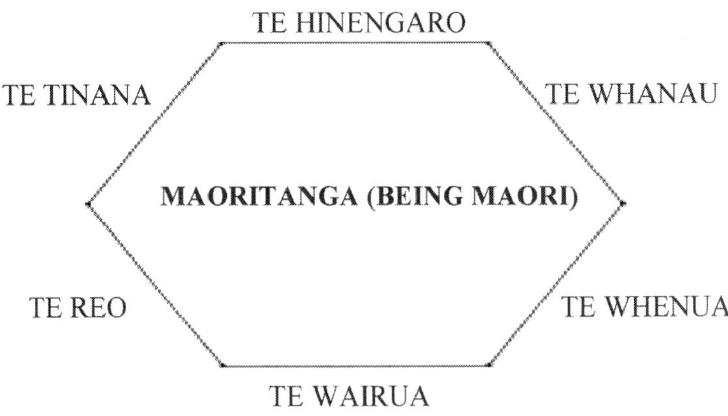

For Maori, mana, or esteem (rather than self-esteem) is gained by one's relationship to six elements. As an individual, a Maori's esteem is based on how he or she can effectively complement and add to the whole. The areas are:

1. Te reo: the language of one's own tribe, together with a knowledge of tribal protocol, whakapapa (geneology), lore and culture.
2 . Te whanau: the family, which could include relations other than immediate family, for example aunts, uncles, cousins and grandparents. Kinship ties.
3. Te whenua: the land and environment, and its relationship as kin through Papatuanuku (mother earth). Maori families buried the placenta and birth cord in a special place at their kainga (home ground). 'Whenua' also means 'placenta', 'umbilical cord' and 'afterbirth'.
4. Te wairua: wairua is spirit, including the human spirit. This is linked to Mauri (life force), ihi (strength/ confidence), and mana (esteem).
5. Te hinengaro: emotions and thoughts.
6. Te tinana: the physical being, i.e. body.

Individual and group esteem

Te Hata Ohlson's description emphasises the importance to Maori of one's relationship to larger wholes. In contrast, in Pakeha culture it is often assumed that esteem can be achieved by celebrating one's personal successes. Joan Metge (1986) describes how a Maori woman, Pat King, went to see a Pakeha counsellor at Marriage Guidance. The counsellor suggested she build up her selfesteem by making a list of the things she was good at. King explained: 'I couldn't do it. We were brought up not to look down on anyone, but to look up to the people who had mana, to the kuia [female elders] and koroua [male elders], and above all to be whakaiti [modest, with humility], not to push yourself'.

To be whakaiti is not the same, Metge explains, as being whakamaa (a word which implies shame, shyness, withdrawal, and loss of mana). She quotes Maori researcher Anaru Penrose: 'Whakamaa is not taking a lowly position, it is being put in a lowly position. One does not seek whakamaa. Whakaiti is a lowly position that one might seek, adopt, incorporate into your philosophy, but a lowly position of honour. Whakamaa is a lowly position of dishonour'.In fact, then, the modesty or humility of whakaiti is an important part of esteem for Maori.

Metge adds: 'Whakaiti goes with being secure in your identity, not simply as an individual but as a link in a descent line and a member of a descent group, and as a result of close association with older relatives in childhood".

This is the part of the challenge of building esteem, in Maori terms, which the Pakeha counsellor was unable to pick up. It involves reforging the links with all six elements of Maoritanga. Esteem does not exist in a vacuum. It can only be built successfully on the basis of a person's own cultural values.

Sources of Pakeha identity

The situation of Pakeha in New Zealand is rather different. Even if someone were to wear a tee-shirt saying 'Speak Maori or die!', it could not have the effect on me, as a Pakeha, that 'Speak English or die!' has on Maori people. After all, my language is spoken 99 per cent of the time on TV; in parliament, in our schools and in the streets. It is a fairly safe bet that English will survive.

Nonetheless, many Pakeha do feel uncertain about who they are. As we learn about the injustices involved in the colonisation of New Zealand, we, as Pakeha, search for ways to respond without being paralysed by guilt. In our search, we often ask: 'Who are our people anyway?", and 'Why are we here?'

Richard's ancestors

My own ancestors came to New Zealand from Wales, Norway, Ireland and England. In each case, they were escaping the poverty of Europe and hoping for a more egalitarian society where they could own their own land. Hans Hansen and Christiane Pedersdatter (who took the name 'Bolstad' after leaving Norway in 1872) were leaving their feudal life as farm labourers for a section in the new 'town' of Norsewood. Within a few years they had lost their struggle with the totara forest and were once more labouring on other people's land.

Forty years later, my mother's father, Richard Watkins, left for the new colony 'down under'. Like so many other settlers, his dreams of self-sufficiency eventually had to fit into the restraints of a suburban quarter-acre section.

It was the Treaty of Waitangi which enabled these people to settle here. The Maori tribes accepted earlier settlements, trusting the Pakeha would honour their side of this deal. The Bolstads, for example, were given a formal welcome by Paora Rerepo and the Ngati Kahungunu people. But the land companies, in their eagerness to sell, were less careful about the treaty. Thomas Chapman and Mary Ann Hicks, ancestors of mine who arrived at the Nelson settlement in 1842, found that much of the promised land there had never even been bought from Ngati Toa. Within a year, the determination of the New Zealand Company officials to enforce the illegal subdivision of Nelson land had resulted in the first battle between settlers and Maori, at Wairau.

Maori, Pakeha and the Treaty

I believe my ancestors made the best choices they could, to find a better life for themselves and their families. But they, of all people, could have understood how important land can be to a people's self-esteem. I share my forebears' dream of a fairer society. Now, 160 years later, I think it's time to recognise that in New Zealand this fairness has to include a respect for the Maori people's special relationship with their land. This special relationship is acknowledged clearly in Te Tiriti o Waitangi, the Treaty by which Maori permitted European colonists to settle here. I consider it important to my self-esteem as a Pakeha, that we honour our side of that deal.

Women's reality

There are similar issues when we consider self-esteem for men and for women. New Zealand Auckland University of Technology professor Max Abbott pointed out in 2013 that women are still twice as likely to be diagnosed with mental illness - one in five woman compared to one in 10 men.

We don't have to look far to find social sources for the lower self-esteem of women. One is the attitude that has been called 'sexism'. just as racism is present when one culture assumes its superiority and is able to implement this; so sexism involves one sex (usually men) assuming a belief in their own superiority and acting to put this into practice. This includes:

• Unequal sharing of decision-making power. Even in New Zealand's parliament, the number of men has remained at twice the number of women over the last two decades. This statistic is reflected in other decision-making bodies throughout the world.

• Unequal sharing of resources. Even when women's work is paid for (which it isn't in the case of housework, for example) the average hourly earnings for women is 11.8% lower than earnings for men (New Zealand Ministry for Women).

• Unequal sharing of work. In March 2015, University of Canterbury business and economics associate professor Annick Masselot reported research suggesting that even though New Zealand men participate in domestic work more than men in other industrialised countries, women in New Zealand do more than double the unpaid house-work and childcare.

• Men's violence against women. In 2012 72% of the 87,622 family violence investigations by New Zealand police involved male perpetrators: almost 3 times as many as women. Most of their victims are women. (statistics from the New Zealand Family Violence Clearinghouse)

• Pressure on women to conform to a very narrow ideal of attractiveness. One aspect of this usually unattainable standard is body shape. A 2010 study shows the average BMI of Miss America winners has decreased from 22 to 16.9 in the last 80 years. A normal BMI is classified as between 18.5 and 24.9, so this means that the ideal is now below the healthy normal level. (Reported in 2013 by Lynn Grefe, president and CEO of the National Eating Disorders Association in the USA).

Sexism in Language

Sexism is also expressed in the way men and women talk with each other. This produces some rather subtle assaults on women's self-esteem, which will be discussed in more detail. In the English language, even the words we use assume male superiority.

(Maori, on the other hand, is an example of a language virtually free of sexism.) In English, the average person can be called the 'man in the street", and the achievements of our species are the achievements of "mankind'. A very sexually active man is a 'stud' (complimentary) while a very sexually active woman is a ‚slut' (insulting). 'Sissy' (from the word sister) is an insult, while 'buddy' (from the word brother) is a compliment. 'Being a man' means acting strong (complimentary), while 'behaving like a woman 'means being ridiculously weak (insulting). One of the challenges of effective communication, then, is to find ways of talking which are inclusive, rather than male-centred: for example to avoid saying 'he' when we mean to include any person; to avoid saying 'man' when we mean to include all people. Using inclusive language supports everyone's self-esteem, and that is the first step towards successful relationships.

Women's talk and men's talk

Research shows some important differences between the ways that women and men talk in groups. Reviewing the research about this, sociologist J.E. Baird notes that studies have shown the following:

MEN	WOMEN
Start conversations more	Respond to others' conversation more
Talk about the task or goal more	Talk about social relationships more
Give more information	Express warmth and helpfulness more
Talk more and use more words	Say less as men talk more
Interrupt people more often	Avoid unpleasant conversations more
Talk about themselves more	Talk about others more
Say more statements about 'what is'	Use more questions
Describe 'objective' facts more	Express personal opinions as opinions

Response to the two styles

Women opposed to sexism have responded to this difference in conversational style in two ways. One response (epitomised originally by therapist Anne Wilson Schaef's book Women's Reality) has been to affirm 'women's talk' as part of an emerging female way of relating to the world. The other (represented in books such as Desire: the Politics of Sexuality, by Ann Snitow, Christine Stansell and Sharon Thompson (eds)) has been to call for an end to the division between 'female' and 'male' ways of relating.

John Gray initiated a popular third response to the difference with his book Men Are From Mars, Women Are From Venus. He suggests that men and women are 'supposed to be different', and that by appreciating these differences they can learn to live together more successfully. He recommends learning about how each sex thinks as a prerequisite to being able to effectively ask for what we want. As a small example, Gray says that men are frequently turned off by a request for assistance from a woman, if it begins: 'Can you help me...'. Gray suggests that the words 'can' or 'could' trigger a challenge, whereas 'would' doesn't. When Gray was challenged on a television show about this hair-splitting, he gave an example. 'Imagine,' he said 'if a man came up to a woman and said 'Can you marry me? Would that be different to asking 'Would you marry me? Most of Gray's suggestions for more effective communication are covered in Part 3 of this book.

The doctor-nurse game

Some of the ways in which men and women relate damage women's self-esteem. These include what Anne Wilson Schaef calls 'peacekeeping talk'. In peacekeeping talk, women are careful not to rock the boat.

Nursing researcher R.A. Hoekelman notes that peacekeeping talk is common when female nurses deal with male doctors. She calls it 'the doctor-nurse game.

Here is an example quoted by nursing researcher Loland Menikheim. A doctor re-prescribed librium (a tranquilliser) for one of his patients. After thanking the doctor for the drug prescriptions, the nurse added: 'Oh, Doctor, I forgot to tell you that the night nurse reported that Mrs M. was nauseated after each librium. Did you want to write a new order? The doctor, who had forgotten the night nurse's report, then replied: 'Yes, thanks Trudy. I did want to change the order'.

Notice how the nurse's comments fit precisely with the research about women's style of talking. Instead of stating her disagreement with the doctor, she asks a question and suggests he has made the decision. She thus comes across as helpful and non-threatening, and appears to be simply responding to his comments.

Menikheim points out how similar 'peacekeeping talk' used by women such as housewives and secretaries, preserves the pattern of male control. Women's wisdom, skill, and contribution to society is covered up in this process, and women are deprived of opportunities to feel good about themselves. And yet when women do not cooperate with the game they are usually viewed as rude, aggressive and domineering.

Men's changing identity

Chapter 8 discusses alternative ways for individuals to cooperate, without one person using their power over the other. For now it's also important to realise that men's control of conversations and of society is not just a personal issue. It is a social issue, and the solutions need to involve major changes in the way we raise children, present men and women in the media, structure our government, and so on.

What do men think about all this? Are they eager to protect their power; to go on playing the doctor-nurse game? I don't think so. Social workers Ken McMaster and Peter Swain use the analogy of a bully to describe men's tendency to control others (1989). They say: 'We have met and worked with many men who have the strength to take on the challenge and explore the bully in themselves. These men are clear that the rules and roles of being a bully no longer fit. It hinders them from being cooperative, nurturing, sensitive towards and caring for their partners, family, children and friends. We haven't yet met a man who deep down enjoys being a bully. Many of the men we meet are afraid of themselves and feel guilty about how they are within their families. They know at heart that there must be a different way.'

McMaster and Swain say that they are 'challenging all men to join us in stopping men's violence to women; and we ask, are you man enough?

It's a new definition of 'being a man" that such people promote. One which asks men to find their self-esteem not from power over others, but from a greater power - power over their own lives.

Activity 2.6

AIM: to affirm the significance of ancestry and sense of place

Note: give group members one or two weeks to research their ancestry. Members who are adopted may like to research their adoptive family or their birth family, depending on circumstances. Some people, of course, simply may not be able to collect much information.

1. Get into pairs and discuss:

• Who were your ancestors and where did they come from?
• What customs and values do you imagine your ancestors had which are still part of your life today?

2. Change partners and discuss:

• In which parts of your country has your family lived?
• What parts of this country are special to you and why?

3. Everyone: choose one place in your country which is special to you.

Create an imaginary map of the country on the floor, and get everyone to stand where their special place is. Share with the group where each person is standing and why.

4. Sit down again, and take time to write down individually some of the customs and values you have experienced in your family, and in the culture you are a part of. (Values simply means things that are important to you, such as family support, individual rights, respect, freedom, and equality.)

5. In pairs, look at your lists and discuss which things are precious to each other, and which customs or values are important enough that they be passed on to your children and to people living in this country in the future. Then collect ideas from the group.

Activity 2.7

AIM: to affirm your sense of gender identity

1. Divide into two groups (if there are men and women, try to include both in each group). Give each group a pen and a sheet of newsprint.

Reading the sheet, one group thinks of all the women they know from media contexts such as movies, and lists the characteristics they have in common. The other group should do the same with the men.

2. Report back and discuss:

- What are the main differences?
- What would you expect to happen if a group of people with the characteristics listed for women and a group of people with the characteristics listed for men tried to work together?
- Which group (from the lists) appears to have the best self-esteem?

3. Everyone: take time to think back through your life, and find an action which (a) you feel proud of, and (b) you could only have done as a person of your gender. Such actions could include being a son or daughter, a mother or father; being a supportive same-sex friend; being involved in a helpful way with a group or class where only people of your sex were members, and so on. Ensure you have plenty of time to fully recall such an action, then find a word to describe the personal characteristic you demonstrated at that time.

4. Share these words. (You may want to make two new lists from them, or to invite people to share the events themselves.)

Activity 2.8

AIM: to help you to understand the social origins of body image, and affirm your own body

1. By yourselves, list six individuals from your past or present life who have probably had an influence on how you feel about your body.

2. Relax and close your eyes, then tune in to the way you think and feel about your body.

3. Group leader: repeat the following instructions six times: 'Imagine that one of those six people comes into the room now and walks around you... Watch what that person looks at and hear what they would say about your

body if you asked them... Check how what they say affects your feelings about your own body... Ask yourself whether there is anything you have swallowed from their comments which you would like to spit out... If there is, actually imagine yourself spitting it out, and hear yourself saying something strongly positive about the aspect of your body concerned. Take time to ensure you have done this if you needed to.

4. Share in pairs what this was like, and then report back to the group. Questions might include:

- In what ways was your body image affected?

- How easy was it to reject comments you didn't want to swallow?

Resolving internal conflicts

AIM: to be able to move from inner conflict to a sense of integration and congruence.

Incongruity: when people don't make sense

- A friend tells you that he wants to cut down on his drinking because it's causing him too much trouble. But two weeks later he's caught driving while drunk, and loses his licence.

- A student you're teaching tells you she really wants to study more, but somehow when she gets home, all she does is watch TV.

- You try to get on with the people you work with, and to respect their own ways of doing things. But sometimes, for no reason, they just irritate you, and you find yourself yelling angrily at them.

These are situations of incongruity. Incongruity means that two different states in a person don't fit together. All of us have times when we've been incongruent. Times when you planned to do an exercise program every morning, but never got round to it; or when, even though you believe in honest relationships, you told your friend you couldn't go out with him or her, when actually you just didn't want to. These are small incongruities, but some people struggle with far more serious ones. Being an alcoholic for example. In such a case, a person may well tell you that they can give up drink any time - in fact they may say they plan to soon... but somehow it never happens. Or having a phobia where, even though the person knows in theory that they're safe in an elevator, they go into a frenzied panic when they try to step inside one.

When a person is incongruent, it's as if one 'part' of them wants to be in one state, or to get one result, while another 'part' of them wants another., opposed state or result. For example, part of them wants to be drunk and part of them wants to be sober; or part of them wants to be energetic and part of them wants to rest. By struggling inside, these two parts use up much of a person's energy.

Also, the person who is incongruent is sending out two different messages to other people, who may be confused about which message to believe. Does the alcoholic really want to give up drinking? Did you really mean to do that exercise program?

Resolving incongruity isn't only the single most interesting thing you can learn about communication; it's also the most important key to feeling good about your life. Imagine if there were ways to quickly solve internal conflicts like these. What would you do with the extra energy you'd have, if you weren't fighting with yourself in those ways? In this section we'll learn a process from NLP to resolve conflicts between internal states. This process is a simplified version of one described in Core Transformation (1994) by NLP trainers Connirae and Tamara Andreas.

The peaceful country

To understand how to resolve incongruity, it's useful to know how serious incongruities begin. Let me tell you a story about that.

Once upon a time there was a country; a very young country. It was idealistic, and the people there had great dreams about what the country would be like. It would be a country without war. It would be a prosperous country. They wanted to live together in cooperation and peace.

Unfortunately, in the early history of this country, there was an unexpected attack from outside. And not just one attack, but several. The people didn't know how to respond, and the whole country was thrown into turmoil. As they considered the best way of dealing with the situation, someone suggested: 'Lets ask for volunteers, and then we can set up a small group of people in charge of defending the border.' As they seemed to have very little choice and, at least by doing this most of the people would be able to carry on living their normal peaceful existences, they agreed on this course of action and sent a small group to defend the border.

The group knew that they were there to control the border. That was their job, and they wanted to do it as well as they possibly could.

After a while, very disturbing news began to come back from the border. It was said that the small group there was causing chaos, doing things of which the people in the centre of the country didn't approve of at all - things that were damaging to the community. Naturally, the people in the centre were really concerned about this. They just hadn't seemed to be able to find a solution that worked in every way.

Time went on, and unfortunately more problems occurred. The small group started sending messages saying that, to defend the border, more territory was needed. In other words they wanted to control more of the country. At first the people agreed, but wondered whether this situation would go on and on. And they began to wonder... 'who is really in charge here?

It was time to seriously consider what to do. So they organised a meeting with the people out on the border, and they called in a negotiator to assist them. The people from the centre, the small group and the negotiator began to communicate. The people from the centre said that some of the things going on at the border really concerned them, and they wondered if the small group had good reasons for them. (The way that they said this was very important, because they really wanted to understand the small group's highest intentions. They were therefore careful to express their worries in a way that showed that.)

They asked the small group about their intentions, and the group said that, of course, they were defending the border. They had to get tough, they explained, because it was so critical that this was done well.

The negotiator asked them what they aimed to achieve by defending the border in that way - if the border was fully defended, what would they gain by getting tough that was more important than the defence itself?

The group replied that the country would be safe - that's what they were trying to achieve.

Then the negotiator asked them what would they gain from having that safety that was even more important than the safety itself. The small group thought about it, and explained that it would enable them to live in peace, harmony and cooperation.

The people from the centre said that they now understood what had been happening, and explained: 'That's really interesting, because that's what we want, too. And do you notice that some of the things that have been happening really don't seem to get us to that state of peace and harmony very often? How would things change if we started off from a state of peace and found some new ways to protect it?'

So they were able to really begin to cooperate and find ways, together, of getting to a state of peace and harmony.

And you know the really important thing about this story? The most important thing to know is that the attack had been finished many years ago. That's right... it had been over for years.

Helping Stewart find his real intention

I've worked with a great many people who have incongruities, using the principle behind this story. One example was a young businessman I'll call Stewart, who complained that he felt 'driven' in his life. He really wanted to be able to relax, but it was as if part of him kept pushing him to succeed, to keep trying to prove something. This didn't fit in with his main intention - to relax - and when he tried to do a relaxation exercise, he would get more active!

Stewart knew, rationally, that he was achieving all he needed, but he kept getting into a pressured state. I explained to him that he could consider metaphorically that there was a part of him that was creating this pressured state. I asked him to imagine that part, because I knew it would have developed at a time when something important was going on in his life; I believed that the part had some reason for what it was doing (like the small group defending the border). I wondered, out loud, what that part might look like if he could visualise it, and what it might say to him.

Suddenly, Stewart said he had an image of himself as a schoolboy. I asked him to thank the part for communicating with him, and got him to ask the part: 'What purpose does this compulsive behaviour achieve? What do you want through being pressured and driven?' and to wait for an internal answer.

Stewart replied: 'I'm getting a picture of a situation with a teacher at school. I wanted to prove something to him. The part says its purpose is to prove something; to get revenge.'

I asked him to thank the part for telling him this. It's important that, although Stewart might not approve of revenge, he appreciate and listen to the part.

'Now imagine you could get that fully and completely. When you get your revenge fully and completely,' I asked him, 'what do you get, or what does that do for you, that's even more important?'

I waited for him to step into that imagined experience.

"Peace" he replied.

"And when you have that peace, fully and completely, what does that get you that's even more important than that?'

He nodded. 'A sense of wellbeing.'

'And when you have that sense of wellbeing fully and completely, what even more important thing does that give you?'

This time, as Stewart experienced the higher outcome, he flushed red and his breathing changed. Almost awkwardly, he explained: 'It's amazing...'he struggled to find the word... 'emptying'.

Already I had the sense that Stewart was aware of a what I'd call,a 'core state'; a state as central to his life as peace and harmony were to the country that was attacked in the story. To check, I asked again: 'When you have that "emptying"" fully and completely, what even more important thing do you get through having that?

'There's nothing further' he said, with total calmness.

Stewart's 'part' had been causing him to feel driven, yet ultimately it intended to bring him to a state of profound peace and emptying. It was as if the part couldn't accept that it was permissible simply to be in that state of peace now.

I drew his attention to this: 'So somehow this part has come to believe that being driven is a way to create emptying. And often, parts of us get, unconsciously, the belief that they have to do something else in order to experience their real outcome. But actually it doesn't work very well. When parts believe they have to go through a sequence to get there, for example:

being driven - revenge - peace - wellbeing - emptying

they don't get there so often. So now that you know what that part actually wants, is it OK to start from there and find out how that changes things?

He agreed. I asked him how his life would change if he just had that core state as a way of being in the world. How would it change his feeling about peace, his feeling about revenge, his need to be driven? Stewart agreed that now he felt as if there was no need for revenge, and he could find other ways to get that peace.

'That's great. It's gone. It's totally changed. I feel much calmer. Thanks, Richard.'

Positive intentions and core states

Notice that what I asked Stewart to do was to find the intention behind the behaviour. What need did it meet? What was it trying to get?

His first answer was a 'negative' intention - to get revenge. I therefore asked him what he would get through achieving revenge - what the intention of revenge was. This time he described a more 'positive' intention - peace.

Even when a person has a very negative first intention (for example, I used this process with someone who smoked cigarettes and got them to discover that the part of them that smoked wanted them to die!), I can always find a positive intention by asking: 'And when you have that fully and completely, what do you get through having that which is even more important?' Eventually they say: 'freedom', or 'an end to the struggle', or something else that leads to a positive intention.

As I keep asking for the intention, we shift towards more and more important intentions (or, to use a term from Chapter 9, 'higher values'). If the person tells me something more detailed and less important, I ask again, emphasising that the aim is to find out what's even more important. For example, if Stewart had said that the reason he wanted 'peace' was to be able to watch TV comfortably on Sundays (a more detailed result of peace, instead of an even more important reason), I would have asked: 'And if you get peace and are able to watch TV on Sundays comfortably, what do you get that's even more important?

The person begins to remember what is really, deeply important in their life. These states that are deeply important to a person are called core states. Sometimes the person will discover that their core state has a spiritual significance, such as 'communion with God' or 'spiritual enlightenment'. Whatever the result, this process will seem very special to the person. And many people find that this simple exercise clears up a challenge they've had for a long time.

Once the person knows that both 'parts' inside them have a positive intention, it's as if there's no need for the existence of separate parts any more. They can act as a whole person, and find solutions which work for the whole of their experience.

Activity 2.9

AIM: to find the positive intention behind a challenge, and generate new solutions to an internal conflict

If you have a group leader, he or she can guide the group through this process, pausing at each step. Otherwise it can be done in pairs or individually

1. Identify an emotional response (a state you get into sometimes) or a behaviour pattern that you want to change: something you do that you wish you didn't. Write this down (step 1).

2. Use the relaxation process from activity 2.3 to get into a relaxed state.

3. Ask yourself the following question: 'If there was a part of me that created this feeling or behaviour, what would it feel like, look like and sound like?' Close your eyes and be aware of the part. Thank it for communicating with you. If you need to, assure it that your only purpose in communicating with it is to assist it to meet its highest intention.

4. Ask what the part's intention is for you. Just allow the answer to enter your mind in whatever form it chooses. Write this answer down (step 2). Thank the part for communicating, whatever the answer is.

5. Now ask: 'When you have that outcome, fully and completely just the way you want it, what do you get through having that which is even more important?' Go slowly and gently, allowing the part to fully experience what it would be like to have this outcome, so that it can notice what even more important thing having this outcome will give you. Write down the answer below each of the previous ones, numbering it as step 3.

6. Repeat 5, above, numbering the answer and writing it down, until your answer feels so special, so positive and so complete that there's nothing more important. Enjoy this state. Check that the part understands that its longwinded attempt to get to this 'core' state by doing or feeling other things is not as successful as just being there. At the time when it decided it wasn't OK to just have that core state, it was too young to realise this.

7. Ask yourself: 'So how does just having [insert your own core state] change and transform [the step you wrote down just before the core state]? Keep asking: 'How does already having this core state transform the experience of...' for each outcome back to step 1.

8. Notice how, when you think of the situation that was a challenge, it feels different now. You may even already know some new solutions you could think up that would work for the whole of you in the situation that was a challenge.

Summary

This chapter has considered the state of mind you're in from three different angles. Firstly, you learned four powerful techniques for creating the state you'd like to be in, whether it be relaxation, motivation, confidence, caring, or whatever. The four ways are:

1. visualisation: using your ability to imagine and picture things
2. affirmation: the way you talk to yourself
3. body position and breathing style, and
4. anchoring yourself into the desired state using a stimulus linked to it.

Secondly, we discussed the effects of cultural and gender differences on your state of mind. Equalising power in society can make it easier for all of us to be in a state of mind where we feel good about who we are - a state of esteem. For Maori, this process involves making links to the wider context of Maoritanga. For women, it requires an increasing respect for women's rights and contributions.

Thirdly, we considered the situation where a person has an incongruity - two states in conflict - and looked at how to heal incongruity by identifying the higher positive intention of each part of a person.

Chapter 3: The Context of Communication

KEY CONCEPTS

- Proxemics (closeness)
- Body language and culture
- Gestures and body language
- Sensory system use (visual/auditory/kinesthetic)
- Rapport

Approaching others

AIM: to be able to recognise someone's intimate and personal zones according to Edward Hall's model.

Context

As you know, reading a book is very different from talking to someone. For instance, if I say 'Hello' to you here on the page, all you'll get is the word 'Hello'. In real life you might have received hundreds of other messages as I said that one word. Check it out and you'll see what I mean. Pause now and remember a time when someone you really liked, someone you were strongly attracted to, said 'Hello' to you... Most likely, as you remember that, you're aware of the tone of voice they used, and how fast or slow they said it. You can probably see that slight smile on their face as their lips form the word, and even feel the rush of interest inside you as you move physically a little closer to them.

What's different? The answer concerns the context of the word they said: the things happening around and at the same time as the word Hello. Talking to someone is high-context communication. By comparison, using an automatic teller machine to get money from your bank is low-context communication. The machine does the same thing whether you smile or not, and no matter how sensitively you touch its keyboard: it's not interested in the context. Human beings usually are. In this chapter we'll explore the context of human communication; often called 'body language".

The value of body language

You'll understand the reason for learning about body language when you think back to meeting that person you were strongly attracted to. As you spoke with them, you were probably very interested in understanding how they felt about you. It may have been important to you to know how they reacted to whatever you said and did. That's one good reason to learn body language: so you can tell what effect you're having.

Another good reason is so you can create the sense of 'rapport" which I mentioned in Chapter 1: the ability to make that other person feel really understood by you, and for you to understand them. That sense of understanding doesn't just come from saying the right words to each other. It comes from using the right tone of voice, the right body gestures, even the right movements of your eyes (by 'right' I mean right for both you and the person you are with). That's what you'll learn in this chapter.

Although we are dealing with body language in this particular chapter, it's useful to remember that body language is the most important part of all person-to-person communication. Albert Mehrabian (the author of *Silent Messages*) suggests that only about seven per cent of the impact of a message comes from the words you say. The other 93 per cent is context. This is particularly amazing when you remember that most people are not even aware what messages they are sending nonverbally. Think about it. Most of your communication is happening at an unconscious level!

Pupil size

Some of the messages you're sending aren't even under your control (ever tried to stop yourself blushing once you've started?). A good example is the size of the pupils in your eyes. Professor of psychology Eckhard Hess (1975) researched pupil size and found that even three-month-old babies smile more when their caregiver's pupils are dilated (large) than when they are constricted (small).

Adults tend to describe people with dilated pupils as 'open", 'warm' and 'gentle', and people with constricted pupils as 'harsh", "cold' and 'sneaky. So people are sending messages every time they look at someone; messages that even a three-month-old baby can pick up.

Of course, you may have realised this already. Sometimes people use the term 'bedroom eyes' to describe a person whose pupils are dilated in a way that reminds them of sexual attraction; or 'beady little eyes' to describe someone whose constricted pupils make them seem 'sneaky' or 'reserved'. In parts of southern Europe (for example Spain), women used to put diluted juice from the poisonous plant belladonna (the name means 'beautiful woman') in their eyes to attract men. Why? Because belladonna dilates the pupils. In the same way, poker players sometimes wear dark glasses so that the excitement of a winning hand can't be detected from their dilated pupils.

Intuitively, people realise that they are sending and receiving messages just by the size of their pupils. If you've ever noticed this, you can congratulate yourself on your skill at reading body language. And you'll find it easier to understand that communication is continuous: it's always going on. The moment you look at someone, your eyes are sending messages - like it or not! Most of the time you haven't even been aware that it's happening, let alone been planning what message to send.

Proxemics

Let's think again about how you're communicating as soon as you've met someone. Even the distance you stand or sit away from them is communicating things. It was anthropologist Edward Hall (1959)who first called the study of how far apart people stand 'proxemics'. Hall observed that, for every person you meet, there will be a distance between the two of you with which you feel comfortable. If they come closer than that, you will feel as if 'your space' has been invaded; you may feel cramped, anxious, even suffocated. Obviously, the distance at which you can relax will be closer for a friend than for a person you've just met.

For most people, the close intimate zone (area A in above diagram) and the intimate zone (area B) stretch out to about 46 cm from the body. Generally, in cultures of British origin, people expect only very close friends and family members to stand or sit this close to them.

Of course, what you expect and what actually happens are two different things. Other people are forced to move into your intimate space when you stand in a queue, in a lift, in a crowded place, and so on. If you are a health professional, your job requires you to move into other people's intimate space quite soon after meeting them. Even in these situations, people usually feel anxious about their personal space being invaded. They may cope by avoiding eye contact more than usual, not talking, and so on. Watch next time you are in an lift or a queue, and be aware of your own response as others move closer than 46 cm from you. You'll understand quickly why, in cultures of British origin, this is not the best distance to stand from a person you're just meeting.

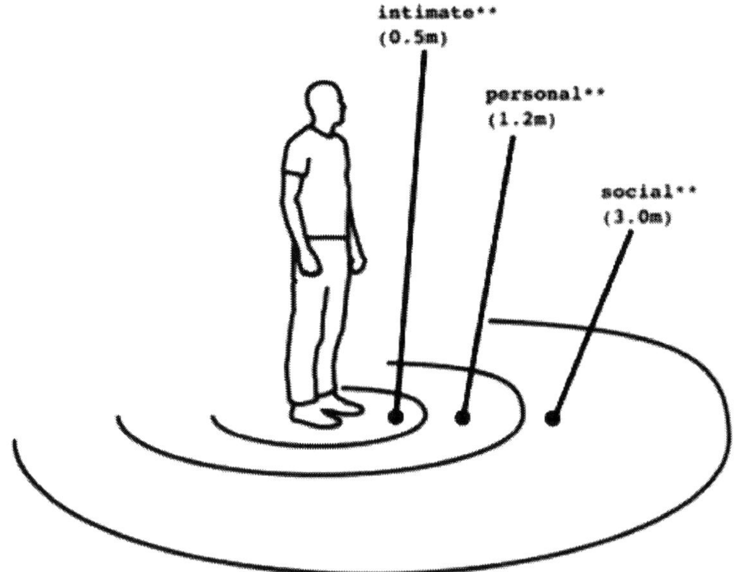

Personal and social zones

The personal zone (area C in the diagram) stretches from about half a metre to a metre out from the body. This is the distance at which people usually stand at friendly gatherings such as parties. Being this distance away demonstrates a deliberate interest in getting to know someone, whereas strangers and people not known so well tend to stand one to three-and-half metres away (area D, the social zone).

When you meet someone new, standing somewhere between one and three metres away from them will usually tell them you are friendly, without making them feel invaded. Exactly how far away you stand will depend on both your cultural origins and on whether you grew up in an urban or rural setting (people from the country stand further away than city people).

Area E is the public zone, used for speaking to an audience, for example. If you work in a group and sit more than three-and-a-half metres away, you will almost certainly create a sense of distance which makes it harder for others to share with you. Many group leaders prefer to seat people in a circle so that each person is actually in the personal zone (or even closer, as with the person beside them).

Activity 3.1

AIM: to get used to the difference between the intimate zone, personal zone and social zone

1 Get into pairs and stand three metres away from each other (this requires either a large space, or people standing in two lines facing their partners). Discuss with your partner:

- In which situations would you stand this far away from your partner?
- When was the last time you remember talking to someone from this distance away, and what relationship did you have with that person?
- What does it feel like, now, to talk to someone from this distance?

2 Move closer together - one metre apart - and discuss again the three questions above.

3 Now stand about 40 cm apart and answer the three questions above, plus the following: What things are you doing right now, if any, to manage being at this distance?

4 Return to the group and report back. You may also discuss the distance people usually sit or stand from each other in this group. Which zone are they usually in?

Spot the difference

AIM: to be able to specify one male-female difference and four AIM cultural differences in body language.

Culture and gesture

In their book Talking Past Each Other, Joan Metge and Patricia Kinloch recount the beginning of a fight in a hotel bar. A person from the Pacific culture of Niue accidentally bumped into a Pakeha (New Zealander of European origin), spilling his glass of beer. The Niuean apologised, and the Pakeha replied: "It doesn't matter', waving his hand away and down towards the floor to emphasise the point. Recognising the Niuean gesture for 'Come here, the Nuiean moved into the Pakeha's intimate zone. Such a sudden move could only mean a fight, the Pakeha realised. He decided to get in the first swing, and hit the Niuean.

just as surely as verbal language varies from culture to culture, so does body language. To a Pakeha New Zealander, the gesture 'come here' tends to be waving the hand up and towards the head. In most Pacific cultures (and in Japanese and some European cultures), the hand is held palm down and waved in towards the body to say the same thing. Knowing such a simple thing can make the difference between a friend and an enemy.
Showing respect

In most cases, when people meet each other, they are searching for ways to show each other friendship and respect. Both people in the ill-fated meeting in the hotel bar wanted exactly that. And yet, even aside from the different understanding of the downward wave, they probably misunderstood each other's most basic ways of showing respect.

Eye contact is a very important way of demonstrating respect when listening to someone in European or Pakeha culture. Body language expert Allan Pease describes in his book Body Language (an excellent study of Pakeha body language) the downturned eyebrows and sidewards glance, as well as the closed eyes gesture, as evidence of a negative or critical reaction. For Pakeha, someone who can 'look you in the eye' is honest and respectful of what you are saying; someone who does not is shifty and hostile.

Maori and Tagata Pasifica (Pacific Island Polynesian) speakers, on the other hand, consider it impolite to look directly into another person's eyes while talking to them. To do so is a gesture of conflict, whereas looking down, looking to the side and closing the eyes while speaking are often used to show respect and friendliness in these cultures.

Most Pakeha will appreciate how invaded a Maori or Samoan speaker feels by the Pakeha level of eye contact, if they think of the relentless (to a New Zealander) eye contact many North Americans expect. In some North

American cultural settings, a speaker may keep their eyes fixed on the listener's throughout an entire speech, pursuing the New Zealander's eyes as they shift to look away while thinking. This is comparable to the Pakeha-Maori difference.

Standing or sitting

Another important difference in showing respect involves standing or sitting down. In Pakeha culture, to stand up for someone shows respect, for example a student may be expected to stand in front of a teacher, and the court stands while the magistrate enters. In these cases, respectfulness means not sitting down until a seat is offered.

Metge and Kinloch point out that in Samoan and Maori culture, the opposite is often true. People do not stand up in front of an important speaker (even if they must leave the room, they tend to do so in a crouching, bended over position); and the best way to show respect upon entering a room may well be to sit down and lower oneself.

If you are working in a people-centred job, it will be a relief to know that both the Pakeha who comes in and stands rather stiffly above you, and the Maori who comes in and slips down into their seat may be gesturing respect. In both cultures brief body lowering (a nod or a bow) tends to indicate respect.

Other cultural differences: the Japanese example

Whichever cultural setting you live and work in, it pays to check out the meaning of gestures and the context of what people say. In our time in Japan, I experienced the Japanese system of gestures. There, when speaking to each other, people put slightly more space between themselves than westerners do, and touch each other far less. Research shows that the Japanese use about a third of the eye contact used by Americans (which places them somewhere near New Zealanders!). On the other hand, when listening, the Japanese person will nod more, to indicate attention.

One basic principle behind the Japanese use of nonverbal communication is that Japanese people tend to value calmness and centredness, so that open displays of anger or frustration are avoided. In fact, the Japanese sometimes distinguish two kinds of truth: tatemae (public truth) - what they would like others to receive in order to preserve harmony; and honne (private truth) - the person's actual feelings. Some gestures, such as a smile when something embarrassing has happened, are expressions of tatemae. Other gestures are similar to their western counterparts, such as the placing of a hand on the back of the neck to indicate discomfort about what is being discussed.

Some Japanese gestures have specific conscious meanings. For example, fanning the right hand in front of the face as if brushing away a fly is a gesture meaning "no'. Belief that someone is lying can be indicated by licking the index finger and smoothing an eyebrow. For women, embarrassment or modesty is indicated by covering the mouth.

Cross-cultural gestures

Luckily, some gestures do work cross-culturally. The smile is an example: genetically coded as a response to pleasure, it occurs even in those who are deaf and blind, and is understood in every known culture.

The handshake has some universality, despite its European origin. However, in their book Te Marae, Pat and Hiwi Tauroa caution that the clasping of the hand or forearm with the left hand, while shaking the right, may come across to Maori as a sign of insincerity. Allan Pease (see page 54) advises that clasping the arm or shoulder while shaking hands can seem insincere to Australians as well, so this may be a result of our general suspicion of people who seem too eager to reassure us.

Of course, the above points do not mean that, for example, every Maori will prefer to look down more while talking than every Pakeha. I am merely describing what Metge and Kinloch found to be common patterns. One of the delightful things about human beings is their individual uniqueness. What we can learn from body language is that each gesture is unique to that person and that moment. However, some gestures are common enough, and it is therefore worth knowing their usual meaning - it could prevent a lot of bar fights, for a start!

Understanding Maori/Pacific Island gestures

There are several situations in which a Maori or Pacific Island Polynesian might choose to use body gestures to convey a message that a Pakeha would always say in words:

- A nod or an upward movement of the head and/or eyebrows conveys 'yes' to all Maori/ Pacific Island cultures, whereas for Pakeha the word 'yes' needs to be spoken to be polite. To Maori, the gesture alone may be perfectly adequate, and the Pakeha's lack of understanding could easily seem a refusal to acknowledge.

• In a Polynesian culture, shaking the head or staring unresponsively down may clearly indicate 'no'.

• To catch someone's eyes and then move the head and eyes sideways can say quite clearly: 'Go over there please.

With such sensitivity to body language, it's possible, for Pakeha to get the impression that 'a lot is going on without anyone talking about it'. The raising of eyebrows, which so obviously means 'yes' to a Samoan, may be understood as puzzlement to a Pakeha; the fixed downward stare which says 'no' may be taken as agreement. Pakeha expect words to be added to clarify the intention. In the Maori or Samoan situation, the gesture is used more precisely.

There are a few gestures which have caused difficulty for Maori students in the Pakeha school system, and Metge and Kinloch comment particularly on the following three:

• Hunching the shoulders up round the ears which, in a Maori context, may well mean: 'I don't know', but to Pakeha also suggests '... and I don't care'.

• Rapid, repeated frowning which can indicate: 'I'm uncertain, please assist me', but is often read by Pakeha as straight disagreement.

• A sniff can mean acknowledgment of a mistake (sort of "OK, I goofed. Sorry'), and yet can be taken as: 'Who cares?" by Pakeha.

You can well imagine how these three gestures, used by a Maori student, could easily spoil their chances with a culturally unaware Pakeha teacher. It's another case of people's best intentions being sadly misread.

In many such situations the Pakeha expects a verbal explanation, whereas the Maori prefers a nonverbal gesture this is the case in the expression of feelings generally. This means that a touch or hug accompanies Maori communication of sympathy, gratitude or apology more often than for Pakeha. The model of intimate and personal zones around someone, which we discussed before, needs to be modified when moving from Pakeha to Maori culture.

Activity 3.2

AIM: to develop your skills in recognising the non-verbal expression of feelings

1 Use two decks of playing cards, or enough to enable each player to have six cards with at least six left in the deck. Shuffle the cards, give six to each player, and put the deck face down in the middle of the group. Keep your cards hidden from view.

2 Each card represents an emotion. Write down the following list and place it where everyone can see it:

Ace	love	8	shyness
2	joy	9	respect
3	hope	10	agreement
4	loneliness	Jack	apology
5	sadness	Queen	disagreement
6	fear	King	confusion
7	anger		

3 The player on the dealer's left begins. This player selects a card from their hand and lays it face down in front of them. Their job is to express the emotion represented by that card, without speaking.

4 All other players then check their cards. If they think they have a card matching the emotion expressed, they place it face down in front of them. If not, they do nothing this round.

5 When all the cards are down, everyone who has placed a card down (including the person who expressed the emotion) turns their cards face up.

a If one or more of the group have matched the emotion exactly, then they and the expressor put that card into the deck. Any player who put down a wrong card keeps it, and draws another from the top of the deck.

b If no-one matched the card of the person expressing the emotion, then all other players simply keep their cards and do not need to pick up another. The expressor must now keep his or her own card and take another one from the deck.

6 It is now the turn of the person on the left of the last expressor. The aim of the game is to get rid of all your cards by accurately expressing and recognising emotions.

7 As a variation, you could play assuming the context of a particular culture known to you.

8 Discuss:

- How easy was it to recognise /express emotions?
- Were you aware of cultural differences in expression?

Men and women

Even within a culture, people's body language varies depending on, for example, gender (male or female), and style of thinking (visual, auditory or kinesthetic - to be discussed at the end of this chapter).

Research shows that, in most cultures, men and women use different body language from a very early age. Allan Pease refers to the fact that when a man and a woman have to edge past each other in a narrow space, the man tends to turn towards the woman, while the woman turns away from the man. In her book Invisible Women, Dale Spender observes that men sit and stand so that they take up more space than women. This even happens at primary school, where little boys' wide-spread knees form an obstacle down the rows of desks, while little girls" generally do not.

Space-taking

People sometimes rationalise this difference in space-taking by saying that it's a result of women wearing dresses, or of men being naturally bigger. But if you compare, for example, a tall woman wearing jeans with a short man, you'll soon realise that this can't be the complete answer.

The most convincing evidence that space-taking is a result of our modern society's attitudes to 'manliness' and 'womanliness' is found in history. Only a few hundred years ago, when women in Europe always wore dresses, they satvery wide-legged. Take a look at a statue of 'Britannia' or a similar older model of womanliness and you'll see that it's true.

Similarly, we tend to assume that for a man to put his arm round a woman's body and arms (actually pinning her arms to her sides) is a normal way for two people to walk together, while for a woman to do this to a man is odd. Ancient Egyptian statues, however, always depict the woman (as mother and protector of humanity) holding her partner in this way.

Spender describes men's extra space-taking as part of their general tendency to grab more attention, resources and control. This may not be their intention; however, it happens and is therefore important for us to be aware of. Men working in helping professions, for instance, will be able to increase their level of rapport with women clients and colleagues if they share the space and time available more fully.

A hopeful gesture

Increasing our rapport with others is important to all of us, male and female, from every culture. And an awareness of the meanings of body language can sometimes bridge the most extraordinary differences.

In her book My Friends: The Wild Chimpanzees, Jane van Lawick-Goodall, an anthropologist working with wild chimpanzees, gives a graphic illustration of how the use of gesture can bridge such a gap: 'I was alone with David, a chimp, that day, deep in the forest. I held out a palm nut to him and, although he did not want it, he accepted my offering. For a full ten seconds, he held my hand gently and firmly in his. Finally, with a last glance at the nut, he let it fall gently to the ground. In that brief exalted moment, I felt a thrill of communication with a wild chimpanzee... He had reached out to reassure me by the pressure of his fingers. Although he rejected my gift, he gave me one of his own.'

Reading this story, it occurs to me that if a chimpanzee can reach across the gap between two different species, surely you and I will find ways to cross the much smaller space between human and human.

Activity 3.3

AIM: to consider how 'masculine' and 'feminine' postures relate to 'male' and 'female' social roles

1 Close your eyes and think of the most feminine body posture you know, using your own ideas about what 'feminine' means. The posture may be seated or standing. Still with your eyes closed, get into that posture.

2 Open your eyes and look around. Remaining in your posture, discuss:

- What are the similarities between postures?
- How comfortable is the posture?
- How confident do people look in their postures?

3 Repeat steps (1) and (2) using the most masculine posture you can think of.

4 Discuss what this tells us about men and women in our society?

The General Impression

AIM: to be able to recognise common gesture clusters for attraction, anxiety, dishonesty and confidence.

Two first impressions

There is a surprising similarity in the way people first meet and begin successful friendships.

Marie Skodowska was a Polish woman living in France late last century. One day in 1894, at the home of a Polish friend, she was introduced to a 35-year-old French scientist named Pierre. She later wrote: "When I came in, Pierre Curie was standing in the window recess near a door leading to the balcony... I was struck by the expression of his clear gaze... His rather slow reflective words, his simplicity, and his smile, at once grave and young, inspired confidence'.

A year later their friendship and scientific partnership blossomed into marriage, and Marie took the name under which she would, within six years, make the most important scientific discovery of the decade: the discovery of radium (Described in Birch, 1988).

In 1942, George Adamson was working as a game warden in Kenya, when he was introduced to a young Austrian woman, Joy Bally. He describes his first impression of her in his book: 'Joy... who turned out to be Austrian, was quite uninhibited. Fair-haired and slim, she wore a slinky, silver dress, and seemed entirely unaware that her growing animation accentuated the distortions of her curious English... Within a few days I sensed a growing attraction between us, which Joy seemed to encourage.'

Upon their next meeting six months later, Joy told him: 'she had decided I was just the kind of man for her. Our few days on safari together had confirmed it. She fixed me with her blue eyes, and smiled an unspoken question.'

Over the next 40 years, until their deaths at the hands of elephant poachers, George and Joy Adamson's friendship, and their work protecting African wildlife (as immortalised in the film Born Free), were testimony to the power of that first meeting. (Adamson, 1986)

Attraction

The nonverbal signals of attraction (sexual or not) are usually quite strong. Both Marie Curie and George Adamson refer in their accounts to the other person's smile, eyes, and apparent openness. These, along with other, briefer gestures, would have come together in what Allan Pease calls a cluster.

A cluster is a series of nonverbal signals which back each other up, enabling others to be more certain of their actual meaning. Someone smiling, for example, may or may not be pleased to meet you. They may be smiling to cover up nervousness, or because they've just remembered a joke someone told them. However, if someone smiles while giving you slightly more eye contact than usual, with their pupils relatively wide, pointing their body towards you, gesturing with open arms and holding their palms outward... such a cluster is fairly convincing evidence of friendly interest.
Sexual interest

When sexual interest is being expressed, two other types of gesture will probably be added. First, there are preening gestures (similar to a bird preening its feathers). These may include stroking, smoothing or tossing back the hair, and straightening clothing such as a collar, tie or belt. Even the muscle tone of the body is enhanced as the person 'presents' themselves well for the other.

The second type of gesture expressing sexual interest is one which draws attention (directly or by mimicry) to the sex organs. This includes widening the distance between the legs (or crossing and uncrossing them), stroking the thighs, putting a thumb in the pocket or under a belt so the hand points to the genitals, opening the mouth and moistening the lips, and fondling cylindrical objects such as wine glasses. At the same time, the person expressing interest may allow their gaze to wander down to the other person's chest or lower (whereas in most social encounters, it remains on the face).

There are, of course, two reasons for understanding these signals. One is so you can recognise them in someone else. The other is so you can choose to send them or not. There are, after all, some situations where you will choose not to express sexual interest, as well as some where you will want to.

Resistance/anxiety

Resistance or anxiety about meeting someone is also expressed in clusters of gestures. These gestures will usually include facing the body away from someone and leaning back, constricting the pupils, and using the arms and legs to form a protective barrier in front of the body.

The meaning of the last of these gestures has probably caused more disbelief in body language than any other, so let's discuss it. Are people who cross their arms, or clasp one arm/hand with the other, or cross their legs really anxious? The easiest answer is: 'not necessarily'. They may be cold, or just in the habit of using that gesture. Again, the cluster of gestures is important.

Another answer, however, is that it doesn't matter: either way, other people will react as if the person is anxious. Research (which you can easily repeat yourself) indicates that, when people are shown photos of someone with their arms or legs crossed, they identify them as more anxious, more reserved, and more resistant.

If you want to appear open to others, it's to your advantage to have an open posture. And if you want to ensure that others can relax and open up to you, it may be useful to encourage them to assume an open posture (for example by giving them a task which is easier to do with unfolded arms, such as holding a page of information).

Lying and uncertainty

Related to the situation of anxiety is the situation of lying, or being uncertain about what you are saying. The most significant body signals displayed in such situations are hand to head movements: covering the mouth, rubbing the nose/ eye/ ear, scratching the neck, and pulling at the collar. Anthropologist Desmond Morris suggests that such movements both cover up the tell-tale signs of insincerity, and deal with the physical discomfort felt by the person constructing a story. If you observe these gestures in someone you're talking to, it would be useful to check their statement. Remember, these signals do not always mean that a deliberate lie is being told - they may simply indicate uncertainty.

Confidence

At the opposite extreme from signals of uncertainty are the gestures of extreme confidence and dominance. These include forming a steeple shape by pressing opposite fingertips together; clasping the hands together behind the back (not to be confused with actually clutching the arm behind the back, which is often a sign of frustration); displaying the thumbs while folding hands under a coat collar or into pockets; hands on hips; and leaning back with hands clasped behind the head. Most of these gestures expose the front of the body 'fearlessly'. Their meaning can vary from sexual confidence to dominance, or simply general self-assurance.

When you see these gestures in others, you will need to interpret the meaning based on the situation. For your own behaviour, be aware that these signals can come across as arrogant and overbearing. The gestures for openness and attraction will give you much safer ways of showing confident interest.

Also, while hand gestures which move away from your body appear more confident than self-enclosing gestures, some of these so-called "baton' gestures will again create that impression of overbearing intention. Waving your finger at someone may seem to you to be simply a way of emphasising your point. To others, it may well carry associations of being told off. Open palm gestures will enable you to add similar emphasis, without being so threatening.

Subtle changes

So far we've listed various gestures which, in a cluster, would disclose attraction, anxiety, dishonesty and confidence. You'll remember from the last chapter (on states of mind) that, as a person moves from one emotional state to another, they change in a great many subtle ways. Larger-scale gestures are only one of the sources of information. Other, minute changes occur, and these tend to be very individual.

The changes which can be observed fit into five categories. Remember, as you read this list, that you already recognise and respond to all these subtle changes. We're just giving them names so you can be more consistently aware of them:

1 Voice changes: the speed of talking, the loudness, the tone of voice (high and low), and the type of words used all vary

2 Eye changes: these include pupil dilation (discussed previously) and eye movements (discussed in the next section).

3 Changes in posture and gesture: large-scale movements.

4 Changes in breathing: the speed of breathing, the type and number of pauses in breathing, the amount of air taken in, and the area of the chest/abdomen used, all vary.

5 Skin changes: these include colour, moisture on the skin, and apparent muscle tension, as shown by tightness of the skin. Some areas of skin (especially the lips) may expand or contract with different emotions.

Practice

Generally, information comes in recognisable clusters, otherwise it would be too much to be aware of at one time. Imagine meeting someone for the first time, in a polytechnic or university cafeteria. You ask if the place beside her is taken, and she shakes her head. "Help yourself', she says, smiling and gesturing with an open hand towards the seat, while sitting up and leaning forward a little. In the course of a brief chat while eating, she explains that she works as a chef at a local hotel. As she describes this job, she leans over the table, pressing her fingertips together so her hands form an inverted V shape. She raises her head and speaks more rapidly and fluently, still smiling.

'Are you doing a course here?' you ask. She frowns slightly while nodding, and closes her hands into a clasp. Looking down now, she explains: 'My boss asked me to do this course. They say it's really useful for the general hotel staff '.

Her arms are now folded, and she is speaking more slowly. Some of the colour has gone out of her cheeks. 'I guess I'll learn a lot from it. Should be quite interesting', she adds, her hand covering her mouth slightly. 'Anyway, what are you doing here?' Her smile returns as she waits for your reply.

What happened? That's right. Almost certainly she's happy to meet you, feels good about her job, and isn't enjoying the course. Not so complicated in real life is it?

The only way to really develop this skill that you have is to practise observing people in various situations. The television is a wonderful tool for this. To observe the visual changes, try watching for a quarter of an hour with the sound turned off, and see how many of the things you've been reading about you can find.

Activity 3.4

AIM: to remind you of your ability to correctly identify states of attraction and dislike from non-verbal cues

1 In this exercise, even though we reduce the available information to a minimum, observers will still be able to recognise the subtle body cues as

someone changes state. The exercise could be done first with the whole group observing, and then in pairs. In each case one person (the subject) should sit in a chair facing the observer/s. To reduce their anxiety, as well as the cues available to the observers, get the subject to close their eyes. Ensure observers can see both sides of the person's face, and their whole body.

2 Ask the subject to think of someone they are strongly attracted to; someone they really like. Say to them:

- 'Get a picture of the person's face and see them in front of you.'
- 'Hear the kind of things they commonly say, in the tone of voice they'd use.'
- ‘Get a sense of what it would be like if they were beside you right now.'

Get them to keep repeating the three steps above, while observers mentally 'take of photograph' of them in that state.

3 Ask the subject to clear their mind and then think of someone whom they strongly dislike, or strongly disliked at some time. Examples could be superiors with whom they've had conflicts, villains from TV series, or politicians with whom they disagree. Using the same words as in step (2) above, giving the instructions to see, hear, and feel that memory. Get the observers to take a new photograph of this state.

4 Ask the subject to clear their mind once again, and now to think of one of the two people at random, without saying which one they have in mind. Again, use the same instructions to encourage their full recall. Ask the observers to guess which person they are thinking of, then to tell you how they know.

5 Repeat step (4) until most observers can detect the nonverbal changes, then do the exercise with another subject. Emphasise that the cues will differ from person to person.

Just Thinking

AIM: to be able to recognise sensory accessing from gesture, breathing, skin changes, eye movements and voice changes.

Sensory system use

Most people can tell when someone else is 'thinking'. For a start, they often don't look at you or the things around them while they do it: their eyes are "somewhere else'. And often they touch their body with their hands, for example rubbing their forehead, stroking their chin, or clasping their hands on their tummy.

In the early 1970s, NLP developers John Grinder and Richard Bandler (1979) found a way to be rather more specific about this. They discovered that it was possible to tell how someone was thinking from their body language.

What we call 'thinking" involves seeing mental images (visual processing), talking to yourself and sounding things out (auditory processing), walking yourself through situations and getting the feel of things (kinesthetic processing), and even sniffing around and getting the flavour of a situation (olfactory/ gustatory processing). In New Zealand, most people use one or more of the first three ways of processing information, but in some cultures, a lot of people's thinking is done by smell and taste. For example, the Yolngu people of Northern Australia can distinguish, by smell, minute amounts of the poison cycasin in cycad nuts. Anyone else needs a chromatograph machine to find which nuts are poisonous and which are safe to eat. The Yolngu way of understanding the world involves an acute sense of smell (Yunupingu, 1994).

Other cultures encourage mental processing using the other senses. The Russian psychologist Alexander R. Luria (1969) spent decades studying a person he called 'S', whose extraordinary visual memory enabled him to almost instantly memorise a list of say 50 numbers and recall them 17 years later by 'seeing' the list again in his mind.

While European cultures have cultivated vision in this way, in Polynesia, auditory memory has been enhanced. Hohua Tutengaehe, previously Kaumatua (elder) at Te Whare Runanga o Otautahi (Christchurch Polytechnic), was one of several Maori Tohunga (experts in Maori lore) who can accurately recite tribal genealogy (whakapapa) for several hours in a row.

Preferences

All of us who can see, hear, smell, taste and feel will also think using these ways of accessing and representing information, and in a particular context we may have a preference. Those who prefer the kinesthetic (body feelings) system will tend to move and talk more slowly. Their voices will have a deeper tone and they will talk about 'getting in touch' with 'something solid','feeling' that things are 'deep' , "shallow', 'close', 'distant', and so on.

People whose preference is for the auditory (sounds and words) system will move and talk in a measured, rhythmic way. Their voices will be resonant and they will talk about whether things 'sound right', 'click", 'tune in with each other harmoniously', 'grate, and so on.

Those whose preference is for the visual (pictures and images) system, will move and speak quickly. Their voices will be higher, and they will talk about the way they 'see' things, whether they 'get the picture", 'take a dim view' of something, have 'brightened up', and so on.

Conflict and sensory preference

In my work as a coach, I frequently counsel couples, and more often than not one of the issues is their different mode of thinking. A couple whom I'll call Carol and Ed came for counselling one day with just such a challenge. Ed began speaking. He looked up to the right and said, in a fast, relatively high-pitched voice: 'One of the things I see wrong is this: I can't imagine what Carol does all day. When I get home, all bright and looking forward to seeing her, the first thing I face when I open the door is the mess in the kitchen. If I've tidied up the hall cupboard that morning, by evening it'll be spread all over the show again. I mean, sometimes Carol doesn't even look like she's brushed her hair that day. It doesn't look to me like she cares about us at all.'

Carol, looking down to the right, replied in a low slow, quiet voice: 'Well of course I care. I care about our family. I want it to be a warm, comfortable place for us all to live, and that's what I put my energy into during the day. Perhaps I'm just not so in contact with those things you describe. But when you come home you're so distant, I don't feel as if you really care at all. You just rush past us.'

One way to understand this conflict is to realise that these two people love each other, but they are speaking different languages. Ed, whose main sensory system is visual, looks to see if Carol loves him, but can't find the evidence (no matter how warmly and lovingly Carol holds him). Carol, whose preference is kinesthetic, reaches out to feel whether Ed is caring about her., but she doesn't 'pick up' very much (no matter how bright his manner or sparkling his smile). Each of them sends the messages they "know" will tell the other person they love them, but the 'words' (to use an auditory expression) fall on deaf ears. Once I pointed this out to them, both of them had tears in their eyes. They had just never heard what the other was saying.

Other differences

Conflicts between visual and kinesthetic ways of processing the world are very common in western society: men are often encouraged to pay attention to visual images, while women nourish the feeling side. Even advertising plays along with this, providing flashy, visual presentations to motivate men, and aiming images of someone stroking themselves with a towel or running a hand over a tactile object, at women.

The western education system is still mainly visual in its approach (books, diagrams and so on). This creates needless difficulties for many women, and for people from more auditory-kinesthetic cultures. If you find learning from a book (like this) hard work, relax. It's not because you're dumb; it's because your strengths lie elsewhere. Talking over the material and doing the activities described will enable you to learn more easily. Does that click into place for you?

Cues to observing sensory systems

You can actually tell which system someone is using to think even before they begin to speak. Remember that body language information comes in five main categories. As you read how each category changes depending on the sensory system, notice how this fits in with what you already know intuitively.

1. Voice: as already mentioned, when thinking visually people use a high, fast voice; when thinking auditorally they use a rhythmic, resonant voice (it may be melodious or a monotone), and when thinking kinesthetically they use a deep, slow, sighing voice.

Usually, the words people use to represent their thoughts (their 'representational system') will match the other cues you see and hear (their 'accessing system'). When they don't, you know that the person is getting information from one sensory system and explaining it to themselves in another. For example, a person may look up left and say in a high voice: 'I don't know why, but I just feel bad in this place. In this case it is the picture of what happened before that causes the person to feel bad. The picture is 'unconscious' and only the feeling the person gets from looking at it is 'conscious'.

The words people use (their representational systems) will be discussed in greater depth in Chapter 6.

2 Eye movements: this is the easiest way to recognise which sensory

system someone is accessing. Each sense is stored in its own special area of the brain, and the eyes tend to move involuntarily to different places as different areas are used. In 2015 research confirming this emerged out of studies of REM (Rapid Eye Movement) sleep, the phase when dreaming happens. It had always been known that eye movements to the sides occur during this sleep, and it was hypothesized that maybe sleepers are scanning things in their dream images. However even people blind from birth have these movements. The next part of the puzzle was that researchers noticed that these eye movements during sleep are similar to those that happen when awake people imagine a new image. Scanning people's brains while asleep, researchers from Tel Aviv University found that there was a burst in the activity of neurons that occurred just after the person's eyes flickered. This activity reflected a change of concept or scene (not image processing) during sleep. The scientists demonstrated that this was the same brain activity that occurred when awake patients were shown pictures, especially those related to their memories, or asked to think about concepts. Researcher Dr. Nir explained "Every time you move your eyes, a new image forms in the mind's eye." (Andrillon et alia, 2015).

Sometimes the eyes just flicker to the side; sometimes they stay there as the person thinks. Here's how it looks on most right-handed and some left-handed people (the rest usually have the same system, but with right and left sides reversed).

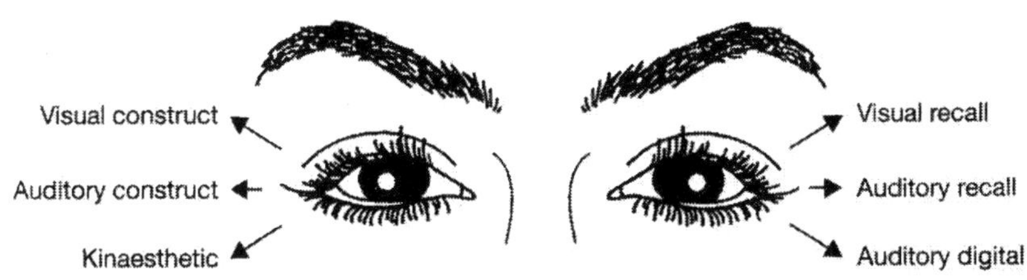

The specific areas, identified in NLP, are:

- Visual constructed: seeing pictures made up by the person, or seeing things differently to how they are in real life (for example get a picture of how you look reading this now) .

- Visual remembered: seeing images of things seen before (for example remember which colour is at the top of a traffic light).

- Visual: a general visual image can also be formed while staring straight ahead with defocused eyes.

- Auditory constructed: hearing words or sounds put together in new ways (for example imagine the sound of a parrot singing your favourite song).

- Auditory remembered: hearing sounds heard before (for example think about which door in your house slams the loudest).

- Auditory digital: talking to oneself (for example say one of your favourite sayings to yourself, in your own voice).

- Kinesthetic: feeling emotions and sensations of touch (for example think about which carpet in your house is the softest).

3 Posture and gestures: when people think, they physically stimulate the sensory system they're using. To see pictures, they rub their eyes and forehead, and raise their eyebrows, using gestures which point upward. To talk to themselves, they rub their mouth, stroke their chin, fold their arms over and press on their chest, and lean their head to one side to hear the messages. To contact feelings, they bend over and contact the body itself, gesturing downward, towards and away from the body midline.

4 Breathing: to think visually, people breathe fast and shallow into the upper chest, often holding their breath to get a picture. When thinking auditorally, people breathe into the chest, fully and rhythmically. Kinesthetic breathing is slower, and deep, using the tummy muscles.

5 Skin changes: in general, people's skin colour is paler or even greyer when they visualise, and when they are aware of feelings their skin is flushed and more coloured.

There are many ways in which you can use the above information about how people think. One is to enhance your own memory. For most people, looking up to the left is the best way to get the brain to remember visual images (how to spell words, where the right labels go on a diagram, and so on). Studies by F. Loiselle, social sciences lecturer at the University of Moncton, Canada, show that teaching students to look up and left immediately increases their ability to learn and remember the spelling of words by 61 per cent. Thomas Malloy, Professor of psychology at the University of Utah, USA, showed that teaching this simple strategy was twice as effective as drilling students in the older auditory phonics spelling method. (See Dilts and Epstein 1995, Loiselle 1985, Malloy 1989, Malloy et alia 1987)

Perhaps an even more important use of this information, though, is that now you can avoid the difficulty Carol and Ed encountered, by using gestures and language which make sense to the person you're with. Have you ever felt that someone could really see what you meant, was really tuned in to your wavelength, or had really made contact with you? That's the power of rapport. It isn't just 'chemistry'. It's a skill you can develop, and that's what I'll discuss after the following activities.

Dr Michael Yapko worked with 30 graduate students in counselling, and had them listen to three separate relaxation tapes. Each tape used language from one of the main three sensory systems (visual, auditory and kinesthetic). Subjects were assessed before to identify their preference for words from these sensory systems. After each tape, their depth of relaxation was measured by electromyograph and by asking them how relaxed they felt. On both measures, subjects achieved greater relaxation when their preferred sensory system was used. (Yapko, 1981) In other studies, counselling clients have been shown to prefer a counsellor whose word use matches their own representational system (visual, auditory, kinesthetic or auditory digital) by a ratio of three to one! (Brockman, 1980).

Activity 3.5

AIM: to recognise sensory accessing cues in others

1 This activity can be done in a group with three people as subjects, or in pairs. Seat the subjects so that everyone else can see their eyes clearly (if they have glasses, consider the lighting in the room). Check for lefthandedness.

2 Ask the subjects the following questions and observe for accessing cues (particularly eye movements) as they think of the answer and then reply.

a. Visual

- How many windows are there in your house?
- What colour was the last bicycle that you owned?
- How would you look with blue hair?
- Imagine the Prime Minister wearing a pink polka-dot dress. Does it suit him/her?

b. Auditory / Auditory digital

- What's the seventh word in the national anthem?
- Who in this group has the quietest voice?
- If you had to give a speech about body language, what would your first sentence be?
- What would it sound like if a window in the next room was smashed?

c. Kinesthetic

- How cold was the sea last time you went to the beach?
- How warm do you like the water in a shower or bath?
- Where is the most uncomfortable place to be sunburnt?
- How did you feel when you first woke up this morning?

3 Now ask them to tell you what they like and don't like about where they live (use those words).

Check

- What accessing cues they used, and
- What sensory system they talked about.

Activity 3.6

AIM: to discover which sensory system gives you the most important information about being loved

1 In pairs, take turns to ask the other person the following question: 'Think of a time when you really knew you were loved, when you felt inside that you were fully loved (or make up such a time if you can't recall one). As you remember that time, seeing what you saw, hearing what you heard, feeling what you could feel, decide what is the one thing that is absolutely necessary for a person to do, say, or show you so you know you are loved. You don't need to tell me; just decide what it is, and from which sensory system it is. Is it something you'd see (for example a look on their face, places you'd go and see, the beautiful things they'd give you); something you'd hear (the tone of their voice, the right music, certain special words); or something you'd touch and feel (the way they hold your hand, the kind of hug they'd give you, and so on)? You'll know when you have the right thing because you'll realise that, even if the information from the other systems was not available, you'd know you were loved with that one key thing.'

2 As a group, draw an imaginary triangle on the floor, with kinesthetic, visual, and auditory at its comers. Get everyone to stand near the comer from which they get the most important information about being loved. Notice where everyone is, and discuss:

- Are people where you expected?
- Who could benefit from knowing this information about you?
- Is there anyone you'd like to know this information about?

3 Discuss in pairs: what was it like to do this exercise?

Rapport

AIM: to be able to pace someone using visual, auditory or kinesthetic behaviour.

What is rapport?

When it comes down to it, creating rapport is so simple it can be summed up in a single sentence: to create rapport with someone, you pace or mirror enough of their behaviours for them to get the sense you understand them, elegantly enough so it doesn't distract them. (The words 'pace' and 'mirror' are used interchangeably to mean copying the other person's behaviour).

The only complexity is knowing what to mirror or pace. The answers lie in: postures and gestures, breathing, skin changes (a little hard at first), eye movements and voice.

If you observe two people who are getting on well together, the chances are they'll be talking at a similar speed, at a similar volume and in a similar tone. To do that, they probably breathe at a similar rate. Their posture and gestures will tend to be mirror images of each other (when one waves to the side with their right hand you'll see the other's left hand flick across a little), even to the extent that, as one looks down, the other will gaze that way too. As we will learn in Chapter 6, they will also be likely to use similar language, and to restate each other's main points before adding their own.
Mirroring

If you're involved in any kind of group, watch people over the next sessions and notice who is in rapport with who. Mirroring isn't mimicking (which usually means exaggerating someone's body language to make a joke of it): it's something more subtle.

If you are just learning to use rapport, you'll be safer to copy one or two things at a time, and to understate your own version slightly (so as to be sure not to overdo it). You'll know it has worked because, when you gently change your behaviour, the person you began to mirror will change with you.

For example, parents often have excellent rapport with their young children. When the parents are getting ready to go out, their pulses start to speed up, they breathe faster and so on. Their child starts to speed up, too (and is thus difficult to put to sleep). Parents of young children often discover that the easiest way to get a child to sleep is to physically lie down beside them and to go to sleep. (Once you realise how it works, you can choose just to gradually slow down your breathing to a sleeping rate, thus saving on wasted time).

In his book Unlimited Power, which covers much of the content of this chapter, NLP trainer Anthony Robbins gives several examples of his use of rapport. In one situation, he went to New York's Central Park to relax. Noticing a man sitting across from him, he began (without giving it much thought) to sit in the same way as this man, breathe the same way, sway his head a little in the same way, and so on. As the other man fed the birds breadcrumbs, so did Robbins. Soon the man came over to sit beside him. Robbins continued to mirror his voice tone and phraseology. Within a few minutes the man expressed a belief that Robbins was ,a very intelligent man' and that he felt he knew Robbins better than people he'd known for 25 years. Soon after this, he offered him a job!

Difficulties mirroring

What would Robbins have done if the man had told him to stop copying? This is something that often worries people learning pacing and mirroring skills. My. guess is that he would simply have apologised. He might have explained that he was trying to more fully understand the other person. Certainly, as he apologised, he would have continued to pace the man's use of sensory representational systems (talking about seeing, hearing, or feeling depending on which the other person used), just as he would have continued to use English, not German. Everyone expects to be mirrored to some extent; the only question is how much.

The power of rapport: pacing and leading

Once you have mirrored someone to the extent that rapport is established, then the two of you are connected almost like two magnets. When one moves, the other will tend to move. This fact can be used to assist someone to change. For example, if I'm talking with someone who is depressed, I begin talking at their rate, sitting in a similar (slumped) position to them, and so on. Then, once I've acknowledged their depression verbally and nonverbally (so rapport is established), I very gently begin to adjust my own voice, position and breathing back to my normal level. They will tend to follow.

In NLP, this process is called pacing and leading. If the other person doesn't follow my 'lead', I simply return to 'pacing' (mirroring) them some more.

There's no such thing as a person who's resistant to change. In every situation where someone else doesn't change in the way they've chosen, more pacing is the solution to get them on board with the leading you are doing.

Of course, this raises an ethical issue. A salesperson can pace and lead someone to buy something they don't actually need. The person would buy it 'because the salesperson was so nice and I just wanted to cooperate'. Using pacing and leading in this way is something successful salespeople have always done. However, unless the technique is used to help someone make decisions which suit their own goals, it can backfire. The person who bought five vacuum cleaners last week will feel angry this week, and this so-called 'buyers' remorse' is not good for sales. The only sure way to use pacing and leading is to use it to help people reach goals which they've chosen themselves, and that's what the next chapter is about.

How Rapport Happens In The Brain

Research studies using the empathy scale of the Barrett-Lennard Relationship Inventory show that mirroring counselling clients' non-verbal behaviour does indeed increase their sense of mutual understanding, of empathy (eg see Palubeckas, 1981 and Sandhu et alia, 1993). But what is happening in the brain at these times?

In 1995 a remarkable type of neuron was discovered by researchers working at the University of Palma in Italy (Rizzolatti et alia, 1996; Rizzolatti and Arbib, 1998). The cells, now called "mirror neurons", are found in the "pre-motor cortex" area of the brain in monkeys and apes as well as humans. In humans they form part of the specific area called Broca's area, which is also involved in the creation of speech. Although the cells are related to motor activity (ie they are part of the system by which we make kinaesthetic responses such as moving an arm), they seem to be activated by visual input. When a monkey observes another monkey (or even a human) making a body movement, the mirror neurons light up. As they do, the monkey appears to involuntarily copy the same movement it has observed visually. Often this involuntary movement is inhibited by the brain (otherwise the poor monkey would be constantly copying every other monkey), but the resulting mimickery is clearly the source of the saying "monkey see, monkey do".

In human subjects, when this area of the brain is exposed to the magnetic field of transcranial magnetic stimulation (TMS), thus reducing conscious control, then merely showing a movie of a person picking up an object will cause the subject to involuntarily copy the exact action with their hand (Fadiga et alia, 1995). This ability to copy a fellow creature's actions as they do them has obviously been very important in the development of primate social intelligence. It enables us to identify with the person we are observing. When this area of the brain is damaged in a stroke, copying another's actions becomes almost impossible. The development of speech has clearly been a result of this copying skill. Furthermore, there is increasing evidence that autism and Asperger's syndrome are related to unusual activity of the mirror neurons. This unusual activity results in a difficulty the autistic person has understanding the inner world of others, as well as a tendency to echo speech parrot-fashion and to randomly copy others' movements (Williams et alia, 2001).

Mirror neurons respond to the facial expressions associated with emotions as well, so that they enable the person to directly experience the emotions of those they observe. William Condon has meticulously studied videotapes of conversations, confirming these patterns. He found that in a successful conversation, movements such as a smile or a head nod are involuntarily matched by the other person within 1/15 of a second. Within minutes of beginning the conversation, the volume, pitch and speech rate (number of sounds per minute) of the peoples voices match each other. This is correlated with a synchronising of the type and rate of breathing. Even general body posture is adjusted over the conversation so that the people appear to match or mirror each other (Condon 1982, p 53-76). As a person adjusts their facial expression and other nonverbal behaviour to match others' they actually use the same pattern of brain activation that the other person is using. When their mirror neurons respond and they copy the person's actions, they thus feel what that person is feeling. This results in what Condon calls "emotional contagion" – what we are calling rapport (Hatfield et alia, 1994).

Empathy: the feeling of rapport

In rapport, the technical skill of mirroring blossoms into a feeling of having entered the other person's inner world, of being tuned into their wavelength, of seeing life as it appears in their maps.

This feeling, often called empathy, is an essential ingredient in all successful communication, but especially in helping. Over the last 50 years, hundreds of research studies have consistently shown that empathy is the key emotional quality required to help another person. Carl Rogers, who developed the verbal mirroring skills discussed in Chapter 5, states: 'Empathy is clearly related to positive outcome. From schizophrenic patients in psychiatric hospitals to pupils in ordinary classrooms, from clients of a counselling centre to teachers in training, from neurotics in Germany to neurotics in the United States, the evidence is the same."

Empathy needs to be distinguished from sympathy. In empathy, it is as if you can experience the feelings of another, feeling these with them. In sympathy, one feels one's own feelings for another. Sympathy means feeling sorry for another, for example, and often has a sense of looking down at the person. Empathy comes with a sense of equality, of sharing this moment.

The feeling of empathy is an important clue that you have mastered the skill of mirroring.

The power of rapport is understood in every field where human beings interact. The field where there has been more research about it than any other is the field in which relationships are most intense of all: couples and marriage coaching. In 2007, Harvard Business Review senior editor Diane Coutu interviewed Seattle's Washington University researcher John Gottman (Coutu, 2007). Gottman has been in the forefront of a revolution in couples work. His in depth research on more than a thousand couples over the last thirty years has debunked many cherished theories about what makes intimate relationships work, and has implications for all work relationships. When couples are videotaped 24 hours a day, the difference between happy couples and unhappy couples is very small. There are subtle differences in the linguistic patterns that successful couples use before, during and after an argument. These differences in linguistic patterns pervade the whole relationship though, not just the arguments.

In 12 year long follow-up studies, Gottman's researchers have shown that they can predict with over 90% accuracy whether a couple will divorce just by listening to a five minute conversation between the couple at the start of the 12 years, by identifying the specific language patterns used and seeing the specific non-verbal responses they make to each other (Gottman and Silver, 1999, p 3). They can predict with 80% accuracy exactly which year the breakup will occur!

Gottman's research demonstrates the power of what we are calling rapport. Successful relationships are founded in a physiological synchronisation, a tuning in at the level of body rhythms. Couples who can understand each other and respect each other's perspectives actually adjust their bodies to experience what the other person is experiencing. They breathe in time with each other, sit in similar positions, use similar voice tonality, and even their heart rates match (Gottman, 1999, p 27). This synchronising creates a powerful feeling of shared trust and understanding that is the basis of all successful friendships, marriages and work relationships: the feeling of rapport.

In a recent experiment, researcher William Maddux tested the impact of this behavior on business negotiations. One portion of the MBA student volunteers were instructed to subtly mirror their partner (e.g. put their elbow on the table if the other person does), while the other half were told not to mirror. The results showed that when one student was instructed to mirror the other, the two parties reached a deal 67% of the time. But when they were told not to mirror, only 12.5% reached a deal.

How well do you think you'll be able to use this skill? Let me remind you. To be reading this page to yourself, you had to learn to talk English. This is a process so complex that we can't yet teach a computer to do it fully. And how did you learn to talk? By reading a book about it? By analysing the muscles of the mouth and throat? Not likely. You learned by mirroring other human beings, subtly, expertly and consistently. You have always had the skills to create rapport. Now you can find new ways to use these skills to build the kind of relationships you want, and to create, for those you live and work with, the sense of being fully understood and valued that they need.

Milton Erickson and George

Dr Milton Erickson was one of the experts studied by the developers of NLP when they first explored the concept of rapport. Erickson's skill with rapport was outstanding. On one occasion he was working in a psychiatric ward where there was a patient with a severe psychosis (in everyday terms he was 'crazy). This man had spoken only six sensible words in the five years he had been in the hospital. Otherwise he spoke in 'word salad' - a long jumble of sounds, words and syllables in no apparent order. Psychiatrists, nurses and others had made numerous unsuccessful attempts to talk to him, or just to find out his full name (his six words included 'My name is George').

Erickson did something different. He got his secretary to record, in shorthand, a sample of the man's "speech'. Erickson then studied this sample until he could improvise a word salad similar in form. Now he was ready. He sat down next to George and introduced himself. George spat out an angry stream of word salad. Erickson replied with an equally long stream of the same type of noise. George appeared puzzled and added more word salad, and Erickson responded in kind.

A few days later Erickson returned, and again George spoke in word salad, this time for four hours. Erickson, aware that George was watching a clock on the wall facing them, replied in kind for another four hours, missing his lunch. George listened carefully, and they then traded another two hours.

The next day George gave only two sentences of word salad. After Erickson returned his own two sentences, George did an extraordinary thing. He said: 'Talk sense Doctor!'

'Certainly, I'll be glad to. What is your last name?' Erickson asked.

'O'Donavan, and it's about time somebody who knows how to talk asked. Over five years in this lousy joint..." and he lapsed back into word salad.

A few months later, George O'Donavan left the hospital and found himself a job. Erickson followed his progress for some years and he was not readmitted. Like everyone else, George needed rapport, needed to feel understood, to be met with his own way of experiencing the world, before he would be willing to move on. For five years no-one had considered this either possible or sensible. It took Milton Erickson one week once George was willing to start. (from Dolan, 1985, p 58-61)

Activity 3.7

AIM: to develop your skills in pacing someone auditorally, visually and kinesthetically

Get into groups of three, and decide who will be: 'speaker', 'listener' and 'observer'.

1 . The speaker makes a simple, short statement, such as 'Rapport is the key to good communication.

- The listener restates this sentence trying to get the exact tone, speed, loudness and emphasis as the original.

- The observer gives the second person feedback on what they need to change to make their voice sound exactly like the original.

- The speaker repeats the same sentence, and the listener again tries to create an identical statement.

- After three or four times, depending on the observer's comments, change positions so that each person eventually has a turn in each role.

2 The speaker talks for four minutes about how they think they could use these skills (or on any other topic of their choice). He or she should change position at least twice in the four minutes. The listener can just listen, or may add their own comments, but he or she should mirror the posture and

gestures of the speaker. Before changing roles, the observer gives feedback about how the mirrorer got on. Again, rotate to give each person a practice.

3 The speaker now simply sits, breathing normally. The listener assumes a mirroring posture and breathes in time with them until the observer is satisfied that their breathing matches for two minutes. (Breathing rate can be detected from subtle movements of the shoulders, chest and tummy.) Rotate roles, remembering to return to your normal breathing rate after each turn.

4 Discuss in your group how each type of rapport was: which was most difficult for you to achieve? Were any of you uncomfortable to continue?

Summary

In this chapter you have dived into the amazing world of nonverbal communication. You'll have realised that the context of what is said is even more important than the words we say.

Like verbal language, body language differs from culture to culture. Pakeha culture for example, uses less physical contact, more eye contact, and less standalone gestures than Maori and Tagata Pasifica cultures. People from different cultures, and even different groups within a culture, may have a preference for physical closeness or distance (the study of which is called 'proxemics'). They may also have different preferred sensory systems. People can process information ('think') using the visual, auditory, kinesthetic or gustatory/ olfactory sensory system. And you can recognise which they are using from their body language.

In verbal language words join together to make sentences, and in body language gestures join together to make clusters. Understanding body language involves noting:

1 gesture changes
2 breathing changes
3 skin changes
4 eye changes, and
5 voice changes.

Once you can recognise these changes, not only will you have a good idea of how a person feels, but you'll be able to build rapport by mirroring them.

Chapter 4: Creating solutions

KEY CONCEPTS
Happiness ownership
Problem-solving/goal-setting process
Learning stages

TRANSFORMING COMMUNICATION

Happiness Ownership

AIM: to be able to recognise who 'owns a challenge', using Thomas Gordon's terminology.

When to use the skills

So far we've considered states of mind and how people can shift from one state to another; we've learned much about what people are saying before they use any words; and we've thought in a general way about how people introduce themselves and get in contact with each other. Once you have reached this chapter you already have a lot of skills for enriching your life and enjoying the good times that relationships bring.

At this point the bad news is: things don't always go well (you probably knew that, though). The good news is: there's a lot you can do about it when something isn't right, either for you or for someone else. In fact, the rest of the book is mainly concerned with helping yourself and others find your way back to enjoyment when something is not going right.

This section is crucial to understanding the rest of the book! Basically, it will help you work out when to use Part 2 (Caring for others) and when to use Part 3 (Caring for yourself). The answer isn't always what you expected. For example, people sometimes think that, because they are a health professional, a teacher or a parent, they mainly need skills to care for others. In fact, a teacher, nurse or parent who knows only how to help others is soon in serious trouble. Helpers need to be just as good at solving their own challenges as they are at helping other people solve theirs. We'll see why in Part 3.

Thomas Gordon

The happiness ownership model is adapted from a framework developed by Dr Thomas Gordon (Gordon, 1970). Thomas Gordon says that his career as an advocate of conflict resolution began during the Second World War. He was a trainer of Army Air Corp flight instructors at Montgomery, Alabama. At that time, Army Air Corp instructors had an authoritarian style of teaching that Gordon says "usually instilled so much fear and tension that students didn't perform well." (Gordon, 1995, p315). Having been a graduate student and friend of counselling developer Dr Carl Rogers, Gordon believed that a more accepting approach would be more successful. He set training goals with this in mind, assigned other trainers their tasks in line with these, and evaluated their progress. He says "To my surprise and puzzlement, within a few months morale was bad, resistance was high, production was low, creativity was nil, and open and honest communication ceased between the group members and me." Ironically, while his intentions and the content of his changes had been co-operative, the process he had used to implement change had been authoritarian. In response, after being confronted by a friend, he began to develop a totally different model for his work. "This changed leadership style had startling and enduring effects: creativity flourished, communication opened up, tension decreased, and the work became enjoyable and satisfying to all of us."

After the war, Gordon went back to graduate studies and began to write a book about his learnings (Gordon, 1995). This gained him a job with a large industrial company in Davenport Iowa. When they adopted his model in their factory, again "Cooperation increased, morale shot up, and the foremen were happier, worked harder, and were more creative. Productivity increased." The book catapulted Gordon into a career as a consultant and therapist, but he continued to feel that his work was remedial, and what was really needed was an intervention at an earlier stage in social events. In the late 1950s he hit on the idea of designing a leadership training program for parents. This course (Parent Effectiveness Training or PET) was the first of a number of specific packages of this training designed for salespeople, women, young people, teachers, clergy and others. Many of the skills you'll learn in this book were first developed as a result of Thomas Gordon's work.

Gordon's basic idea is a very simple one. He points out that in any relationship, at any given time, I am either happy with the other person's behaviour, or not happy (own a challenge, or as he says a "problem") with it.

What Happiness Ownership Means In This Book

Now, this claim is disarmingly simple. Let me first emphasise that the word "behaviour" is a jargon word in Psychology, and Gordon is using it in this precise way. By behaviour he means the things that you can actually see with your eyes, hear with your ears, or touch physically. For example, if I saw a friend tearing up my book and throwing pages into a fire, then I might not be happy with that behaviour. But by "behaviour" I do not mean "John being destructive." Or "John losing his temper." "Destructive" is a word describing my value judgement about what I have seen. "Losing his temper" is my mind read about what is happening inside John. The behaviour is simply "John removing pages from the book and placing them in the fire."

Even "John ruining my book." is not a description of the behaviour. The word "ruining" already implies a value judgement (the judgement that taking pages out of the book is wrong). Furthermore, even saying "John deliberately burning pages of my book" does not describe the behaviour. After all, "deliberately" assumes that I can read John's mind and know that he is planning to do what he does. There's nothing wrong with me having value judgements or trying to guess what someone else is thinking. It is important that I notice when I do, that this is not the actual behaviour that I am seeing, hearing or touching.

So the happiness ownership model begins with the idea that I am either happy with the other person's behaviour (what they did that I can see, hear or touch), or not happy with it. When I am not happy with the behaviour, the model describes this by saying that "I own a challenge" (Gordon used the term "problem" where we will mostly use "challenge"). Now, once again, this phrase is being used in a very specific sense, as jargon. When I say "I own the challenge", it doesn't mean that it's my fault that John is placing pages from my book in the fire. It doesn't mean that I should be the one who fixes things up. It simply means that I am the one who is not happy with what is going on. That I am the one who feel angry, hurt, sad, frightened, resentful, embarrassed, or otherwise unaccepting of the situation. In ordinary language, we use the term "own a challenge" quite differently of course. If we see someone drunk and apparently annoying others, we may say "Boy, that guy really has a challenge!" whereas in these jargon terms, they may have no challenge at all. On the other hand, sometimes when someone is upset about an apparently (to us) small issue, we may say in ordinary terms "Hey, relax; it's no problem!" and yet in this specialist way of using the term, if the person is upset, then they "own a challenge".

I'll use the following diagram to represent the two situations. Above the centre line is the area where I feel fine. Below the line is where I "own a challenge." Of course, this line goes up and down. Even when I see the other person doing the same behaviour (meaning what I can see, hear or touch) it may be below my line when I've had a rough day, and above my line on a good day. For example, let's imagine that my friend asks to borrow twenty dollars. On a day when I just got a pay increase, this may be no challenge at all. On a day when I just got a massive account from the car repair shop, someone asking for twenty dollars may really annoy me. People are not machines. At different times they feel differently. A behaviour that is no challenge when one person does it may result in you owning a challenge when someone else does it. A behaviour that is no challenge at home may be a challenge at work. What counts is how you are feeling right now.

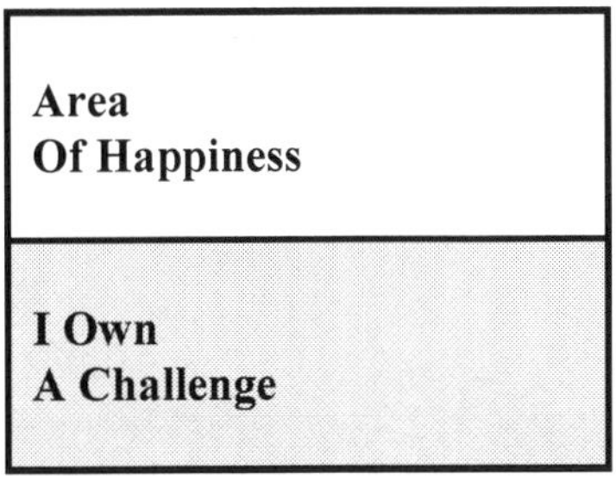

Area Of Happiness
I Own A Challenge

Fig 1: The Happiness Ownership Model: My happiness ownership

This line moves up and down

However, in communication with someone else, I also need to consider the situation from their perspective. I diagram the other person's experience on the other axis of the model.

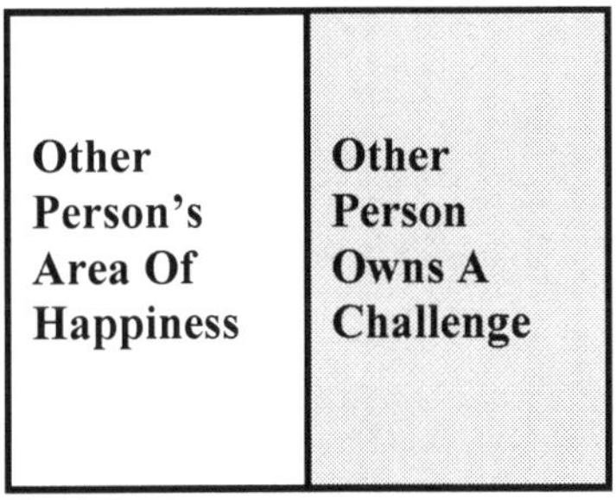

Other Person's Area Of Happiness	**Other Person Owns A Challenge**

Fig 2: The Happiness Ownership Model: The other person's happiness ownership

The Four Areas

As a result, there are four distinct possibilities, as shown in the next diagram.

Area Of Happiness	**Other Person Owns A Challenge**
I Own A Challenge	**Both Of Us Own A Challenge (Conflict)**

Fig 3: The Happiness Ownership Model: Combined model

1) Neither of us owns a Challenge. If both of us are happy with the events occurring, then the focus of our communication can be on our individual and mutual enjoyment; on building rapport. In the situation where neither of us owns a challenge, a larger range of ways of speaking will be safe to use (safe in the sense of preserving both of our self esteem, and preserving the relationship). We can relax and do whatever we have arranged to do together. In the educational situation, this is the area where both teaching and learning can happen. In the consulting situation, this is the area where a consultant can share their expertise and the client can make decisions based on it. In the management situation, this is the area where teamwork happens. This area offers the most potential for us to grow personally, as each of us has energy free from problem-solving to focus on our goals and on discovery.

2) I feel OK but the other person owns a challenge. If I am in a relationship where at this moment I feel okay, and the other person does not (ie they are unhappy, frustrated, worried, angry, sad or unaccepting of what is going on), it can be useful to focus my attention on assisting them to solve their challenge. This process, called Helping, is of course a common one when you are a consultant assisting a client to change. It also occurs when you are listening to your spouse or partner talking about a difficult day they had, or when you offer to assist your co-worker to learn how to perform a new work task that has been overwhelming them. In this situation, as we'll see, it *does* matter what you say. To help another person, I am interested in understanding what things seem like through the other person's eyes and stepping into their experience. The most effective skills for Helping will be ones that talk mostly about the *other person's* experience and desired outcomes, not about mine. I will say, for example, "So what *you* want to

change is..." rather than "So what *I* think you should change is...". The helping situation is discussed more fully in the next section of this book.

3) I own a challenge. If I am in a relationship where at this moment the other person feels okay, and I do not (ie I am unhappy, frustrated, worried, angry, sad or unaccepting of what is going on), it can be useful to focus my attention on finding a way for me to reach my own outcome. This process could be called Problem Solving or Solution Finding. If my challenge relates to the behaviour the other person (if I'm upset or angry or hurt "about something I see or hear them doing"), then this process of solution finding is called Assertion. For example, I could own a challenge where I'm frustrated about my spouse's failure to wash the dishes, or where I'm resentful that I ended up doing extra work when my co-worker didn't attend a meeting. I also could own a challenge at times when a client forgets to turn up to a session. To assert my needs, I need to be able to take what NLP calls "first position", being aware of what things seem like through my own eyes and in my own experience. The most effective skills for Assertion will be one that talk about the challenge and the desired outcomes as existing inside my own experience I will say, for example "What *I* want to change is..." rather than "So what *you* might want to do is...". The assertion situation is discussed in the chapter on Assertiveness.

4) Both of us own a challenge. When we are both unhappy about the situation, a combination of skills will be useful (So what *you* want is... and what *I* want is...). Where we both own a challenge about the same issue, the situation could be called a "Conflict". This doesn't mean that we are necessarily opposed to each other, or that one of us must win and one lose. It simply means that we both are upset, angry, hurt etc about related issues (eg I think we should spend more time together and the other person wants more space. I want to use the company car tomorrow and so does my co-worker). Such situations benefit from a combination of the helping and assertive skills, as well as from specific conflict resolution skills. To effectively deal with these situations I need to be able to take "fourth position" and be aware of the whole system of which I am a part. I need to talk about my outcomes, the other person's outcomes, and the outcomes of the whole system. This "conflict" situation is discussed in the chapters on Resolving Conflict and Values and Metaprograms.

By using all the skills we'll explore here, our aim is to shift back the two lines crossing this diagram, and thus create a much larger area where there is no challenge.

Rapport	Helping Skills
Assertive & Solution Finding Skills	Conflict Resolution Skills

Fig 4: The Happiness Ownership Model: A Method Of Selecting Skills To Help People Reach Their Outcomes

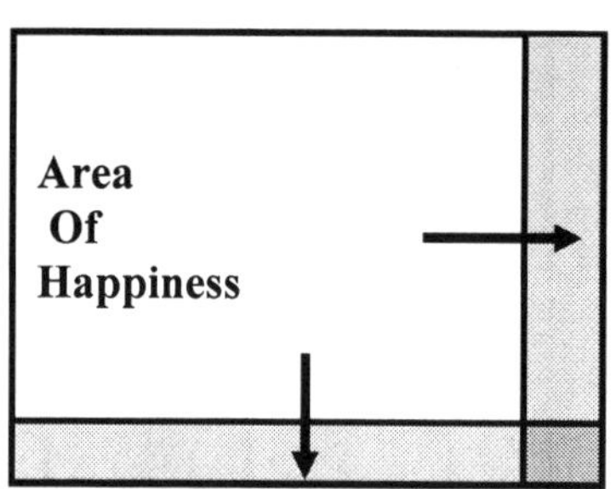

Fig 5: The Happiness Ownership Model: My aim using these skills

Some examples

1. Let's say your teacher enters your class and tells you: 'I'm very disappointed with you all. You're not getting through this work quickly enough. You may be enjoying yourselves, but you're really not treating this seriously enough. Now, who 'owns' this challenge? The question, restated, says who here is feeling unhappy right now? The teacher is, so the teacher owns the challenge. That doesn't mean it's her fault, or that she's the one who has to fix it up: just that she is the one who is upset.

2. As you arrive at your work, you see a young man with a spray-can of paint writing slogans over your workplace walls. He's singing to himself as he writes. In ordinary language, we might well say: 'That guy has a problem", but in this new way of using the phrase, he probably doesn't - he's having a great time, painting the walls and singing.

Who is feeling unhappy at that moment? Possibly you are! It's not your fault, and it doesn't mean you should clean it up. All we're saying is that it is very important to work out in any situation: 'Who is unhappy about this? That's more important to understand than 'Who is to blame? or 'Who will have to fix this up?'

Sometimes people say: 'Well, the guy painting the walls may not own a challenge now, but he sure will once I finish with him.' That may be true. What we're doing here is checking who is feeling unhappy right now.

3. A friend tells you he's lost one of the handouts from a course you're both doing. He says he's really worried about asking the tutor for a replacement. You think he's getting worried about nothing. Does anyone own a challenge? In the sense we're using it, yes. If your friend is worried, he's worried. It doesn't matter how trivial it seems to you. What counts is: 'Who is feeling unhappy right then?

Reasons to use the model

There's a good reason for working out who 'owns the challenge' then. The ways of talking which will help when another person owns the challenge (helping skills) are very different to the ways which help when you yourself own the challenge (assertiveness skills, problem-solving skills). And as you may have realised, there will be times when you both own a challenge (such as when you and a friend both want to use the same textbook at the same time). Those situations, called conflicts, require a third set of skills (conflict resolution skills). When there's no challenge, you have the opportunity to build the sense of rapport in the relationship using the rapport skills we've already discussed.

Relationship researcher John Gottman is famous for his ability to predict with 90% accuracy whether a couple will stay together over the next 10 years, after observing just a 15 minute discussion between them. Differences between successful and unsuccessful couples are not merely present in arguments. As Gottman says, his research has shown that "successful conflict resolution isn't what makes marriages succeed." (Gottman and Silver, 1999, p 11). It is the quality of the friendship between the couple, in every area of happiness ownership, that counts. In discussion with Harvard Business review senior editor Diane Coutu (Coutu, 2007), Gottman explains that research is beginning to identify the same effects in business. He says "Within organizations people have to see each other as human beings or there will be no social glue." Gottman also notes that very different skills work in each area of the relationship.

However, I have another reason for wanting you to know about happiness ownership: that is, to explain to you my role as the writer of this book. It's not my job to tell you when you should or should not own a challenge. I don't intend to tell you which things you should feel accepting of or which things to be upset about. But once you have worked out what you want from your relationships, the skills in Parts 2 and 3 will help you achieve this, expanding the happiness area as above.

This chapter discusses working out what you want. What you want is special to you. Your dreams for your life may be different to anyone else's, and what 'gets on your nerves' may be totally different to what bothers someone else. That's why my invitation to you is to use this book like a supermarket of new choices. Only you can know what choices will work well for you in which situations. If what you're doing already works perfectly, I'd say go for it! If it leaves you or others around you feeling less than delighted, this book contains some new possibilities.

My values about happiness ownership

My belief, on which this book is based, is that when people own a challenge they have a right to get that challenge sorted out. This is a very basic value underlying all the things you're reading. When other people (your family, friends, clients at work, and so on) are upset, there are some things which research shows work better than others. You'll learn those skills in Part 2. Other people have a right to feel good about their life: that's why there's a Part 2 to this book.

When you are upset you have a right to get those challenges sorted out. You'll learn the skills which have been shown to work there, in Part 3. You don't lose that right just because you are a parent, a child, a friend, a teacher, a nurse, a woman, a man, or anything else you might be.

The skills for solving challenges you'll learn in this book are remarkable. I didn't make them up; they are the result of the collected wisdom of hundreds of thousands of skilled communicators and researchers. To use them, the first step is delightfully simple. It is to work out who owns the challenge, by deciding who here is feeling unhappy right now.

Activity 4.1

AIM: to check understanding of the Happiness Ownership Model

1 Individually, read the following situations and decide for each one whether:

a there is no challenge
b you own a challenge
c the other person owns a challenge
d both you and the other person own a challenge.

Note that there is not always one 'right' answer, because different people will find different things a challenge (for example some people are always upset to discover that someone close to them is unhappy, whereas others might want to help but not feel upset about it).

2 Designate four areas of the room to each represent one of the above possibilities (a, b, c or d). Read out each of the situations below in turn, and get group members to stand in the area of the room they think applies to the situation. Discuss the result each time and check that people are using 'own a challenge ' to mean who here is not feeling happy right now.

Situations:

- A person working with you plays the radio so loud you're starting to get a headache.
- Your friend tells you she's trying to cut down the amount of alcohol she drinks, but is finding it hard work.
- Your child begins to cry when you tell him he has an appointment with the dentist tomorrow.
- You need your bike to get to work each day. The repair shop told you they'd have it fixed in a day, but have so far taken three days and still don't have it ready
- One of the people you look after in your job tells you he feels angry with some of the other staff.
- A friend says he is really anxious about a meeting with his boss.
- A fellow student hasn't returned the lecture notes which you need to study for next week's exam.
- Your child forgot to do the dishes last night and you have to wash things before you can cook tea tonight.
- Your mother tells you that you should phone her more often.
- You and your best friend often spend an enjoyable evening debating which sports team is doing best this season.

Setting goals and solving problems

AIM: to be able to describe a challenge or a goal in sensory specific ways; and to list five steps in the problem-solving process.

The uses of goals

It's an often quoted saying that "If you don't know where you're going, you'll probably wind up somewhere else.". The research confirms that the most successful people do indeed take more care working out where they are going. In their study of *Women of Influence* throughout history, Pat and Ruth Williams say that "The successful woman is the average woman, focused. The successful women in this book focused their lives.... They had a mission and they followed through." (Williams and Williams, 2003, p xvii). Dr Harry Alder interviewed more than 150 business leaders to create his study *Think Like A Leader*. He says "Leaders seem to know where they are going in both a personal and a business sense. They are quite happy with goals and objectives.... It appears to the impressed follower that the leader can quickly get to the core of a matter, is able to see the longer term implications, or somehow knows just what the important questions are. All of these often-quoted features of good leadership relate to an ability we all have, to visualize, that can be improved with practice. In people decisions, it comes over as sound judgement. Or a leader might be seen to remain cool in the heat of a crisis. In fact, for the leader, the crisis has already been 'experienced" in the form of visualization – it comes as no surprise. For the leader it is just another scenario that has turned into reality." (Alder, 1995, p 18, 20).

The same is true in sports. Top golfer Jack Nicklaus explains "I never hit a shot, even in practice, without having a very sharp, in focus picture of it in my head. It's like a colour movie. First I "see" the ball where I want it to finish, nice and white and sitting up high on the bright green grass. Then the scene quickly changes and I "see" the ball going there: it's path, trajectory, and shape, even it's behaviour on landing. Then there's a sort of fade-out, and the next scene shows me making the kind of swing that will turn the previous images into reality." (quoted in Hansen and Allen, 2002, p 52)

Edwin Locke and Gary Latham (1990) have surveyed 400 studies of goalsetting, showing that specific goals are the key to high success in fields as diverse as education, management, sport and new year's resolutions. In a long term study of 250 students age 12-15, researchers Judith Meece, Allan Wigfield and Jacquelynne Eccles showed that the best predictor of whether students succeed is not how good they actually are but how good they *expect* to be in future (Meece Wigfield and Eccles, 1990). It is goals, not intelligence or skill, that determine success.

Whether your goal is financial success, a deeper sense of wellbeing, individual pleasure or social change, this section makes the process used by the most successful people available to you. When you own a challenge, you'll be able to use this process to find the very best solutions for you. When you have a conflict, the same process (as adapted in Chapter 9) will help you find solutions which suit both you and the person you are disagreeing with. When your job is to help someone else solve their challenges, understanding this process will enable you to know what stage of the process they are stuck at, and where they need to go next.

On Top Of The World!

Let me give you a specific example of the power of goalsetting. One famous New Zealander describes his first day at secondary school, an experience which, sixty years later he says "still affects my whole attitude to life". He says "When I first went to Grammar, we all had to go along to the gymnasium to be assessed for sporting potential. This gymnastic instructor, who I regard as one of the more unpleasant teachers I ever had anything to do with, looked at me when I stripped off. I clearly remember him staring at me with scorn and saying, "What will they send me next?" He told me I had a bulging rib cage and my back wasn't straight, everything that was terrible about my physical appearance and set-up. I was mortified and this created in me an enormous sense of inferiority."

At first, this experience shattered the young boy, but at home he rebounded. He explains, "I think this incident built up in me - I was after all only 11 at the time - a determination that I would become competent in something." His family were very involved in a movement that we would recognise today as being related to NLP. The movement was New Zealand teacher Herbert Sutcliffe's "School of Radiant Living". They studied nutrition, herbalism, energy healing and the use of "affirmations". Sutcliffe's motto was "Faith in goodness will produce good things. Faith in abundance will draw conditions of abundance around you. Faith in health will establish health in body and environment."

On the 29th of May, 1953, that boy, now grown to adulthood, stood 8848 metres above the snow covered Himalayas, atop the highest mountain in the world. Edmund Hillary had become the first person to climb Mt Everest. A childhood dream, crystalised into an outcome that had seemed impossible. (Booth, 1992, p33)

The process: five steps

The problem-solving process is listed in various books, and is given a wide variety of stages. In other parts of this book I'll refer to particular models as appropriate. The process always involves:

1. defining the challenge
2. setting a goal
3. planning how to achieve the goal
4. acting

5. evaluating how well you got what you wanted.

In this chapter you'll learn, by using the problem-solving process, how to achieve a goal which is important to you personally. This is the very best way to learn this model. You'll understand how to help someone else much better once you feel able to help yourself. You deserve to do this well, so make sure you set aside an hour to work your way through this part of the book. You deserve more than a theory, do you not? As I said in the last section, one of my basic assumptions is that you have a right to feel good about your life, to actually achieve happiness. So before you read another word here, make sure you have a pen and paper ready.

Defining the challenge

a List all the changes you would like to make in your life. Have you ever watched a child try and do a complex jigsaw puzzle for the first time? The trick is to turn all the pieces over and spread them out on the table before you start. It's the same here. We start by getting you to make a list of everything you'd like to change in your life, to improve or do better, to do more or do less. You could call this an 'inventory' or an assessment'. For now, you don't need to work out how you'd achieve this. just allow yourself to dream. Take at least ten minutes. Think especially of what you would like to change about the way you communicate.

b Choose one change you would like to make. Describe in writing the challenge this change would solve. Check through the list and choose one change you'd like to work on in the next couple of months. What we are going to do now is get specific about this one change.

Start by reminding yourself why you want to change. You could call this step "diagnosis' if you wanted to be medical about it. If you know why you'd like to change, you will be more enthusiastic about reaching your goal. What difficulty, what challenge, what limitation in your life would be solved by this change? Write down the answer to this question.

Goal setting: What Doesn't Work?

The purpose of goalsetting is to motivate you to actually achieve what you want in life. It is not to motivate you to avoid challenges, and it is not to distract you so you avoid thinking about the challenges. It is to motivate you to act! Almost everyone believes that they use goals to some extent, but what is different about the way that the most successful change agents set goals? The answer is that they SPECIFY them. What does that mean? It means to make them:

Sensory specific and timed
Positive
Ecological
Choice increasing
Initiated by you... with...
First step identified
Your resources identified

Outside of the field of NLP, most people understand the importance of goals, but not many of them actually use this SPECIFY process. Recently, there has been some dramatic new research about what enables goals to work. This research suggests that the two most common unsuccessful choices people make in goalsetting are:

1) Paying attention to what they don't want all the time, instead of what they do want.
2) Fantasising about having achieved what they want, instead of planning action.

Unsuccessful Choice 1: Focus on the Problem. Focusing on problems and what we don't want is paying attention to the past. It feels very different to focusing on the goal, outcome or solution to those problems, and it has very different results. In 2000, Dr Denise Beike and Deirdre Slavik at the University of Arkansas conducted an interesting study of what they called "counterfactual" thoughts. These are thoughts about what has gone "wrong", along with what they could have done differently. Dr. Beike enlisted two groups of University of Arkansas students to record their thoughts each day in a diary in order to "look at counterfactual thoughts as they occur in people's day-to-day lives." In the first group, graduate students recorded their counterfactual thoughts, their mood, and their motivation to change their behavior as a result of their thoughts. After recording two thoughts per day for 14 days, the students reported that negative thoughts depressed their mood but increased their motivation to change their behavior. They believed that the negative thoughts were painful but would help them in the long term.

To test out this hope, the researchers then enlisted a group of students to keep similar diaries for 21 days, to determine if any actual change in behavior would result from counterfactual thinking. Three weeks after completing their diaries the undergraduate students were asked to review their diary data and indicate whether their counterfactual thinking actually caused any change in behavior. "No self-perceived change in behavior was noted," Dr. Beike told Reuters Health. Counterfactual thoughts about negative events in everyday life cause us to feel that we "should have done better or more," Dr. Beike said. "These thoughts make us feel bad, which motivates us to sit around and to feel sorry for ourselves." So what does work? The study found that "credit-taking thoughts", in which individuals reflect on success and congratulate themselves, serve to reinforce appropriate behavior and help people "feel more in control of themselves and their circumstances." (Slavik, 2003).

Unsuccessful Choice 2: Fantasise About The Solution. Although focusing on the problem you have had does not lead to success, neither does merely fantasising about the future success. Lien Pham and Shelley Taylor at the University of California did a study where a group of students were asked to visualise themselves getting high grades in a mid-term exam that was coming up soon. They were taught to form clear visual images and imagine how good it will feel, and to repeat this for several minutes each day. A control group was also followed up, and the study times of each student as well as their grades in the exam were monitored. The group who were visualising should, according to proponents of "The Secret" DVD and the "Law of Attraction", have a clear advantage. Actually, they did much less study, and consequently got much lower marks in the exam (Pham and Taylor, 1999).

This result is very consistent. There are now a large number of research studies showing that this way of applying "The secret" or "The law of attraction" (visualising your outcome and then letting go and trusting that the universe will provide it) impedes success. Gabrielle Oettingen at the University of Pennsylvania has done a number of studies showing the same result. In one study, women in a weight-reduction program were asked to describe what would happen if they were offered a tempting situation with food. The more positive their fantasies of how well they would cope with these situations, the less work they did on weight reduction. A year later, those women who consistently fantasised positive results lost on average 12 kilos less than those who anticipated negative challenges and thus put in more effort (Oettingen and Wadden, 1991). Oettingen followed up final year students to find out how much they fantasised getting their dream job after leaving university. The students who fantasised more reported two years later that they did less searching for jobs, had fewer offers of jobs, and had significantly smaller salaries than their classmates (Oettingen and Mayer, 2002). In another study she investigated a group of students who had a secret romantic attraction, a crush, on another student. She asked them to imagine what would happen if they were to accidentally find themselves alone with that person. The more vivid and positive the fantasies they made, the less likely they were to take any action and to be any closer to a relationship with the person 5 months later. The result is consistent in career success, in love and attraction, and in dealing with addictions and health challenges

(Oettingen, Pak and Schnetter, 2001; Oettingen, 2000; Oettingen and Gollwitzer, 2002).

Richard Wiseman (2009, p 88-93) did a very large study showing the same result. He tracked 5000 people who had some significant goal they wanted to achieve (everything from starting a new relationship to beginning a new career, from stopping smoking to gaining a qualification. He followed people up over the next year, and found firstly that only 10% ever achieved their goal. Dramatic and consistent differences in the psychological techniques they used made those 10% stand out from the rest. Those who failed tended either to think about all the bad things that would happen or continue to happen if they did not reach their goal (what NLP calls away from motivation, and what other research calls counterfactual thought) or to fantasise about achieving their goal and how great life would be. They also tried to achieve their goal by willpower and attempts to suppress "unhelpful thoughts". Finally, they spent time thinking about role models who had achieved their goal, often putting pictures of the role model on their fridge or other prominent places, to remind them to fantasise. These techniques did not work! And the most successful people did not waste their time doing them.

Wiseman warns that visualising what it will be like to have achieved your goal has become a popular tactic. "This type of exercise has been promoted by the self-help industry for years, with claims that it can help people lose weight, stop smoking, find their perfect partner, and enjoy increased career success. Unfortunately, a large body of research now suggests that although it might make you feel good, the technique is, at best, ineffective." (Wiseman, 2009, p 84). This is because, as Wiseman notes, whether you achieve your goals is primarily a question of motivation; of getting yourself to do certain things. Fantasising that everything has already been done reduces motivation.

Goalsetting - What Works?

An important issue comes up whenever people set goals, and whenever they make decisions to purchase something. It is related to what NLP calls a "convincer metaprogram", a personality trait that determines how easily people make decisions. In research, the two extremes of metaprogram (personality trait) are called maximisers and satisficers. Richard Wiseman explains: "Extreme maximisers tend to check all available options constantly to make sure they have picked the best one. In contrast extreme satisficers only look until they have found something that fulfils their needs." The result, from research, is that maximisers actually do get better quality and more for their money, but they cannot turn off their maximising, so they are never satisfied. In one study, 500 students from 11 universities were categorised as either maximisers or satisficers, and then followed up as they sought employment. The maximisers got jobs earning them 20% more money, but they were less satisfied with their jobs and more prone to regret, pessimism and anxiety. (Monterosso et alia, 2002). Wiseman recommends that if you are a maximiser, you may want to set limits around each major decision, so that you know when to let go of the decision.

Once you've decided, what do you do next? The complete inventory of successful strategies that Richard Wiseman's research found fits neatly into our SPECIFY model.

Sensory Specific: Firstly, the most successful people did imagine achieving their goal, and were able to list concrete, specific benefits they would get from it, rather than just say that they would "feel happy". They had what Wiseman calls "an objective checklist of benefits" and made these "as concrete as possible", often by writing them down. He notes "... although many people said they aimed to enjoy life more, it was the successful people who explained how they intended to spend two evenings each week with friends and visit one new country each year." (Wiseman, 2009, p 91- 93)

Positive: Secondly, they described their goal positively. Wiseman says "For example, when asked to list the benefits of getting a new job, successful participants might reflect on finding more fulfilling and well-paid employment, whereas their unsuccessful counterparts might focus on a failure leaving them trapped and unhappy." (Wiseman, 2009, p 92)

Ecological: Here's a surprising result of the research by both Gabriellle Oettingen and Richard Wiseman. After thinking about the positive benefits of achieving their goal, the most successful participants would "spend another few moments reflecting on the type of barriers and problems they are likely to encounter if they attempt to fulfil their ambition.... focusing on what they would do if they encountered the difficulty." (Wiseman, 2009, p 101) Oettingen trained people to do this process, which she calls "doublethink" and was able to increase their success dramatically just with this step.

Choice Increasing: Related to this NLP concept is the fact that successful goalsetters made sure that they felt as if their progress was bringing them rewards rather than limiting their choices and creating work. They did this most of because "As part of their planning, successful participants ensured that each of their sub-goals had a reward attached to it" so that it "gave them something to look forward to and provided a sense of achievement." (Wiseman, 2009, p 93)

The next sections of this SPECIFY model are really part of planning how you'll achieve your goal....

Initiated by Self: Successful goalsetters have a plan. They do not leave their goal up to "the law of attraction" or to someone else who will save them. Wiseman notes "Whereas successful and unsuccessful participants might have stated that their aim was to find a new job, it was the successful people who quickly went on to describe how they intended to rewrite their CV in week one, and then apply for one new job every two weeks for the next six months." (Wiseman, 2009, p 91)

First Step Identified: Wiseman found that it was particularly important to break the goal down into small steps and manage one step at a time. "Successful participants broke their overall goal into a series of sub-goals, and thereby created a step-by-step process that helped remove the fear and hesitation often associated with trying to achieve a major life change." (Wiseman, 2009, p 90-91)

Start by 'brainstorming' -listing ideas without criticising or discussing them. Think creatively and find new approaches wherever you can. There'll be plenty of time to be realistic in the next step. For now you can help your mind think up new ideas by accepting whatever occurs to you and writing it down. Give yourself ten minutes to do this. Actions for achieving your goal may include talking to a resource person, studying a book, practising new behaviour, keeping a diary of your progress, setting aside time or money to use, and so on.

The final stage in your planning involves narrowing down the list of possible actions. Check for each one:

- have I got the resources to do this?
- does it get me closer to the goal I wrote down?

When you know which actions you are going to take, you can list them in the order in which you will act. It's most effective to find a small part of one action which you can do today. People generally feel even better about goal-setting once they have started doing something. Write down now which action you can take today!

Your Resources Identified There are many 'resources' that will help you reach your goal. If you were planning to bake a cake, useful resources might include flour, sugar, eggs, and so on. A recipe book or a friend who knows the recipe would also be a resource. For your goal, resources to list will include:

- friends who can support you to change
- role models (people you know of and can learn from who have achieved this goal themselves)
- time, money, energy
- information sources, including this book
- your character traits, such as determination or an enthusiasm for this goal
- times when you've been in the kind of state you need to achieve this goal - you can use these resourceful states by anchoring them (see activity 2.4)

Evaluating how well you got what you wanted

Each time you do one of the things on your list you'll remember to congratulate yourself. Each small step will add to your confidence. And every time something doesn't happen quite the way you had hoped, that gives you valuable feedback about what else you need to do or how you can change your goal.

At the start, set yourself a time when you can check how you are doing. This involves asking:

- Have I achieved my goal yet?
- Which actions are working? Which should I change?
- Is my goal still appropriate? If not, what is my new goal?

Goal setting and problem solving are 'course correction' models. It's like flying an aeroplane or paddling a canoe. If you find you haven't got where you want, that tells you to adjust the rudder to get back on course. It doesn't mean you've failed; in fact it's part of how you will succeed.

Conclusions

If you have any final doubts about whether goal setting can work for you, here's the answer. Check through your life for changes which have happened in the last ten years. Have you passed any exams, shifted house, started a new friendship, completed any projects, learned something new, even bought new clothes? Almost every positive change in your life began as a goal. Before you did it, you thought about doing it. This process works because it takes what you are already doing, and helps you to do it better. Doing it better means breaking it down into five simple steps:

1. define the challenge
2. SPECIFY the goal

Sensory specific and timed
Positive
Ecological
Choice increasing
Initiated by you... with...
First step identified
Your resources identified

3. plan how to reach the goal
4. act
5. evaluate.

Activity 4.2

AIM: to give group members a supervised experience of the goalsetting and problem-solving process

Group leader:

1 Set each member an individual assignment to define a personal goal as described in the section above. After discussing the plan with them, give them 4-12 weeks to act.

2 Group members should write up individual evaluations of their progress, as a final report.

Activity 4.3

AIM: to experience the value of goal setting

1 Everyone spread out across the room and stand with your feet slightly apart. Each person brings their left arm straight up in front so it's parallel with the floor. Now, keeping your feet still, turn your body to the left, pointing with the finger as far as you can comfortably turn. Notice, by the point on the wall, how far round you are pointing.

2 Turn back to the front. Everyone will now close their eyes and make a picture of what they would see if they turned again, but this time with their hand going 40 centimetres further round. Imagine where on the wall or window that would mean your hand is pointing. Sense what it would feel like to be that much more supple, so that your body just flowed around. Imagine what you would say to yourself if you could go that much further.

3 Now open your eyes and physically turn again to the left.

4 See how much further each person has turned. The difference is due to programming the brain to achieve - the same process we have called 'goal setting'. When people don't achieve in life, it's not 'laziness'. It's just a lack of adequate, compelling goals.

Activity 4.4

AIM: to experience the value of creative brainstorming

1 You have agreed to bake a small, square cake for a children's birthday party. Decide what kind of cake, but ensure it has icing on the top only. There are four children coming, and you are going to cut the cake into four pieces, each the same shape and size. All the cake must be used up in these four pieces.

How many different ways are there of cutting the cake to get this result? Think for a minute or so, and write down your ideas. If you are in a group, one person should collect up the answers.

2 Refer to the answer on page 226. Discuss how our perceptions of challenges often limit the answers we think up.

Learning Stages

AIM: to be able to explain the four steps in Abraham Maslow's learning model.

Learning in communication

Learning communication skills is an amazing business. In a way, little of it involves learning anything 'new' at all: it involves understanding what you already do well, so you can do it whenever you need to. It's like falling asleep. Everyone can do it; you've fallen asleep thousands of times. And yet I'm sure that there have been times - perhaps times when you really needed to sleep, say because you had an exam the next morning - when you couldn't do it. Learning the skills of falling asleep means you can do it every time. It means that if you find it doesn't happen automatically one night, you can do it step-by-step (Maslow 1971, Miller et alia 1988).

Mostly, people's communication skills work satisfactorily. However, when they own a challenge their normal ability may not be available. For example, the person who can't get to sleep: that is the time they need to know, step-by-step, how to do it.

Unfortunately, when people first hear about the idea of learning communication skills, they often suspect there's nothing to learn. After all, you can either talk to people or you can't. Aren't some people just naturally good at it and some not? And isn't it all just theories anyway?

This kind of question always occurs at the first stage of learning something. Remember learning to ride a pushbike? Quite often very young children are eager to get a bike. Perhaps they've had a tricycle before; that's much the same thing, right? Wrong. Going from three wheels to two turns out to be a major challenge. The child who was just waiting to ride off into the sunset suddenly comes to suspect that he or she may never ride a bike. Perhaps it's just not their scene. They have now reached the second stage of learning.

• Stage one: unconsciously unskilled: you can't do it, but you don't know you can't do it.

• Stage two: consciously unskilled: you can't do it, and you know you can't.

A lot of people give up at stage two, but for those of us who stuck at it, riding a bike gradually became more possible. At first, someone pushed you, letting go for a brief time. You could ride at those moments, but you knew you had to hold on for your life. The slightest move to the side and you came off. Some people give up at this stage, too. They say: 'Sure, I can do it. But it's a lot easier to get around the natural way - the way I always have before. Maybe it only works for certain people. I know when I'm doing it I feel really phoney.' This is stage three.

• Stage three: consciously skilled: you can do it, but it's something you have to keep remembering to do.

It's just practice that enables you to get past this stage and on to stage four.

Did you make it with bike riding? Can you ride a bike while thinking about where you're going, while carrying a parcel or waving to someone? If you can, the actual work of keeping your balance on a bike is now something you know so well, it's unconscious.

• Stage four: unconsciously skilled: you can do it and it just happens without thinking about it.

Learning communication skills is exactly like that. Have you ever known someone who got married and was unconsciously unskilled about building a relationship: someone who thought there wasn't anything to learn? Then you watched them as they learned new ways of behaving. They probably felt phoney when they tried to act or speak in new ways: they were consciously skilled.

It takes a lot of practice to change fully. You may even 'fall off the bike' a few times in the early stages. But in the end, it works. The skills you will learn in the next few chapters may seem trivial at first, or they may sound phoney when you use them for the first time - but once you have integrated them into your natural way of talking they will work. They will enrich your life beyond anything you could have imagined before.

Oops!

Does this mean that once you've learned a skill, you'll always use it perfectly? Unfortunately not. In most situations I find myself able to use the skills described here with ease. However, every so often I surprise myself. Some months ago I found myself shouting at a family member to 'shut up' - an approach which differs somewhat from what I recommend in the next chapters. It's always a rather humbling experience. In such a situation, something has 'pushed all my buttons'. To use a way of explaining it from Chapter 2, I've been anchored back into a state where I don't have the skills I need.

I have two ways of coping with this experience. One is to excuse myself from the room and take the 'time out' to meet my needs and return to a resourceful state. The other is to apologise. In my first months as a single parent, when I was learning many of these skills, I did a lot of apologising! One of the really important things for me to remember at such times is this: making a mistake today doesn't prove that I'm doomed to live a life of mistakes. The fact that I've recognised the mistake does mean that I'm learning to respond differently.

Conclusions

Learning happens in four stages:

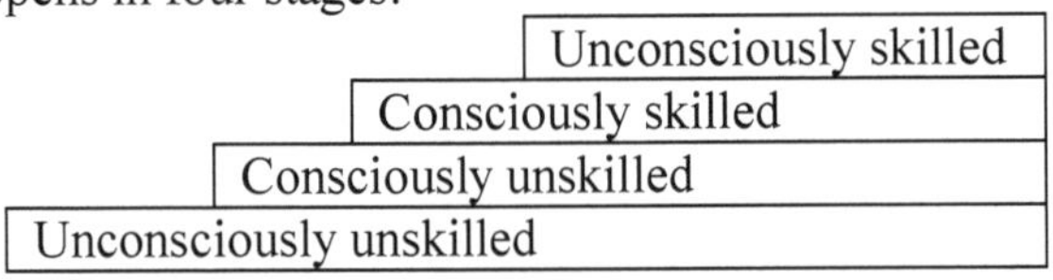

Unconsciously skilled
Consciously skilled
Consciously unskilled
Unconsciously unskilled

Unconsciously skilled: I do it without having to think about it.
Consciously skilled: I need to think about it to do it.
Consciously unskilled: I know that I can't do it.
Unconsciously unskilled: I don't realise that I can't do it.

Summary

In this chapter I've introduced you to a process which is the basis for most of the skills you'll learn in Parts 2 and 3 of the book. Solution finding in communication begins by identifying who owns the challenge (meaning who is feeling unhappy at that moment). It then works through the five steps of the problem-solving process:

1. define the challenge
2. SPECIFY the goal
    Sensory specific and timed
    Positive
    Ecological
    Choice increasing
    Initiated by you... with...
    First step identified
    Your resources identified
3. plan how to reach the goal
4. act
5. evaluate.

Another model presented in this chapter was Maslow's four steps of learning, through which you will move as you learn any new communication skills. These steps or stages are:

1. unconsciously unskilled
2. consciously unskilled
3. consciously skilled
4. unconsciously skilled.

PART TWO

Helping

Chapter 5: Hearing someone else fully

KEY CONCEPTS

- Rescuer/victim/persecutor roles
- Roadblocks to listening
- Non-verbal attending skills
- Open and closed questions
- Reflective listening skills

Rescue, persecution or help?

AIM: to be able to recognise common 'roadblocks' to helping, according to Thomas Gordon's model, and to identify the assumptions of rescue which underlie these.

A life of waiting

The very first person I visited in my work as a public health nurse was an elderly lady. Most of my nursing training had been done in hospitals. It was odd to walk up to her, sitting alone on a tree stump round the back of her little house, and to think of this as 'nursing'.

My visit was essentially routine, but I had the time to listen as well as the intention to get to know her. As she attempted to introduce herself to me her mind wandered over nearly a century of memories.

The youngest child in her family, she had continued to live with and care for her mother until her mother's death a few years before.

When she was about 20 she had fallen in love. The young man involved went off to World War I and then moved to England. He wrote to her assuring her that he would return to marry her soon. She waited faithfully for him - for more than 40 years. Gradually she realised that he was never coming back, and that she was going to be single all her life.

Her mother's last words to her, on her deathbed, were to the effect that she had always been a selfish, lazy daughter, and had never looked after her well enough. At that moment, as her mother's life ended, she understood that she had wasted her own entire life. Now an elderly woman herself, she had never ever lived. 'And now, she concluded, 'it's too late.' I held her hand as she wept for the tragedy of a life given up to the demands of others.

Over an hour had passed while I listened to this woman's tale. I had said only a few sentences but, as I left, she pleaded with me to accept some gift for what I had done and asked eagerly when I would be able to return.

What had I done to earn this gratitude? I had been the only person who happened to have the time to listen for an hour to her sorrow. I was 22 years old. This woman had lived four times that long, and she certainly was not asking for my advice. What she did crave, above all, was to be heard.

How do I help?

All of us will come across people who are hurting, who are unhappy, angry, afraid, or otherwise 'own a challenge'. They will range from those who experience their whole life as 'a waste' to people who are momentarily annoyed. In the next two chapters we will discuss how to respond to these situations.

Have you ever met someone who has been through a distressing event, or who has suddenly off-loaded their anger, their hurt or their confusion in front of you? Perhaps your job involves working with people at times when they are anxious or in pain? In all these situations, people often wonder: 'What can I say?, 'What can I do to help?, or 'How do I show that I care about them?'

One of the temptations of such situations is to forget who really owns the challenge: to start thinking that it's my challenge and I need to find the right solution to it. It's hard to accept, when someone else is hurting, that only they can find the very best solution for them. They have to live with the solution. So it doesn't matter how well my ideas would work for me, if the other person doesn't think they will work for them.

Rescuer role

Once I forget that the other person owns their challenge I start to believe that I can take away their pain for them: that I can 'make them feel happy". I may even think that I have to rescue them from their challenge because they are not smart enough or strong enough to do anything about it themselves. Once I believe these things, I'm in what Stephen Karpman calls the Rescuer role (Stewart and Joines, 1987, p 236). He uses the word Rescuer with a capital 'R' to distinguish it from genuine rescue, which does happen (for example when a firefighter rescues someone from a house fire). The Rescuer believes that helping someone means doing things for them (whether they asked for it or not), even when it creates difficulties for the Rescuer.

Victim role

The elderly woman I described above had spent much of her life being a Rescuer for her lonely mother. The result of Rescue, Karpman says, is to encourage the other person to act like a helpless Victim (again he uses the capital 'V' to distinguish someone in the Victim role from someone who is a genuine victim asking for a specific kind of assistance). The woman's mother began to do less and less for herself; she too began to believe that she was not smart enough or not strong enough to solve her own challenges. She became a Victim.

Persecutor role

Instead of thanking their Rescuer (as an actual victim of a real misfortune might thank their helper), the Victim often comes to resent and complain to their Rescuer. They then move into a third role, the role of the Persecutor. And that's exactly what the woman's mother was doing on her deathbed. The mother had come to demand that she be looked after in every way by her daughter, and was resentful when asked to do something for herself. Calling her daughter selfish and lazy was like a slap in the face: it was action from the Persecutor role.

Rescuers also slip into the Persecutor role. At times, the daughter in our example would begin to suspect that her mother was 'not as sick as she made out'. She would then become angry at being manipulated and decide not to respond to the mother's requests at all. From being her mother's Rescuer, she would shift to being her Persecutor, angrily blaming her for ruining her life. It's a bit like a game of musical chairs; everyone keeps changing places around this triangle.

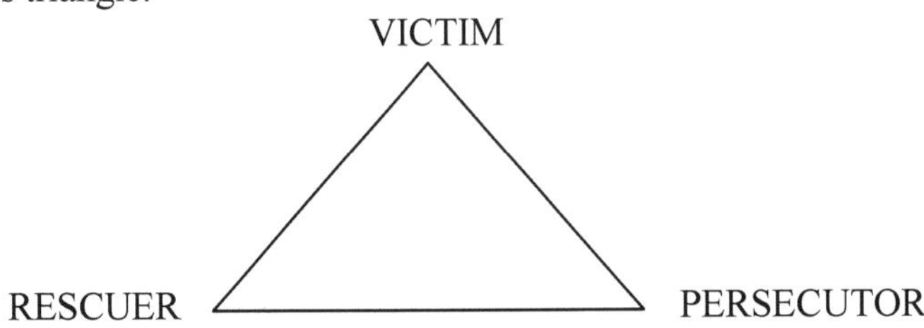

The daughter herself also felt like a Victim much of the time. She dreamed that the young man who had promised to marry her would Rescue her from life with her mother, because she herself didn't feel strong enough or smart enough to get out.

Role theory

The term 'role' is similar to the terms 'state of mind' and 'ego-state' which we discussed in Chapter 2. The word 'role' was borrowed by psychotherapist Jacob Moreno (1892-1974) from the world of the theatre, where actors play various roles. Moreno described a role as 'the functioning form the individual assumes in the specific moment he reacts to a specific situation in which other persons or objects are involved.' This definition emphasises the way a state of mind is a response to a specific situation, to other people or things.

The role of Rescuer is a response to the Victim, and vice versa. They are 'interdependent' - one can't exist without the other. Moreno called this a role set. Victims need Rescuers, and Rescuers also look for Victims to save. Each role has a context or surrounding situation, feelings, beliefs about what is happening, behaviour, and consequences of what the person does. The Rescuer role has a context where someone else owns a challenge; feelings of guilt and responsibility related to a belief that the other person is not able to contribute to solving their own challenge; behaviours such as advice-giving and reassuring, and the consequence that the Victim does even less to help themselves.

The Rescue triangle in action

The Rescue triangle is so common that you can easily think of times when you've been caught in it. In my work training nurses and counsellors, I often find that the people who choose such 'helping' professions are people who have a strong Rescuer role. They're the one who always helps out in their family, who helps sort things out when others are fighting, who's there whenever a friend is in a tangle. The challenge is they feel that they have to do these things, and forget who actually owns the challenge.

If you want to be able to help others when they are upset (and that includes helping your friends, family or clients) the first thing to understand is how to avoid Rescuing or Persecuting them.

Here's an example from parenting: In a long term study of 1000 elementary school children, Dr Eva Pomerantz of the University of Illinois (2001) found dramatic evidence of the harmful effects of parental guilt. Her research showed that children were more prone to psychological disturbances and to depression in particular when their parents felt more responsible for the children's feelings.

Pomerantz used the term "intrusive support" to refer to parents monitoring and helping children deal with emotional challenges when the children have not asked for such help. This is the kind of support parents use more when they feel responsible for their children's happiness. Put simply, when parents feel guilty about their children's unhappiness, they interfere more and things get progressively worse. The more the parents used intrusive support, the less competent their children came to feel, and the less happy they became. Parents who did a lot of intrusive support actually ended up controlling what their children could say about their challenges, denying their children's feelings and deepening any feelings of inadequacy that were there.

Roadblocks

In his book T.E.T Teacher Effectiveness Training, Thomas Gordon points out four basic ways in which people can do damage when someone else owns a challenge. Each of these ways of talking involves a confusion about challenge ownership. Each of them is either Rescue or Persecution. Gordon calls them 'roadblocks' because they tend to block the other person from sorting out solutions to their challenge.

1. Solution giving

This includes straight out advice giving ('Why don't you try...'), lecturing ('Well, the fact is that research shows...'), commanding ('Stop behaving like that right now!'), warning ('If you carry on that way you'll...'), and moralising ('You're old enough now to be more considerate').

When you give solutions as a response to someone feeling upset, there is a high risk that the person will feel put down, that they are too dumb to work it out, and that they are being pushed into something. If someone tells me: 'I'm having trouble with my marriage. I'm beginning to wonder if it's all worthwhile', it is of very little use for me to say: 'Get a divorce or you'll be stuck for life". It's as if someone came to see a doctor and said: 'I'm not well', and the doctor said: 'Take these pills. I was sick last year and they worked for me". The doctor hasn't listened well enough to really understand what it's like for the patient.

In most cases giving solutions just leaves people feeling misunderstood. Even when they agree with the suggestion, they rarely act on it unless they have chosen it. Real helping means enabling people to choose solutions they will act on.

2. Judgements

Included here are blaming ('It's your own fault: serves you right'), name-calling ('You numbskull. You're incompetent"), and analysing ('I think deep down what you're really doing is...'). These kinds of messages simply tell people your theory about how bad they are. They often leave the other person feeling ashamed, insulted, hurt and angry.

Take the person who says to me: 'I'm having trouble with my marriage. I'm beginning to wonder if it's all worthwhile'. For me to reply: 'It's your own stubbornness that's really causing your problem' may make me feel better, but is of very little use to anyone else. People are generally better at finding good solutions when they feel respected and understood than when they are being told off.

3. Denying

Denying that there is a challenge can be done by praising (You don't need to worry. You'll do fine as always'), reassuring ("Never mind. It'll all work out in the end'), and distracting ('Come on, let's think about happier things right now'). The most likely result of such attempts is to leave the other person feeling misunderstood, or sensing that they have been told off for the way they feel. To respond to: 'I'm having trouble with my marriage. Im beginning to wonder if it's all worthwhile" by saying: 'I'm sure it's worthwhile. A nice person like you will work it out', may stop the other person talking about their worry. But it won't stop them worrying. They'll just need to find someone else who really listens to them.

4. Interrogating

Asking a lot of questions, such as: "Why did you do that?, or 'Can't you talk about it with him?', or 'Did you tell her?' is the fourth main type of roadblock. Oddly, such questions produce the opposite effect to what was intended. The person often says less and less, waiting for the next question. They may feel defensive, exposed, and distracted from the things they meant to talk about. By asking repeated questions you take charge of the conversation and stop the person's own natural way of working it all out.

In our example, where someone tells me: 'I'm having trouble with my marriage', to ask, for example: 'Why haven't you gone to see Marriage Guidance?' is more likely to lead to a lot of defensive explanations than to any useful sorting out.

Mostly, people who use a lot of advice giving, judging, denying or interrogating aren't trying to hurt someone. They're more often trying to help in the only way they know how. It's sad, because all of us enjoy helping. Some of your most precious memories of being with others are probably of times when you were able to help in some way.

An example of roadblocking

See if you can recognise the particular roadblocks being used in the following conversation between Tony, aged ten, and his father, John. Notice how John wants to help very much, and yet how far from helpful his comments actually are.

Tony: I'm really worried about this maths test tomorrow.
John: You should be studying for it right now then.
Tony: But I don't understand parts of it.
John: Didn't you talk about it in class? Why didn't you ask the teacher?
Tony: I don't know. just didn't want to.
John: Well read it again. You can do it if you want to. You're good at maths.
Tony: No I'm not. Not this maths anyway.
John: Honestly Tony, how do you expect to get anywhere in life with such a negative attitude? You're hopeless. I don't want to talk about it any more.
Tony: (Begins to cry)

Remember, we're not saying it's never a good idea to ask a question, to praise someone or to give advice. But sometimes it's not the right time (for example when someone is upset). As a rule, the stronger the person's feelings, the more risky these four types of roadblock will be.

Often when I point out the risk of using roadblocks, people say to me: 'But that covers 95 per cent of what I can say when someone is upset!' In the next section we'll discuss the other five per cent.

Activity 5.1

AIM: to provide practice identifying roadblocks and their effects

I Write down five imaginary situations where you could be upset, worried, angry, hurt, and so on: where you would "own a challenge '. (For example, 'I've lost all my money', I can't wake up in the mornings', 'None of my friends came to my party.') Don't use real situations - we are not going to be getting very helpful responses.

2 In pairs, each tell one of your imaginary challenges to the other, who should then respond using one of the four main roadblocks (solutions, judgements, denial or interrogation). The first person imagines how they would feel if this were a real situation and tells the other. Reverse roles so that the other now states one of their own imaginary concerns. Continue until all the situations have been tried.

The listening attitude

AIM: to be able to attend and to ask open questions as an invitation to talk.

People's needs

When people are upset and try to get help from others around them, what do they want more than anything else? Social workers John Mayer and Noel Timms (Mayer, 1970, p 287) studied a large number of people who visited 'helping' professionals, to find out what helped. A few comments they heard were as follows:

'The first time I went, I was there for two hours and I didn't stop talking once. It was marvellous and I felt very much better when I left. I was a completely different person. I just felt like I was talking to an old friend and just pouring out my troubles. She heard all I've got to say and out it goes.'

People talk the same way about their need to be listened to by other professional contacts, such as their bosses, teachers, doctors and lawyers. It's very much the same thing people want from non-professional helpers like friends, parents or spouses. Here's what author and university professor Judy

Katz said about her friend Richard's help, after her experience of being raped:

'He was very understanding and compassionate about the rape. What was particularly helpful was just his being there. He took all the cues from me and responded to my needs, not forcing his own.' (Katz 1984)

Benefits of listening

Not only do people want helpers who can 'just be there' and listen to them, they are actually physically better off if they have someone to do this. James Pennebaker, a psychologist at Southern Methodist University in the USA, studied men and women whose spouses had died suddenly (reported in Love, Medicine and Miracles, Siegel 1988). He found that those who had no-one to talk it over with had a much higher-than-average rate of illness over the next months. Those who had someone to listen stayed well.

Listening is a powerful message to the suffering person. It conveys respect, acceptance, and understanding of their difficulty. Learning how to listen will increase your success in people-oriented jobs, and will help you to be a valued friend, lover, parent or relative. Your very presence around people will help them to heal and protect them from stress-related illness.

Commitment to listening

Listening requires a commitment, though. After all, if you really learn to listen, you may sometimes hear things you don't like or don't agree with. And listening only works fully when you have a willingness to find out what it's really like for the other person (when you don't 'own a challenge" with what they're saying). Listening requires love. The word 'love' comes from an old English word related to the word 'leave', meaning permission to be free (for example to give someone leave, or to take annual leave from work). So to love is to give permission to someone to be who they are, and to find solutions which suit them. In this sense 'love' is a state (see Chapter 2) which you need to be in to listen well.

If you are interested in listening fully, and you have someone who wants to share a concern, what next? What do good listeners actually do? First, they use all the body language skills we studied in Chapter 3 to show the other person that they are listening. This non-verbal skill is called attending.

Attending includes:

1 Being close to the person (how close varies from person to person as discussed in Chapter 3), and at their height. (People from some cultures will find it easier if they are a little lower than you, as a gesture of respect.)

2 Facing the person and/or leaning towards them. (People who get a lot of information visually - through their eyes - will want to face you, while people who get more information from your voice or from how they feel may prefer to sit next to you.)

3 Using open body gestures (legs and arms uncrossed).

4 Mirroring the speaker's body posture, breathing and voice tonality. (This way of creating rapport, discussed in Chapter 3, needs to be done carefully so the other person doesn't feel made fun of.)

5 Nodding your head occasionally as they speak.

6 Having your eyes facing somewhere near them, so they are available for the other person to make eye contact as they need to. (This will be more for Pakeha than for Polynesian people, for example, and more for people who get information visually.)

7 Not doing other things such as gazing out of the window, playing with a pen or reading a book, while the person is talking. (If you need to do something else, perhaps right now is not a good time for you to listen, and you will have to tell the person that.)

This may sound like a lot to remember when it's written down in a list here, but in real life good and bad listening are both pretty obvious. You can probably remember a time when someone didn't listen to you (perhaps a parent, a child of yours, a teacher, a health professional or someone serving in a shop or office). Check through the list and find out which of the six principles of attending they forgot. Once you remember how it feels not to be attended to, you'll realise how very important it is to actually show someone you're listening. It's not enough to know that you can sometimes listen while you do other tasks. People need to feel listened to, and they need to see that you are attending.

Nowhere is this more obvious than in a group or classroom. Try it out. When you and your fellow students lean a little forward and attend, the teacher's energy will improve. And as you know, if you all started packing your books away, the teacher would falter and might even experience 'strong negative feelings'.

Activity 5.2

AIM: to experience the effect of attending

1 Get into groups of three. Each person should think of a topic that interests them, or a book/film/TV programme they've enjoyed recently.

2 One person talks about their interest while a second person listens to them, talking only minimally. The third person is the observer and timekeeper. For the first two minutes the second person (the listener) should break three of the principles of attending. In the next two minutes he or she should use all the principles of good attending.

3 After the four minutes are up, the talker describes what each section felt like, and the observer gives feedback about the listener's ability to attend. (In this case 'feedback' simply means to tell them what you saw.)

4 Change roles and start again. Repeat a third time so that each person tries out each of the roles.

Verbal listening skills

There are times when attending is just about all you need to do with someone who is upset. Someone who is crying may appreciate your silent presence or simply a hand on their shoulder. Remember that at such times you can increase their sense of being understood by the use of pacing (for example breathing in time with them).

However, there are also things you can say which actually increase the other's sense of being listened to and understood. These skills were first identified by people such as Carl Rogers, Robert Carkhuff, Allan Ivey and Gerard Egan: American researchers who developed modern counselling. New Zealand counsellors Anne Munro, Bob Manthei and John Small have written an excellent exposition of them. Others, including communications skills trainers Thomas Gordon, Linda Adams and Robert Bolton, have shown (with courses such as Parent Effectiveness Training) that not only counsellors but anyone who wants to be able to help others can learn these skills.

In this chapter we consider the three most basic verbal listening skills:

• minimal encouragers
• Open questions, and
• reflective listening. (Reflective listening is discussed separately in the next section.)

Minimal encouragers

These are the 'sound effects' for attending - what Thomas Gordon's Youth Effectiveness Training Course calls 'helpful grunts' (Gordon, 1988). They are brief grunts or words of acknowledgment ('Mmm', 'Uh-huh', 'Right', 'Sure', 'Yeah') which tell the speaker that you are still awake and listening. They don't imply agreement or disagreement, just interest. On the phone, they may in fact be the only way you have to assure the speaker that you are still there, without interrupting.

Questions

Questioning can either help or hinder your ability to listen. Overuse of questions (interrogating) is one of the four roadblocks to listening, discussed before in this chapter. Often the challenge to those learning to listen is to use less questions, not more.

Helpful questioning is best understood as an invitation to the other person to talk. Sometimes people will prefer not to talk when they are upset, and just to be nearby may be the very best thing you can do. But at other times, a simple question such as: 'What's on your mind?', 'Tell me about today' or "How do you feel about that? may help them to start talking. Such questions can be used well in the middle of a conversation, too, to help the person say more or to direct them to start again if they got lost. There are two kinds of questions: closed and open.

Closed questions

Closed questions can be answered with the words 'yes' or "no', or with a specific piece of information such as a number. For example: 'Do you like it here?, 'Don't you think you could ask him?", and 'What time is it?' In ordinary conversation when nobody owns a challenge, closed questions usually get perfectly good answers. However, when people are upset, they often reply with a straight 'yes' or 'no', forcing you to ask another question to get the extra information you expected. This easily degenerates into an interrogation, with the speaker saying less and less as the listener asks more and more. Closed questions are best used to check a very specific issue and are a skill to use sparingly.

Open questions

When you are in a listening situation and want to invite someone to talk more, open questions (which cannot be answered 'yes', 'no', or with a specific number) will work better. Open questions usually begin with words such as: 'what' , 'how', or the phrase 'Tell me about'. For example: 'What was that like for you?','How is your new job going?", 'Tell me what happened before that'.

The word 'why' also begins open questions (for example: 'Why did you do that?) but most people find 'why' questions difficult to answer. This is because 'why' asks the person to explain what was happening underneath. It suggests that simple facts are not good enough and deserve explaining or justifying. Often people hear: 'Why did you do that? as a judgement about what they did.

'How' questions get a better response (for example: 'How did you come to do that?), because they ask for a simple description of what went on, rather than a justification.

Before we read on to learn the most important verbal listening skill, let's summarise these basics. Good listening includes both non-verbal and verbal skills.

The non-verbal part is called attending, and includes:

- nearness
- directing your body towards the speaker
- open and mirrored gestures
- nodding
- appropriate eye contact, and
- avoiding distractions.

Verbal skills include:

- minimal encouragers, and
- the use of questions (particularly open questions such as those beginning 'how' or 'what').

Activity 5.3

AIM: to practise forming open questions

In each of the following six situations, the listener asked a closed question. Write an open question which would give you a fuller response. Compare your answers in pairs, and discuss.

1 A 26-year-old woman has been discussing her mother's overuse of alcohol.
Closed question: 'Do you and your mother usually get on OK?

2 An eight-year-old boy has been telling you how he doesn't enjoy maths. Closed question: 'Don't you like anything at school?'

3 A 17-year-old woman is talking over her feelings of resentment about her boyfriend. Closed question: 'Have you told him about this?'

4 A 35-year-old man has just explained that, as a child, he hated social events. Closed question: 'Do you hate social events now?'

5 Having explained his difficulty finding a job, a 19-year-old man says he will have to do a training course on carpentry as that's all that's available. Closed question: 'Do you want to be a carpenter?'

6 Your friend stops talking in mid-sentence and begins to cry. Closed question: 'Are you OK?

Activity 5.4

AIM: to increase awareness of the different effects produced by open and closed questions

1 Get into pairs (it helps if you don't know each other very well). One person is to interview the other with the aim of discovering:
a more about them in general
b what kind of books they enjoy reading, or
c some other similar piece of information.

Ask six closed questions, which you should write down before starting.

2 Now begin again, but this time change each of the closed questions to an open question.

3 Reverse roles and repeat steps one and two.

4 Discuss in pairs the difference between the effects of open and closed questions. Report back to the group.

Reflective listening

AIM: to be able to verbally reflect (a) feelings expressed in words or behaviour, and (b) information described in words.

The crucial skill: the third verbal listening skill

The skill described here is the single most important verbal skill I know. It is the skill which helpers and counsellors use more often than any other. Group leaders use it to help discussions flow, and in conflict situations it has the power to bring the temperature down and get people sorting things out again.

As you'd expect with such a widely used skill, it appears in hundreds of bestselling books, under a wide variety of names (such as 'active listening', 'reflecting', 'accurate empathy', 'responding, 'feedback', 'the helping response', ,understanding response', 'paraphrasing', and 'verbal pacing'). As you'd also expect with such a widely used process, it is something which can be misused or even overused, and in those cases it can feel annoying or condescending.

Research identifying the effectiveness of this method first emerged in 1950, and a summary of the 50 years of continuing evidence for this core helping skill is presented by Allen Bergin and Sol Garfield (1994) in their Handbook of Psychotherapy.

Reflective listening is not merely a prelude to helping. It is by itself a powerful helping intervention. In a series of studies from the 1950s, Fred Fiedler (1951) showed that successful psychotherapists from a number of different therapeutic orientations tended to use empathic restatement of the client's concern more than any other intervention. This marked them out from unsuccessful therapists so much that what they said had more in common with other effective therapists than with others in their own school of therapy. Five decades of research has tended to support Fiedler's conclusion (Lambert and Bergin, 1994, p 181).

Relationship researcher John Gottman's studies identified that reflective listening was the most powerful response offered by members of successful couples relationships when the other person is unhappy (Gottman and Silver, 1999, p 87-89. In discussing parenting relationships, Gottman again emphasizes the importance of "Communicating empathy and understanding of the emotions, even if these emotions underlie misbehaviour." (Gottman, 1999, p 330).

If you'd like to have the ability to establish rapport with others - to fully understand them and for them to value your listening - then learning to use this skill well is a must.

Verbal rapport

In Chapter 3 we discussed how to build rapport by 'pacing' or 'mirroring' enough of the other person's behaviours for them to feel understood, but not distracted. Reflective listening is the verbal part of this process. To reflect you simply restate the basic idea or feeling in what another person has said. This helps each of you to know whether you've understood them. It also tells them that your intention is to understand and accept what they have said. If done well it helps the person clarify their own thoughts and feelings. Naturally, you've done this many times when listening. It's no newer to you than asking open questions, and like questioning, you can greatly improve your ability to do it.

The beach challenge

Consider the following example, in which John, aged 23, is listening to his 25 year-old friend Andrew. John has recently attended a listening skills course where reflective listening was taught. Recognising the situation as one where Andrew ,owns a challenge ', he uses this reflective process to help him clarify the feelings involved.

John: How did you and Beth get on at the beach yesterday? [open question]
Andrew: Oh... not so good I guess. I don't think I'll bother again.
John: Not so interested in her? [reflective listening]
Andrew: Well, I was when we were just going to parties, that sort of thing.
John: So it's the way things were at the beach. [reflective listening]
Andrew: Yeah. Turns out she owns a windsurfer, and .... (shrugs)
John: You're not into windsurfing. [reflective listening]
Andrew: No. Whereas she's really a pro.
John: Uh-huh. [minimal encourager]
Andrew: Hell, I couldn't even stand on the thing. I was a wipeout!
John: Embarrassing, eh! [reflective listening]
Andrew: Yeah, I'll say... But it's more than that. I suppose I always back away from situations where I'll have to learn something.
John: You tend to stay with what you know. [reflective listening]

Andrew: Yeah. Which is stupid really. I mean, I get so worried about what other people will think of me that I give up the whole relationship anyway.
John: And avoiding that embarrassment leads to even worse losses. [reflective listening]
Andrew: Mm-hm. I mean, heck, everyone has to learn sometime. Obviously Beth didn't just climb on a windsurfer and zip across the harbour.
John: Right. [minimal encourager]
Andrew: And, anyway, if I wasn't being so down on myself I'd probably enjoy having her show me.
John: Starting to feel interested in another try? [reflective listening]
Andrew: I guess. She's going out again on Thursday. I think I'll ring up and see if I can invite myself along.
John: Sounds great!

What happened here? Well, Andrew solved his challenge - by himself. All John did was listen.

Possible responses

What would you have been tempted to do? Mostly, when I ask people about this, they say they'd either avoid the issue or give some advice: 'Why not get some windsurfing lessons', or 'Let me show you how it's done'. The saddest thing about this advice is that it may actually work. Sad, because if it does work and Andrew learns how to windsurf, he may well still carry the basic challenge (of embarrassment learning in front of friends) into several more relationships. If the advice doesn't work, Andrew's going to spend a lot of energy convincing John that windsurfing's not for him. He's then worse off than before. Neither advice nor denial will create that sense of safety for Andrew to explore how he actually feels about the challenge.

That sense of acceptance and understanding (or empathy, which means to feel with someone) is uncommon in life. Empathic, reflective listening is like a precious jewel. In a society full of loneliness, anxiety and frustrations, it is rare indeed that you find someone who really wants to listen, someone who trusts that you can find solutions which will work for you. This skill is too important to leave only to counsellors and other professionals.

How to reflect

Obviously, what Andrew does needs to be different from parroting, just as nonverbal pacing needs to be different from mimicking. Take the sentence where John said: 'I was a wipeout'. For Andrew to reply: 'So you're a wipeout' is not very good reflective listening, even though it uses John's own word! Andrew's actual reply is 'Embarrassing, eh!', a shortened version of

'So you felt embarrassed'. He's interested in checking the basic meaning of what the speaker has said.

Content and feeling state

This basic meaning includes the information (or 'content') about what happened (in this case when John tried windsurfing), and the feeling states the person is experiencing. When the person hasn't named the feeling states they are experiencing, the listener needs to ask themself: 'In this situation, how would I be feeling?', and: 'From this person's body language, what do they seem to be feeling?'

Being in a similar body position to the speaker can help you identify feelings (see Chapter 3, on rapport). When you reflect feeling states, you are often less certain of having understood than when you reflect information. Sometimes it helps to explain this in the way you reply, for example: 'It almost sounds like you felt...', 'You feel... is that it?', 'From the way you say that, I get the impression you feel...'.

Having reflected the meaning as you have understood it, your next step needs to be listening for confirmation. If your reflection was accurate, the person will usually nod, say 'yes' or continue talking almost unaware of your presence. If your reflection sounds different to what they meant, they may frown, shake their head, or attempt to re-explain. Either way, your reflection has worked! You now have a better idea what the person meant (or didn't mean) and they know your intention is to understand. If your reflection wasn't accurate, you can listen again and offer a new statement.

To summarise, reflective listening has three steps:

1 Ask yourself what the basic meaning of the person's message was.
2 Put this into a brief statement and say this back, in words that can be understood by the person.
3 Check the person's response to find out whether you understood.

Learning to reflect

Reflective listening makes sure that you really listen. New students sometimes say: 'I always thought I was listening, but when I have to say something back I realise it's actually hard work'. It is, at first. As we mentioned in Chapter 4, when people are first learning a new skill it can feel like work, and it may also sound less natural. With practice you'll integrate reflective listening into your natural way of talking. Once that happens you won't have to think out every response, and - most of the time - no-one will even notice you're using a new process. You can then simply enjoy being fascinated by what the person is saying to you.

Reflective listening itself doesn't require a lot of effort. You don't have to think up the solutions, and you don't have to find smart questions to lead the conversation the right way. In fact, the main mistake learners make when counselling or helping is to work too hard. Christchurch counsellor George Sweet explains: 'It is becoming clear to me that when I am working effectively with a client, I have ceased working altogether, ceased striving to be helpful. My questioning and searching for answers is over. I no longer "leave the room" to go into my head. I am with What Is. Part of the way What Is is flowing. The more I am simply with, the more healing occurs.'

This is a very simple and a very old idea. George Sweet finds it origins in the gentle Chinese philosophy of Taoism. Christians will recognise it in the words of Paul: 'Rejoice with those who rejoice, and weep with those who weep' (Romans 12.15).

Deeper messages

When you are listening to someone, you will certainly discover that what people say to you (especially early on in a conversation) is not always a complete description of what is happening inside them. In our earlier example, Andrew's initial comment about his day at the beach is simply that he didn't get on so well and doesn't think he'll bother again. He doesn't say: 'I felt embarrassed by my difficulty windsurfing and - as usual - am backing away from that situation'. That's how he describes it later on, but first he gives the impression that he has a generally uncomfortable feeling about the day.

Each time John reflects back to him, it acts as a kind of feedback, helping Andrew understand and explain his experience more deeply and more clearly. Often you will find in listening to someone, that the basic challenge the two of you end up discussing is very different from the first thing they presented to you.

Listening is a voyage of discovery for both speaker and helper. I urge you to use it with respect and with affection.

Types of reflecting

Sometimes, in order to teach reflective listening, counselling trainers will divide it up into several smaller 'microskills'. These include:

1 Reflecting content (paraphrasing): this part of reflecting is less intense, and helps concentrate on solving the specific out there challenge. For example: "You had difficulty standing on the windsurfer'.

2 Identifying and reflecting feeling states: a deeper response which focuses the conversation on how the person talking is. Feeling states can be described:

a . using single words (for example: "You feel embarrassed')

b. by comparison to other situations, i.e. metaphor (for example: "You feel as if your pants just fell down')

c. using the body response the feeling causes (for example: 'You went red all over')

d . by the action it makes you want to take (for example: 'You felt like running away and hiding').

Feeling states are not the same as beliefs or opinions. To say: 'You feel she's putting pressure on you' is not actually reflecting a feeling state - it's reflecting a belief about what 'she' is doing. As a simple test, if the word 'that" is or can be put after the word "feel' in your sentence and it still makes sense, you have an opinion or belief. For example:

- 'I feel you're being rude' is a belief, because 'I feel that you're being rude' still makes sense.
- 'I feel lonely' is a real feeling, because 'I feel that lonely' loses the sense of it.
- 'I feel I'm a good loser' is a belief, because 'I feel that I'm a good loser' still makes sense.
- 'I feel like jumping for joy' is a feeling, because 'I feel that like jumping for joy' is not correct English.

3 Perception check: this refers to checking your understanding, not just of what the person said, but of all the "messages' you get from their body language as well. For example: 'You've become very quiet. I have the impression you're feeling sad. Is that right?' As in this example, it helps to specify the non-verbal behaviours from which you made your guess about how the person felt.

4 Summarising and sorting issues: this means restating things expressed over a longer period of conversation, or reflecting several pieces of content/ feelings at once. The listener may invite the talker to do this (for example: 'Well, where have we got so far?') or may do it for them (for example: 'So although you found it difficult to be in that situation yesterday, you'd like to stop telling yourself off and try just enjoying being with Beth there').

Summarising helps the person 'put the pieces together' and clarify their thoughts. A good example occurs in psychotherapist Carl Jung's account of his first interview with Sigmund Freud, in 1907. For three hours Jung talked with great enthusiasm about his own ideas. At the end of this time, Freud interrupted him and, to Jung's astonishment, grouped the content of this talk into several categories. These formed the basis for the rest of their discussion (described in Bolton, 1979, p 59).
Simpler than it sounds

As these descriptions of microskills come from the field of professional helping (discussed in Chapter 6), they may make reflective listening sound more complex than it is. Reflective listening is actually a very simple skill which I use many times every day. Whenever I'm in a discussion with someone, I use it to check my understanding of what they're saying. Usually this involves my saying one sentence.

An example

Some time ago I passed the scene of a fairly serious car accident. After I'd checked each of the people who were injured (including a child with a skull fracture), I saw the driver of the car, who was the father of two of the injured, standing by himself staring blankly ahead. Bystanders were busy assisting each of the injured, but no-one was looking after him. He seemed to be in a state of shock. I stood beside him and said: 'It's a hell of a shock isn't it? Hard to believe it's happening to you'. 'It's a hell of a shock!', he replied emphatically, and launched into an explanation. Mostly I just listened, but my first comment was reflective listening. Had I said nothing, he could have been left to assume I considered him a bad driver or a poor first aider, or he might have just withdrawn into himself. Had I 'reassured' him he could well have felt I didn't realise how serious it was. Reflective listening gave me a simple third choice. It involved:

listening for the basic meaning of the speaker's message restating this to the person, and checking to see whether I had understood.

Summarising reflective listening

Once you have some practice, you can use reflective listening to:

convey understanding and acceptance, and
- help the person clarify and resolve their concern - a concern which may well differ from their original comment.

Reflective responses include:

- reflecting content (paraphrasing)
- identifying and reflecting feeling states perception check, and
- summarising and sorting several comments.

Reflecting feelings involves:

- being able to distinguish beliefs from feeling states, and
- having a wide variety of ways to describe a feeling.

Activity 5.5

AIM: to practise developing reflective responses

1 Read each of the ten statements below. For each one, write a response which reflects the information (content) the person is talking about. Check the responses in pairs.

2 Next, go through the examples again. For each one, identify the feeling state involved, using:

a a single word
b a metaphor
c the body responses you'd expect, and
d the actions a person with this feeling feels like taking.

Discuss in the group and collect ideas on a whiteboard or a large sheet of paper.

3 Write a response for each statement, reflecting the feeling state. Check your responses in pairs, and report back to the group.

a A student in your class asks: 'Do you think it's fair the way half the class is late like this? I mean, you and I get here on time, why can't they?

b A 39-year-old friend with a teenage son confides: 'I thought it was bad enough when he was a kid. But now! I never know what he's doing in the evenings. He won't talk to me. He could be on heroin for all I know!'

c A client who is seeing you for counselling explains: 'I've talked about this so often - including with my last counsellor. Nothing seems to help, and I guess I've just given up on ever feeling better'.

d A 25-year-old woman whose son died in a car crash explains tearfully: 'I play those minutes over and over in my mind. Could I have swerved away? I don't know. But I don't think I'll ever really forgive myself'.

e A friend announces: 'Amazing! I passed my biology exam! Honestly, I'm just over the moon. Wait until I tell my mother. She'll do a flip'. (Note that this is not a situation where the other person owns a challenge. Use it for practice anyway.)

f A 64-year-old woman explains haltingly: 'Since Mathew - that's my husband - died, I've been aware of how big the house is. Some days I just wander around from room to room, listening to the sound of my own footsteps and wondering where everybody is. She begins to cry.

g A friend explains: 'I thought I'd decide what I was doing this year – that I'd just be doing the university course. But this new information has thrown all that into confusion. I can't decide which thing to pick up: worse, I don't even know how to choose!'

h I'm no good at parties', a friend tells you. 'Just go without me. I always feel so awkward, and I'm sure everyone else is staring at me.'

i A 27-year-old-man, discussing his wife, complains: 'I've had it. Every time we make an arrangement to share the housework, it ends up being me who does the extra! This is the last time. Either something changes or this relationship is over!'

j A 56-year-old man who has recently lost his job confides: 'Most mornings I just stay in bed and sleep. I wish the day would go away. There's nothing to look forward to, and I just don't have the energy to keep on trying.'

Activity 5.6

AIM: to practise reflective listening in a group setting

I Beginning with the group leader, go around the group checking in (saying how each person is, how their week has been). Before you describe your own week, restate the essence of what the last person said and check that you have understood it.

2 As a group, choose a topic for discussion about which people are likely to have different opinions, such as euthanasia or a current issue. Set aside 30 minutes for discussion, using the following rule: anyone may state an opinion, but before they do so they must reflect the comments of the last speaker to that person's satisfaction. (If the previous speaker doesn't feel understood, they can help the new speaker to rephrase their reflection.)

3 Discuss the effect of reflecting on:

- the previous speakers (did they feel more understood), and
- the next speakers (did they find they had to listen more carefully than usual?)

Activity 5.7

AIM: to practise reflective listening in a one-to-one situation

1 Divide into groups of three (triads). In each triad, one person will be the speaker, one the listener, and one the observer.

a The speaker talks for six minutes about any actual concern of theirs. (If your group repeats this exercise, extend the time to ten minutes on the second round.) If you are speaking it may help to choose one
of the feelings identified in activity 5.5 above and talk about a recent time when you felt that way - unless you are an excellent actor, roleplaying an imaginary situation will not give a useful practice.

The issue you discuss does not need to be a major challenge or life crises: we're only doing a six-minute practice.

When you talk, pause after each couple of sentences and give the listener a chance to reflect: remember, they are learning. If you take up the full six minutes talking, they won't have a chance to practise their skill.

As you listen to their reflection, think about whether it sounds as if they have understood, and check what else comes into your mind to continue talking about.

b The listener listens and uses reflective responses. He or she should check first of all that they are in an attending posture - ask the person who will be speaking what feels right for them. Remember, the listener doesn't have to "solve' the concern the person raises. His or her job is simply to understand. Use only reflective listening, so you get the chance to really learn this new skill. At the end of the six minutes, give a summarising response.

c The observer keeps time and observes the listener. At the end of the six minutes he or she should encourage the speaker and listener to say how they found the experience. The observer can then tell the listener what they seemed to do well. If you are the observer, remember that it helps the listener to hear specifically what was said or done that was useful. It also helps them to know if they lost track of what they were doing or used any of the roadblocks (denial, judgements, solution giving or interrogating).

2 Swap roles and repeat the activity twice more, so each person has a practice.,

Summary

This chapter has discussed listening fully when someone else is upset. The four most common roadblocks to listening were considered: solutions, judgements, denial and interrogating. These approaches treat the person with the challenge as a helpless Victim and put the would-be helper in a Rescuer or Persecutor role.

In contrast, real listening begins with non-verbal attending, such as directing your body towards the speaker. Minimal encouragers like 'uh-huh' emphasise this attending, and open questions invite the person to begin talking.

When listening it is most important to make a comment which restates the basic meaning of what the speaker has said. This comment tells the other person that you are interested in understanding and 'feeling with' them. This is called reflective listening.

Chapter 6: Helping someone change

KEY CONCEPTS
Models of helping: motivational interviewing and RESOLVE
The place of emotions in helping
Ethical issues in helping
Other perspectives: Maori and women's models
Refining the listening skills
Advanced helping skills: confronting incongruity, reframing, metaphors, immediacy, managing feelings

The helping process

AIM: to be able to explain the ways in which helping skills can be used to promote:

- creating solutions,
- emotional resorting,
- an ethical 'contract' between helper and client, and
- a reintegration of personal, social, and spiritual life.

Listening and helping

The situation 'where someone else owns a challenge ' covers a wide field. In your personal life, for example, it covers everything from a 30-second chat in which your child tells you they grazed their knee at school today, to which you reply: 'Ouch, that must have hurt!', to a three-hour evening spent with a friend whose marriage is ending and who feels like committing suicide.

For most of those situations, attending, minimal encouragers, open questions and reflective listening are all you need to use. These are the simple listening skills discussed in Chapter 5.

Mostly, people don't want you to use fancy counselling techniques to help them find new solutions and resolve lifetime challenges. They just want you to listen, so they can identify their own solutions. They'll do the rest of the work from there. This chapter discusses the times when someone wants more. People like coaches, consultants, teachers, managers, nurses, doctors, lawyers, social workers, clergy, physiotherapists, naturopaths and counsellors are all helpers. They're around at some important times in people's lives. They deal with people who have major issues to resolve, decisions to make, and future actions to plan. In my opinion their clients have a right to expect high-quality helping from them.

The Sperry Rand Corporation owns companies like Univac Computers and Remington. Their studies estimate that 40% of a professional's salary is earned by listening. The percentage increases as you climb the corporate ladder, so that 80% of a CEO's salary is earned by listening. Understandably, Sperry Rand spend more on listening skills training than on any other training (McKenna, 1998, p 30).

Someone who has recently learned they might die of cancer deserves a doctor who won't deny they're upset. A person who has just managed to get out of an abusive marriage has a right to a social worker who doesn't dump a load of judgements on them. An executive who is deciding whether to go ahead with a $100,000 contract deserves skilled support from his or her management team.

This chapter is for people who want to refine their listening ability and become excellent helpers. I will present two models for helping, and discuss some of the issues that arise in helping relationships, and then present a set of advanced new skills. Helping is a serious business. Counsellor Robert Carkhuff (Carkhuff and Berenson, 1977) has shown through research that, left alone, people with a major challenge tend to 'struggle on'. But when they receive 'help' they tend to get either much better or much worse. He points out that, in more serious situations, a person will not always be able to find and enact solutions if they have only been listened to.

When helping doesn't work

If helping skills are skills to use 'when someone else owns a challenge, then helping is a process of finding solutions. Most people in distress have been thinking about what's wrong - about their challenge. They often have no idea what they want instead. Effective helping means getting them to plan for what they actually do want to happen in their life. It's a real change in direction.

As Carkhuff notes, not all counselling provides this change in direction. When it doesn't, 'helping' can bind people into the very problem focus that has been creating their pain. In 1951, psychologists E. Powers and H. Witmer published An Experiment in the Prevention of Delinquency, one of the most extensive and welldesigned studies of the results of counselling and therapy. In this study, 650 high-risk boys aged between six and ten were chosen and grouped into pairs based on various demographic variables. One of each pair was then assigned to counselling (either clientcentred or psychoanalytic), and linked up to support services such as the YMCA. After an average of five years' counselling, the boys were followed up (Powers and Witmer 1951). The counsellors rated two-thirds of the boys in their care as having 'benefited substantially' from the counselling, and the boys agreed, saying it gave them more insight and kept them out of trouble.

What a success! Or was it? In fact, the treated boys were more likely to have committed more than one serious crime, and had higher rates of alcoholism, mental illness, stress-related illness, and lower job satisfaction than those left untreated. This remained true at a 30-year follow-up. The researchers lamely suggested that there 'must have been' some positive benefits, but they were unable to find them. reach their goal (in Zilbergeld, 1983, p 132-134). Just because counsellors believe that counselling "feels good" doesn't mean it helps. This 1951 study demonstrates the risks of dependency-producing models of treatment in general. The boys and their therapists valued "their relationship", but it did not empower the boys to change; it disabled them.

What would have worked? In 2000, O'Donohue and colleagues investigated the qualities of all the therapies identified by the American Psychiatric Association as "empirically valid." (ie all the therapies that had actual research showing that they worked). Questionnaires were sent to a number of researchers in the field. Their responses indicated that all the effective therapies:

- Involved skill building rather than focusing on understanding the past or on venting emotions;
- Had a specific rather than general focus;
- Included regular, ongoing assessment of progress;
- Were relatively brief in duration (20 visits or less).

Three boy scouts

We've all met people who seem to "enjoy their problem" and don't want to leave it. They may be happy to talk about how bad it is, but when it comes to changing, somehow they "aren't ready yet". Remember from the section on rapport that this is just an indication that they don't feel fully in rapport with you as a helper yet.

You may have heard the story of the three little boy scouts. At the end of the day they reported to their troop leader. It is, of course, a boy scout tradition to try and do one good deed every day.

'Well?' the leader asked, 'and what was your good deed for today, Johnny?'
'Please sir,' smiled Johnny, "I helped an old lady across the road.'
'Very. good,' the scout leader encouraged. 'How about you, Timmy?'
'Please sir,' said Timmy, just a little less certainly, 'I helped the same old lady across the road.'
'Well,' said the leader thoughtfully, 'that was very good too.' After all, he considered, some old ladies require a bit more assistance than others.
'How about you Andy?', he asked of the third little boy scout.
'Please sir,' said Andy, 'I helped the same old lady across the road.'
'Now hold on', said the scout leader, suspecting some mistake here. 'This can't be right. How come it takes three little boy scouts to help one old lady across the road?'
'Please sir,' explained Andy, 'You see sir, *she didn't want to go.*'

This does not count, in my terms, as 'helping'. Helping begins when the person being helped chooses to change.

How people change by themselves

Effective helping starts with building rapport and gently guides the person through the goalsetting and change process. It focuses the person's attention on what they have achieved, what they can achieve, and what they will achieve. Motivational Interviewing is a model based on the way people change by themselves when they do so successfully (Finney and Moos, 1998, p 157). James Prochaska, John Norcross and Carlo Diclemente interviewed 200 people who quit smoking on their own, to find out what happened (Prochaska et alia, 1994). How did these people change a behaviour that psychotherapists have found so hard to alter? The researchers followed up with studies of people who had given up a number of other self defeating behaviours, finding the same patterns.

Their results confirm that people are quite good at changing their own behaviour *in certain circumstances.* This is even true where the behaviour is a serious "addiction". Over two thirds of those addicted people who stop drinking alcohol, do so on their own with no help. 95% of the 30 million Americans who have quit smoking in the last decade or so, did so without medical or AA style help. (Prochaska et alia, 1994, p 36). These people have better long term success than those who choose treatment programs: 81% of those who stop drinking on their own will abstain for the next ten years, as compared with only 32% of those who are going to AA (Trimpey, 1996, p 78; Ragge, 1998, p 24). . What has happened in the lives of successful self-changers? Research on 2700 British smokers showed that, at the time they stop, they often change their job, alter their relationship or otherwise solve some lifestyle challenge. Also, they stop when they "lose faith in what they used to think smoking did for them" while creating "a powerful new set of beliefs that non-smoking is, of itself, a desirable and rewarding state." (Marsh, 1984).

The same seems to hold true for lifestyle based "addictions". In 1982, Stanley Schachter announced the results of a long term study into obesity. He set out in the early 1970s with the idea that while most overweight people can lose weight, few ever keep it off. In two separate community based studies, what he actually found was that 62% of obese people succeeded in taking off an average of 34.7 pounds and keeping this weight off for an average of 11.2 years. Those who never entered weight loss programs showed better long term weight loss. Incidentally, he stumbled on the truth that many smokers give up smoking on their own. He followed up this variable too, and again found that those who attended treatment programs did not do as well as those who gave up on their own! (Schachter, 1982, p 436-444).

If we look beyond the addictions field we find the same story of successful self-change. For example, 80% of individuals suffering major depression will "spontaneously" cease to be depressed in 4-10 months (Yapko, 1992, p 16). People normally find their own way out of depression. Michael Yapko points out that this also means that if any type of "assistance" continues for ten months it will seem to have solved the challenge of depression in 80% of cases. Genuinely successful strategies for assisting are those that can show benefits in the short term.

The same pattern occurs even with severe disorders like schizophrenia. Recovery rates from schizophrenia vary depending on where people live, but World Health Organisation studies show that in Nigeria, 58% of diagnosed schizophrenics fully recover within two years, and in India 50% recover within two years. In Denmark, only 8% recover within two years, despite having vastly more drug treatment. (Jablensky et alia, 1992). Nonetheless, if we follow up even western people with “well diagnosed and severe forms of schizophrenia” we find that within 20-30 years a full 50% will be functioning normally (Kopelowicz and Liberman, 1998, p 191).

Motivational Interviewing

To return to the question this research raises, what do successful self-changers do, that much of psychotherapy fails to replicate? Prochaska and DiClemente (Prochaska et alia, 1994) found that successful self-changers cycle through a series of six stages. Helping a person in one stage, they say, requires an entirely different approach to helping someone at another. Part of what makes therapy less successful is that everyone is being treated as if they were at the same "stage". The methodology of Motivational Interviewing does not focus on the content of the challenge (eg by educating an alcoholic about the dangers of drinking) but on the process of becoming motivated to quit. The authors describe "resistance" as a result of applying a change strategy designed for the wrong stage of change (eg treating a person in the contemplation stage as if they should be ready for action). The stages can be diagrammed in a cycle as below.

The Motivational Interviewing Self-Change Model

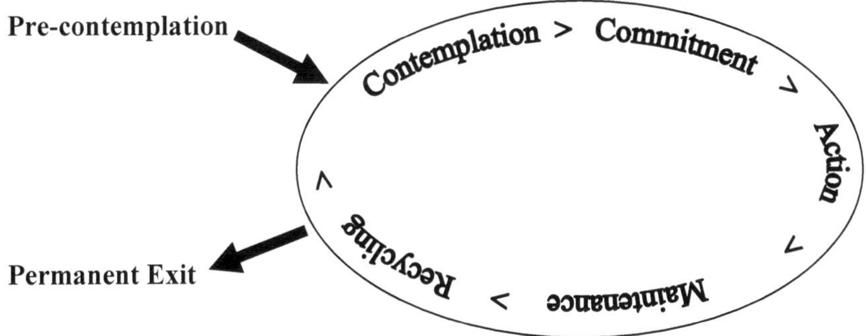

Summarising, the stages and the effective responses to each stage are:

Pre-contemplation. The person doesn't consider the challenge an issue at this stage. Helpers can refuse to collude with the challenge, and simply seek permission to give information.

Contemplation. The person seesaws between wanting to change and keeping their old pattern. Helpers can assist the person to explore and clarify their values (what's important to them) and to use decision-making processes.

Commitment. The person says they really want to change. Helpers can assist the person to set goals, and can provide preparatory tasks for the person, to check out their intention to act.

Action. Once the person is ready to act, a helper can elicit and alter their old strategy for creating the challenge, and integrate the conflicting neural networks to resolve the challenge.

Maintenance. At this stage the person needs to build a new lifestyle by integrating change at the level of their life mission, values, and time line. Helpers can also teach interpersonal skills, state changing skills, and other useful new strategies to back up their change.

Recycling. Finally, it is important to have the person think through how they would respond to possible future "lapses" into the old patterns and have them check that they can continue supporting their new choices.

Planning a session of helping

When you help someone to change, then, you are aligning yourself with their own innate ability to change. In my training of counselors and business consultants, I use a seven step model based on the acronym RESOLVE, for planning this process (Bolstad, 2002). Each step in this model has research supporting its inclusion. This same model can be used in any planning process, and in teaching. This model checks at each step to ensure that the relevant stage of the self-change cycle has been reached. The steps are:

1. Resourceful State Of Mind For The Helper. Begin by getting yourself into a confident state where you have plenty of energy available to attend to and assist the person. If you own a challenge right now, choose another time to help, or another person to do the helping. If the other person does not agree that they own a challenge, choose another time to help. They are at the "precontemplation" stage of changing. Helpers who function poorly in their own life actually influence clients to deteriorate in their functioning! (Carkhuff and Berenson, 1977, p 5, p 35). Carkhuff and

Berenson likened most psychotherapists to professional lifeguards with extensive training in rowing a boat, throwing a ring buoy, and giving artificial respiration, but without the ability to swim. "They cannot save another because, given the same circumstances, they could not save themselves."

2. **Establish Rapport**. Breathe in time with the person, align your voice with theirs and use reflective listening to acknowledge and clarify their situation. These are the skills we discussed in the last chapters.Verbally, this involves empathic restatement. This helps the person clarify their challenge and move through the "contemplation" stage. Remember that in a series of studies from the 1950s, Fred Fiedler (1951) showed that successful therapists from a number of different therapeutic orientations tended to use empathic restatement of the client's concern more than any other intervention. This marked them out from unsuccessful therapists so much that what they said had more in common with other effective therapists than with others in their own school of therapy. Five decades of research confirms Fiedler's conclusion (Lambert and Bergin, 1994, p 181).

3. **SPECIFY The Person's Goal.** Once you have a sense of shared understanding of what the concern is, help the person identify their goal, using the principles of the SPECIFY model (See Chapter 4). You're helping them get specific enough so they know how to check later, whether the challenge has disappeared, and whether they have reached their goal. Check that the outcome is ecological; okay for all of them. This is the "commitment" stage of changing. The amount of discussion of solutions and outcomes in the first session is strongly correlated to the chances that the person will continue with the change process (Miller et alia, 1996, p 259). William Miller has done an overview of the research into successful psychotherapy, in which he identifies that enabling the client to set their own goal for therapy significantly increases their commitment to therapy and enhances the results (Miller, 1985). Successful helping is a solution-focused process.

4. **Open up their Model of the World**. At this stage, you will help the person come to an understanding of how change will be possible. If they are dealing with a "challenge", find out when the challenge occurs (the things that "anchor" or trigger the challenge) and when it doesn't occur (the "exceptions"). Explore with the person what steps they need to take, to increase these exceptions, and reach their goal; what they need to change about their response to the triggers; and what inner resources they have to reach the goal (see the section on Goalsetting). Ask them how serious the challenge feels right now (on a scale of 1-10) so you can come back after

and check the amount of change. This whole process causes a change (a "reframe") in the person's way of thinking about this situation, from being something that just "happens" to them, to being something they are in charge of. Clients who believe that they are in charge of their own responses do far better in numerous research studies with a variety of different models of therapy (Miller et alia, 1996, p 319, 325). Furthermore, research shows that this sense of being in control is not a stable "quality" that some clients have and others do not; it varies over the course of their interaction with the helper. Successful therapy has been shown to result first in a shift in the "locus of control", and then in the desired success (Miller et alia, 1996, p 326).

5. **Leading to the Desired Outcome**. Together with the person, choose which change process to use, to help them reach their goal. Change processes are steps on the way to the goal. There are several examples of NLP change processes described in this book. They include the visual swish (activity 2.2, see page 26), resource anchoring (activity 2.4, see page 28), the positive intention process (activity 2.11, see page 48) and the phobia/trauma process (activity 6.3, see page 118). Learning and practising new skills in real life is also a powerful change process. For example, a person having a challenge getting their own needs met in a relationship may choose to practise with assertiveness skills (see Chapter 7). Once you've found an exception to the challenge (in the last step), you can invite the person to practise recreating that exception. Setting tasks such as this one is also a change technique in itself.

6 **Verify the change**. Check, after using the process, that the person experiences the situation differently. (This kind of check is usually described in the activities, and involves asking the person to 'try and react the way you used to, and notice that you've changed.') You might ask the person again to rate how far they've got towards their solution (on the scale of 1-10 used before). Compliment the person on successes - celebrate with them! Learning to notice and to celebrate their positive results is a powerful change process, too. If the situation is not yet fully changed, decide together which process is likely to move the person forward from here. . In studies replicated several times, psychotherapy researchers have found that if they ask follow-up questions which imply the possibility of failure (eg "Did the change process work?") they get a different result than if they ask questions which presuppose success (eg "How did that change things?"). When asked a question that presupposes change, 60% of people will report success. If the question presupposes failure, 67% will report that their situation is the same as it was before (Miller et alia, 1996, p 255-256).

7 **Exit process.** Check that the changes you have made still suit all of their intentions, by getting them to imagine future situations where, in the past, they would have had the challenge, and noticing that the challenge has now disappeared. This is just a future extension of verifying that the change has happened. In NLP it's called futurepacing, and it is discussed more fully under that name in Chapter 11. In futurepacing, you are helping the person plan the "maintenance" and "recycling" phases of change. Allen Ivey and others have their clients write a "future diary" of their success a year into the future. Alan Marlatt has clients step into the future and fully consider what might make them change their mind about their changes, and then has them plan to prevent that. Both approaches have been shown to deliver far more robust change than parallel programs which skip this futurepacing stage (Mann et alia, 1989; Marlatt and Gordon, 1985). Of course, if any undesirable consequences of the change are detected at this stage, the process shifts back to clarifying outcomes.

Helping as emotional re-sorting

In some situations (for example in a business setting), helping may simply involve a rational process for planning objective changes. However, whenever resolving emotional issues is central to the desired change, it's important to notice how your use of language can assist change. When a helper reflects feelings, he or she is giving their client permission to become aware of, recognise, and express those feelings. By naming a feeling, you make it obvious that acknowledging feelings can be safe to do. By sharing your own feelings respectfully, you further demonstrate that having feelings is not only normal, but is an important part of healthy living.

The therapeutic release of strong feelings is known as emotional catharsis. The word catharsis comes from the Greek katharsis, meaning to purge or to clean out. A cathartic drug is a laxative. In 1971, Fred and Brenda Forster (reported in Crying: The Mystery of Tears, by W.H. Frey) studied the responses of nursing students to crying patients. They found that the students generally behaved in the following ways:

- offered a ready-made solution, such as turning on the television
- belittled the patient's reaction, for example by saying that other people had just as big a challenge as theirs
- ignored the crying, changed the subject, or told them not to worry.

These are, as you probably realise, the first three main types of roadblock we studied in Chapter 5 (solutions, judgements and denial). William Frey urges helpers to directly give permission to a crying person (It's alright to cry',

'That's it, let it out'), and assist by silently staying nearby while the person weeps. Creating space where a client can allow themselves powerful feelings such as grief, anger, fear, love and joy is one of the most precious gifts of helping.

Releasing feelings is not enough

Being able to feel is crucial to healthy living. But in itself, it is not enough. Being able to feel is useful because it motivates us to act in ways that meet our needs.

William Frey had a large and varied population of adults keep a diary for 30 days and note the effects of any crying. The majority of women and men reported a decrease in negative emotions as a result of crying (Frey et alia, 1983). These self-reports do not tell the *full* story however. Virtually every study so far that has monitored people over the actual time of crying has found the opposite effect. The most popular form of study has used a crying stimulus which many people in Frey's diary project used: watching sad films. Such films evoke tears, and often restimulate sadness in relation to similar life events in the watcher's previous experience. When people watch a film and are monitored, the physiological and emotional results are far more negative for those who cry than for those who do not (see for example, Gross et alia, 1994). Crying is associated with increases in heart rate, other measures of arousal such as raised skin temperature and body tension, as well as increases in feelings of depression, frustration, anger, and pain. Furthermore, it is associated with decreases in immunoglobulin A in saliva (Labott et alia, 1990), ie it reduces immunity.

These unpleasant effects continue after the event. Susan Labott researched crying as a coping device amongst university students and found that although they thought crying helped, those who cried often were more likely to report high levels of mood disturbance, such as anxiety, depression, anger, fatigue and confusion (Labott and Martin, 1987). What about longer term health effects? There is some evidence in the literature that people who struggle to *suppress* crying suffer badly longer term. They are more prone to cancer (Gross, 1989) for example.

However people who spend long periods of time in cathartic therapies are also at risk of illness, as a study by Dr Hans Eysenck shows (Eysenck, 1992, p 117-118). He describes his longitudinal study of 7000 inhabitants of Heidelberg, from 1973 to 1986. This study was designed to discover the health effects of psychotherapy. Clients in psychotherapy were able to be matched by age, sex, type and amount of smoking etc with controls. The results showed that cancer and heart disease were most prevalent in the group who had had two years or more of "therapy", less frequent in the group who had one year or more in "therapy", and least frequent in the group who had no "therapy".

How do we explain this paradox? Both suppressing crying and crying regularly seem unhealthy.

How crying works

In a study of the literature on crying and health, Ad Vingerhoets and Jan Scheirs (2001, p 241) conclude that scientific studies "have yielded little evidence in support of the hypothesis that shedding tears improves mood or health directly, be it in the short or in the long run. This is not to say that crying is a useless behaviour. It has strong effects on the environment, promoting comforting and helping behaviour, and possibly strengthening attachment".

Randolph Cornelius has done a number of studies supporting this hypothesis. The idea is that crying evolved as a social message, not as an intrinsically healing mechanism. When a baby cries, the crying itself may not help it much, but the effect of the crying is to elicit support from others (and rather quickly at that, as those readers who are parents will know). We do not have to hypothesise that "crying is good for babies" and leave the baby to cry each day to release the pain (something that psychotherapists actually recommended for a time in the twentieth century). We know that the purpose of crying is to elicit action.

Dr Cornelius has asked people to describe in detail a crying event where they felt better after crying, and a crying event where they did not feel better. The events need to be similar in type and in intensity of crying. The results are clear (Cornelius, 2001, p 207). People feel better when the issues that led them to cry are resolved (eg "Hearing her say that we'd work out the financial situation."). Cornelius sites a number of other studies in which the same factor is clearly the key to the "success" of crying. The point of catharsis is to get change, not just to feel bad. Once we understand this, we can see that both ongoing cathartic therapy *and* the suppression of crying can be cancer-promoting. They are both ways that people can avoid taking action in their real life, asking for what they want, and getting things to change.

The lesson of crying is one every baby knows: "change me!" Crying is a highly stressful activity which is designed to send this message both to the crier and to others. Cornelius concludes (2001, p 209) "Crying, except perhaps when due to organic brain damage, is always about something and has a social context.... Crying may not have cathartic effects if the issues that have moved one to tears have not been resolved or if one receives negative feedback from others about one's tears."

Family Therapist Virginia Satir said "For me the symptom is analogous to a warning light that appears on the dashboard of a car. The light, when lit, says the system required to run the car is in some form of depletion, disharmony, injury or impairment.... My treatment direction is to release and redirect that blocked up energy." (Satir and Baldwin, 1983, p188). This is true in relation to crying. The point is not to suppress the crying (like disconnecting the warning light). On the other hand, the point is not to leave the car in such a chronic state of disrepair that the warning light shows every day (on the grounds that seeing the warning light is somehow releasing energy itself). The point is to change things.

Paying attention to the positive

In 2000, Dr Denise Beike and Deirdre Slavik at the University of Arkansas conducted an interesting study of what they called "counterfactual" thoughts. These are thoughts about what has gone "wrong", along with what they could have done differently. Dr. Beike enlisted two groups of University of Arkansas students to record their thoughts each day in a diary in order to "look at counterfactual thoughts as they occur in people's day-to-day lives." In the first group, graduate students recorded their counterfactual thoughts, their mood, and their motivation to change their behavior as a result of their thoughts. After recording two thoughts per day for 14 days, the students reported that negative thoughts depressed their mood but increased their motivation to change their behavior. They believed that the negative thoughts were painful but would help them in the long term (Slavik, 2003).

To test out this hope, the researchers then enlisted a group of students to keep similar diaries for 21 days, to determine if any actual change in behavior would result from counterfactual thinking. Three weeks after completing their diaries the undergraduate students were asked to review their diary data and indicate whether their counterfactual thinking actually caused any change in behavior. "No self-perceived change in behavior was noted," Dr. Beike told Reuters Health. Counterfactual thoughts about negative events in everyday life cause us to feel that we "should have done better or more," Dr. Beike said. "These thoughts make us feel bad, which motivates us to sit around and to feel sorry for ourselves."

So what does work? The study found that "credit-taking thoughts", in which individuals reflect on success and congratulate themselves, serve to reinforce appropriate behavior and help people "feel more in control of themselves and their circumstances." This is the understanding that Solution Focused approaches to changework (Miller et alia, 1996) are based on.

The fact is that simply expecting things to work out well tends to produce success better than thinking about what might be wrong. K. Thomas is a British General Medical Practitioner who has written a number of articles on his use of the placebo effect in clinical practice (Thomas, 1987, 1994 also quoted in McDermott and O'Connor, 1996). In one study he took 200 patients without any specific diagnosis, but with general ill-health. Half of them were told they had a definite complaint, and given a reassurance that they would get better. The other half were told that he was not sure what was wrong, and to return if the situation did not improve. Two weeks later, 64% of the first group had improved, while only 39% of the second group were better. Thomas had almost doubled his success by simply talking positively to the first group.

Helping as an ethical process

When helping is part of your job, the person you help can be considered your client. just as you may expect them to arrive on time for appointments, for example, they have a right to expect certain standards from you. 'Ethics' is the study of the standards of behaviour to which you keep. Important examples are touch and confidentiality.

Touch

In the professional helping situation, the issue of the non-verbal part of listening - physical touch - often comes up. Anthropologist Ashley Montague, in his book Touching, points out how powerfully healing human touch is. He quotes evidence that a 'course' of regular human touch will cure such illnesses as asthma and eczema, as well as enhancing children's physical growth.

In some professional situations (such as in hospitals), helping routinely involves physical touch, therefore holding someone's hand or putting an arm around their shoulder may be an accepted way to offer comfort. Similarly, some cultural settings allow more touch than others (for example, according to psychiatrist Mason Durie, physical touch is an important part of any Maori greeting).

There is also a difference in the way people in our society feel about being touched by men and by women. In Counselling: The Skills of Problem Solving, New Zealand counsellors Munro, Manthei and Small suggest that female counsellors ,may still be seen more naturally and effectively to initiate such contacts with both males and females'. The same is true of other helpers, such as supervisors.

But there are two concerns that helpers need to think about when using touch. The first is that your client needs help, and therefore may find it difficult to ask you to stop touching them if they don't feel right about it. Secondly, in our society there is often some confusion about whether touch has a sexual meaning. How do you balance the value of touch and the risk of a client feeling uncomfortable with it? A good general principle is only to use touch when (a) you sense that the client will appreciate and benefit from it, and (b) you feel comfortable with it yourself. Once you have a sense of rapport, or empathy, with a client, the very best way to find out what they feel right about is simply to ask.

Confidentiality

When you listen to a friend talking over their worries, you will often have a sort of understanding that you won't tell anyone else what they have said. As a professional helper, of course, this becomes even more important.

At times it will help clients to know exactly how much confidentiality they can expect. Do you need to report back about your discussion to your colleagues, superiors or teachers? And what if you find out that your client is planning to drive off a cliff tonight?

For me, these are the two main limits to my confidentiality:
• professional requirements, such as reports or supervision
• someone's life being endangered.

If I thought I was in one of these situations (where I needed to discuss a client with someone else), I'd aim to tell the client as soon as possible about my intention,

Other than in these three situations, I think clients have a right to know that their helpers won't discuss their affairs with others. This commitment is often acknowledged by a helper at the start of their time with a client, as part of their making a 'contract' . When considering what helpers do say to others (for example in case discussions), the sense of respect is important. A client's information is precious, it is a treasure, and not an amusing story for the curious. When I go to a doctor, a lawyer or a counsellor, my hope is that they have this sense of respect and affection for what I share with them. In some cases, who they tell is not so important to me as how they tell my story. The New Zealand law comes down firmly on the side of confidentiality in counseling unless it can be shown that someone's life has been endangered by this (see Robert Ludbrook's book *Counselling and the Law*).

Discussing ethics

The skill which enables you to discuss ethical issues like touch and confidentiality, is called immediacy. When you explain your limits and check your client's limits about what is happening between you, that's immediacy. It's also part of the process of maintaining a contract (see Chapter 1).

Whenever you begin a helping relationship, the questions 'what will we do here?', 'What are the rules?', and 'What will I get out of it?' need to be answered. As was pointed out in Chapter 1, it helps to set aside a little time at the beginning to ensure these questions are answered for both of you. In some cases the agency you work for will do this routinely. When both you and your client know what to expect from each other, this sense of contract adds to the feeling of safety which you are building.

Helping as a holistic process

'Helping', as we have been discussing it here, developed out of western (particularly American) male culture. Initially, it has taken for granted the western, male tendency to approach life by dividing things into even smaller pieces. For example, we have accepted so far that helping is something one individual does for another individual. In fact, people are almost always part of families, teams, organisations and other groups. It doesn't make any sense to try and fix up one person in a system without thinking about how they relate to the others (as the theory of ego-states in Chapter 2, and roles in Chapter 5 both emphasise).

There is often an assumption in western cultures that to be totally independent is to be mentally healthy. Fritz Perls, who founded Gestalt Therapy, summed up mental health by saying: 'You do your thing, and I do mine. I am not in this world to live up to your expectations and you are not in this world to live up to mine. You are you and I am 1. And if by chance we find each other, it's beautiful. If not, it can't be helped.'

Most helpers nowadays would question the absoluteness of this. Robert Bolton, for example, says quite simply: "You can't be human alone'. If Bolton is right, and 'by chance' we don't find each other, we'd better damn well discover why not!

Another part of our tendency to divide things into small pieces concerns the separation between mind and body. In Chapter 2 we discovered that mind and body are completely interrelated, so that a person's 'state of mind' is also their physical state. We must ask ourselves how much sense it makes, then, to help someone 'emotionally' without nurturing their body, or at least considering their posture. In this sense, touch (although culturally sensitive) is an important helping skill. To communicate "acceptance' while staying physically aloof from someone is almost self-contradictory.

Connection with the universe

The other major example of the western dividing process is the separation of humans from the universe which surrounds them: from nature; from what we might call 'the spiritual side of life'. Consider psychiatrist Viktor Frankl's initial response in his account of his visit to a young woman in a Nazi concentration camp (from his book Man's Search for Meaning: An Introduction to Logotherapy). Her own comments are a moving reminder of the healing power of a sense of unity with the universal life-force:

'Pointing through the window of the hut, she said: "This tree here is the only friend I have in my loneliness. "Through that window she could see just one branch of a chestnut tree, and on the branch were two blossoms. "I often talk to this tree", she said to me. I was startled, and didn't quite know how to take her words. Was she delirious? Did she have occasional hallucinations? Anxiously, I asked her if the tree replied. "Yes." What did it say to her? She answered: "It said to me, "I'm here - I am here - I am life, eternal life"'.

All this dividing is quite odd, because the very concept of 'healing' comes from the old English word haelen, meaning 'whole' (the same word from which our words 'holy' and 'whole' come). In old English, to heal was to reunite with the universe, to join together all your parts, to reconnect body and mind, to reestablish your relationship with others. The word 'holistic" is being used today by many health professionals to describe care which has this aim of reuniting. What does it mean in practice? Two fresh perspectives on counseling have raised this issue. One is the voice of indigenous counseling providers; the other is the feminist counseling movement.

A Maori model

Psychiatrist Mason Durie (1972) discussed helping from a Maori perspective in conference of the Association of Counsellors. Holism, he suggests, has always been central to Maori culture (although it is the Americans who are marketing it most enthusiastically). Helping, for Maori, needs to incorporate (using Durie's key words):

- Whanaungatanga: family involvement
- Whakamanawa: encouragement, including the sharing of food and other supports (manakitanga) as well as the physical embrace (awhi). This could mean welcoming clients with a hug and an offer of a cup of tea, for example.
- Mauri: vital or life force, including the spiritual element (wairua) and the genealogical background (whakapapa) of the tribe and subtribe.

These elements are treated as significant in any 'personal' concern, whether a 'business' concern, a 'health' concern or an 'educational' one. Durie also points out that in a holistic culture, 'talking about' feelings is less valued. Actually experiencing the feelings or doing something about them is more appropriate, and being asked to name feelings may even pull a person away from this.

Even the division between professional helper and client is culturally specific. The very words 'helper' and 'client' come from American counselling models. Maori counsellor Hinekahukura Barrett-Aranui states (in Counselling: The Skills of Problem Solving) that:

'Counselling as a one-to-one relationship between a professional and a client is a concept foreign to Maori culture. In Maoridom, helping involves the whole whanau (family) and beyond in an intense sharing which takes physical, emotional, spiritual, and practical forms. The essential elements are the family network (whanaungatanga), the help given by the people (manaakitanga), and the spiritual dimension (wairuatanga).'

While it may be appropriate for people to receive help from those who share their own culture (for example in New Zealand for Maori to assist Maori and Pakeha to assist Pakeha), all helping is obviously enriched by the recognition of the unifying trend of holism. As the word haelen reminds us, English culture too had it's roots in the holistic world view.

Empowering: a feminist model

Feminist counselor Miriam Greenspan's description of feminist helping is also about holism. In her book *A New Approach to Women and Therapy*, she says the helper needs to go beyond 'the old divisions between feeling and thinking, emotional release and theory, love and work, male and female. The therapist must know how to combine the feminine skills of empathy, intuition and relatedness with the masculine skills of discipline, distance and theory'.

NLP trainer and media expert Maia Freeman and I discuss this emerging women's model of helping in our article "Maybe We Should Ask For Directions, Dear?" (Freeman and Bolstad, 2003). In her comparative study of masculinity, *New Mens Magazines,* Freeman (as Snell, 1992) noted that "In the men's magazines, the most dominant values emerging from the men profiled were their Work, their own Self-concept, and their Status... put bluntly, men seemed more concerned about themselves than about others." Observing that only one of sixty articles had friendship as a dominant value, she says "The loneliness of the male's world is emphasized in the lack of items under this category.... Only one profile placed value on a male-male friendship; the other occasional incidences were presented as a field for competition."

Miriam Greenspan suggests that becoming totally independent in this way is a male ideal of mental health. She is critical of Fritz Perls' individualistic definition of health, saying: 'A female-style model of therapy must acknowledge that not only children but adults have legitimate needs for caring, reassurance, nurturance and support.'

She says that the fact that women ask for and give support has often been used to suggest that they are less independent and therefore less healthy than men. Both extremes (being a 'rugged individual' and always being dependent on others for feeling good) may be equally unhealthy Helping women understand how the male definition of mental health (as being alone and unemotional) has left women feeling inadequate is part of 'listening for the connections between personal and political in women's stories'. A helper, she suggests, needs to understand the way social pressures affect self-esteem (see Chapter 2).

In the same way that reflecting feelings helps a person recognise their own feeling states, reflecting people's experience of what it is like to be a woman, a man, poor, Pakeha, Maori, Samoan, and so on, helps them recognise their own identity. Understanding the social causes of their situation, they are less likely to blame themselves and more able (empowered) to change things.

Virginia Satir's example

Therapist Virginia Satir gives a great example of working in a way consistent with this principle. "Some years ago I took on an assignment in a southern county to work with people on public welfare." She explains (Satir, 1993, p 204-206). "What I wanted to do was show that everybody has the capacity to be self-sufficient and all we have to do is to activate them. I asked the county to pick a group of people who were on public welfare, people from different racial groups and different family constellations. I would then see them as a group for three hours every Friday." Satir asked each person what their dreams were and what stood in the way of their reaching them. "One woman shared that she always wanted to be a secretary.... She said "I have six kids, and I don't have anyone to take care of them while I'm away." "Let's find out," I said. "Is there anybody in this group who would take care of six kids for a day or two a week while this woman gets some training here at the community college?"

The results were dramatic. Satir reports "Everyone found something.... The woman who took in the children became a licensed foster care person. In 12 weeks I had all these people off public welfare. I've not only done that once. I've done it many times." By accepting their need for mutual support, Satir demonstrated their ability to change the social context in which their challenges occurred, and hence solve their challenges. (Satir, 1993, p 379). Note that Satir's aim was to demonstrate that people could be self-sufficient. However, for her, this self-sufficiency, this being "at cause", included their acting socially and asking for assistance from each other. She is encouraging interdependence rather than isolated independence.

The human electrical field

One traditional way of directly experiencing the interconnectedness of human beings is by training yourself to feel the electrical field around yourself and others. Evidence (Rosa, 1998) suggests that this experience is entirely subjective, but it is also widely accepted in indigenous cultures, and subjectively pleasant.

To help people get used to feeling this subtle electrical field, NLP trainer Robert Dilts uses a 'biofeedback' machine which measures changes in skin electricity (or 'GSR'), like a lie detector. As he points out, though, certain people in almost every culture around the world have discovered by themselves how to feel, and even see, changes in the electrical field around the body (Dilts and deLozier 2000). Like the people he teaches, these 'naturals' have learned to increase the power and stability of their own field, often using breathing techniques. Here, the research is solid. People who breathe less, such as depressed people, have a lower amplitude GSR, while people in a state of anxiety have a high amplitude, erratic GSR (Lader, M. The Psychophysiology of Mental Illness).

Wide use of the bio-electrical field

In Maori culture, for example, the ability to see and feel a person's energy field is well respected. There are also numerous descriptions in religious sources, such as the Bible, which may be related to this natural phenomenon. Once people realise, or imagine they can feel this field and even direct this energy so as to help someone else 'recharge', it often produces a deeper respect for the interconnectedness of all life.

This process is taught (by Dr Dolores Krieger, Dora Kunz and others) as part of basic nursing training in a number of hospitals in the USA, where it is called 'Therapeutic Touch'. In my training with them in New York, I observed several examples of the almost magical results of their technique. Their research (see Wager and Kunz 1996, Wirth 1990, Wirth and Cram 1993, Bush and Geist 1992, Peck 1998, Hinze and Louise 1988, Macrae 1988) supports its healing benefits, whether these are due to actual electrical changes or simply to the placebo effect created by rapport between practitioner and client.

No particular beliefs about the 'meaning' of the electrical field (for example a belief that this is a 'spiritual aura' or 'real electricity') are necessary to learn to use this process. In China, the use of the energy field is known as Chi Kung (Tai Chi is a small spin-off from the science of Chi Kung). In my training in Thailand and China with Chi Kung experts, I learned techniques which are shown by research to prolong life, enhance recovery from serious illness and neurological damage, and increase vitality. I have included a simple Chi Kung exercise for you to experiment with here.

Helping: A Recap

So far in this chapter we have discussed the following four frameworks:

1. Motivational Interviewing. This is a framework for identifying which stage of the change cycle someone is at (precontemplation, contemplation, commitment, action, maintenance, recycling)
and responding appropriately.
2 . Creating Solutions, using a model of helping (RESOLVE) that flows from being in a resourceful state and establishing rapport, through specifying a solution and opening up the person's model of the world, to change processes which are then verified before the exit.
3. Understanding both the value and the limits of emotional catharsis
4 . Maintaining an ethical 'contract'. Clarifying what the 'rules' in your helping relationship are and how these rules are working.
5 . Reintegrating body and mind, personal and political, individual and family, or human and universal. To make helping a holistic process may mean changing the physical setting (involving family and other support systems, offering food, using touch). It also means using other helping methods such as energy work.

Activity 6.1

AIM: to feel human "electrical energy" 1-10 cm out from the body

While the research suggests that this experience is largely imaginary (Rosa et alia 1998) it is used in many cultures because of the positive subjective effects and included here purely for this purpose. The group leader should use the relaxation process described in activity 2.3 (see page 27) then give the following instructions:

- With each in breath, imagine that energy of some kind is flowing from the area above your head, down the centre of your body to your heart. If you like, you can imagine this as an electrical energy or as a spiritual energy which you know and trust. Actually feel the flow down to the area of your heart.
- Continuing to 'breathe in' energy, imagining that, as you breathe out, the same energy flows out from your heart, down your arms and out of your fingertips. Think of this energy as being as abundant as' the air you breathe. You may be aware of tingling in your fingers.
- Get into pairs, continuing to imagine the energy flow, and sit facing each other. Lift your hands, palms facing each other and about 5-10 cm apart. You may feel your own energy as you move the hands a little. Get your partner to move one of their hands down through the space between yours, then back and forth several times. Check for the feeling. Once you are aware of what this feels like, you may be able to feel the field a similar distance away from your partner's body in general.

Activity 6.2

AIM: to practise the use of touch as a helping process (shoulder massage)

This activity can be done in pairs, taking turns to do the massage, or in a group, simultaneously. If you are in a group you can all stand in a circle, facing the back of the person in front.

Relaxing the shoulders, upper back and neck has a calming effect on the body in general. Massage strokes can include tapping using the finger tips, gentle pounding with knuckles or fists, kneading (grasping areas of the shoulder and squeezing), and pressing firmly in a circular rubbing motion with the hands /thumbs /fingertips. When pressing with one hand, you may find it helps to steady the shoulder with the other.

Activity 6.3

AIM: to re-energise your body and appreciate your internal organs

This visualisation exercise is included for its subjective benefits, with no claims made about the validity of traditional Chinese exercise/meditation (chi-kung). It is done sitting on a chair.

1 Sit on the edge of the chair with your feet flat on the floor. Your back needs to be straight but relaxed; an effect which you'll get by imagining that your head is suspended by a cord, from the crown up to the ceiling. Close your eyes and gently press your tongue against the top of your mouth. Clasp your hands together gently.

2 Remember a time when you felt caring or loving, that you feel comfortable recalling (perhaps when you were caring for a child, animal or plant). Imagine that you can see this time, and the gentle smile of caring it brings, as a picture about a metre in front of your eyes. Allow your forehead to relax, and draw the energy of caring into the place between your eyes. Experience it as a limitless source of caring energy flowing to this place, and from there flooding through your body as a smile.

3 In the Chinese system, each of the organs has an emotional balancing function. We are now going to flow this smile through the body and its organs. As you flow the smile, check for a 'feeling' that each organ is smiling back. Take the time it needs to allow this to happen. The whole process may take 20 minutes at first, but with practice it will happen in a few seconds.

- First allow the smiling energy to flow across your face, relaxing it. Smile into the neck and throat, through the thyroid and parathyroid glands (which control your metabolic rate and keep your bone tissue balanced).

- Smile down to the thymus gland (which co-ordinates your immune system) in the upper central chest area. From there spread the smile back to the heart, allowing it to relax and blossom: the job of the heart is transforming hastiness and irritation to joy and love.

- Flow the smile out on each side to the lungs, enhancing their ability to take in energy from the air and transforming sadness and grief into the ability to discriminate in favour of what's right for you.

- On the right, flow the smile down through the liver, enhancing its hundreds of cleansing and organising functions, and transforming resentful anger into an assertive kindness to yourself and others.

• On the left, flow the smile through the pancreas (which assists in digestion and the regulation of blood sugar). The far left is the position of the spleen, which forms and stores blood cells, and here rigidity and stuck thinking are transformed to openness.

• On each side the smile now flows to the back at waist level, flooding through the kidneys, which filter the blood, and the adrenal glands on top of them, which give your body the energy burst of adrenalin. As these glands relax, feel, in the kidneys, fear transformed into a gentleness.

• Now flow the smiling energy down through the urinary bladder and through the sexual organs, including the glands (ovaries or testes), which balance the cycles of your life.

• Finally, flow the smile to a place just below the navel and a couple of centimetres in from the front. Feel the energy spiral into this centre (which in China is called Dan Tien), as a storage for the day.

4 Again, draw the smile into the place between your eyes. This second time, flow the smile down your nose and mouth into the digestive tract, swallowing as you do, and imagining that the saliva you swallow is also full of smiling energy. Smile through the stomach, just below the ribs and through the intestines, feeling stress transformed into relaxation in the cavity of your abdomen. Having flowed the smile down to the anus, draw the energy back to the Dan Tien centre below the navel.

5 The third time, draw the smile into the centre between your eyes (actually called upper Dan Tien) and circle your eyes nine times clockwise (as if watching a speeded up clock right in front of your eyes) and nine times anti-clockwise. Draw the smile back through the brain itself, smiling deep into the brain tissue, where the glands which co-ordinate your entire hormonal system reside. Here, mood swings, delusions and the feeling of being a victim are transformed into radiant happiness. Flow the smile down the spinal column, and through the neurons (nerve cells) out to every part of the body. Beyond the body, imagine that the smile, flowing into you from an infinite source of love and healing, flows out across the whole room, out across the whole city or town, out across the entire country, and across the whole planet. Draw the energy from your body back to lower Dan Tien, feeling it spiral in there as a store for the day.

Skills of helping

AIM: to be able to use the seven helping skills listed below.

Attitudes and skills

I'd have to be crazy to believe that helping was nothing more than a set of skills: 'Do this, do that, and someone will feel better'. No amount of fancy communication skills can replace the attitude of affection which is the basic principle in helping someone. But, on the other hand, without skills a whole lot of nice ideas about love, holism, or anything else can end up as 'just nice ideas'. Once you feel confident with the listening skills described in Chapter 5, you will have many of the skills to express that love. We will, however, discuss several more skills. These are:

- refining your questioning skills
- refining your reflecting skills
- confronting incongruity
- reframing
- telling a metaphor
- immediacy
- using language to help someone associate or dissociate.

Refining your questioning skills: the metamodel

In Chapter 1, we learned that what usually causes pain in people's lives is not so much the actual events around them, as their internal beliefs - or maps - about what happens.

Based on their study of the remarkable family therapist Virginia Satir, NLP developers Richard Bandler and John Grinder (Bandler and Grinder 1976) developed a method of recognising which parts of a person's map create difficulty for them, and of asking open questions to help the person change that map. They called this method the metamodel, and it is useful not only in helping relationships, but in all relationships. For example, in the book Precision: A New Approach To Communication, John Grinder and Michael McMaster teach the use of these skills in a business context (1993).

To use these open questions effectively, it's important to use reflective listening first, to acknowledge what the person said, and then to gently inquire. Here are some examples of using the metamodel questions.

1 Sometimes a client's map of the world contains beliefs that are 'supernatural', such as mind reading, (for example: 'I know what he thinks of me). The metamodel suggests you ask how this illogical process is happening: 'How, specifically, do you know? What do you see or hear?'

2 When a client says something is 'wrong' or 'right', 'good' or 'bad', they often don't say who is performing this value judgement. You could ask: 'According to whom?' For example: 'It's wrong to accept charity. "According to whom? Who believes it's wrong?' This question helps the person identify whose map of the world they are using: is it their own? Is it their parent's? Who is the 'lost performer' of the value judgement? Whatever the answer, the question reminds them that it's only a map .

3 Another 'supernatural' belief is that one person can make an emotional response happen inside another person's body - that one person can cause effects in another body without touching them. For example: 'You make me feel very powerless.' (This belief is challenged by activity 1.1, see page 4). A metamodel response might be: 'How, specifically, does what I do cause you to feel powerless.'

4 Sometimes a client claims that an event has a meaning way beyond what it needs to mean. For example: 'He never hugs me so he obviously doesn't love me', or 'If we argue it means the relationship is over.' These claims suggest that 'love' is an equivalent of 'hugging', or that 'arguing' is an equivalent of ending a relationship. A metamodel response to challenge this 'equivalence' is: 'How does ... mean ... ?, for example: 'How does an argument mean that the relationship is over?'

5 If a client claims that something 'always' happens, 'never' happens, happens with 'everyone' or with 'no-one', the metamodel suggests you ask about this ,universal quantity, by repeating the same word, for example: 'Always?' 'No one?'.

6 Sometimes a client talks in a 'mode of impossibility': they believe that certain things are 'impossible' for them. If a client says 'I can't.. ' , the metamodel response could be either: "What stops you? or 'What would happen if you did?' For example: 'I can't tell my husband what I really think of his jokes'. 'What would happen if you did?'

7 At other times a client talks from the 'mode of necessity' (of 'have to' or 'must'). If a client says 'I must...' or 'I have to...", the metamodel response would be: 'What would happen if you didn't?' In both modes of impossibility and modes of necessity, the person's map of the world assumes that things have to be the way they are. Your question challenges that limit to the map.

8 A client may also describe what happens in such general terms that you don't know who did what to whom. The verbs (action words) in their sentences are unspecified. You could, then, ask for this information, for example:

• 'My brother annoys me all the time.' 'How, specifically, does he annoy you?'
• 'You've hurt me very much.' 'How, specifically, have I hurt you?"
• 'People are always picking on me.' 'Which people are picking on you, and how, specifically, do they pick on you?'

9 Sometimes a client simply misses out important parts of a sentence, leaving you to guess what they have deleted. The metamodel suggests you actually ask what these deleted things are. For example:

• 'I can't cope with this.' 'What, specifically, can't you cope with?'
• 'The things I do really confuse me.' 'What things do you do?'
• 'I'm sad. 'What are you sad about?' Such questions help the person explain what is wrong in a sensory specific way (see Chapter 4 on goal setting for an explanation of 'sensory specific).

Practise using the metamodel to respond to these statements:

- 'I can't face my teacher ever again."
- 'I must spend more time with my family.'
- 'It's not right for a woman to argue with a man.'
- 'This is hopeless.'
- "My children push me around a lot.'
- 'I can tell you don't like me.'
- 'My mother makes me so angry!'
- 'No-one cares about my feelings.'
- 'She didn't smile so she must be angry!'
- 'I'm angry.'

Refining your questioning skills: solution-focused questions

If your open questions focus only on the challenges the person has, the person will be directed to think more about what's gone wrong. If your questions focus on the solution they want, the person will think more about what they want to achieve. This in itself enables them to become more resourceful, and to take charge of making the changes they want.

Based on this understanding, psychotherapists Steve de Shazer, Insoo Kim Berg and others (Miller et alia, 1996) have developed a model of change called the Solution-Focused approach. The following are examples of their questions, which guide the person to identify what they want and how to get it:

1 Ask for a description of the person's outcome. For example:

- 'What has to be different as a result of you talking to me?'
- 'What do you want to achieve?'
- 'What would need to happen for you to know this challenge was solved?'
- 'How will you know that this challenge is solved?'
- 'When this challenge is solved, what will you be doing and feeling instead of what you used to do and feel?'
- 'How do you think this session will help you move towards your goals?'
- 'What made you decide that now is a good time to make some changes?'

If the person has no goal of their own because they have been sent or asked to come and see you, then ask:

- 'Since they sent you here, what will you need to be doing differently for them to realise that you don't need to come back?'

2 Ask the person about the times when the challenge doesn't occur (the exceptions). For example:
- 'When was a time that you noticed this challenge wasn't quite as bad?' 'What was happening at that time? What were you doing differently?'
- 'How have you managed to remain this resourceful as you coped with all these challenges?'
- 'What have you learned so far from these challenges and from the responses you've used either successfully or unsuccessfully?'

If there are no exceptions, ask about hypothetical exceptions using the 'miracle' question: 'Suppose one night there is a miracle while you are sleeping, and this challenge is solved. Since you are sleeping, you don't know that a miracle has happened or that your challenge is solved. What do you suppose you will notice that's different in the morning, that will let you know the challenge is solved?'

After the miracle question, you can ask other follow-up questions such as:

- 'What would other people around you notice was different about you?'
- 'What would other people around you do differently then?'
- 'What would it take to pretend that this miracle had happened?'

• 'On a scale of 1-10, where 10 means this is totally solved, where are you now?... and what will you be doing differently when you move up to….?'

Refining your reflecting skills

The aim of reflective listening is to verbally create that sense of shared understanding called empathy or rapport. This works better if you use similar language to the client. For example, if an eight-year-old child said to you: 'I'm sick of my brother. He always gets his way', to reply: 'You have a sense of resentment about your sibling's interpersonal persuasiveness" is not as useful as: 'You don't think it's fair'.

One way in which you can make your language more understandable for clients of all ages is to use your knowledge about sensory systems (explained in Chapter 3). When someone speaks mainly about what they see (visual system), your reflective reply can do the same. This applies equally to auditory and kinesthetic responses. For example:

Client: 'I can't see any way forward. It looks really gloomy to me.'
Reply: "There's no light at the end of the tunnel.'

Client: 'I tell myself we can just tune into each other again, but all the conflicts keep echoing round my head.'
Reply: 'Sounds like you keep hearing the past arguments replaying, and that stops you listening to what she's saying now.'

Client: "It's too much. I've been carrying this relationship for years, and I just have to have a bit more distance from it.'
Reply: 'You want to stand back from it more and share the load with your husband.'

Research by psychotherapist Michael Yapko (1981) shows that when you use the sensory language favoured by your client, they will follow suggestions more effectively. In his study of relaxation exercises, he found that clients relaxed more fully (measured by electromyelogram) when the helper used the sensory system used most frequently by the client.

Practise matching sensory systems

Write reflective replies using the client's sensory system, for the following examples:

- "When I spoke to her, we just clicked. She's really on my wavelength.'

- 'It's been a long, hard struggle, ploughing through all these decisions, but I feel like I'm almost there now.'
- 'The way I see it, it's black and white. Either he wants to be in this scene or not.'
- 'Wherever I look, I see problems obscuring the way forward.'
- 'It was so quiet before. Now I can hardly hear myself think!'
- 'I don't feel like I make contact with her any more. She's so distant.'

Words Sorted by Sensory System

Unspecified	Visual	Auditory	Kinesthetic
attitude	view, perspective	opinion,comment	position, stance
consider	look over	sound out	feel out
persevere	see through	hear out	carry through
demonstrate	show, illustrate	explain	walk through
absent	blank	silent	numb
plain	lacklustre, dull	muted	dull
ostentatious	flashy, showy	loud, screaming	striking
attend to	look after	listen in on	care for, support
ignore	overlook	tune out	pass over, slide
understand	get the picture	tune in, click into	catch on, grasp
conceive	imagine	call up/attention	get a hold of
remind one of	look familiar	ring a bell	strike as familiar
reconsider	review, reflect	repeat, recall	rerun
teach	illuminate	instruct	lead through
refer to	point out, focus	call attention to	touch on/contact
attend to	look at, focus on	tune into	get a feel for
insensitive	blind	deaf	unfeeling
imitate	reflect, mirror	echo, play back	bounce off, pace
equalised	symmetry	harmony	balance
intensity	brightness	volume	pressure
motivate	add sparkle, flash	tune up	move, into gear
decide	see the options	hear the options	weigh options
unperceptive	blind	deaf	numb
make aware	make them see	convince	hammer home
perceivable	clear as day	clear as a bell	solid, concrete
meet with	see	talk to	touch base with
considering	in the light of	on that theme	bearing in mind
rapport	seeing eye to eye	harmonise, tuned	connected

Confronting incongruity

Here are some common human experiences:

• someone talking to you says something that doesn't fit with what you see of their body language
• someone says one thing one day and the opposite the next day
• someone tells you they plan to do something, but then never quite get round to it.

In all these cases, the person is sending you two conflicting messages. The jargon term for this is 'incongruity', which we discussed in Chapter 2.

1 once had a counselling client who came to see me each week, and always began by starting to cry. As she sobbed, she would say to me: 'Well Richard, I'm feeling a lot better this week,' (pause to wipe her eyes) 'and I think I've really got over the separation now.' Of course, a reflective listening response might be: 'You feel on top of it all now', but this would miss a lot of what she was telling me.

When someone is incongruent, to ignore the incongruity is not the most useful helping response. Another approach that's not very helpful is to believe that one of the messages is 'real' and the other is 'phoney. Using that approach I might have said to my client: 'You say you're fine but obviously that's not true. You're pretending to be OK, but I can tell that really you're still upset'. As you can guess, this approach ends up with an argument: it's actually a judgemental roadblock (interpreting).

Acknowledging both messages

The most powerful response to incongruity is to acknowledge (and reflect) both messages, that is, literally to 'believe all things'. My opinion is that both things are, in some sense, true. The woman who tells me that she feels better may well be aware of more positive feelings. There is certainly a part of her which wants to feel better. I don't want to deny that part, just because there is another part which is still feeling her grief.

My comment will therefore be something like: 'On the one hand you say you feel a lot better. On the other hand you still cry as you talk about it'; or: "There's a part of you that has got over it and a part of you that still cries as you say that.'

What will the person make of my reflecting both messages? I can't be sure. She may come to understand the way in which both things are true, or she may decide she isn't fully over her separation. My job was simply to confront her with the difference between the messages. When I use the word 'confront', I mean to put it in front of her clearly enough so she cannot pretend that one message doesn't exist. The name of this skill, 'confronting', sounds a little aggressive, but in fact this is simply an extension of the basic skill of reflective listening. By helping the person to identify the part of them that is different from their preferred state, we can begin using the positive intention process to resolve the difference (activity 2.11, see page 48).

Confronting addiction

Another example might be my response to a client who begins drinking gin and tonics at eleven o'clock each morning and who is routinely drunk by tea time, but who tells me: 'I'm not an alcoholic. I could stop any time. I just need to relax lately'.

I might respond: "You say you're able to stop if you want to, and at the same time you've been drinking every day for several weeks because of a "need to relax"'. To emphasise the confrontation I might explain my awareness of the difference by adding: 'Those two things don't seem to fit together'.

The first example (crying and saying 'I'm fine') was an incongruity between words and body language. The second (alcoholism) could be described as an incongruity between words and actions or between one statement and another. Any of these incongruities is a signal to the helper to use confronting incongruity - if there is enough sense of rapport built up. To use this skill before the person feels listened to in a more gentle way will create resistance.

Practise using confronting incongruity

Write your own confronting responses to the following statements:

- A 15-year-old boy, laughing enthusiastically, tells you: 'I guess I do push my brother around a lot. Poor kid. I feel sorry for him. He never gets a break'.
- A 31-year-old man tells you: 'My wife and I have a good relationship really. It's surprising because, as I say, she can be a real bitch at times'.
- A 21-year-old woman who told you last week that she intended to give up smoking before her next visit, comes in. Lighted cigarette in hand, she explains: 'Well, I've decided for sure now. I'm stopping smoking... sometime soon, mark my words'.

- Smiling, and speaking in a quiet, musical voice, a 25-year-old man tells you: 'I'm absolutely furious about what my father said, and I mean to tell him, too'.

Reframing

Some pictures look cold and dark in one frame, but warm and bright in another. The colours may clash when you put a picture up on one wall, but harmonise with the wall next to it.

A person's life experience is like that, too. Put it in one frame and they feel powerless or meaningless; put it in another and they discover all sorts of new ways forward.

Think back to a time when you made a major decision in your life: perhaps a decision about what job you'd do or a decision to begin or to leave a relationship. Once you'd made that decision, it reframed the rest of your life. Maybe it gave you a whole new perspective on what was possible; maybe it restored the balance you needed to move ahead.

In helping, to reframe means to reflect what the person has said, but to put it in a different context or give it a different meaning. This new meaning should offer more choices or create a more positive state of mind. All the reflective listening skills are really a kind of reframing. When someone says: 'My mother is really stubborn', and I respond: 'You're annoyed with her', I've given quite a different meaning to the statement. The person says something about their mother. I reframe it as something about them. This reframe is useful - they may not be able to do much about their mother's stubbornness, but they do have choices about dealing with their own feeling of annoyance.

From problem to goal

Reframing is also used to help move someone to the goal-setting stage of finding a solution. If someone says: 'Im hungry', I may reply: 'You'd like something to eat'. They've defined their challenge, but I've said back something about their goal.

If someone says: 'I can't stick up for myself', I may say: "You'd like to learn how to be more assertive'.

This challenge -to-goal reframe will only work once the person understands their challenge enough to start thinking about what their goal might be. Most reframing will work best later in the helping process. Used at the beginning, it may come across as a denial of the person's real challenge.

Finding usefulness instead of blaming

To create a meaning reframe I ask myself: 'In what way could this experience have a useful meaning?' If I offer a reframe and the person seems to resist, then I need to go back to listening again, and more simple reflection.

Many people who come for help have a judgemental or 'blame' frame. When they talk about their challenge they talk as if either they or someone else are bad, at fault, and to blame. The "blame frame' is not much use for working out what to do next, so I usually offer them a reframe.

An example would be the man I described in Chapter 1 ('Culture and Meeting') who came to me and explained that he was 'no good' at communication because (for instance) he couldn't make eye contact as much as his wife wanted. I encouraged him to reframe this situation by comments which, in essence, said: 'Sounds to me like you're a good communicator with a Maori cultural experience'. Did this mean his wife was the 'bad' person? No. She was just a communicator with a Pakeha cultural experience. Our reframe put the personal situation in a social or even 'political' context, instead of one in which individuals are at fault.

Symptoms and society

Symptoms such as depression, anxiety or a stress-related illness can also be reframed as social events rather than as an individual's challenge. Such symptoms have usually been very sensible choices which the person first made early in their life. At that time, to be depressed may have been the only safe way to shut down feelings of hurt and anger which were not allowed in the person's family. To develop an illness may have been the only way to get quality time with preoccupied parents. Now, however, the person may be able to find other, even better ways of dealing with hurt, anger or loneliness. But we don't need to blame them for a wisdom which has just outlived its time of usefulness.

Let"s say someone tells me: 'I feel really worried about it. Ever since my childhood I've had an explosive temper'. I may reframe: 'Sounds like you learned at the time that the best way to cope with that situation was to be aggressive, and now you're really choosing to learn new ways that are suited to the kind of relationship you'd like to have now'.

There are two reframes here. I reframe the person's temper (which they saw as a challenge) as something that 'worked' in one context. I reframe their worry about it (which they felt as a weakness) as 'choosing to learn new things' (a strength).

Practise reframing

There are as many ways to reframe as there are stars in the sky. In this chapter I've reframed "helping" as:

- listening
- a set of skills
- finding solutions
- emotional re-processing
- healing
- love,

and now as:

- reframing.

Read the passage below and write reframes of it as:

- a feeling (reflecting feelings)
- a goal instead of a challenge
- an example of a social situation
- a good choice which has outlived its usefulness
- evidence that the person is choosing to change.

A 26-year-old woman explains: 'My problem is that when my husband Karl gets annoyed about something, I just shut down. It's the same as it was with my father. When he got angry - boy, nobody had better say a word! I know Karl's not like that, but I suppose I'm still stuck in the same response. So I say less and less, and Karl gets even angrier. It's odd, because with some feelings I'm fine. I'm quite supportive when someone's sad. But I realise now that I can't seem to handle anger.'

Context reframes

A reframing question related to 'What else could this mean that's useful?' is: 'In what other time or place, in what different context, would this be useful?' This question creates a context reframe.

In 1975, a man named Greg Newbold was sent to Paremoremo prison to begin serving a seven-and-a-half-year sentence for a drug offence. Most people in his situation find their daily life too limited to be of much use. However, by 1978, Newbold had presented his Masters thesis on the social organisation of prisons. By 1982 he had published a book on his prison life (The Big Huey). In 1987 he became Doctor Greg Newbold of the Sociology

Department at Canterbury University. He had found one remarkable answer to the question: 'In what other time or place would this be useful?'

Many brilliant inventions are context reframes. On a September morning in 1928, Scottish scientist Alexander Fleming was checking a culture plate that he was using in his study of bacteria. The culture plate was spoiled: a mould was growing in the corner. Fleming was about to throw the plate out, and was complaining to his friend D.M. Price about the nuisance, when he noticed something odd. 'That's funny', he muttered, and took the plate off to study it. Everywhere in the area near the mould, the bacteria had died. Although Fleming showed this phenomenon to many other scientists that day, none was interested. (McFarlane 1984)

Only Fleming had made the context reframe. The penicillium mould, which was a nuisance in the culture plate, would be a lifesaver if you could apply it to infections in human beings. Fleming had discovered Penicillin, the first antibiotic. He did it with that key question: 'In what other context would this be useful?"

When a client complains that they are 'too (something)', I can ask myself where else that would be useful. If someone says: 'I'm too quiet, I might say: 'I imagine that would be great if someone needed a person to listen.'

If someone says: 'I'm too ugly', I might say: 'I think that would be useful in a relationship, because you'd always know that the other person loved you for who you are.'

Now, create a context reframe for the following statements:

'I'm too laid back. I never get things done in my job.'
'I'm too selfish. People are always telling me I should do more for them.'
'I'm too critical. I always notice minute mistakes, even in my own work.'
'I'm too much of a tangential thinker. Instead of staying on task, my mind wanders off on tangents.'

Telling a metaphor

This skill involves sharing my own experiences and stories with the person I am helping. By 'metaphor', I simply mean a story which the client could think of as similar in some way to their own story.

This is a high-risk skill, in the sense that, unless I use it carefully, the client may feel as if I'm giving them advice or sorting out my own personal challenges instead of listening to their concerns. And yet there are times when telling a story from my own life, or from the life of someone else who has met a similar dilemma and resolved it, can let the client know that I've understood, that solutions are possible, and can help them find their way to their own solutions.

Many people have had the experience of hearing how someone else coped with a difficult situation, and then finding that they came across new solutions for their own situation. Even reading this book may have produced that experience for you, as there are many metaphors in it.

Two things make this skill safer to use:

a. When telling the story, I make it clear that I am telling a story about what happened to me or to someone else. I don't intend to say: 'This is what you should do', but rather: 'This is what someone else did.' That leaves the client free to decide what they might learn from the story.

b. After sharing the story, I want to encourage the conversation to shift back to its focus on helping, not to become a two-way 'chat'. Often I will include a question or comment at the end of my metaphor which does this, for example: 'So where does that leave you now, as you think through your own situation?' or: 'I don't know what meaning that has for your situation, but hearing your story reminded me of it.'

To practise using metaphor, identify a story from your own life about overcoming a challenge, which you could tell a client who was: doubting their ability to learn something, or trying to resolve a conflict between two different desires, or afraid to tell a friend about some behaviour that annoyed them.

NLP Trainer Joseph O'Connor gives a fascinating example of conversational metaphor use (O'Connor and Seymour, 1994, p 184). " I went to the newsagent's the other day and found a very traumatised elderly lady telling the shopkeeper how she had just been mugged. The story went on and got worse. Awaiting my moment, I interrupted and recounted the tale of my friend who was beaten up in her home and could not seem to get the incident out of her head. Then, a few weeks later, when she realised what she was doing, she said, 'Being beaten up is bad enough, but I'll be damned if I'll give them the satisfaction of ruining my life' and she decided to push the whole incident so far away that it was as though she had forgotten all about it....' Can I have a Guardian please?' The old lady paused, her eyes focused off into the distance, and then her state changed and she calmly walked out of the shop. The unexpected thing was that as I left with my paper, the person behind me smiled and said two words: 'Nice work.'."

Immediacy

Immediacy means talking about what's happening right here and now, in the 'immediate' situation. When I am "up front' in this way, I honestly but respectfully tell the other person how I feel, or what response I have to the things they've said and done. This can encourage them to be more open and 'honest' with me. It can also give them important real-life feedback about how others react to them.

Most people have certain ways of behaving that invite a similar reaction in each person they meet. Someone who is depressed, for example, may behave in ways that invite others first to feel sorry for them, but later to get annoyed and frustrated (see Chapter 5, 'Rescue, persecution, or help?). When I am helping this person, it's quite likely I'll start having these feelings, too. Instead of telling myself: 'I shouldn't feel this way I'm the helper and I need to be gentle and caring'; immediacy is another choice. I might say, at various times:

- 'As I listen to your story, I feel a real sadness inside me.'
- 'I'm starting to get frustrated here. You said you wanted to explore this, but you're saying less and less. I begin to feel as if I'm left to do all the work.'
- 'You've stopped talking, and I really don't know right now what you want from me.'
- 'I appreciate you telling me about this.'
- 'I'm really inspired by your ability to continue in spite of all these difficulties.'
- 'I've enjoyed being with you as you find new ways to live a more enjoyable life.'

All of these comments are examples of immediacy. One important function of immediacy is to help us to clarify the 'contract'. I might say such things as:

- 'Mostly my intention is to listen to you and help you find your own solutions.'
- 'I intend to treat this conversation as confidential. Unless I think your life is in some kind of danger, I won't discuss this outside this room.'
- 'I need to stop in ten minutes.'

As with self-disclosure, my language in immediacy makes it very clear which are my thoughts and feelings, and which are the ones I've heard from my client.

Using immediacy

Immediacy is powerful. It needs to be used gently, and with a good understanding of how a comment will help the other person. To develop your skill with immediacy, take time after practising the use of helping skills to talk with the person who was your 'client'. You could discuss what your feelings were as you listened to them, how you chose which things to say back to them, and so on. Then check - would any of what you've just discussed be useful for you to say while you were helping?

Assisting people to distance themselves from painful emotions

Talking about what's wrong with life once a week for years is not healthy. Evidence is mounting that such therapies are particularly unhelpful to those who have traumatic backgrounds. Such people already know how to feel pain; in fact they are doing it involuntarily throughout their life. They may be coping with it by taking drugs or by severe internal splits in their personality (called 'dissociative disorders' in psychotherapy).

When an emotionally healthy person remembers past traumatic events, they tend to do it in a particular way. They remember the event as if they were observing it from the outside, seeing and hearing themselves in a movie, at a distance, and feeling calm. By contrast, when they remember enjoyable events, they remember them from the inside, so they get all the good feelings back.

Someone who is depressed, or suffering from a trauma or phobia, does the opposite. They step right inside the unpleasant memories and feel bad about them. They may even step out of the good events, so that good events always feel a little bit unreal and distant to them.

Thus there is a particular way of viewing the previously traumatic event which is characteristic of recovery. The event appears small, distant, and viewed from the outside, and the person usually has full recollection of what happened 'almost as if it happened to someone else". They also have the ability to remember other, pleasant experiences, as if inside the experience. This is a healthy shift in perspective; a change in the submodalities, which allows the flexibility to dissociate from pain and associate into pleasure. This is very different from the uncontrollable shutting down from all experience that a dissociative disorder brings.

Using language to help someone associate or dissociate

The words you use, and which you encourage your client to use, affect whether they remember a situation as if they were experiencing it from the inside (called, in NLP, 'Associated'), or as an observer (called, in NLP, 'Dissociated'). Remembering an experience Associated is useful if you want the person to recontact the feelings they had then - for example to get a realistic sense of what it was like there, to rehearse something they plan to do or say in that situation, or to get back into a resourceful state they had at that time.

Remembering an experience Dissociated (meaning seeing an experience from outside, rather than being cut off from it) can be useful to help the person get a new perspective on things, or to get a sense of distance from undesired feelings. So, to restate the meaning of the terms:

When you remember an experience Associated:

- You see the things you saw through your eyes at the time.
- You hear the things you heard through your ears at that time.
- You feel the feelings you felt in your body at that time.
- It's easy to practise being in the situation in a realistic way.

When you remember an experience Dissociated:

- You see yourself in the picture as you would have looked to an observer.
- You hear your voice from over there where your body appears to be.
- You don't feel the feelings in your body, so you feel calm.
- It's easy to get a detached perspective on what was happening.

To encourage your client to associate into an experience, you can get them to:

a use the gestures and body positions they would use in the situation (act in the situation)
b imagine being in their body and looking around them
c refer to the experience as if they are experiencing it here and now. Ask them: 'How do you feel now as you remember being here?' (meaning in that experience)
d 'say what you want to say to that person now' (meaning in that situation).

To encourage your client to dissociate from an experience you can:

a get them to relax back in the chair and imagine it
b tell them to see themselves out there
c ask them: 'How is he or she feeling over there at that time?' (meaning in that experience)
d ask them: What do you think would have been useful for that you over there to have said?' (meaning in that situation).

The exception questions for developing solutions (see page 124) are an example of associating a person into the experience of their desired outcome. The skill of associating someone into an event by getting them to speak about it 'in the here and now' was first developed by helpers such as Jacob Moreno and Fritz Perls. It gives the power of immediacy (see page 131) to situations from outside in the rest of the person's life. Notice, in the following example, how much more impact the 'here and now' statement has than the client's earlier 'there and then' statement.

Client: 'I wish I could tell Lisa how much I love her, but I never do. It's kind of sad. I suppose she wonders'
Helper: "Imagine she was sitting beside us here. Try saying that to her now.'
Client: 'Well... OK... Lisa, I never say it but...' [begins to cry]. 'But I really do love you. I know this is a hard time for you, and I want to be here for you.,
Helper: 'That sounds great. How do you think she'd respond?'

The NLP Phobia/Trauma process

The NLP phobia /trauma process is a simple 15-minute process for teaching people how to shift perspective from associated to dissociated. Research shows it is more effective in resolving phobias than several months of behavioural or cathartic psychotherapy (see Bolstad and Hamblett, 1995). Other studies show its effectiveness in working with the victims of rape and other trauma (see *The Trauma Trap* by Dr David Muss MD, who used the process with the survivors of the Lockerby plane bombing in Scotland).

In 1998 and 1999 I had the privilege of teaching this technique to psychiatrists and aid workers in the city of Sarajevo. This was soon after that city had been through an extremely traumatic civil war, and while civil war continued to rage in nearby Kosovo. It was exciting to be able guide people through a one session process which stopped the persistent nightmares and flashbacks of “post traumatic stress disorder”. Since then I have trained health practitioners in, and used the process in the Russian Caucasus (near

Chechnya), in Samoa and Japan after Tsunami, in Christchurch, New Zealand after Earthquake etc.

In 2001, after the 9/11 attacks, New York NLP organisations offered free dissociation trauma cure treatments for New York citizens. their results, over hundreds of people, were so promising that they gained the attention of authorities. In 2014, NLP Trainers, Dr Frank Bourke, Dr Richard Gray and colleagues received a $300,000 grant from New York state and over 5o War Veterans Organisations referred clients to begin a pilot study on the method. 58 veterans were interviewed and evaluated for treatment (52 diagnosed with PTSD). Nearly all of them were combat vets, and they ranged from Vietnam veterans suffering for almost 50 years to vets from Iraq and Afghanistan. Of 33 clients who entered treatment, 26 (using the national PTSD norm of 45 points as cutoff) no longer test as having PTSD; their symptoms were fully alleviated in under five sessions. There were six others who either dropped out or had missing diagnostic scores; one more did not respond to the treatment.

As the protocol was tested under strict scientific standards for the first time, it produced results that matched previous success levels. In this study 75% of the treatment pool and 96% of program completers terminated treatment with complete and permanent elimination of the symptoms of PTSD in less than 5 hours of treatment as verified at the two- and six-week follow-ups. The researchers say "According to combined behavioral and instrumental measures, this pilot completely removed the PTSD diagnosis in 96% of those who completed treatment. Current VA and Army treatments "statistically improve" PTSD scores 35% of the time (Steenkamp & Litz (2013, 2014). No currently approved treatments for PTSD remove the diagnosis; at best, they only improve the symptom scores." For more information on this technique and memory reconsolidation, read Richard Gray and Richard Liotta's article (Gray and Liotta 2012)

I do not recommend you use this process on serious challenges without full training. But you can use it to cure your own minor anxieties and mild phobias very easily (an activity to do this is included later in this section).

The following example of the use of NLP phobia/ trauma cure by NLP trainer Margot Hamblett gives a sense of what can be achieved with such techniques.

Using the NLP trauma/phobia process

Jane is a mother of three primary-school-age children. Four years ago her younger son, then aged two, had a very painful and gruesome accident while playing at home. He soon recovered, both physically and emotionally. However, since that day, Jane had suffered typical symptoms of Post Traumatic Stress Disorder.

When Jane tried to describe to me what had happened to her son, she immediately started crying and getting very distressed. I reassured her it was OK to tell me later. She told me she was unreasonably anxious about her family, especially her children, but also her husband. She was continuously imagining awful things happening to them, and was constantly watchful, needing to know their every move. She could only relax if the children were still and quiet, so she was tending to stop them, or yell at them, if they did any normal boisterous activities. A child's yell in play caused her to panic. If her children had minor childhood accidents, cuts and scrapes, she was immobilised with panic and could not help them. So she was reorganising her whole life so that she would never be left alone with her children, and there would always be a back-up adult there.

Jane very much wanted to relax with her kids, enjoy and encourage their adventurousness, take them skiing, and also let them have some space to themselves.

I asked her to imagine she was sitting comfortably at home, sitting where she would usually sit to watch a video on TV: 'Make that TV screen one of those really small ones, almost like a toy one. Now, on that small screen over there, imagine you can see a still picture of yourself, just like you are now, and make it black and white. Is that easy?"

'Yes.'

'Great. Now imagine you're standing right outside the house some distance away, looking through the window. You can see that other you, sitting inside on the couch, looking at the screen. As you stand outside the house, notice that you have in your hand the remote control. You are going to watch her inside, on the couch, as you show her some special videos. Is she comfortable over there? Can you see the back of her head? Great.

'Now get her to look at a still black-and-white picture of herself, in a safe time just before the accident happened, while she's relaxed and happy at home. And now put up a picture for her, of herself in a safe time after the accident time, when she knows it was all over. She might feel relieved to know its over now. OK?

'Now play through for her the video of what happened, from the first safe picture to the end safe picture. Play it quite quickly, and you just watch he as she watches and learns what she needs to know to let it all go?

Jane looked a little bit tense at times as she did this, but she remained fairly comfortable, and completed this step.

'How was that?' I asked.

'Not too bad. Easier than I thought.'

'Great. Now, I'd like you to imagine you could float right over into that end safe picture, as if you're right inside that experience, seeing through your own eyes, hearing through your own ears.

'Turn up the colour. Now come backwards inside that experience very quickly, like a video on rewind, to the first safe picture. Take 1-2 seconds. Zip! Then be standing, looking in the window again. How was that?'

'Fine', she nodded.

I guided her through this last step again, then asked her to repeat it by herself very quickly, a few more times, until the picture began to disappear or disintegrate, ‚so you can't do it any more.'

After a few moments, she nodded: 'OK'

'Great. Well, that's pretty much it really.

She laughed in disbelief.

'Well, let's see. Try and remember the accident, and find out how it's different now.'

'It's just gone back into the past' she said, with a shrug. 'I know it happened, but it's just over there.'

'Can you get back the feelings you used to have? Really try and see if you can, or can't.'

She laughed and said: 'I've never felt so relaxed.

I asked her to imagine a kid yelling and shouting outside in play. She shrugged again and said: 'It's just normal. just a kid playing'.

As we tested and confirmed the changes she had made, Jane found she could easily and comfortably imagine tending effectively to her kids after minor cuts and scrapes, and enjoying their more adventurous sports and games. She was really excited about looking forward to a relaxing week-end with the family. She even practised how she might explain to her kids how very different she was around them now, because she was sure they would wonder what on earth had happened!

'So what did happen to your little boy?' I asked. This time she told me the story quite calmly. When she finished she said she felt a bit sad, telling it, and that that was OK. She was amazed to be able to talk about it now and feel so calm and relaxed.

Summary

Now you have been introduced to seven 'advanced' level helping skills appropriate to situations such as counselling. These skills are:

1 Using the metamodel to develop questions which challenge the limits in a client's map of the world. These limits include unquestioned beliefs about what can't be done, what must be done, what is wrong or right, and people's ability to read minds or cause feelings in each other, as well as missing information.

2 Matching the client's use of sensory systems, when you use reflective listening.

3 Confronting the incongruity between two messages a client has sent (by restating both messages).

4 Reframing - that is, suggesting new contexts where a client's behaviour might be useful, and offering new frames for understanding the meaning of what the client is exploring, for example:

- changing a comment about events into a comment about feelings
- changing a description of the challenge into a description of a goal
- changing a blaming statement into a description of social causes
- changing a description of a challenge into a recognition of a solution which worked in an earlier situation
- changing a story of failure into an affirmation of the person's intention to change.

5 Sharing metaphors - stories of your own or other people's experiences, which may assist the client to find solutions.

6 Immediacy - talking about what is happening right at the moment, between helper and client.

7 Choosing whether to use language which directs the client to re-experience an event, or to get some distance from an event, including using the NLP trauma/phobia process.

Activity 6.4

AIM: to practise the use of helping skills and receive specific feedback

1 Follow the procedure described in activity 5.7 (see page 102), but extend the time to 10-15 minutes. The listener may use the full range of helping skills as appropriate.

2 After each practice, the observer can give the listener feedback using the following chart. Functioning at level 3 could be considered a successful or 'pass' level.

Skills	Level 1 Dangerous	Level 2 Unhelpful	Level 3 Helpful
Attending	Not in an attending posture. Distracted by other activities.	Mechanical use of attending posture. Gestures and smiles absent. No pacing of client's gestures.	Posture and gestures are relaxed and appropriate for attending. Some indications of rapport (eg simultaneous gestures)
Reflective Listening	Comments are often unrelated to client experience. Repeated use of roadblocks (denial, advice, judgements, interrogation.)	Reflects some of the feelings expressed. Occasional use of roadblocks.	Accurately reflects all major feelings expressed. All comments come from a basis of empathy.

Continued over page ...

Skills	Level 1 Dangerous	Level 2 Unhelpful	Level 3 Helpful
Metaphor and Immediacy	Either overwhelms the conversation with own stories and views or denies and lies about own feelings.	Avoids personal material or shares own "feelings" incongruently.	Congruent non-verbal & verbal responses. Shares own feelings and experiences respectfully if relevant.
Confront-ation & Reframing	Ignores important incongruities or use of blaming by the client, or reacts to these only with roadblocks. repeatedly confronts or reframes in ways that break rapport.	Reflects the feelings or incongruity in client blaming statements, but does not fully utilize these statements by confronting and reframing.	Able to specifically and empathically challenge client incongruity or blaming statements and finds useful new ways to reframe the challenge situation.
Solution creating skills	Uses roadblocks (advice, interrogating) to direct client's solution seeking, or responds with abstract and vague statements.	Asks the client to be specific and to seek solutions but does not model this process as helper.	Uses open questions, reflecting skills etc to model specific language and assist the client to focus on solutions.
Emotion sorting skills	Associates person into distress they did not choose to explore, or avoids emotional issues altogether.	Unable to identify any positive emotional content, and uncertain which emotions to associate the client into.	Helps client to explore emotions, then associate into positive emotions and step out of unpleasant ones.

Activity 6.5

AIM: to practise the individual skills of: a) metamodel questioning, b) solution focused questioning, c) matching sensory systems, d) confronting incongruity, e) reframing, f) metaphor use, and g) immediacy. Complete the questions at the end of each of the relevant sections above.

Activity 6.6

AIM: to alter the way the brain codes an unpleasant memory using the NLP phobia/trauma process

Note: the following exercise is completely safe. However, unless you have professional NLP training, it would be appropriate to do this exercise only on yourself and only on an issue which you know you can manage, although it is less-than-comfortable to think of. Examples might include:

- a 'traumatic' exam which has left you anxious about further exams
- a small specific fear of spiders /mice /elevators, etc.
- a minor -physical injury which makes you 'cringe' or feel nauseous when you think about it.
- a time you remember with embarrassment

1 For this activity you need two chairs, one facing a blank wall, the other behind it, facing the back of the first chair. Sit in the first, front chair.

2 Identify a particular time when you had to cope with the thing that "makes you anxious' (for example the time of the injury, the exam, a time when you saw a spider or mouse or rode in an elevator). Once you have identified the time, put that memory totally away for now.

In this activity we'll use the imagery of a cinema. (In Margot's description she used watching a TV screen. Both work perfectly.)

3 Begin by getting yourself into a relaxed and resourceful state (you may like to do the relaxation activity from Chapter 2). Remember a time when you felt incredibly resourceful and confident about a very enjoyable, satisfying experience, and step into your body at that time, feeling all those good feelings completely.

4 Pretend that you are in a cinema. On the wall in front of you is a movie screen and on it, in black and white, imagine you see a still picture of

yourself before the event which made you anxious: a time when you can see yourself looking safe and OK

5 Next, leave the cinema and move back to sit on the chair behind. This second chair is actually in the projection booth from where they show the movie. There's a thick glass screen between you and the auditorium. If you look in front of you, you can see yourself sitting on the first chair, watching the movie screen. Imagine what the back of your head looks like, and that you look up at the picture of the earlier you on the screen, looking safe and OK

6 From inside the safety of the projection booth, you are now going to run a black-and-white movie. In the movie, that earlier you on the screen will go through the event you're changing, right from the time when he or she was safe before it happened, to a time afterwards when he or she was safe again, after the event, and maybe away from it. As you run this movie, instead of watching the earlier you on the screen, I want you to watch the you in the movie theatre, watching the screen. That other you may have some reaction to seeing the movie, but just run it through to the safe end, and to a still frame of yourself safe after the event.

7 OK! Now, from inside the projection booth, I want you to imagine something. Stay seated on the second chair safe inside the projection booth, but imagine that you float out of there and into the earlier you on the screen, safe at the end of that event. In a minute I want you to be inside that earlier you, seeing through his or her eyes and hearing through his or her ears. You'll turn the picture back to colour and run the movie backwards, all the way to the start where you were safe before the event. Have you ever seen a video played backwards, with people walking backwards and so on? Well, that's almost how it will be. One difference is that you'll be in this movie. The other is that you're going to rewind the whole film in one second flat. Zzziiipp! Right back to the safe time before the event happened. Once you've done that, you can float back into your body in the projection booth. OK, go ahead and do that. Zzziiipp!

8 Now, from the projection booth, try and get back that black-and-white picture of the earlier you, safe before the event, on the screen. You're ready to repeat steps 5 and 6. Repeat these two steps until you absolutely cannot get back a picture on the screen. Some say it gradually whites out. For some people, at a certain point, it's as if the tape just snapped. Usually this takes 3-10 times, but do it until you know it's gone. Notice that the feeling goes too. You cannot have a feeling state without the representations that cause it.

9 After completing the process successfully, wait for five minutes. Do something else: read a book, watch TV, or go outside. Give your brain time to adjust. Then come back and think about the thing that used to scare or upset you. Some people have an uncontrollable urge to laugh when they realise how different it is. Others just smile.

Summary

There are times when simply listening is not enough to help another person regain their sense of wellbeing. This chapter has explored four different ways of understanding this 'helping' situation, and has suggested several verbal skills you can use to help someone change. We have considered helping as:

1. A natural progression from precontemplation, through contemplation, commitment, action, maintenance and recycling
2. A step-by-step use of the solution-creating (RESOLVE) process.
3. A process of exploring emotions and then of dissociating from traumatic emotional events.
4. An ethical commitment to assist another in ways respectful of them.
5. A holistic process which relinks body and mind, personal and political, and human and universal.

As was noted, each of these four models suggests particular advanced helping skills. I then explained the following seven skills:

1. Questioning to loosen the limits in the person's map of the world, and to uncover solutions.
2. Matching the person's use of sensory systems.
3. Confronting the incongruity between two of the person's messages.
4. Offering new reframes of the person's situation.
5. Telling of your own and others' experiences in metaphors.
6. Talking about what is happening at the moment (immediacy).
7. Choosing your language to assist the person to associate or dissociate.

PART THREE

Meeting your own needs along with the needs of others

Chapter 7: Assertive Communication

KEY CONCEPTS

• The assertiveness model
• Addiction and co-dependence
• Assertive . messages
• Sources of anger
• Using listening skills in assertive situations

Assertiveness

AIM: to be able to discriminate between assertive, aggressive, and unassertive behaviours.

The need for assertive skills

As a counsellor I have sometimes been called out to visit a family where communication has 'broken down'. Like an ambulance driver, perhaps, I often don't know what sort of help is needed until I get there.

In the case of one family I visited, a woman (whom I'll call 'Kerry') had phoned out of concern for the way her husband ('Sam') dealt with their kids.

'He loses his temper', Kerry explained as the three of us sat down to talk. 'Social Welfare have warned us that if he hits our oldest girl again like he did last month, she'll be taken off us.'

Sam nodded: 'The thing is, I know what I have to stop doing, but I don't know what I'm supposed to do instead. It's easy for the Social Welfare people to say "Don't hit her". They don't hear how she goads me, how she hassles me'.

I replied: 'You really want to change, and the question is what do you do to cope with her at those times. Tell me about what happens when she '"hassles" you.'

He shrugged his shoulders. 'I guess I mainly just try and ignore her. I'll be sitting here, just like now, watching TV say, and she'll come up to me and thump me or something. I might say "Be a good girl and sit down. You don't want to get daddy mad." But honestly - it's as if she does. I take it for as long as I can, just pretending I don't notice it. And then I can't take any more. I explode. I let her have it - in words as well as hitting.'

Kerry leaned forward. 'That's right. It's not just the hitting. He calls her all the names under the sun. And I think that can't be very good for her either. Most of what he says to her is telling her she's no good.'

A key skill

Already I knew a lot of ways in which this family could change, in order to create relationships which boosted each other's self-esteem instead of wrecking it. But in that first hour I needed to leave Sam with something he could use. Rather than impose my own solution, I listened until he was certain he knew what he most wanted - the ability to send what I call an assertive 'I message. When I explained how to use this skill, Sam was elated. It was exactly what he'd been trying to find.

Having never been to a counsellor or read anything about 'communication skills" before, he'd had to get to a crisis before he risked talking to me. At that stage, even I wasn't sure how much use assertive skill would be to him. He seemed a pretty down-to-earth, no-nonsense kind of guy, and I wondered if this new way of talking would be too 'middle class', too text-book sounding, for him to really get into. However, within a few minutes he'd convinced me that he was going to be an expert. As he said: 'What I've been wanting is a way to get my message across, to tell her what I want, but not put her down, eh! And this is it. It's fantastic!'

Most of us want exactly the same thing for our own lives. We're searching for ways to get our needs met, to express our opinions and concerns, and we don't want to hurt or humiliate those around us in the process. What's missing is often the skill to achieve this.

When I own the challenge

Let's think about Sam''s situation using the challenge ownership model introduced in Chapter 4. When Sam's daughter comes up and hits him, he 'owns a challenge' in the sense that it's him who is immediately annoyed. He's the one whose needs are not being met; the one who is unaccepting of the situation. In this situation, helping skills - such as we discussed in Chapters 5 and 6 - won't work. Helping skills are the most effective response when someone else owns the challenge, while assertive skills are the best choice when I myself own the challenge. Far from just listening, which is useful when the other person owns the challenge, when I own the challenge I want others to listen to me. When the other person owns the challenge I'll help them find solutions that suit them, but when I own the challenge, the solution has to suit me.

You messages

If it's me who owns the challenge, you might expect that most of what I say will be about my concern. In fact, many people respond to this situation by saying a whole lot of things about someone else. Look at what Sam tried. He says: '[You] be a good girl and sit down'; 'You don't want to get daddy mad', and 'You're just a little bitch!''. All his messages are <u>you</u> messages. They may tell his daughter she's good or she's bad, what she wants to do or what she must do, but they don't say anything much about what his challenge is.

There are four main kinds of you message:

• denials: for example, 'You don't want to get daddy mad.'
• solutions: for example, 'Sit down!'
• judgements: for example, 'You're just a little bitch!'
• interrogating: for example, 'Why do you do these things?'

These are the same types of response which cause difficulty in the helping situation, when someone else owns a challenge. Thomas Gordon (1978) calls them 'roadblocks' (see Chapter 4). Some roadblocks may work quite well when no one owns a challenge, but in the area where I am not happy about something, they are likely to:

• create resistance to change

• leave the other person feeling bad about themselves, and
• damage my relationship with the other person.

As they are you messages, they actually encourage the other person to think more about themself ('Am I a bad person?', Do I have to do this?', Why did I do that?') at a time when I'd like them to consider my own concerns.

Unassertive behaviour

Denial statements, and what Sam called 'pretending I don't notice it', are unassertive ways of behaving. They don't tell others that I'm upset; they expect others to guess what I'm upset about (an unassertive person will sometimes say: 'You should know I was upset. I shouldn't have to tell you'), or they suggest that my needs aren't as important as other people's. The likely results of unassertive behaviour are:

• the unassertive person builds up resentments until they explode
• the unassertive person becomes depressed (shutting down their feelings) or develops physical illnesses (from the stress)
• others avoid the unassertive person because they can't work out what they want
• others walk all over the unassertive person: they decide to meet only their own needs because they can't work out what the unassertive person wants.

Aggressive behaviour

Judgements, interrogation and solution sending (ordering), along with actions such as hitting, are aggressive ways of behaving. They violate others' rights, use more force than is necessary, and suggest that others' needs are not as important as mine. The likely results of aggressive behaviour are:

• the aggressive person becomes anxious about others' resentment
• the aggressive person feels guilty about their 'overkill'
• others avoid the aggressive person because they feel abused by them.

Although unassertive and aggressive behaviour seem very different, they are really only the opposite sides of the same coin. Both unassertive and aggressive people believe that things can't be sorted out so that both theirs and others' needs are met. Both of them think that 'someone has to lose'. Both are afraid to take the risk of discussing the matter openly. In fact, many people (like Sam) swing between unassertive and aggressive and back. When they are unassertive they build up resentment which pushes them to explode aggressively. When they've been aggressive they feel guilty and resolve not to be so violent again, and so become unassertive.

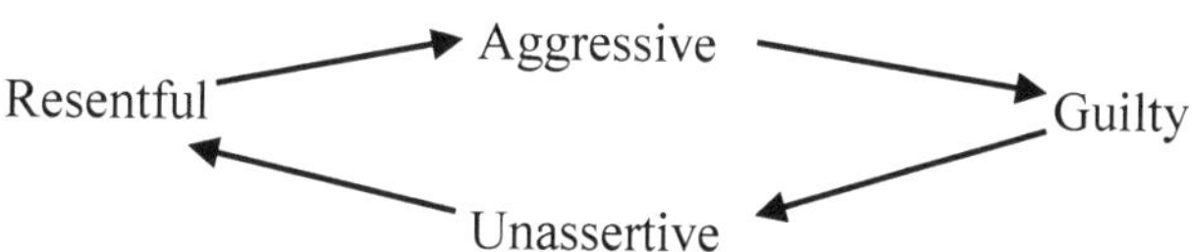

Being assertive means stepping right out of this system, and expressing your own opinions and feelings in ways that don't put others or yourself down. Assertive messages suggest that my needs and the needs of others are equally important and worth meeting. They invite others to act in ways that also respect both sets of needs. The likely results of assertive behaviour are:

• the assertive person becomes increasingly confident of their rights, and trusting of relationships
• most other people are attracted to the assertive person because of the mutual respect and honesty they offer. Some others will avoid the assertive person because they are not willing to risk such relationships.

This last comment reminds us that there is a risk in being assertive. The risk of using listening and helping skills is that you will hear what people are saying, and sometimes that may not be what you wanted to hear. The risk of using assertive skills is that others will hear what you think and feel, and there are times when they may not want to. Relationships which have been unhappy but 'stable' can be destabilised when only one person learns communication skills. Of course if you learn assertive skills and then discover that one of your friends or family doesn't want to hear what you think and feel, you could just choose to stop using the skills.

Mostly, though, people who learn to be assertive begin to realise that they can build the relationships they want, and they can create the kind of life they'd really enjoy. They then either work to change or to leave those relationships which deny this. We'll discuss that situation in Chapter 9.

Assertiveness and whakaiti

Interestingly, the word 'assertiveness' may refer to an attitude similar to the traditional Maori quality of 'whakaiti' (humility). Consider Maori teacher Tipene Yates' description (quoted in *In and Out of Touch* by J. Metge) of his kaumatua (Maori elders):

'I observed them and watched them, and they all had one thing in common, whakaiti. To me that is how these old people conducted their whole way of

life. You didn't see them abusing people; you saw them talking fire, not abuse. Always they were polite and humble. But they made their points and they would not turn away from them. They would say, "Well, I am sorry. You say this is white, I know it is black, and you are misguided". Something nice like that in Maori.'

The assertive attitude

So far in this chapter, we've talked about assertive, aggressive and unassertive ways of responding to the situation where 'I own a challenge '.

An assertive response does what Tipene Yates suggests: it makes the point politely, neither backing down nor abusing the other person. We'll discuss this issue later in this chapter. The assertive attitude (or state of mind, to use a term discussed in Chapter 2) can be thought of more generally. An assertive attitude is one which values my own feelings and opinions, my own needs, and also those of others. Such an attitude is 'confident' and includes a sense of 'self-esteem' (see Chapters 2 and 3). Like other states, the state of assertiveness is one you can develop using body language, visualisation, and self-affirmation. For example, assertiveness is helped if you:

1 Use postures, gestures and voice qualities which express confidence, including:

- open hand gestures and open arm/ leg positions
- culturally appropriate eye contact
- a voice with a relaxed tone and a steady delivery, loud enough to be heard
- posture, gestures and voice which are congruent, that is which fit with the words you're saying.

2 Visualise situations, from your memory, in which you were relaxed and confident. Use all your senses to fully recall these times (associated) and anchor yourself back into that sense of confidence: remember what you could see, hear, smell, feel and even taste.

3 Tell yourself beliefs about your situation which are realistic and supportive of your assertion. This was discussed in Chapter 1 in relation to the skill of introducing yourself to someone else. People are more able to assert themselves when they believe that assertion is likely to work, for them and for others. This means reminding themselves of the differences between assertion, and aggression and non-assertion.

Assertive rights

Another way of thinking about the beliefs that support assertiveness is the model of assertive rights. You will behave more assertively when you fully believe you have the right to:

- have and express feelings and opinions
- be different from others, and set your own priorities
- ask others for information or help
- say 'no' when others ask you for things - without feeling guilty
- change your mind or recognise you've made a mistake without feeling guilty
- choose not to express feelings and opinions.

Others around you also have these same rights. As you reread the above list, think about the very specific everyday rights which are a part of these six main rights. For instance, 'the right to have and express feelings and opinions' may mean, in your actual daily life, such things as:

- the right to tell your parents you disagree with them
- the right to say you felt insulted by a certain joke
- the right to a religious belief your friends don't share
- the right to really enjoy your favourite music.

Basic right

New Zealand trainer Marjorie Manthei (1981) suggests that such assertive rights all spring from one basic or ultimate assertive right. She says: 'You have the right to be the final judge of your own behaviour, thoughts and feelings. You must, however, take responsibility for them.'

Assertiveness, then, is about the right to be who you are. There's an old Jewish saying which suggests that: 'You don't give glory to God by trying to be more like Moses. That was Moses' job. You give glory to God by being true to yourself.'

Whatever the most important thing in the world is to you, this saying is likely to make sense: giving glory to that most important thing means being true to yourself.

Addictive, codependent, and integrated behaviour

In the last few years, several writers have used the addiction model to explain how destructive communication happens. In *Women, Sex and Addiction,* psychotherapist Charlotte Davis Kasl (1994) points out that people who have an unmanageable desire or compulsion (whether for alcohol, food, sex, power, or whatever) become increasingly concerned only for themselves and for winning. The addict is, in that sense, aggressive. Kasl describes addiction as often being an escape from the opposite pole of feeling empty, as if one has no self to be concerned for.

This opposite pole is one she names 'codependency'. The codependent is concerned almost entirely with other people's happiness, unable to live their own life and ensure their own needs are met. The codependent, then, is unassertive.

Men's conditioning, Kasl points out, usually moves them towards the addict position, while women's conditioning usually moves them towards codependency. But both positions are based on the same sense of low self-esteem, and are interchangeable.

In her book *When Society Becomes An Addict,* addictions therapist Anne Wilson Schaef suggests that many of the institutions in our society are addictive systems: they require people to function either as addicts (for example workaholics) or codependents; to be one up or one down in relation to others.

Recovery

If your aggressiveness or unassertiveness is a result of addiction or codependency, how do you find your way to 'recovery' and what Charlotte Davis Kasl (1994) calls 'integrated behaviour'? Traditionally, organisations like Alcoholics Anonymous have recommended a series of twelve steps. Kasl says that she finds these steps themselves to be full of one up/one down assumptions. Her book *Many Roads, One Journey: Moving Beyond The Twelve Steps* offers a reframing of these steps. Her new 'twelve steps' involve acknowledging that your addiction has been controlling you, being willing to tune in to your own inner wisdom and spirituality, examining your life and committing yourself to resolve issues in an assertive way, and sharing this understanding with others. Most of all, Kasl invites us to 'move from recovery to discovery. Then we can break through the limitations imposed by hierarchy, work together for a just society, and free our capacity for courage, joy, power and love').

Loving yourself

Helping skills begin with the attitude of love for others. Assertive skills are founded on the ability to love yourself (on self-esteem, to use the term we discussed in Chapter 2). To discover this ability in yourself, what I'd like you to do right now is to search through your memory for someone who you know loves you. This person need not be someone present in your life today; they need not even be someone you love; but it is extremely important that, as you think of them, you know they love you. Continue thinking until you've identified this person, and then read the next paragraph.

Get a picture in your mind of this person, with the kind of look that reminds you of who they are. Listen to the sound of their voice, saying the sort of thing they might say to you; remembering their particular tone of voice and way of saying things. Sense what it would be like if they were with you now, nearby. Feel the feelings which pass through you as you remember their particular personality, their idiosyncrasies, all the little things that make them who they are.

And now, gently feel yourself change your position. In your imagination, float out of your body and over to the form of the person who loves you. See the altered perspective as you look back out of the eyes of that person. Hear from their ears as you now become aware of their thoughts - the thoughts that occur in the mind of someone who loves you. If you listen carefully, you will hear how they describe the you that is in front of them, with your particular personality, with all the little things that make you who you are. Seeing yourself through the eyes of this person who loves you, you may notice qualities in yourself which these eyes, understood in this person's words, you can recognise what it is that makes you lovable; what it is that enriches this other person's life just by being you.

Take all the time you need, now, to look at yourself through the eyes of this person who loves you, and to hear how they would describe the unique person that is you.

Gathering this understanding, holding it deep inside you, and, remembering what you have seen or heard, return to your own body, slowly, gently, respectfully.

You may like to reread that first list of assertive rights and check how much more you can accept them, when you hold this new understanding. (Adapted from an exercise in Solutions, by Cameron-Bandler).

To recap

So far in this chapter we have considered the general concept of assertiveness. Assertive behaviour means expressing your own feelings and opinions in ways that don't put down either others or yourself. Assertiveness can be thought of as a state, with body language, feelings and thoughts which back it up. Amongst the thoughts which back it up is a belief in your assertive rights, including the ultimate assertive right to be the final judge of your own behaviour, thoughts and feelings. The feeling of self-love is an important basis of assertive behaviour.

Assertive behaviour can be contrasted with unassertive behaviour in which a person denies their own feelings and opinions, and aggressive behaviour in which a person overrides others' opinions and feelings. When I 'own a challenge', assertive ways of talking explain my challenge, while unassertive or aggressive responses tend to be 'you messages'.

Activity 7.1

AIM: to assertively give and receive compliments

1 Give the group time to prepare for this activity by inviting each person to look around and remember what they genuinely like about each of the other persons in the group. Whether you like someone a lot - or even dislike them -there are always things you can genuinely appreciate. To be genuine is important in this activity

2 Think about how (1) above shows that we cannot 'measure' how much people like us, based on how many things they say or how long they take to find the words to compliment us. It is worth reminding yourself of this as we do this activity.

3 Each person takes a turn being the focus of compliments from the others. (The order may simply be the seating order, or could be decided at random.) When it is some one's turn, the others should speak in no particular order (and it is not necessary for all to speak). Note again the point made in (2) above. Compliments could begin with statements such as: 'One thing I value about you...'; 'I like ... '; or 'I think it was really good the way you...'. Note that compliments are most effective when delivered congruently (that is, without a tone of voice or side comment which makes fun of or contradicts the compliment). Carry on until it appears that everyone has said what they want to say.

4 The person who is the focus can receive compliments most effectively by not denying them, and by maintaining an open, attentive body posture. Having heard the compliments, the person writes down all those comments which they can accept as being valid in some way. They may like to add their own self compliments, describing qualities or actions not obvious to

those in the group.

5 After each person has had a turn, discuss:
  * How did it feel to give compliments?
  * How did it feel to receive compliments?
  * Was people's body language assertive? How could it improve?
  * What effect does this activity have on the group?

'I' messages

AIM: to be able to write and say assertive 'I' messages, using reflective listening to deal with the other person's response.

Before discussing I messages, we will look at three examples:

Example 7.1

Sam has an important exam coming up in two days' time, so tonight he's set aside five hours to revise his work. He's a little uneasy when, at 6.30 pm, Eliot rings him up to tell him about the party they're having. 'Come on', Eliot urges, 'you're always wound up in that study. The exam will come and go, but your friends are here for keeps. It's about time you remembered us.' Consider his choices, using the model of assertive-aggressive-unassertive from the last section. Which of the following responses fits in which of the three categories?

1 'Ah, um, well, I don't know Eliot. I may come over in an hour or so then. Don't wait up for me though: I've been feeling ill today so I might not make it.' (After an hour of study, feeling guilty, Sam leaves for the party.)

2 'Oh yeah? Well, how about you guys spare a thought for me once in a while. How do you think I feel stuck here with my study? You've got a lot of nerve. Get off my case Eliot.' (Slams phone down.)

3 'Well I certainly don't want to lose your friendship. I am studying for this exam in two days though, and if I leave the study now, I'm worried that I'm going to end up with even more pressure next year.'

Example 7.2

Marge has an arrangement that her kids will take turns doing the dishes, because she cooks the meal each night. But it's now the third night in a row that they have forgotten the arrangement and watched TV all evening instead. Seeing the dirty dishes, she considers what to do about the situation. In terms of assertive, aggressive, and unassertive options, her actions might include the following (check again that you recognise which is which):

1 Walking quickly into the TV room, turning off the TV and announcing: 'There'll be no TV until the three of you have got into the habit of doing your jobs. You're the most ungrateful, selfish slobs a mother could ever be cursed with.'

2 Walking into the TV room during an ad break, turning the TV down and explaining: 'We have an agreement that you'll organise the dishes, and I feel really resentful when I end up having to remind you each night. This is the third night they haven't been done.'

3 Doing the dishes and resolving not to cook anything the kids enjoy for tea the next night.

Example 7.3

Andrea and her husband John are going out to tea this Friday with some of the people from John's work. She's fairly tense about this. Last time they went out with John's workmates, John got pretty drunk and told some rather embarrassing stories about their sex life. Andrea doesn't want to end up in another situation like that. Which is the most effective way for her to express her concern?

1. Not mention the subject and encourage John gently to slow down with his drinking, hoping it won't happen again.

2. Find a time when he seems able to listen and tell him: 'I'd like to talk about Friday I think I'll enjoy the dinner, but it's really important to me that I don't end up feeling embarrassed there. Last time I found some of the things you said about me hard to handle.'

3. Catch John as soon as he gets back from work that day and tell him: 'Your one-track mind has got me all tense about this Friday dinner. So help me, if you carry on like last time, I'll walk out then and there.'

Usually, people find it easy enough to recognise an assertive response (such as the third of Sam's choices, the second of Marge's options, and the second of Audrea's possible actions). What people have more difficulty with is actually working out the right words to use in their own real-life situations. In this section we'll learn a simple three-step process for making up your own assertive messages, and we'll think about how to carry on talking when the other person disagrees with your message.

Remember that assertion is about expressing your own opinions and feelings; for example telling someone when you 'own a challenge' as discussed in Chapter 4. This means that assertive messages are mostly 'I messages' (to use a term coined by Thomas Gordon 1978). Instead of focusing on what you think of the other person, they describe the situation you yourself are in. This includes:

- the actual behaviours which are a challenge to you
- the concrete effects (if any) that these behaviours have on you, and
- the feeling states you have about those effects and behaviours.

You don't have to 'cover up' your feelings when you use an I message. In fact, using an I message is a more direct way to express your feelings than a you message.

The behaviour

In the assertive I messages in the three examples, the behaviours which were a concern were described as follows:

'I am studying for this exam in two days though, and if I leave the study now...'
'We have an agreement that you'll organise the dishes... This is the third night they haven't been done.'
'... some of the things you said about me...'

The important thing about describing the behaviour is to describe things that you can see, hear, or physically touch - not opinions or guesses. In the terms we discussed in Chapter 4, this means being 'sensory specific'. 'The dishes haven't been done' is a description of a behaviour, whereas 'You kids are being ungrateful, selfish slobs' is an opinion or a guess about what goes on inside them. When you describe the behaviour you're unhappy about, check that the other person is likely to agree that those things did happen. (The kids probably won't agree that they were being 'selfish slobs', but they can agree that 'the dishes haven't been done'.)

It's just good 'tactics' to describe behaviour this way. Otherwise you'll end up arguing about what actually happened, instead of telling the other person your challenge and getting their help.

For the same reason, avoid saying 'you never...'or' you always...', for example: 'You never do what you've arranged'; 'You always say things that embarrass me.' Those words just get you into an argument about whether there are any times when this wasn't true.

A second set of words to avoid includes 'deliberately' and 'on purpose'. These are guesses about the other person's intention. The aim of assertiveness isn't to argue about whether your friend 'deliberately' said things that embarrassed you, or did it by accident. The aim is to get them to stop! If you're uncertain how to describe the behaviour, a simple beginning suggested by Thomas Gordon is the word 'When...', for example: 'When I give up my study two days before an exam...'; 'When the dishes don't get done...'; 'When you tell your friends details about our sex life...'.

Concrete effects

Once you've explained exactly what behaviours concern you in this non-blameful way, the next step is to check whether the behaviour has any <u>concrete</u> effects on you. Does it cause you more work, cost you money, physically hurt you, and so on. Or do you believe it will cause these effects in future? Not all challenges cause actual effects that will make sense to the other person. Sometimes you just have feelings about them.

In example 7.3, Andrea probably doesn't have to do more work or pay more money as a result of her husband's comments about her personal life. She just feels embarrassed. However, people have just as much right to get challenges solved when there's no concrete effect on them as when there is an effect. (These 'no effects challenges' are values conflicts and will be discussed further in Chapter 9.)

Sam, whose friend Eliot rang about the party, is worried about the possible concrete effects of leaving his study ('I'm going to end up with even more pressure next year'). And Marge is already experiencing concrete effects when her kids leave the dishes ('I end up having to remind you each night'). I messages which include a clear description of the concrete effect are much more likely to produce results. They help people understand exactly how their behaviour causes you a challenge.

Feeling states

The really powerful part of an I message, though, (and the part most important to remember for people learning this skill), is the feeling state. Sam feels 'worried', Marge feels 'resentful', and Andrea feels 'embarrassed'. Remember from Chapter 5 that feelings are not opinions or beliefs: 'I feel that you are very mean' is not a description of a feeling state - it's a description of a belief. Feelings can usually be described in one word (for example: 'sad', frustrated', 'afraid', 'discouraged'). If you can put the word 'that' in front of the word 'feel' in your sentence, you have a belief or an opinion. To discover a word for your feeling, you might ask yourself: 'How does someone who gets those effects feel?', or 'How does someone who experiences that behaviour feel?'

Marshall Rosenberg, author of the book *Nonviolent Communication* (1999), points out that many words we use instead of describing feelings are actually

1) descriptions of our opinion about what the other person is doing: for example “I feel abused”, “I feel attacked”, I feel let down”
2) descriptions of our opinion about ourselves: for example “I feel stupid”, “I feel incompetent”

Feelings		**Non-Feelings**	
Angry	**Sad**	**You're not good**	threatened
irritated	lonely	abandoned	trampled
agitated	troubled	attacked	tricked
furious	helpless	betrayed	unaccepted
enraged	gloomy	blamed	unheard
infuriated	grieving	caged	used
pissed off	overwhelmed	cheated	violated
resentful	discouraged	controlled	
disgusted	distressed	criticized	**I'm not good**
	disheartened	distrusted	inadequate
Confused	depressed	dumped on	incompetent
frustrated		hassled	invisible
hesitant	**Scared**	ignored	stupid
troubled	afraid	insulted	unimportant
uncomfortable	fearful	intimidated	
torn	terrified	isolated	
hopeless	startled	left out	
hurt	nervous	let down	
uneasy	panicky	manipulated	
irritated	anxious	misunderstood	
embarrassed	worried	overpowered	
	anguished	overworked	
Tired	lonely	patronized	
exhausted		pressured	
lethargic		pushed around	
weary		put down	
worn out		rejected	
sleepy		smothered ...	
overwhelmed			

Using I messages

A clear I message has three parts, which describe:

• the behaviour, in away the other person can recognise, without blaming words such as 'always', 'never' or 'deliberately'
• the concrete effects which are happening or will happen in future to you, and
• the feeling you have.

Some people ask: 'Shouldn't I suggest the actions I'd like the other person to take - the solution?' Our experience is that solution suggesting is only helpful when the other person resists acting because they have a challenge of their own. This situation is a conflict, and we'll explore it further in the next two chapters.

Suggesting solutions in your first I message runs a high risk of leaving the other person feeling cornered, insulted and ordered about. It's as if you said: 'I'm going to spell out step-by step what you must do to solve my challenge, because you're too dumb or too selfish to understand'.

Often, an I message won't solve your challenge instantly. It's not the complete answer - that's why there are more chapters in this book. But an I message is a lot more effective a way of starting to assert yourself than a you message. The I message:

• explains exactly what your challenge is instead of leaving the other person to guess
• does not put the other person down, so protecting their self-esteem, and
• opens discussion rather than closing it, so protecting the relationship.

When to use I messages

I messages can be used:

1 when you own a challenge, i.e. when you are unhappy about some behaviour that's already happening (for example in Marge's case with the dishes)
2 when you think you may own a challenge in the future (for example at Andrea's dinner)
3 when you want to say 'no' to a request which could cause you a challenge (for example in Sam's study situation).

As with any skill, you will need to practise to be able to use I messages well. At first it may help you to write out your I messages and even roleplay sending them (as in activity 7.3, page 156) before doing so. In a short time, I messages will feel more natural than you messages.

You won't always need to say all three parts of the I message. Let's say you are standing in a queue and someone stands on your foot. A full I message might be: 'When you stand on my foot [behaviour] the bones get pushed into the floor [effect] and it hurts [feeling]'. Instead, you'll probably get a good response by describing only the behaviour: 'Excuse me, you're standing on my foot!' (If the person looks puzzled and nods, though, I'd recommend sending the full message and moving!)

Why I messages are not enough

More often than not, an assertive I message in itself is not enough to ensure that things change. In fact, I messages are best thought of as a heading in a newspaper article, rather than the full article. They simply anounce that there is something to discuss.

In his research on couples, American psychologist John Gottman found evidence again and again that the first thing someone says in a disagreement is crucial. He notes about couples "The bottom-line rule is that, before you ask your partner to change the way he or she drives, eats or makes love, you must make your partner feel that you are understanding. If either (or both) of you feels judged, misunderstood, or rejected by the other, you will not be able to manage the challenges in your marriage. This holds for big s and small ones…There's a big difference between "You are such a lousy driver. Would you please slow down before you kill us?" and "I know how much you enjoy driving fast. But it makes me really nervous when you go over the speed limit. Could you please slow down?" Maybe that second approach takes a bit longer. But that extra time is worth it since it is the only approach that works." (Gottman and Silver, 1999, p 149).

Gottman recorded hundreds of thousands of hours of marital conflicts. He found that in 96% of cases, the emotional tone of the first one minute of a conflict could predict exactly how that conflict would go overall, and also predict whether the couple's marriage would survive. The first statement in a conflict will decide what the entire conflict turns out like (Gottman, 1999, p 41). It is worth thinking carefully about the precise wording of your first sentence when you ask someone to change. The choice of those few little words will decide whether your relationship survives or not. The most important aim of your first sentence is not to win the argument, it is to keep rapport so that you can get what you want **and** preserve a cooperative relationship with the other person.

The key to the I message working is that you do not include in your first statement a claim that "I know what is going on inside you and it is "bad" and "wrong". This implication, called blaming by Gottman, has a 96% chance of going to a place you did not intend! Even so, there are four basic reasons an I message may not work by itself:

1. The I message wasn't a complete I message as described above.
2. The other person felt upset when they heard the I message and their upset wasn't listened to.
3. The other person has a challenge of their own: a conflict of needs.
4. The other person doesn't believe their behaviour affects you: we call this a conflict of values.

We'll discuss (3) and (4) in the next two chapters. Here we'll think about (2): how a person feels when you send them an I message.

If you've ever been 'told off' or had it pointed out to you that another person is finding your behaviour a challenge, you'll know that it can feel pretty uncomfortable. Remember some of the times when someone has complained to you, criticised you or asked you to change. What did you do? You might have defended yourself, argued back, or got angry. You may have been embarrassed, gone silent, looked down more, shrugged your shoulders, cried, blushed, or even laughed nervously. Whatever you did, all these responses are clues that you 'owned a challenge '.

The person who complained to you started off owning a challenge about some issue. When they told you, you owned a challenge.

Listening to the other

I messages minimise this effect, but they don't eliminate it. If you send an I message to someone, they'll experience feelings such as embarrassment, anger, hurt, confusion or even guilt.

If you have read Chapter 5, you'll already know the skills which are useful in this situation (where someone else owns a challenge). They work just as well when the challenge concerns your behaviour as when it concerns some outside situation. The skills are:

* attending: physically paying attention
* minimal encouragers: 'ah-huh', 'yeah', 'mm', 'right', and soon
* questions, especially open questions which begin 'how', 'what', or 'tell me

about'
* reflective listening: this restates the person's meaning, acknowledges their feelings, and summarises or sorts the various issues they've raised.

Using reflective listening after I messages

The easiest way to respond to someone's distress caused by your I message, is to acknowledge it using reflective listening. Use reflective listening until the other person nods, says 'yes', or otherwise tells you that they feel understood. You can then repeat your I message if you have to. This is a kind of a dance, where you first step forward with an I message, and then wait for your partner to step too, before continuing. Here are a couple of examples:

Example 7.4
Jennifer: 'I've really enjoyed being out with you this evening Gary, and that's why I want to explain something I've been uncomfortable about. When you put your hand on my breasts in front of other people, like earlier on, I feel really embarrassed. I wanted to say so then, but couldn't think how to explain it.' [I message]
Gary: 'Hey; I was only joking around. Nobody was watching anyway!'
Jennifer: '*You* don't think anyone could see, and you were just kidding.' [reflective listening] *Gary nods.* 'Well, I did feel uncomfortable.' [I message] 'It may seem silly,' [reflective listening], 'and I do find it embarrassing.' [I message]
Gary: 'Okay, I'll remember. No problem.'
Jennifer: 'Thanks.'

Example 7.5
Father: 'Tim, I get tired of picking up people's clothes so I can walk through the main room. Your shoes and socks are on the floor there now.' [I message]
Tim: 'Oh, dad!'
Father: 'It just seems a nuisance to get up right now, huh?' [reflective listening]
Tim: 'Yeah. I'll do it later.'
Father: '*I* believe you mean to do it later, and I also know you forgot before' [reflective listening; confrontation],'... and I want to make sure I don't have to step round them again.' [I message]
Tim: 'But I'm tired now.'
Father: '*You* think I should have told you before.' [reflective listening] Tim nods. 'The thing is, I only came across them just now. I'm also really tired, and I don't want to end up doing your work as well as mine.' [I message]

Tim: 'Well .... OK.'
Father: 'Great. Thanks, Tim.'

In each case, the person who is told the I message doesn't have a really strong reason to disagree (that would be a conflict, see next chapter). They just have an initial challenge accepting the I message. When the other person listens to them, it makes it easier for them to listen as well. The assertive person has shown them the basic assumption of assertiveness: my feelings and opinions are important, and so are yours.

Using reflective listening in this way kind of 'takes the wind out of the other person's sails'. Instead of wasting your energy arguing with their feelings, you can accept them and still express your own concern. This works a lot better than sending a second I message about their complaint. Imagine that difficulty:
Father: 'Tim, 1 get tired of picking up people's clothes so I can walk through the main room. Your shoes and socks are on the floor there now.' [I message A]
Tim: 'Oh, dad!'
Father: 'And another thing I don't like is when I tell you about something like this and you don't listen to me. I end up wasting five minutes to get you to do a ten-second job.' [I message B]

Now the father has sent two different I messages. He's trying to solve two challenges at once, and Tim is twice as upset. The chances are he'll lose at least one argument by being sidetracked. Reflective listening helps keep your I messages concentrated on solving the challenge you wanted to solve. When you send an I message, you are stepping out of rapport with the other person. Reflective listening enables you to bring them back into rapport, so they feel safe enough to actually hear your concern and change. Sending one I message after another would just keep increasing the metaphorical distance between you.

In the following diagrams, I have represented this change in metaphorical distance by having the person who sends the I message step away from the person as they send it. I am not, of course, recommending you step away from a person as you send the I message. Merely saying that this is what happens in terms of rapport. When the person feels understood as a result of your reflective listening, they step back close to you again. This makes sending an I message a kind of a dance. In my training I call this the “two step” (a term first coined in this way by Australian communication skills trainer John Lizzio).

The Two Step: Three Results Of I Messages

If you follow it with reflective listening, your I message will have one of three results. These results are diagrammed in the following charts. Imagine that Jane is a teenager who gets up late in the morning. Her father, Jack, finds that this results in him having less time to tidy up before he leaves for work.He decides to send an I message to explain his challenge. In the diagrams, when Jack sends his I message, we will have him symbolically move out of rapport by stepping down the page. When Jane feels understood as a result of Jack's reflecting, we will have her move down the page back into rapport. This is a kind of "dance" that I call the "Two Step".

1. Jane agrees congruently to change to solve Jack's challenge.

2. Jane and Jack identify that they both own a challenge. While Jane can understand that their behaviour concretely affects Jack, she is not willing to change because it would cause *her* a challenge. (Conflict of Needs)

3. Jane considers this matter to be "none of Jack's business". Jane is thus not willing to negotiate the issue. (Conflict of Values or Metaprograms)

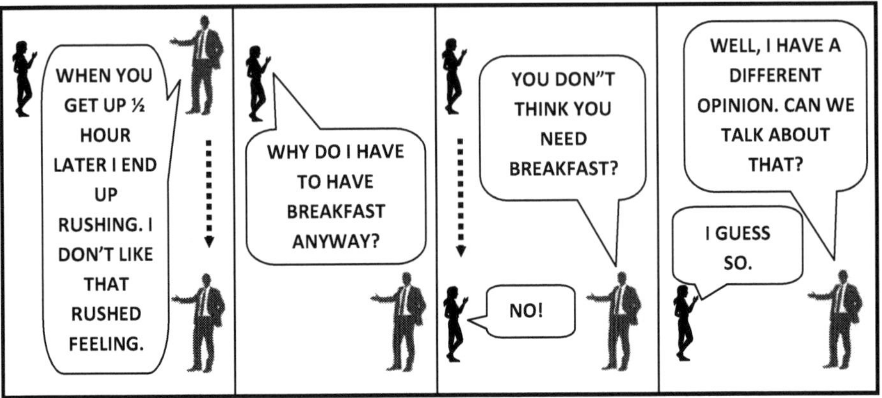

A 4th Possibility?

In some cultures (Japan and New Zealand are examples) conflict is avoided and the other person may not be willing to explain their challenge, and will hide their situation. This is far less common in European cultures. While the other can understand that their behaviour concretely affects you, they are not willing to change because change would create a challenge for them, **and** also they are not comfortable explaining this. The result is that the other superficially agrees, but fails to change their behaviour. This needs a little more care to find out what the other person's needs actually are so you can begin to think up solutions that will meet them and motivate the person to cooperate. (Hidden Conflict of Needs)

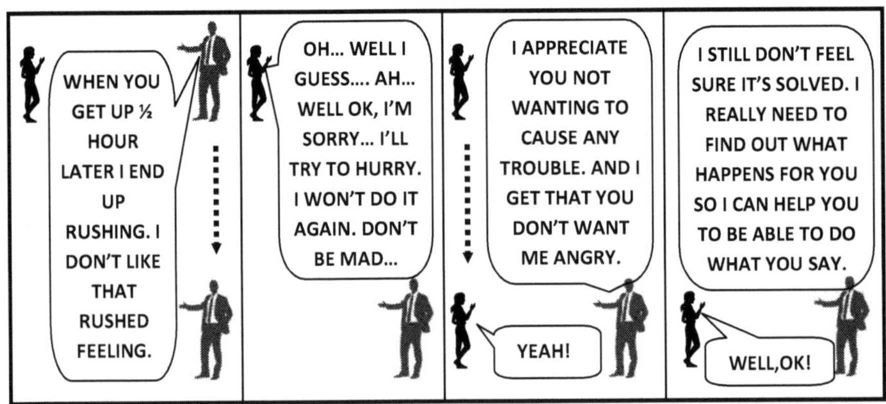

Any of these three outcomes is a successful result of sending the I message and reflective listening. We will discuss what to do in conflicts of needs or in conflicts of values/metaprograms in the following chapters.

What if they leave?

If the person's reaction to your I message was to leave the room, of course you wouldn't be able to send a reflection of their feelings (which may be along the lines of: 'You don't want to hear about this'). There's no magic way to stop someone leaving the room.

You need to then decide: will you try and resolve the issue later on? Will you bring up the issue of leaving the room during conflicts later on? Or will you find some way to change your relationship with this person to protect you from their non-communication (such as seeing less of them or getting help from a counsellor)?

Other assertive uses of listening skills

Assertion means respecting others' feelings and opinions as well as your own, so listening skills have an important place in general assertive speech, too. If you want another person to listen to your challenge, it makes sense to 'show them how it's done' by attending and listening when they disagree with or criticise you. In such a situation, questioning may include checking specifically what they disagree with, as in the following examples:

Example 7.6
Employer: 'Lisa, your work just isn't up to standard.'
Lisa: 'You're not happy with it. [reflective listening] What things do I need to improve on [open question]

Example 7.7
Jan: '*I* didn't like those creeps you invited round the other day.'
Phillip: 'You didn't enjoy them being here. [reflective listening] What were the things that annoyed you about them?' [open question]

Sometimes, when someone is upset, they offload a whole collection of challenges at once. The reflective listening skill of sorting issues may help select one issue at a time to discuss. Consider the following examples:

Example 7.8

Sylvia: 'Why do you always have to take the car when you go to town? It wastes petrol. And you can bet it's me who ends up having to refill the tank

when it gets low. I always end up being the one who checks on it - just like with putting out the rubbish bags.'
Bob:'So, there are two things we need to sort out: the use of the car, and my remembering to check for the petrol, rubbish bags, and so on. Can we discuss the car use first, then come back to the other?'

Example 7.9
Mother:'Gail, I wish you'd tell me where you're going when you leave the house. Honestly! Last night you had two phonecalls I had to answer. And the first time I didn't even know you'd gone out! I went into your room looking for you. Not that I'd be able to find you if you were in there, piled high with mess like it is!'

Gail:'Well, I know you'd like the room tidy, but the main problem is telling you where I am - right?'

When someone criticises you, they own the challenge. These listening skills will work best if you use them gently and with a genuine interest in understanding what that challenge is. If you simply can't put aside your own feelings in response to their criticism (if you own a challenge too) it may be more helpful to explain that in an I message.

Anger as a signal

When I teach groups to use I messages, I often check what words they are using to describe the feeling they have. In more than half of all cases, their word will be 'angry' or a word meaning angry (for example 'enraged', 'furious', 'mad' , 'pissed-off', 'annoyed', and so on).

Obviously, anger is a very common response when someone owns a challenge. In fact, counsellor Harriet Goldhor Lerner (author of *The Dance of Anger)* describes anger as: '... a signal, and one worth listening to. Our anger may be a message that we are being hurt, that our rights are being violated, that our needs or wants are not being adequately met, or simply that something is not right.'

She suggests that it is particularly important for women to give themselves permission to recognise and feel their anger. The force of anger, she points out, Ican motivate us to say "no" to the ways in which we are defined by others and //yes" to the dictates of our inner self.'

While feeling angry alerts us to the fact that we own a challenge, and gives us the energy to do something, it does not in itself explain what the challenge is. This is why Lernor suggests that, rather than giving vent to anger, we need to feel it and discover the challenges that cause it.

Anger and men

A similar description of the importance of anger for men comes from two Christchurch trainers, Tim Williams and Ken McMaster, in their article *Anger Management: A Course For Aggressive Men* (1984).

They say of their courses for men that: 'The primary principle underlying many aspects of the course is that many of the outbursts of violence reported by men in our group related to them not recognising anger when it builds up, or trying to ignore anger. This latter course occurs as they have usually had violence modelled to them as the only appropriate expression of anger.' (Williams and McMaster, 1984). The extra power conferred on men in our society (think about the numbers of men and women in Parliament, for example) often seems to give permission for the use of violence as a male expression of anger.

The feelings underneath anger

Like Lernor, Williams and McMaster encourage their course participants to discover the feelings which underlie their anger, for example: 'Almost all the men in the group reported being particularly angry and prone to violence at times when they felt rejected.'

While rejection may underlie much of these men's anger, Lernor finds that, for women, feeling as if their individuality is denied underlies much of their anger.

Recognising the feelings which produce the anger signal means you can send even clearer, more concrete I messages. Let's say you've arrived late for your class or course. The tutor sends you an I message: 'I feel really angry when you arrive so late.'

The message tells you about the force of her feeling, but it doesn't actually tell you what she feels. Compare it with an I message explaining: 'I feel really worried about whether I'm going to get through the material when we start so late', or 'I'm getting very frustrated with having to stop and start so often'. It's easier to want to help someone who is 'worried' or 'frustrated' than someone who is 'angry', because:

* you know more about what's causing their challenge, and
* you can hear the feelings as being inside *them* rather than 'about' you.

Similarly, a father who has trouble with his kids running round the supermarket while he's shopping will get a better response by explaining: 'I feel embarrassed about the people staring at me', than 'I feel angry at your running'.

The volcano model

Christchurch counsellor and NLP trainer Bryan Royds, suggests that anger can be thought of as the top hole in a volcano. Usually the volcano has side vents, and when pressure builds up lava runs out of these side holes - holes like frustration (the feeling of being blocked), fear, embarrassment, resentment (the feeling of doing more than a fair share), pressure, rejection, and powerlessness (Bryan Royds, 1990, Personal Communication).

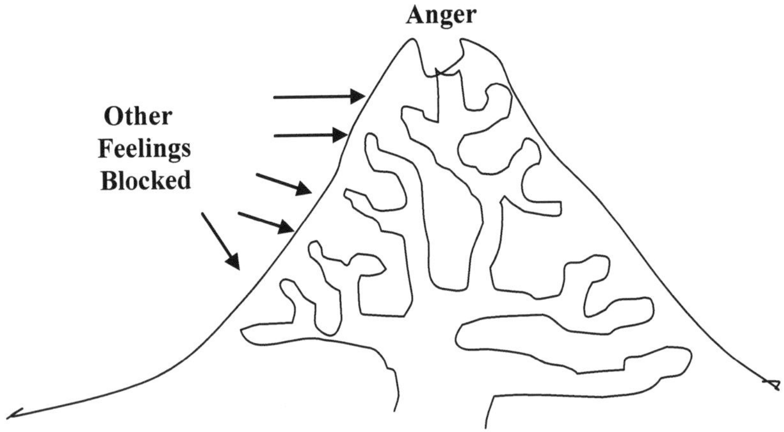

When these feelings aren't permitted (when your upbringing closes off those vents), the force which was behind those feelings doesn't just go away. It builds up and finally explodes out of the top.

Someone who is constantly angry needs to re-open the other vents so that more appropriate feelings can be expressed. This is what I messages do. They take the pressure off the system, leaving more time to enjoy life.

Using I messages to compliment others

So far, we've talked about I messages as a skill to use when you own a challenge, or think you may soon own a challenge.

Expressing yourself in an I message is also an excellent way to tell someone what you appreciate about them. This makes your praise or compliment easier for the other person to accept, and so reduces the chance of the following type of confusion:

Nurse: 'You're doing really well with those crutches Mr Smith.'
Mr Smith: 'Not really. I can't seem to do it the way the physiotherapist showed us.'
Nurse: 'No, you are. You've only just started. You're going great!'
Mr Smith: 'Rubbish. I've never been any good at these sorts of things. It's no use pretending.'
Nurse: 'Don't be so negative.'
Mr Smith: 'Don't be so bloody pushy!'

Lets try it again using I messages and reflective listening, instead of you messages.

Nurse: 'I'm impressed with how quickly you're getting around the ward on those crutches Mr Smith.' [I message]
Mr Smith: 'Well, I get around, but not the way the physiotherapist showed us.'
Nurse: '*You* think you're doing it the wrong way?' [Reflective listening]
Mr Smith: 'Well, I think I'm doing it correctly, but I'm a bit clumsy with them. The physic, made it look rather easier.'
Nurse: 'Compared with her you're not so fluent, eh?' [Reflective listening] 'Well as I say, I'm impressed.' [I message]
Mr Smith: 'Oh well. Maybe I'm not doing so bad then.'

Appreciating the other person is as mportant as resolving conflicts, for the survival of a friendship. John Gottman's research on couples who stay together shows that happy couples saying approximately 100 more words of positive comment per day (a mere 30 seconds more of positive talking) compared to unhappy couples. But those 30 seconds are crucial (Gottman, 1999, p 59-61).

The power of I messages

A good I message is difficult to argue with. Mr Smith is able to hear the nurse's comment as a fact about her. It becomes easier for him to feel good about himself when her compliment isn't a you-message judgement.

Every parent who has tried to praise a child's painting can understand how much safer it would be to say: 'I love the blues and greens in your picture', than: 'What a good painter you are'.

I messages are powerful. It's more powerful to say: 'I love you' than to say 'You're lovable' - 'You're lovable' is a mere judgement; 'I love you' is a personal revelation.

Positive I messages can be written using the same format as those concerning a challenge: behaviour, concrete effects and feelings. For example:

* 'When you do the dishes without being asked, I feel really cared about. It means I can relax for the evening.'

* 'Thanks for getting your work in to me on time. It meant I was able to finish my part of the job without any rush. I enjoyed doing it more and I think I did better work.'

* 'I really appreciated the way you listened to me when we had that argument. It felt like our friendship was safe, even though we disagreed.'

An example from business

In business, millions of dollars often depend on the communication skills used in a few short minutes at a negotiation. A few years ago, the telecommunications company AT&T (affectionately called Ma Bell in America) was negotiating with Boeing airlines (described in Ury, 1991). The purchasing director at Boeing was pleased with the $150 million telecommunications system proposed by AT&T, and asked AT&T to put all their promises in a written contract so AT&T would be liable for any losses. At this point, the AT&T sales chief said "Well, we'll do our best, but you can't hold us liable for the results of lightening strikes and so on." The Boeing director became angry. "You're fooling around with us; you're not willing to commit yourself to what you promised." And when the AT&T sales chief said "Well, lets talk about it; maybe we can put *some* things in writing." the Boeing director and his team walked out the door. Over the next few days, as you can imagine, the AT&T sales chief had a lot of time to think over what he could have said differently. It had happened so quickly. The Boeing people had made a request, and he had a challenge with that request. He needed to find a way to explain his challenge, without arousing mistrust and hostility.

The AT&T sales chief knew that with the Boeing director angry, he was already half way through the I message process. So he began by reflecting "I've been trying to understand your concerns. Correct me if I'm mistaken, but as you and your colleagues at Boeing see it, we've been misleading you, saying we're prepared to give all this service, but not to put it in writing and be held liable for it. ... So naturally you get angry and don't see the point in continuing. Is that right?" "That's right!" exclaimed the Boeing buyer, and after he'd restated that, he asked "So why won't you agree to put your promises in writing?" The AT&T man replied "We will of course put our promises in writing. First, I want to see if I can clear up what's gotten us stuck. I think I'm only beginning to understand it myself." He then explained in I message form how the two companies had different traditions about promises. "We make oral promises and fully expect to deliver on them.... It's a new experience for us to meet with a demand for damages from a client." The negotiations were back on track. The $150 million deal was concluded successfully within a short time.

Summarising

Whether you use I messages to express your appreciation, to tell someone a challenge you are experiencing, or to explain a problem which you want to avoid, they are an ideal first step in assertiveness. An I message may have three parts:

• a non-blameful description of the behaviours and events involved
• an explanation of any real concrete effects on you, and
• a naming of the feeling you have about these behaviours, events or effects. If this feeling is anger, it can help to identify the other feelings which underlie this anger.

When another person has a challenge as a result of what you do or say (for example when someone criticises you, or when a person 'resists' your I message), listening skills can be used. The person's feelings can be acknowledged using reflective listening, before you restate your I message. At times you may use the reflective skill of sorting issues, or ask a question, to clarify the other person's challenge.

Activity 7.2

AIM: to practise writing I messages

1 Write an I message you could send in each of the situations below.

2 Get in to pairs, and check your answers with your partner, ensuring they fit the definition of an I message given in the previous pages.

3 Discuss what the other person's likely reaction to your I message would be, and write a reflective listening response you could make to that reaction.

4 Report back to the group.

Nine situations

a Your flatmate has the stereo turned up so loud that you find it hard to concentrate on the study you're doing in your room.

b Your eight-year-old daughter borrows your hammer and leaves it out in the rain. When you eventually find it a week later, it is already rusty.

c You are a nurse, and you observe a fellow nurse changing a patient's dressing without washing her hands first, thus risking infection. (Note that there may be no concrete effects on you in this situation.)

d You are working in a psychiatric unit and one of the clients there has been interrupting your staff meeting every five minutes, to ask about their medication, check whether their relatives have rung, and find out if you've finished yet.

e A client of yours arranges an appointment for 4 pm - the time you usually leave work. You wait for half an hour and then realise he's not coming. The next day he rings to ask for another 4 pm appointment, without mentioning the previous day.

f Your family has one car and you are hoping to be able to use it this Saturday evening to go out to a friend's place. You want to tell your spouse, to ensure he or she doesn't have other plans.

g You plan to watch live TV coverage of a sports game at 3.30 pm today, and want to advise the rest of the household so that others don't interrupt you.

h When you arrive home from work you find that one of the others in your household has rescued all the clothes you had out on the clothesline from an afternoon downpour. He or she has also folded them ready to be put away. You plan to thank them.

i You are writing to thank a work colleague of yours who wrote excellent notes explaining what phonecalls you received during your two days off work earlier this week.

Activity 7.3

AIM: to practise saying I messages

1 Think of a recent situation in which you owned a challenge about someone else's behaviour (for example a friend, a relative, or someone you met in the course of your work). Work out a non-blameful description of the behaviour, the concrete effects on you (if any), and the feelings you had. Write an I message you could send if that situation occurred again.

2 Check your I messages in pairs, and ensure they fit the earlier definition of an I message. Discuss what the other person's likely reaction to your I message would be (assuming for now that they stay in the room). Write down a reflective listening response you could make to that. Check your responses in pairs to ensure you have used reflective listening and not a roadblock (see page 88 for the definition of a roadblock).

3 In your pairs, practise sending the I message, hearing the other person's response, and using reflective listening. Continue for a few minutes, using only these two types of response, and check how it goes. Initially, get your partner to roleplay the person to whom you're sending the I message, while you act as yourself. If you find your partner's roleplaying less convincing, reverse the roles so that your partner plays you, and you act as the person you have the concern with.

4 Discuss in a group how these roleplays, went. You should have reached one of three conclusions:

a agreement that the person will change

b a conflict of values or metaprograms: the person doesn't believe their behaviour has any concrete effect on you; they think it's 'not your business'

c a conflict of needs: each of you has a challenge. They don't want to change because it creates a new challenge for them.

Activity 7.4

AIM: to rediscover the side vents on your 'anger volcano'

1 Individually, write answers to the following questions:

a. In which situations do you most often get angry?
b. Who do you most often get angry at?
c . What body feelings do you have when you are angry?

d. What do you say to yourself when you are angry?
e. What images flash through your mind when you are angry?
f . In what ways do you act when you are angry?
g . Considering all your answers to the above questions, to what other feelings is your anger related, further down in the 'volcano'?

2 Discuss in pairs the answer to question (g), and check what else you learned doing this exercise.

Summary

It's exciting to realise that you can express your own feelings and opinions in ways that don't put down either others or yourself.

In this chapter you've learned the skills that go with this assertive attitude. They begin with acknowledging your own assertive rights and learning to love yourself. This includes recognising inside yourself the feelings that underlie anger (such as hurt, fear, frustration and powerlessness), so they can be more directly expressed. It includes giving up the codependent concern entirely with others' happiness, and the addictive compulsion only for one's own 'fix'.

The concrete expression of the assertive attitude is the use of non-blaming I messages to express your opinions and feelings. In dealing with others who own a challenge about your behaviour (such as people who are upset by an I message you've sent), the most useful assertive response is to use listening skills. Reflective listening and open questions not only help the other person feel understood in the assertive situation, they also make it easier for them to listen to you and change.

Chapter 8: Resolving conflict

KEY CONCEPTS

- Recognising three types of conflict
- Conflict prevention: environment and communication style
- Effects of using power over others
- Win-win conflict resolution skills
- Resolving internal conflicts

What is conflict?

AIM: to be able to distinguish conflicts of needs from conflicts of values, and to identify two main methods of preventing conflicts.

Conflict

Whenever I ask people why they've come to one of our communication skills courses, 90 per cent of the answers will concern conflict.

You don't have to look far internationally to realise that resolving conflict is the single most important social challenge of our age.

For me, teaching conflict resolution is a delight. The skills that help people resolve conflicts are easy to understand, and learning them always produces a kind of 'aha' experience. 'So that's how it all fits together', is a common comment, as people realise that the skills we've studied so far (especially reflective listening, I messages and problem solving) are the ingredients for this next process. Once you've learned to use those skills as taught in Chapters 4, 5 and 7, this chapter will give you the most crucial step to successful relationships.

Simply stated, a conflict is a situation where two or more people each 'own a challenge ' about the same situation. Usually, as one of them tries to solve their challenge, it creates a challenge for the other, so each resists accepting the other's solution:

* You want to go shopping, but your three-year-old daughter wants to stay at home and watch TV
* You want to wear some new shoes to town, and your best friend says she won't be seen in public with someone wearing that colour.
* You're trying to study and the people in the house next door are having a party
* You think your spouse should spend more time with you, but he or she wants more space to be alone.
* You and a friend want to watch different TV channels and there's only one TV set.

Types of conflict

Interestingly, all conflicts fit into one of the three following categories:

- closed communication loops
- conflicts of values or metaprograms, or
- conflicts of needs.

The simplest to resolve are closed communication loops, which are misunderstandings' resulting from when people forget to use I messages and reflective listening. We'll discuss these later in this section.

Sometimes, even though you've sent a clear I message and listened fully to the other person's response, there is still a disagreement. This could be because the other person doesn't believe your complaint is any of your business. They don't think you have a 'real' challenge at all. An example would be if you told your partner you wanted them to change their hairstyle. Your partner would probably suspect that their hairstyle really had no concrete effect on you and was 'none of your business'. This situation is a conflict of values or metaprograms (we'll define and discuss these terms in the next chapter).

At least one of the people in a conflict of values or metaprograms does not believe the other person is concretely affected. (Even though you may be convinced that your partner's hairstyle gives you serious headaches, if they don't believe it, it's a values issue). Such conflicts include disagreements about religion, sexual activity, clothing styles, use of language, amount of time spent together, standards of work, and standards of behaviour. John Gottman found that 69% of all relationship conflicts were conflicts of values, in both successful and unsuccessful relationships (Gottman and Silver, 1999, p 130).

Conflicts of needs are usually easier to solve. An example would be you and your partner each wanting to watch a different channel on the one TV: each person can understand that the other is affected by the situation, but it seems as if when one of them gets their way, the other will lose out.

Conflicts of needs are the main subject of this chapter. They will be fully discussed later, in the section 'Conflict resolution'.

The following examples show how various situations fit into one or the other category:

Conflict of needs	**Conflict of values/metaprograms**
You want to go shopping but your three-year-old wants to watch TV	You think your spouse should spend more time with you, but he or she wants more space.
You're trying to study and the people next door are having a party.	You think one of your work colleagues needs to be more polite with clients. They disagree.
Both you and your best friend want to use the same library text book to study for an exam.	You don't want your children to swear, but they say everyone does it nowdays.

Preventing conflict - the environment

Most people would agree that the very best way to sort out any conflict is not to create it in the first place. In fact, there are two main ways we can prevent conflicts:

* we can change the environment, or
* we can change our communication.

Communications experts Thomas Gordon and Linda Adams have developed a very simple way of thinking up new ideas for changing the environment. They say that conflicts can be prevented by:

* adding things to the environment
* removing things from the environment
* reorganising the environment, or
* planning better use of time in the environment.

Take the average home. Depending on what the common sources of conflict are:

* adding might include inviting people to tea, doing a project together, adding a room, or getting foldaway furniture to create more space

* removing could mean agreeing on rooms where food won't be eaten, turning off radios and the TV, using headphones to listen to music, or giving away unused furniture

* reorganising could involve rearranging furniture to provide useful room areas; changing tea time to fit in with people's other interests; keeping a list of phone numbers by the phone, or sorting the books on the bookshelf

* planning might include writing important dates on the calendar, precooking some meals and keeping them in the freezer for emergencies, or prewarning others when you are planning to go out for the evening.

All of these ideas reduce the chance that people will have conflicts of needs. When a group begins its time together by working out a contract (see Chapter 1), it is changing the environment to reduce conflicts. Understandings about confidentiality, starting times, and so on are important ways of planning ahead to prevent disagreement.

A communication model

So far, all the communication skills we've discussed in this book have been important ways of preventing conflicts. Many disagreements are the result of people not expressing themselves in assertive I messages, or not listening fully to others and checking their understanding with reflective listening. The following diagram was developed by communications researchers Claude Shannon and Warren Weaver (1963) to explain how such misunderstandings happen.

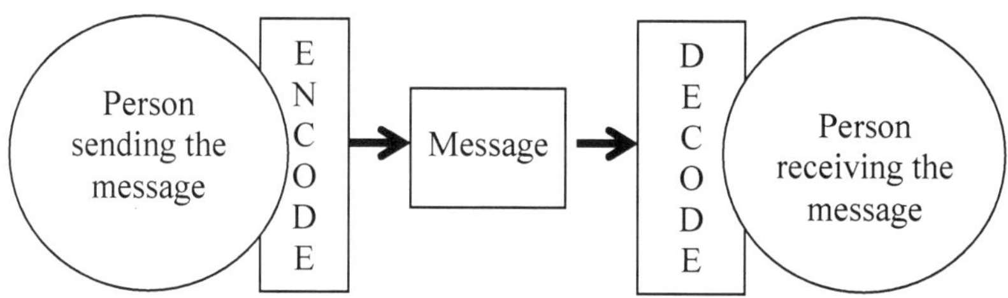

As this diagram shows, when one person sends a message to another, the person sending the message (represented as the circle on the left) has to 'encode' their thoughts and feelings -they have to find some words or actions that will be a code for their meaning. The person receiving the message (in the circle on the right) can't read the sender's mind: they have to 'decode' the words or actions to understand what was meant. In the following example, a person who feels hungry asks the person cooking: 'When is dinner?' The words are their code. The receiver has to decode the message to understand what was meant.

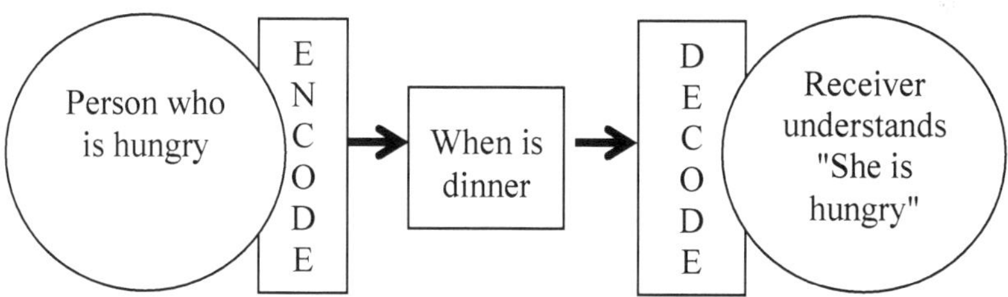

But what if the receiver decodes wrongly? Perhaps this receiver can remember another time when someone asked: 'When is dinner?', and that person was angry about dinner being late. This memory now"interferes" with the decoding process. The receiver might well now decode this message as meaning that the sender is angry. After all, 'When is dinner?' is not a very clear code for this message -'I'm hungry' (an I message) is a clearer code. A smart receiver could also check that they got the right message by using reflective listening, for example:

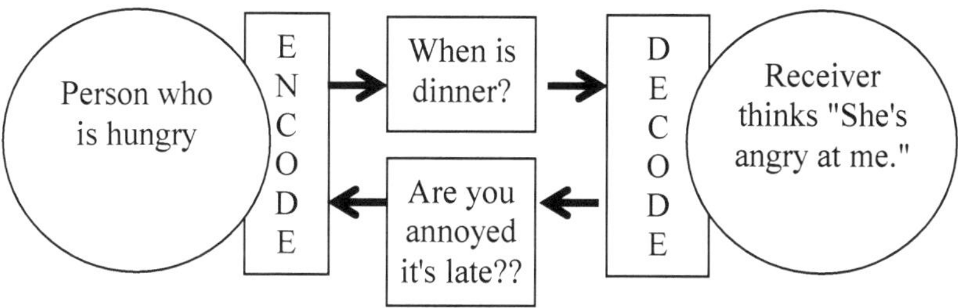

This will help the sender to know whether they've been understood. The sender's next coded message will then be a clearer' l message' code (for example: 'No, I'm just hungry, and that sure smells good!'). Reflective listening encourages clear I messages.

Closed communication loops

What happens when nobody bothers to send clear I messages and nobody checks their understanding using reflective listening? Messages go back and forth, and each person *thinks* they know what is happening.

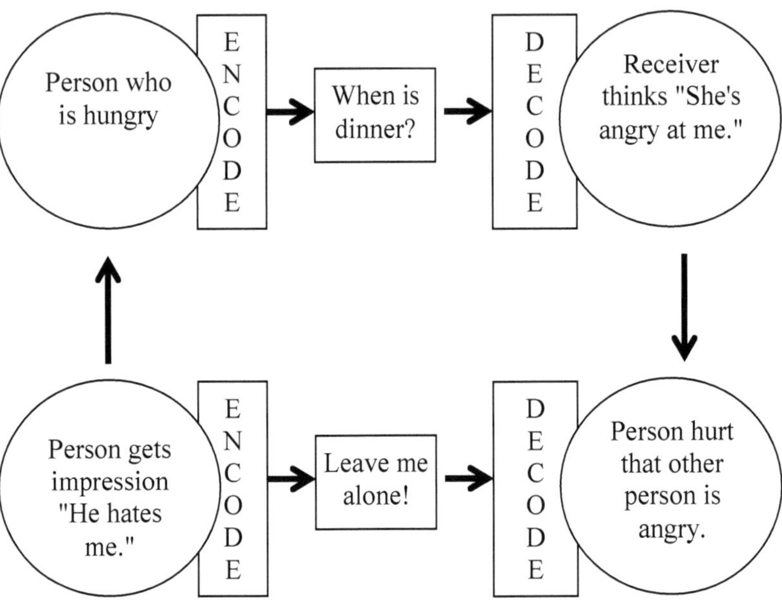

Following the diagram above, the person who was only hungry ends up believing that the other person hates her. She might well then storm out of the kitchen slamming the door. This will 'prove' to the cook that she was angry all the time. When the cook avoids the other person later that evening, this will 'prove' to the questioner that the cook really does hate her.

This is a closed communication loop. Sometimes the unclear message is not even sent in words. It may be just the way the person raises their eyebrows, looks away, frowns or sighs that is decoded as 'he or she is attacking me'.

In Chapter 3 we discussed several examples of closed communication loops based on body language. If you think carefully about your own relationships, you can probably recognise this sort of misunderstanding. When 1 counsel couples, most of what I do involves helping them identify such loops. The solutions are very simple. Whenever a person feels hurt or 'under attack' they need to check carefully what the message was, in sensory specific terms (i.e. what did they see, hear or touch that they decoded as an attack). They can then use reflective listening and I messages to 'open up' the communication loop.

Activity 8.1

AIM: to use Gordon and Adams' model for modifying the environment to prevent conflicts

1 Choose an environment that everyone is familiar with (for example a workplace you all work in or the environment the group meets in).

2 Individually, list ideas for ways to modify that environment, under the headings: a) adding, c) reorganising, b) removing, d) planning.

3 Collect the ideas on a whiteboard or large sheet of paper.

To recap

A conflict occurs when two or more people 'own a challenge' about the same situation. This may be:

* a closed communication loop, where reflective listening and I messages will clarify the situation
* a conflict of needs, where each person can understand that the other owns a challenge, but fears that if one gets their way, the other will lose
* a conflict of values or metaprograms, where one person doesn't believe their behaviour concretely affects the other.

Conflicts can be prevented by:

* changing the environment (adding, removing, reorganising, and planning)
* using I messages and reflective listening.

Power over others

AIM: to be able to describe the three basic effects of solving conflicts by using power over others.

Obedience

A psychology experiment is taking place in a central city building (this could be in a New Zealand city: the experiment has been repeated in several western countries).

In one room a man sits strapped to a chair with an electric wire attached to his wrist. He is memorising a list of words, and has been told that when he makes a mistake he will be given an electric shock.

In the next room sits the 'teacher' at a control panel. He/she (the experiment has been done with both men and women) has come to these rooms in response to a newspaper advertisement. The teacher has been told that this is a study in the use of punishment. Beside him/her stands a lab technician psychologist in a grey technician's coat, who says when to give the electric shocks.

They can see the man strapped to the chair through a one-way mirror. As the experiment goes on, the psychologist instructs the hired teacher to give heavier and heavier electric shocks. They turn up the dial to a level which is marked 'Danger - Severe Shock, 330 Volts'. As the shocks become more severe the man strapped to the chair says he wants to stop. He begins to beg to be let out. He explains that he has a heart condition. Finally, he appears capable only of emitting agonised screams, and then he is silent.

The psychologist does not threaten the teacher in any way, but he calmly insists: 'It is absolutely essential that you continue the experiment...'.

Obedience is not a virtue

In fact, the person strapped to the chair is a trained actor, and he is not receiving any shocks. The real aim of this disturbing experiment is to find out how long the hired teacher will continue giving what he/she believes are severe shocks.

How many people in this situation would obey the psychologist's orders and 'murder' the man in the chair? Psychologist Stanley Milgram, who ran this experiment, asked psychiatrists how many people they thought would obediently kill in this way 'One in a thousand', they told him. The true answer was always more than 60 per cent.

Most people in our society are obedient enough to make excellent Nazi concentration camp commanders. The horrific behaviour we witness in war could be done by most 'normal' human beings.

Milgram's teachers often told the psychologist they wanted to stop, trembled, stuttered, laughed nervously or groaned... but they went right on pressing the button. One said afterwards: 'I believe I conducted myself behaving obediently, and carried on instructions as I always do. So I said to my wife "Well, here we are. And I think I did a good job." She said: "Suppose the man was dead?" [The man replied]: 'So he's dead. I did my job!' (From Obedience To Authority by Stanley Milgram, 1974.)

Dr Jerry Burger, of Santa Clara University, replicated this experiment in 2007. Again, the vast majority of the 29 men and 41 women taking part were willing to push the button knowing it would cause pain to another human. Even when another actor entered the room and questioned what was happening, most were still prepared to continue.

Obedience is not a virtue. Obedience means giving over to someone else's control every virtue you might otherwise have. Obedience is the death of virtue.

Effects of power over others

The word power can be used to refer to energy or 'personal power'. In the former sense, everyone can become powerful without endangering anyone else. But power over others is a different matter. Power over others refers to the ability to reward and punish, to meet someone's needs, or not to meet them. It is the ability to create obedience.

We all have a certain amount of this type of power. Most of us know ways in which we could reward or punish our friends if we really wanted to. When we choose to use that power, though, the risks are horrendous.

Power over others is what Anne Wilson Schaef (see page 35) calls a key part of the White Male System. In many of our organisations power over others is routinely used as a way of dealing with conflicts. It so happens that most of these power holders are white and male. They are also often middle-aged, wealthy, able bodied and heterosexual.

But power over others can be, and is, used by people of every description. What happens when a person with power over you uses that power to get you to do what they want? Some people have a belief that being ordered around 'never did me any harm!' However, it's different when, in our communication classes, we ask people to remember a specific time when someone else coerced them by using rewards or punishment. They may recall a time when a teacher, police officer, parent, government official, boss, spouse or friend used power over them. As they think back over exactly what they heard and saw, remember how they felt, and check what they did in response to this situation (for example how they behaved with that powerful person in subsequent situations), they remember that needs and feelings don't simply disappear because someone else won the battle.

Their reactions fit into three categories:

1 Fight reactions: such as arguing, paying back later on, taking it out on others, ganging up with others, and feeling angry.
2 Flight reactions: such as lying, hiding feelings, cheating, and withdrawing into themselves.
3 Obedience: which includes conforming to the rules without thinking about it any more, avoiding taking the initiative, and 'greasing up' or 'crawling' to the person in power to try and get in their good books.

Punishment

When people want to stop someone from doing something, one obvious and ieasy' way is to punish them. At times this achieves the desired result, and certainly it often makes the punisher feel better because they have got their feelings out (though more often the punisher feels guilty that they have caused pain). But what results does it have for the person who is punished?

Since the 1940s an enormous number of studies have looked at the actual effect of punishment. The most important fact, confirmed again and again, is that punishment produces feelings of anger (although these feelings may be hidden), and this anger is often expressed as aggression. Increased violence is the most guaranteed effect of physical punishments in particular. Research also shows that people who are punished will do everything possible to avoid contact with the person whom they see as punishing - everything from avoiding answering questions, or sulking, to running away physically. The 'lesson' that punishment teaches most effectively is that others are powerful and can hurt us. (From Spare *the Rod,* by Ritchie, J. and Ritchie, J. 1981)

Rewards

We know from research, of course, that rewards are more successful than punishment in achieving obedience. But people who use such rewards need to be aware of how limited the success of even this method is. Research shows that people who are paid for playing with enjoyable puzzles soon play less with the puzzles than people who play without being paid. Children promised a reward for using a particular toy find they want to use it less. Social psychologist David Myers (1983) explains that when rewards are overused 'as happens in classrooms where teachers dictate behaviour and use rewards to control the children, child-driven learning may diminish.... My younger son eagerly consumed six or eight library books a week - until our library started a reading club which promised a party to those who read ten books in three months. Three weeks later he began checking out only one or two books during our weekly visit. Why? "Because you only need to read ten books, you know".'

This doesn't mean it's wrong to praise people or give presents; simply that using this as a technique to control them will, at best, produce obedience, not enthusiasm.

The power user

Power is not even very pleasant for the person who uses it. I have worked with hundreds of men, parents, teachers, bosses, and others who use power in their relationships. All of them come to recognise the fact that their use of power is building resentment in others. They often feel guilty about the threats and punishments they use, and resent the constant struggle to stay on top. 'But what can I do?' they explain, 'I can't just let the other person win. I have to use power.' This may be true. Even if you recognise the damage that using power over others causes, you may still decide it's worth it. We'll discuss that situation in a moment. The saddest thing about the use of power over others is that, usually, it simply isn't necessary. In most conflicts you can use the skills we explain in this chapter and the next to resolve your conflicts so both you and the other person win. Neither the authoritarian 'I win -you lose' style, nor the permissive 'you win - I lose' method is worth making a way of life.

When is power necessary?

In the real world there are some situations where you will try and control another person's behaviour by using power. Thomas Gordon (1974) suggests that these could include:

* situations where you don't have any say in the rules: if you work for a company you won't be able to negotiate solutions that give away their property; if you are a teacher you won't be able to arrange for someone to break a school rule. (You can, of course, work to change such rules.)

* situations where your own need is overriding, for example, you don't have to put up with a child repeatedly hitting you - forcibly preventing them may well be worth their response of frustration or resentment

* situations where another person is obviously in danger: it wouldn't make sense to calmly watch someone walk in front of a speeding car while sending the clear I message: 'I'm really worried that that car will hit you'! Their initial annoyance at being grabbed and pulled off the road will usually be worth coping with.

* situations where there is no time to discuss the matter: if a conflict arises ten minutes before your plane is due to take off, you may decide it's worth temporarily refusing to sort it out

* situations where talking to the person is impossible. This will include many conflicts involving children less than two years old, and conflicts with people who are drunk or fully unconnected to reality.

Minimising the effects

Even in these cases, it's worth remembering the damage power over others causes. You can reduce the damage to your relationship by:

* using only the minimum force necessary to solve your challenge. A child who is hitting you may need to be held, or even confined to a space away from you, until they can agree not to hit you. They don't need to be hit (which is much the same behaviour you're trying to stop), have insults yelled at them, be shut in their room for the afternoon, and so on. Doing these extra things would increase their resentment and make more work for yourself.
* explaining afterwards how you came to use power, and assuring the other person that this is not your usual intention
* using reflective listening to acknowledge their resentment, and spending time rebuilding your relationship
* planning how to avoid that situation in future.

These last three steps can be done quite simply, for example by saying: 'I'd like to talk about what happened before. I don't mean to push you around - I only did that because I couldn't find a way to safely sort it out at the time. I guess you felt pretty annoyed, and I'd like to try and sort out some agreement so we don't get into that situation again'.

To recap

When you use power over others - that is, your ability to reward or punish them they will respond by either:

- fighting back
- flight and avoidance, or
- the shutting down we call obedience.

You yourself are likely to feel resented by them, and frustrated with the constant struggle.

It may be necessary to use power over others, when:

- there is a rule outside your control
- your own need is overriding
- the other person is clearly in danger
- there is no time for discussion
- talking with the person is impossible.

In such cases you can use the minimum force necessary, and discuss the event afterwards using I messages and reflective listening.

Activity 8.2

AIM: to recognise our personal style of responding to the use of power

1 Relax, using either the relaxation exercise (activity 2.3, see page 48) or a similar process.

2 Now recall an incident from your adult life when someone used power (the ability to reward or punish) to get you to do what they wanted. This could be a teacher, parent, boss, spouse, friend, or a person in a position of authority in some agency. Such events come in big as well as small sizes, so bear in mind that you can choose an incident which feels safe to remember and that, if some other incident intrudes, you will be able to I place' the unwanted incident in a box beside you, lock it in, and move the box far enough away so you can feel comfortable and find a more useful example.

3 Recall in detail the events of this incident: the time of day, the air temperature, the surroundings you were in, and whether you were sitting or standing as events happened. You can rerun the story like a video film, listening to how you and others talk, and watching what happens. Then, after about a two-minute pause, check how you felt about these events and what things you did then or later as a result.

4 Now return to the room you are in - become aware of your surroundings - and recall the effects of the use of power on you. Discuss in pairs.

5 Report back to the group. The group leader could list people's responses under the three headings 'Fight', 'Flight', and 'Obedience'.

Conflict resolution

AIM: to be able to resolve internal and interpersonal conflicts of aim needs, using win-win problem solving / solution finding

Win-win solutions

Conflicts of needs are inevitable in any relationship. They happen between people who work together, between workers and their clients, between friends, between relatives and between lovers. But it isn't inevitable that someone will lose in such conflicts. Here you'll learn the key to creating caring relationships where everyone wins.

In a conflict of needs, two people have each developed a plan to meet their need or solve some challenge, and the plans don't fit together. Let's say I plan to use our family car this Saturday night to go out to a sports club meeting. When I tell my partner, she says she also planned to use the car this Saturday night to go and visit a friend. Obviously we can't both use the car for the whole evening.

In such a situation, most people don't despair. They realise that what really matters is that I get to my sports club meeting and my partner gets to visit her friend. Using the car for the night is just the particular plan: the solution each of us thought up to achieve these more basic goals (or, to use other words, meet these more basic needs: the word 'need' here simply means a basic 'want', or goal).

Once we realise this, we can invent several solutions which will fully meet both our basic goals. For example:

1. I drive my partner to her friend's house and pick her up after the meeting.
2. My partner drives me to the meeting and picks me up after their visit.
3. I use the car and my partner's friend visits our place.
4. My partner uses the car and we arrange the meeting at our place.
5. Someone else picks me up on the way to the meeting and my partner uses the car.
6. My partner's friend picks her up and I use the car.
7. One of us gets a taxi and we share the taxi fare, while the other uses the car.

No compromising

None of these solutions is a compromise, in the sense that none of them results in one of us giving up any part of our basic goal. And none of these solutions is a win-lose solution where one of us uses our power to win at the other's expense. (A compromise might be: I go to the first half of the meeting, and my partner goes for the last half of the evening - we both give up a little. Compromises are the result of talking at the level of solutions. Win-win conflict resolution results from talking at the level of needs.)

This win-win method is really a variation of the solution-finding process (discussed in Chapter 4). Here are the steps which Thomas Gordon and others identify as win-win conflict resolution, compared to the basic solution-finding model we described then.

Win-win process	Basic solution-finding
1. Define conflict in terms of goals- needs 2. Brainstorm solutions to meet all needs 3. Check how well these meet all needs 4. Choose the best solution/s 5. Act 6. Evaluate how well it worked	1. Define the challenge 2. Set a goal 3. Planning actions Planning actions, continued 4. Act 5. Evaluate how it worked

An example

I used the win-win method to resolve conflicts with my son Francis from when he was three and-a-half years old, so by the time he was six he understood it fairly well. (Even though he couldn't have listed the steps, he knew 'intuitively' how it worked.)

Like everyone, I'm not perfect, and sometimes I forget how easily conflicts can be solved to suit everyone. One evening, when Francis was six, he reminded me of this very skilfully. We were out visiting a friend of mine, and it was later than the bedtime Francis and I had arranged for him (we'd arranged this using the win-win method: Francis liked to be read a short story to help him relax at bedtime; I didn't want to be reading or entertaining him after eight o'clock. Having a regular eight o'clock bedtime suited us both). On this occasion, I'd chosen to visit the friend as she was upset - I planned to use my listening skills. I figured I'd be willing for Francis to stay up later this one night, so I suggested he should watch TV while we talked.

Unfortunately, Francis seemed to want to climb over me as I listened to the friend (being climbed on is an occupational hazard of early parenthood). I sent him a strong 'I-you' message: 'You can go and sleep in my friend's spare bed, or you can watch TV, but I'm trying to listen here and I can't do it when you climb over me.' 'Well,' he said, 'I'd really like to sort this out so we both get what we want.'

Now, I'd been all set to order him out of the room (after all, I figured, there are some times when maybe you have to use power). But this statement of his really hooked me. It's a very good way to start win-win conflict resolution. If he'd said: 'Well I want to get my way', I'd have simply said 'Forget it!' Instead, he began by saying he wanted to meet my needs too.

Francis' solution

This was a bit embarrassing, in front of my friend, but I knew there weren't any other solutions, so I told Francis: 'Yeah, I like to sort things out that way too, usually, but there isn't any other way this time.'

'Well, I'd like us each to say what the challenge is', he suggested (step one of the win-win process).

'OK', I agreed, thinking I'd quickly prove to him that the win-win method couldn't work and get back to listening to my friend, 'my challenge is that I want to be able to listen to my friend, and yours is you want to play with me. Right?' (This was my attempt at an I message and reflective listening.)

'No/ he replied, 'I'm really tired. I'd like to go to sleep but I don't want to sleep in the spare bed because it's a strange room and it scares me. But I don't want to watch TV.'

Wow. This stunned me! It reminded me how easily I assume I know what others want, when I haven't really listened at all.

'Fair enough,' I countered, 'but even so, we still can't solve it. Either you watch TV or sleep in there.'

'Do you have any other ideas for solutions?' he asked.

'No', I replied, annoyed at such a silly question.

'Well, I have a few', he offered, and then listed five possible solutions, each of which would solve both our concerns (step two of the win-win process). 1 was now even more embarrassed. He was right - there are always more ideas (see activity 4.4, page 82).

'OK, do any of those', I agreed.

'Well, I think we should check which one will work best', he suggested (step three of the process).

So we did. The solution we chose (steps four and five) was for him to wrap up in a blanket and lie down on the floor by my feet. In five minutes he was asleep, safe and rested, perfectly meeting his need and mine. Naturally, the next day I checked how the arrangement went (step six of the win-win process): 'Well I guess I solved that challenge last night pretty well, eh Francis?' There was an amused smile.

How to start

Dr Dudley Weeks (1994) has worked with conflicting parties in over 60 countries including Rwanda and Bosnia. He emphasises the importance of viewing conflict as one part of a relationship; a part that sheds light on the rest of the relationship, and that can best be resolved by bearing in mind the resources of the rest of the relationship.

Weeks says that your initial opening comments have a lot to do with setting the "frame" or atmosphere within which conflict resolution occurs. Remember that in his conflict with me, my son Francis began by saying "I'd really like to sort this out so we both get what we want." Dudley weeks has explored such opening comments more fully. While opening comments need to be short enough not to sound like a monologue, and naturally phrased, he suggests that these comments can:

- establish partnership "I believe we are in this together, and need each other to work it out"
- refer to the whole relationship "This is only one aspect of our relationship."
- Affirm possibilities "I'm sure together we can generate many options for solving this."
- Accept disagreement "Disagreeing doesn't mean we can't remember things we agree on."
- Acknowledge specific difficulties "I know in the past we've had trouble due to our tendency to.... This time lets experiment by..."

The way to get people from talking about their particular solution to thinking about basic goals or needs is simple. To define my own needs I use I messages. To define their needs I use reflective listening. For example, Francis' statement: 'I'm really tired" is a nice clear I message. . His invitation: 'Do you have any ideas how we could solve this for both of us', is an example of how an open question can be used to move on to step two, once feelings are aired and the challenge is defined for each of us.

Sometimes, having people unload their feelings in step one is the most important part of the whole process. At the start, people in a conflict are often so upset that they don't believe things can ever be sorted out. When they realise they're being listened to, however, they begin to remember that their 'opponent' is only another human being, who may also have needs and goals of their own. Win-win conflict resolution cannot be fully used until you have understood its building blocks: I messages and reflective listening. Once you have those skills, it's child's play, as Francis proved.

In the family

Conflict resolution can be used in every area of your life: we use it routinely to solve challenges in my family. I've heard people theorise that' women like to know who's boss', or 'kids like to have limits set', but I've never yet met a person of any sex or age who prefers to have their needs overridden.

It's certainly true that some people are wiser, more knowledgeable and more experienced than others. But no amount of experience means you know more about how someone else feels, or what their challenge is, than they do: on that subject, they are always the expert. You'll get better decisions by understanding everyone's actual needs than you will by using only your own knowledge.

Remember, win-win conflict resolution doesn't mean you have to compromise or give in. If you feel as though you've lost something, then you don't yet have a real win-win solution, and it would be best to sort it out again.

I train instructors for Dr Thomas Gordon's Parent Effectiveness Training (PET), which teaches parents the win-win method described here. Our experience, based on working with hundreds of New Zealand parents, is that the method works even with very young children.

In a review of 26 separate studies comparing PET to other methods (by Robert Cedar of Boston University), the PET approach was significantly more successful, especially in increasing children's self-esteem and willingness to cooperate with their parents. Even with a child too young to discuss their needs (say younger than three years old), you can still use the win-win attitude when in a conflict. This means asking yourself: 'What was this child's more basic need or goal, and how could I help them meet that in a way that suits me too?' (Gordon, 1970)

Here are some examples of using this win-win attitude with younger children (as discussed in *The Aware Baby,* by A.J. Solter, 1990):

Situation	**Parent's need**	**Child's need**	**A possible solution**
1. Shopping. Child pulls things off supermarket shelves.	Not to have to put things back on shelf.	To feel he is involved and helping.	Point out one or two things he ca get down for you.

2. Child refuses to let parent put clothes on her. Parent is in a hurry.	To get out as soon as possible.	To put on her own clothes.	Find 1 or 2 clothing items she can put on herself while you do the rest.
3. Child draws on the wall with crayons.	Not to have to repaint the wall.	To enjoy drawing on a large surface.	Get some cheap newsprint paper and pin it on an area of bedroom wall for her to use.

This simplified approach has also been shown to be useful in relating to anyone with intellectual impairment.

In work situations

'Excuse me, Richard, can we talk to you?' Three students from one of my nursing classes peered in through my office door.

'Sure, come in.'

'We're wondering if you'd be able to cancel our class tomorrow. It's the only class we've got all day, so if you cancel it we can use the day to study for Friday's test.'

I nodded, getting out my diary. 'Hmm. Well, I see the challenge. It's a nuisance to have a class from one to three in the middle of the day.'

'Yes,' one of them added, 'and some people have to bus in to town just for that session, so it virtually wipes out their day'

'The challenge is,' I continued, 'that it's the only time I have to go over the instructions for next week's fieldwork visit. I really need that two hours this week.'

'Oh well.' Looks of disappointment. 'It was worth a try.' They turned to go.

'Well, hold on. Maybe we can sort it out, though. What other time do you have free this week? If it's a time when I don't have another class to teach, 1 don't mind doing the session then.'

One of them got out her timetable. 'How about tomorrow from three to five?

We've got psychology then, but I know we're going to get a study guide to do, so maybe we could use that time.'

'Suits me/ I agreed, 'providing you check it out with your psychology tutor first, and get back to me with her "OK".'

'Great! We'll be back in a few minutes.' They left hastily.

Situations like this arise continually in work relationships. Technically, it seemed either as if the students had to put up with a 'wasted' day, or I had to ruin my fieldwork plans. But once we recognise our basic goals, many more solutions are possible.

Schools

In my experience, my willingness to use win-win processes creates a sense of cooperation which I can rely on when I need my students' or workmates' help. Studies of its use in schools (under the name 'Dr Thomas Gordon's Teacher Effectiveness Training') show results such as a 90 per cent reduction in discipline problems. The New Zealand Roper report on violence recommended that all New Zealand teachers learn TET. (Ministerial Committee of Inquiry Into Violence *1987),*

In research at a New Zealand High School, the late Margot Hamblett and I taught our 26 hour course in co-operative communication to ten teachers. We taught the same skills explained here. We studied seven classes (200 students) three of which had these trained teachers taking more than half their sessions. At six month follow-up, we were able to show marked differences between the classes who had our trained teachers and those who did not (Bolstad and Hamblett, September, 2000). Firstly, students' attitude to school was different. The teachers we trained reported that their biggest problem, low motivation, had simply ceased to be an issue in their classes. Their students agreed; the number who rated themselves as "not at all" wanting to co-operate at school dropped from 6% to 4% in the non-trained teachers' classes, but from 6% to zero in the classes experiencing the trained teachers. The number of students who said that they asked questions in class "whenever they could" dropped in the control group from 12% to 3% -they became less motivated as the year went on. In the group with trained teachers, it rose slightly to 13%.

But the most interesting information was not about the relationship between the teachers and the students. It was about the relationship between the students themselves. The school had been very concerned about student-student violence (bullying), and instituted its own program to reduce bullying. We asked students to confidentially rate how often they saw a student threaten, hit or injure another student in the last week. The number who said this never happened remained stable at about 40% in the control group, but rose to 64% in the group with NLP trained teachers. This and other similar results strongly supported our hypothesis that students would model effective communication skills from their teachers. When you learn these skills, not only will you achieve better results, but others around you will benefit and change their style of relating too.

Julie McCracken is an NLP trainer and high school teacher who teaches these skills to high school students for their use in mediating student-student conflicts. She describes using the method to create class agreements about how to work together. In the first class she used it, she says "The previous academic record of many of these students indicated that approximately 50% would not pass the exam and 25% of them should not have been in the class at all. Despite this, at the end of the year, 90% passed the final bursary exam and the class average was well above the national. In addition, for 85% of students, this subject produced their highest bursary exam result. For me personally, the situation changed from being stressful and frustrating, to a relaxing and enjoyable experience where I could concentrate fully on my goals of facilitating learning and building self esteem. Students supported and helped each other and I became the last person they sought assistance from rather than_the first. As a result, my workload actually went down. This simple process changed the entire nature of the class and was the single most important step towards creating a co-operative learning environment. I now use this process with all of my classes, usually within the first two weeks of the year, depending on how quickly I can establish rapport with the students." (McCracken 2000)

In large organisations, the results are similar. Pehr Gyllenhammar, president of the Volvo corporation, reported that its use in his Swedish plant resulted in absenteeism dropping by 50 per cent, employee turnover being cut to 25 per cent of previous levels, and the quality of the product improving (described in Thomas Gordon's book *Leader Effectiveness Training,* 1978, p 1-4).

The results

Notice that win-win conflict resolution doesn't produce standard solutions. Each agreement is specifically designed for those people at that time. What suits one person perfectly may be a plan which another person would feel compromised by. What counts is that you find the best solution for you.

Win-win solutions don't need policing. That's their beauty. People are motivated to keep up their end of the bargain when they know it meets their own needs perfectly. This is a very old principle, on which all human societies depend. It is summed up by the English saying: 'You scratch my back and I'll scratch yours', and the Maori proverb: 'He kai, he kai' ('some food for some food'), said by the chief Rakai-paka when messengers came from his coastal Whakatane relative, Tamatea-rehe, asking for forest delicacies.

Therefore, the win-win method will end up saving you time. When my son was three, we had an argument every mealtime about how much he would eat. It not only took up a lot of time every day, but it spoiled my own meals to have to supervise, hassle and bribe him into eating. Sure, it took us about a quarter of an hour to sort out the conflict - but that time was well invested. We never had another fight over his eating the meals.

Earlier in this chapter we discussed the side effects of using power to resolve conflicts. Are there any side effects to the use of the win-win method? There certainly are. Increasingly people become more creative in thinking up solutions, and take more responsibility for helping everyone to have their needs met. The feeling of mutual respect and love grows deeper with every conflict resolved. Those are the kind of side effects worth having!

An Example on a larger scale: Israel and Egypt

One of the most remarkable stories of the Middle Eastern conflict is the successful peace negotiations between President Anwar El-Sadat of Egypt and Prime Minister Menachem Begin of Israel. These negotiations took 13 days from September 5 to 17, in 1978, brokered by American President Jimmy Carter at his Camp David retreat in Maryland near Washington DC. Israel and Egypt had fought four wars in the previous 30 years, and in 1967, after the so called Six Day War, Israel had occupied the Egyptian Sinai peninsula. Since then, they had built Israeli settlements there, and the Israeli Prime Minister told Carter's National Security Advisor Zbigniew Brzezinski, "My right eye will fall out, my right hand will fall off before I ever agree to the dismantling of a single Jewish settlement." (Cullen, 2003, p 59). President Sadat was convinced that the talks would be over soon because “He would present his position. Israel would reject it.” explained his diplomatic official of the time, Boutros Boutros-Ghali. Each expected a win-lose or even a lose-lose result.

Carter began with idealistic expectations that peace could be reached in two or three days, but there were a number of challenges. The two negotiators had very different personalities. Sadat preferred visions and hated detail; Begin loved detail and preferred to trust biblical prophets for vision. As a matter of fact, Carter later said, one of the first "creative solutions" proposed by a key member of the Israeli team, Aharon Barak, was to avoid holding direct meetings between Sadat and Begin after it became obvious that the two men couldn't stand each other.

Carter could not simply force an agreement. He needed to preframe the process as a problem to be solved cooperatively without coercion (step 1). When he told the Israeli Prime Minister that Egypt wanted the agreement to acknowledge that seizing land by force was unacceptable, Begin refused. “You will have to accept it.” said Carter. But Begin dismissed this claim and clarified that Carter was only a mediator, saying, “Mr President, no threats please.” Again and again, maps were drawn up showing the Sinai divided in two as a compromise, but every time they were rejected. The discussion was being done at the level of solutions instead of at the level of basic needs or intentions.

Why did Sadat want an acknowledgement that land should not be taken by force? Most of all, his intention was that Egypt retain its security and its land. For Begin, holding the Sinai was most of all about securing a buffer zone on his border. At one point on the third day, Sadat emphasised that he could understand the problem at the level of these basic intentions rather than at the level of individual solutions. (This is step 2 in the win-win process). He pounded the table and shouted “Security, yes! Land, no!”

Carter began searching for an agreement which would guarantee Israel the security it wanted by having the Sinai as a buffer between it and Egypt, while restoring the land Egypt wanted. This is a creative brainstorming process (step 3 in the process). The final result was the Camp David Accords. Israel would agree to withdraw from the Sinai and restore it to Egyptian control. In return normal diplomatic relations would be established with Egypt, with guarantees of freedom of passage through the Suez Canal and other nearby waterways, and with a restriction on the number of troops and the type of armaments Egypt could place on the Sinai peninsula.

Even so, the settlements issue continued to threaten the talks' success until nearly the last day of negotiations. At this point, Aharon Barak finally convinced Begin to accept another possibility: Begin need not personally make the decision to dismantle the settlements, but would ask the Israeli Knesset (parliament) to vote on the issue instead. Begin phoned his Minister of Agriculture Ariel Sharon, considered the driving force of the Israeli settler movement, who said he would speak in the Knesset advocating dismantling the Sinai settlements, because reaching peace with Israel's largest Arab neighbour was far more important for Israel's survival.

Sharon recognised that Israel's survival was the more basic need or intention behind the settlements and the occupation of the Sinai. In this way, Israel and Egypt were guaranteed the aims they most hoped for, and even Begin personally did not need to step back from his position (and lose his right eye, his right hand or his personal dignity). In the win-win process this was step 4, 5 and 6. Thirteen days had achieved what four wars and repeated threats had failed to achieve; a lasting settlement that each side would live with.

The success of finding a solution which met each side's basic outcomes or needs was demonstrated over the following thirty years. In September, 2003, NPR's interviewer Bob Edwards spoke with former president Carter and Carter emphasised, "The treaty that we worked out with Israel and Egypt... not a single word of it has been violated on either side." (Step 7 of the process). Furthermore, the success of Camp David demonstrated to other Arab states and entities that negotiation with Israel was possible: that progress could result from sustained efforts at communication and cooperation.

Deepening The Win-Win Business Model: The Theory Of Constraints

Transforming Communication is not the only business model teaching the win-win process described above. In 1985, Eliyahu Goldratt introduced a new theory of business management called the Theory of Constraints, which describes the same method. The Theory of Constraints is based on the simple understanding that it is always useful to know the goal of a system such as a business, and to know what the current main constraint holding you back from reaching that goal is. Everything else in the system can then be considered a resource which can be focused on releasing that constraint. Frequently, the constraint involves a conflict between two courses of action. Goldratt's solution to this situation of conflict is called dissolving clouds.

As an example, consider a common business situation. My company produces audiocassette tapes. How many should we produce at one time? If we produce a large batch, we will need to setup for copying only once, and so the cost per tape will be lower than if we produce several small batches. But if we produce a small batch, we can hold it in storage for less time, and so we save money on storage and save the money that it takes to produce something without getting any return on it. Most people, faced by such a situation, try to compromise between the two choices. Goldratt points out a number of other solutions, which occur once we understand that both choices are attempts to reduce the cost per tape. He diagrams this "conflict cloud" like this (Goldratt, 1990, p 43-45):

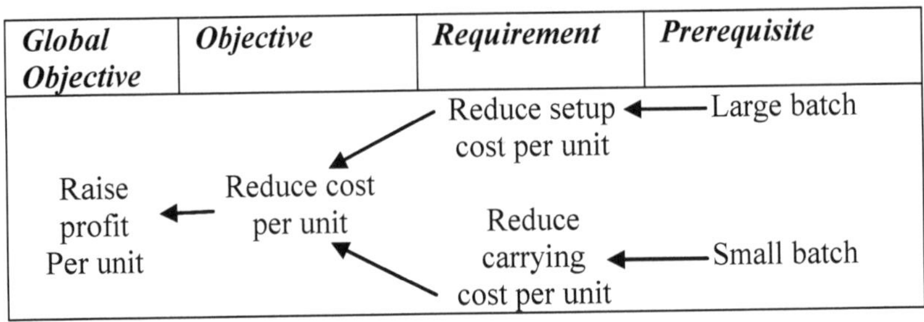

Reducing the cost per unit is in turn best reframed as raising profit per unit (a shift that NLP practitioners will recognise as moving to towards motivation). This final goal is what Goldratt calls "the global objective". This, points out Goldratt, is the only thing that really matters in this plan. In fact, it is important to question what he calls the logical connections represented by each of the arrows above. Is a low setup cost per unit really best achieved by making large batches, for example.

To understand how such connections can be questionable, Goldratt gives the example of reaching the top of Mount Everest. Let's say that reaching the top of Everest is our objective. And lets assume that one of the requirements we are "balancing" is that "participants must be expert mountain climbers' (Goldratt, 1990, p 48). Is this requirement the best way to reach the top at all though? The unstated assumption is that we must reach the top by climbing. Why not use a helicopter? All logical connections in a conflict cloud contain such presuppositions. In the above diagrammed cloud, for instance, we have presupposed that setup for copying inevitably costs money. It may not. The conflict "dissolves" as soon as we focus on the global objective rather than the prerequisites and requirements.

Dissolving Clouds Between People

The same method can be applied to solving conflicts between people and conflicts between the system "rules" and individual peoples desires. Domenico Lepore and Oded Cohen give an example from a medium size company (Lepore and Cohen, 1999, p 140-142). The maintenance manager is assessed based on how much time the factory machines spend not working. He wants the best quality spare parts he can get, so that they need replacing less often.

At present, the purchasing manager is the only person allowed to purchase spare parts. And he chooses spare parts that are cheaper, because he is assessed based on how much money he can save while purchasing needed parts. The cloud is diagrammed as below.

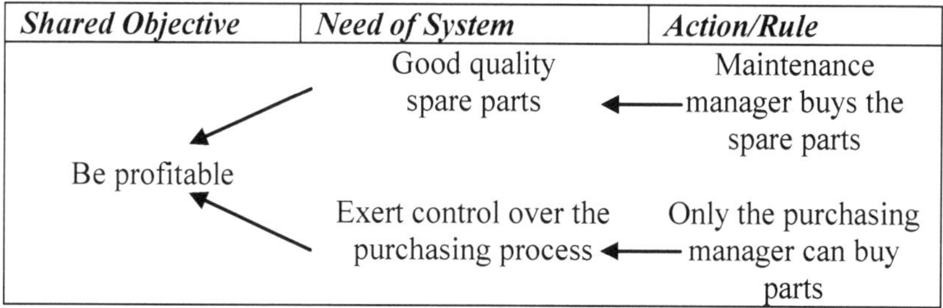

Shared Objective	*Need of System*	*Action/Rule*
Be profitable	Good quality spare parts	Maintenance manager buys the spare parts
	Exert control over the purchasing process	Only the purchasing manager can buy parts

Amongst connections that could be challenged is the notion that the purchasing manager can strike the best deals with spare parts manufacturers. Another is the notion that giving someone else permission to purchase would mean that the purchasing manager loses control over the buying and the prices accepted. By keeping the focus on the shared outcome of being profitable, the two managers can create win-win arrangements that meet each of their needs better than their old approaches did.

Lepore and Cohen point out that Goldratt's work restates much of what the earlier business theorist W. Edwards Deming had advocated. Deming argued that business had been on the wrong track by trying to solve (intra-organisational and inter-organisational) problems competitively. He urged "It would be better if everyone would work together as a system with the aim for everyone to win." (quoted in Lepore and Cohen, 1999, p 15).

First, Second and Third Positions

The power that advanced conflict resolution skills give you is partially explained by the way they increase your ability to "stand in another person's shoes" and "see the world through their eyes". The NLP developers discovered that all highly successful communicators are able to view any interaction from three distinct positions:

- First Position: seeing through their own eyes; their own responses
- Second Position: seeing through the other person's eyes; understanding how it feels to be the other.
- Third Position: seeing the interaction from an observer position, like a "fly on the wall".

Cythia Barnum, IBM consultant, recommends that business people doing business with Japan make a particular point of understanding the cultural differences this way. She has her clients read representative books from each position eg:

- First Position; Edward T. Hall's book, "Hidden Differences, Doing Business With Japan"
- Second Position; Shintaro Ishihara's book "The Japan That Can Say No"
- Third Position; Norwegian author Karel von Wolferen's book on Japanese/English speaking world interaction "The Enigma of Japanese Power"

People in power

When you use this method with someone who has more power (to reward or punish) than you do, it will help to get well prepared:

1 Work out a clear I message to explain your own needs, and make a few guesses as to what the other person's basic goals are (so you're ready to use reflective listening with them).

2 Always reframe the other person's behaviour as 'the best way they can understand right now to meet their needs' (see Chapter 6 for a fuller explanation of reframing). No matter how aggressive their words or actions may seem, when you reflectively listen to them, restate their basic intention as being to solve their own challenge rather than believe their aim is to cause you challenges.

For example: a supervisor tells you: 'There's no other way. Next month you have to work at least one-and-half times as fast as you usually do. We must get that work contract completed. You slobs only work half-speed anyway!'

You respond: 'It's vital to you that we get the work done on time. I'm happy to work with you to find ways to make sure we all keep our jobs, and I see how telling us to speed up has been the most obvious solution to you. I think we can come up with even better ways to solve the challenges you've had, by bearing in mind some of the things we cope with at our end.'

3 Protect yourself from being pushed into an agreement you don't want to live with. To do this, ask yourself: 'What would I do if I couldn't reach a satisfactory agreement?' In the example above, the worker's answer might be:

- stay at this job but immediately begin looking for a better one
- leave the job
- organise industrial action, or
- stay in the job, continue working at a comfortable level and accept the possibility of being fired.

Once you know what your best option outside the conflict discussion would be, compare any of the possible solutions to this 'best outside option'. In so doing, you can tell whether it's worth continuing to work with the person in power to create solutions you both accept. Knowing your other choice, you are less likely to start giving up on your own needs, or to start accepting the other person's way of defining the issues. You can help give yourself more equal power by strengthening the 'best outside option' (the worker in our example might contact the union to plan action, or check out other job possibilities while the issue is still unresolved).

Internal win-win solutions

Of course, the win-win method also works for conflicts between different needs inside yourself. Have you ever wanted to go on a diet but also craved cream cakes? Or intended to study each night but ended up watching TV? Perhaps you've had to choose between two courses of study, or two jobs, both of which interested you. What about times when one part of you is determined to push you into extra work, and you find you've got the flu and end up having to rest?

Situation	Part "A" needs	Part "B" needs	Possible solutions
1. John wants to go on a diet (Part "A") but overeats on cream cakes when he gets home from work (Part "B")	• To feel attractive when in company • To feel energetic and healthy.	• To feel nutured and rewarded after work. • To sleep in at least once a week and recharge.	• Keep to the diet & build in evening rewards: videos, friends, massages, music etc. • Eat the cream cakes, and arrange a regular exercise class as well. • Find a low calorie alternative to cakes.
2. Cynthia works 50 hours a week to save for her university course. She gets the 'flu and has to take a week off work.	• To raise the money for the universit y course.	• To spend time socially one night a week.	• Keep the job, put aside housework, get sleep and social night. • Delay university course one year and reduce work hours. • Keep job, plan sleep-in hours, have friends for social evenings. • Get better paying job.

In all of these situations, one part of you wants one thing while another part wants something contradictory. These are conflicts of needs. Some people deal with them by using rewards and punishments to force obedience from themself. You now have a better choice. Discover what the basic need or goal is for each part, and you can find solutions that work for all of you. This was the subject of the section on resolving internal conflicts in Chapter 2. Here are two examples:

Wider uses

How far can you go with the win-win method? Would it work in whole communities? Could it one day replace much of what we now call government?

Amory Lovins (reported in *Unlimited Power,* by A. Robbins 1988) is director of research at the Rocky Mountain Institute, in Colorado, USA. His particular political interest is promoting environmentally safe energy projects. He achieves this with the use of what he calls 'Aikido politics'. He finds out the basic goals of the electricity companies and the public, and works to prove to them that projects such as nuclear power plants aren't very good ways to meet any of their needs.

In onc case he spoke at a hearing where a local council was planning a huge nuclear power plant. The company had already spent US$300 million (twice that number of NZ dollars) on this plant, but Lovins convinced them that smaller, alternative energy sources would work better for them and the public. The company accepted its $300 million loss and took up his suggestions. Since then he has been hired as a consultant by other electricity companies.

In another case in which Lovins was involved, a local council decided to start a drive for fuel conservation and weather-proofing houses. This cut their use of electricity drastically, so they paid off their debts and made three rate cuts over the next two years. Meanwhile customers saved $1.6 million in fuel costs each year.

Lovins and others like him are literally creating the basis of a new culture. The world desperately needs new models for resolving conflict. If you can solve the disagreements between yourself and your friends using the win-win method, then you have already added to the chances that humanity will survive into the 21st century. Humanity, by the way, means you, your children, and your friends' children. In Chapter 10 we will consider the use of win-win conflict resolution in groups.

To recap

The win-win process of conflict resolution has six steps:

I define the conflict in terms of basic needs or goals, not solutions 2 brainstorm possible solutions to meet both sets of needs 3 check how well these solutions meet both sets of needs 4 choose the best solution/s 5 act 6 evaluate how well the solution/s worked.

I messages and reflective listening are the tools which help you to clarify each person's needs, but the same attitude can also be used to find win-win solutions when someone is too young to use these skills with, or has an intellectual impairment.

When you use the method with someone who has power over you, reframe their intention as meeting their own needs, and work out your' best outside option' to compare possible solutions against. The win-win method can also be used to find solutions to internal conflicts of needs.

Activity 8.3

AIM: to develop the win-win way of thinking about conflict

For each of the following situations, describe the two conflicting sets of needs and then list at least three possible solutions which would meet these needs.

I Each night Rosanne cooks the family meal so that it's ready at 6 pm when her husband Jacob gets home from work. Rosanne likes spending this time together with her family, but their six-year-old son Tom has a favourite TV programme which begins at 6 prn each night. As a result, Tom hardly touches his meal and rushes off to watch TV.
2 Rick has been looking forward to his accounting course for a while. It runs on Thursday evenings, and he hopes to learn a lot that will help him in his new job. Unfortunately, the first night the teacher is rushing through the material too quickly for him to make good notes. 'Sorry,' the teacher explains, 'I've had the course hours reduced by a quarter, so I need to speed up. You'll just have to write faster.'
3 Sandra wanted to make sure that in her second marriage she would share the housework with her husband. Soon after their wedding she told Mike: 'It's very important to me that you pitch in and do your share of the housework on Saturday mornings'. 'But my weekend is really important to me/ he complained, 'I like to keep it free so I can recover from the week.' Sandra shrugged: 'That may be, but in my experience doing the tidying up

together is the only way to be sure we're both doing an equal amount.'
4 Susan definitely intended to do the ten hours study a week which she thought her course needed. She set aside two hours after tea each weeknight and was careful not to arrange any other engagements for that time. Unfortunately, after tea she found she was often quite tired. As a result, she'd sit down in front of the TV to have a rest, and slip into a sort of half-sleep (or even a full sleep). By the time she remembered her study plan, it was often too late to concentrate, and she'd just give it up as a lost cause and carry on watching TV until near closedown.
5 Choose a recent example of a conflict in which you have been involved and write it up in this way.

Activity 8.4

AIM: to practice win-win conflict resolution

In the following exercise people will be in pairs, in which one person will use the Transforming Communication skills, and one person will respond just as they imagine the person they are roleplaying would. Both will get the benefit of experiencing win-win conflict resolution.

1. Get people into pairs and summarise who the two people they'll roleplay are. Have the pairs decide which of them is the person who will use the skills. Have that person get a pen and paper, to keep track of proposed solutions.
2. Give out the instruction cards (copies shown below) and have each person read their role first.
3. Invite them to work through the win-win process. Tell them they have 15 minutes.
4. At the end of this time, ask them to stop, and discuss what progress they've made, and what it was like in the role (4 minutes).
5. Have them stand up and leave behind the role they had when sitting in that seat. Have them remember that they are now themselves, and look at the other person in their pair and remember that person is also back now.
6. Play the other roleplay through, reversing the roles of the skilled person (The person who was the manager in roleplay 1 becomes the teenager in roleplay 2)
7. Take 10 minutes to discuss in the large group, what they learned from the exercise, and any questions they have.

Roleplay 1: Instruction Card: Salesperson
You are a salesperson working in a team which meets once a week to discuss new models of sales, product lines, communication skills etc. Before each meeting, your manager circulates information about the discussion

topic for this week, but at the meeting you seem to be the only one who actually reads this. Succeeding in sales is very important to you. You want to be the best you can at your job. The meetings are beginning to bore you though, partially because the depth of discussion doesn't explore the issues that really interest you. You resent the others' lack of motivation, and have started to let them know that you're sick of their coming unprepared to the meeting, and annoyed with their lack of understanding of the issues in their own job. Your manager has asked to talk with you about what's going on. You respect her/him, and are interested to help her/him out.

Roleplay 1: Instruction Card: Manager
You are the manager in charge of a team sales team which meets once a week to discuss new models of sales, product lines, communication skills etc. There has been rising tension in this discussion group the last few weeks, because one of the salespeople has been increasingly annoyed with the other team members. She/he answers any questions before others get a chance to respond, criticises others' comments, and particularly complains that other participants are not studying the notes you circulate before each meeting to give the meeting focus. You know that this person is a highly motivated and productive salesperson, but at the last meeting no-one else contributed much, and you want to be able to maintain an effective group environment. You want to tell the salesperson that you have a challenge with the way things are going in the discussions. Listen fully to her/his comments, and once the situation seems clearer, invite her/him to search for solutions that could work for both of you.

Roleplay 2: Instruction Card: Parent
You are a parent of two teenagers; Julie (age 14) and Robyn/Robin (age 17). Lately Robyn/Robin has been staying out late at the weekends, arriving home at midnight. As long as you know where he/she is (usually at a particular friend Francis/Frances' place), it doesn't cause you a challenge. However, when he/she arrives in, the sounds of a car arriving, and the banging of the front door (next to your room) often wakes you up, which you resent. You usually go to bed around 11 pm. Also, Robin/Robyn often gets a snack after arriving home, and leaves the mess spread across the kitchen bench. You have learned win-win conflict resolution, and want to find a solution that works for both of you. It's now Sunday afternoon and you've just asked Robyn/Robin if she/he could talk with you about the weekends. Begin by sending a clear I message and reflecting your teenager's responses.

Roleplay 2: Instruction Card: Teenager
You are a 17 year old with a younger sister (Julie, age 14). The last few weeks, you've taken to going around to your friend Francis/Frances' place

on the weekends. Francis/Frances has a sleepout separate from the house there, so you and your other friends can stay up there without disturbing anyone. You generally finish up about 11 pm, but it takes time dropping off people in Francis/Frances' car, so often it's midnight when you finally get dropped off at home. After a snack, you go to bed. You've noticed that your parent is often awake at that time, and have wondered if it was bothering them that you arrive at that time. But you consider it your right to be out with friends, especially on the weekend. After all, midnight is hardly late! It's now Sunday afternoon, and your parent has just asked if she/he could talk to you about the weekends.

Summary

By using the communication skills described in Chapters 1-7, and by changing the environment you live or work in, an enormous number of potential conflicts simply won't happen. This is particularly so of closed communication loops: misunderstandings that I messages and reflective listening will solve.

However, conflicts of needs and conflicts of values or metaprograms will still occur at times. In this chapter a remarkably successful model for resolving conflicts of needs was explained.

In a conflict of needs, you will occasionally have specific reasons why you are unable to discuss the issue and find a solution which meets both your needs and the other person's. However, the effects of one person winning while the other loses are not worth it. For the person who loses, these effects of power include resentment, fighting back, and avoidance of the winner. The win-win process is considerably easier to live with. It involves defining each person's basic needs or intentions (using I messages and reflective listening) and generating new solutions to meet both sets of needs. This same win-win approach can be used to resolve internal conflicts where you seem to have a difference of opinion with yourself.

Conflict resolution brings together the skills of several previous chapters (particularly Chapters 4, 5 and 7).

Chapter 9: Values and metaprograms

KEY CONCEPTS

- Clarifying values
- Metaprograms
- Influencing others' values: consulting
- Modelling your values

Values and metaprograms

AIM: to be able to define values and metaprograms, and describe the processes of:

* identifying shared values
* modelling values
* values-based consultation, and
* identifying and utilising metaprograms.

What are values?

Imagine a situation where a friend buys a new set of clothes which you think looks terrible on them. They ask you for your opinion. Is it the right thing for you to be truthful to your friend, or to make sure they don't feel hurt?

How about the situation where you and your best friend are graduating from nursing training, and you are both looking for jobs in the same area of nursing. By chance you learn of an ideal job opportunity in that field. Do you tell your friend about the job? Is friendship or a career more important? These are questions about values. Values are your personal ideas about what is important or not important, what is right and what is wrong, what is good and what is bad.

The importance of values

In this book you're learning a great many skills. Such skills have the potential to make your life rich and fulfilling; to increase your happiness a hundredfold - but only if you use them in the service of things you really value. People who have the power to make their wishes come true must be careful what they wish (as several stories about magic wish-granting genies remind us). If you use these skills to achieve wealth and power, when you really value friendship and the quiet life, the skills won't bring you happiness at all.Unfortunately, a lot of our values are unconscious - we don't think about them, we just act on them. Sometimes it's only when we meet someone with different values that we realise what is important to us.

What are metaprograms?

Metaprogram is a term from NLP for what people sometimes call 'personality traits'. Metaprograms include, for example, being an introvert or an extrovert, and deciding things either mainly by thinking logically or based on your feelings.

Like values, metaprograms help you decide what to do through the day. But whereas values tell you what things are valuable and what things aren't, metaprograms tell you which things to notice and which things not to notice something that happens even before you check your values. For example, a person who makes decisions based on logical thinking might not even notice that they had feelings about the decision. They might think about which things they value, but never notice that their feelings told them something else. So:

* metaprograms are the ways your mind sorts out which things to pay attention to, and
* values are the ways your mind sorts out which of those things you're paying attention to are valuable.

An example of a metaprogram difference we've already considered in this book is the visualauditory-kinesthetic metaprogram. Some people pay attention more to what they see, some to what they hear, and some to what they touch and feel. We'll consider more examples later in this section.

A values hierarchy

What's important may change according to the area of your life concerned. Let's take friendship. What's important to you about your friendships? List at least six things right now, for example: love, fun, support, challenge, shared goals, honesty, respect, time together, loyalty, and freedom to be yourself.

Once you have a list, compare the items two at a time so you can discover which are your highest values. For example, to compare love and fun you'd ask: 'Which of these things is most important to me? If I had to give up one of these two things in a friendship, which would be the most difficult to give up?' Imagine yourself in each of those situations and decide which value feels most important. Then go down your list and compare the next one to each of those first two.

Once you have a hierarchy listing your values from most important down to less important, you'll know a lot about why you act like you do. Think about what you've discovered. Does this tell you why you make friends with certain people and not with others?

In Chapter 3 we discussed the concept of rapport. Rapport happens on the level of values as well. A group of people who share at least one major value can achieve amazing things, especially if they agree about the sensory specific ways to express that value. (You and I might both agree that fun is very important in our friendship, but if I'm thinking of the fun we get from talking together while you're planning skiing trips, our rapport will be short-lived.)

Identifying shared values

If you are interested in building a relationship with someone, one of the most powerful things is to find at least one value which you both share. Once you know what that is, you can plan together ways to express that value. I'm sure you've used this principle before. For example, let's say you're going over to a friend's place. This friend has a six-year-old son and you really want to get on well with him. What would you do? You'd probably find out what he's interested in - what he values. Perhaps it's computer games, chewing gum and musical instruments. You may not like chewing gum or music, but you've played a few video games in your time and enjoyed that. Video/computer games are a shared value. If you want to get on with your friend's son, you'd plan a way to spend time together expressing that value.

In 1990, in New Zealand, Reckitt and Coleman put out a new group of household cleaners called *Down To Earth.* Although these cleaners were sold in non-returnable plastic bottles, they were advertised as 'taking good care of the environment'. Their contents were biodegradable and were not tested on animals. Why did this major company put out a whole new range of cleaners? Because they recognised the growing power of a new 1990s value -'care for the environment'. All advertising appeals to shared values.

The search conference model is a step by step methodology for guiding a group to the discovery of a co-operative future based on shared values. Rita Schweitz, for example, was the co-ordinator of a 1991 search conference on the use and quality of water from the upper Colorado river basin (Weisbord, 1992, p 215-228). This issue concerned local, municipal, state and national government organisations, water provider companies, agricultural and industrial water user companies, conservationists, first nations and recreational user groups. Decades of bitter values conflicts lay behind the issue. State agencies were involved in taking private firms to court over their use of water at the time. Now all these warring parties were together in one room. Enormous care needed to be taken to build rapport safely and set ground-rules on the first day of the conference, when several members arrived with their lawyers in tow!

Rita Schweitz and the other organisers were very careful to structure the process so that arguments didn't erupt and get out of hand at the meeting of 48 people. On the second day, when each "stakeholder group" presented its own perspective and the others listened, only reflective listening and clarifying questions were permitted. The atmosphere in the first part of the conference process was described by the organisers as one of pessimism and challenge, but all that changed when peoples values in the area under discussion were listed. A dramatic collection of *shared* values emerged, including an attraction to the mountains, the outdoors and enjoyment of the quality of life in Colorado. Talking about these values, one participant made a heartfelt plea that it was "time to change our ways", and the whole conference seemed to nod together. The rapport built by this apparently irrelevant personal sharing inspired major changes in attitude. On the morning of the third day, as participants breakfasted together, one remarked to Schweitz, "This must be the paradigm shift people talk about." A collaborative decisionmaking structure was set up for future planning, progress was made towards legislative reform proposals, and a second conference was set for a year later.

Using shared values

If you're trying to befriend - or even to persuade - someone, you can use this same principle. Say you want to convince a 14-year-old not to smoke cigarettes. Will discussing the risk of her having a heart attack in her thirties work? Probably not. You'd be better talking about how the smell of cigarettes can turn off potential friends. You need to find a shared value.

In the book *Reframing,* Richard Bandler gives an interesting example of the use of shared values to resolve a conflict over non-shared values. A father has just told his daughter: 'If you don't listen to me and don't come home by ten o'clock, I'll ground you for a week...'.

After checking that this message (a 'you message' and 'a threat to use power') doesn't get a very good response from the daughter, Bandler asks the father what the value is behind his command. He replies: 'Well, I care. I don't want her hanging out with hoods. I don't want her out in the street. There's dope out there. I want her to be in the house, safe and sound. She's my girl, and I want to make sure that she has the kind of experiences that she needs to grow up like I want her to grow up.'

The daughter explains her values: 'But it's my life!'

Bandler then points out a value that both of these people share. 'OK, Sam. Is part of that image that you have of your daughter growing up for her to be independent? Do you want her to be a woman who knows her own mind, who can stand on her own two feet and make decisions for herself based on the realities of the world? Or do you want her to be pushed around by other people's opinions?' (Bandler and Grinder 1981)

Once these two people realise that they share the value of 'independence', they will probably find more useful ways to behave. In a sense, they want the same thing, only their methods differ. The father may now be willing to alter his way of discussing the matter, the daughter may be willing to alter her evening pattern. They may, in fact, be prepared to resolve the challenge using the win-win method discussed in Chapter 8.

When values differ

However, in most conflicts over values issues, at least one person will not be prepared to negotiate a win-win solution. This is because they do not believe it's the other person's business to discuss this issue. As Sam's daughter said (above): 'But it's my life'. In this case the person does not believe that their behaviour has any concrete effect on the other person. Sam may send his daughter a nice clear I message ('When you arrive home after ten o'clock I get really worried that you've been hurt') and she just says: 'You worry too much dad. Perhaps you could talk to a counsellor about it'. What can he do?

The real questions are: 'How important is this relationship to him?', and 'How important is it to him that he actually changes his daughter's value?'

If his relationship is not as important as stopping her going out, he could use power. The use of power over her (for example 'grounding' her) will damage their relationship, as we saw in the last chapter. The use of power also has very little effect on her values. Sure, it stops her going out. But it doesn't stop her wanting to go out. Power only changes what people do, not what they value. Nonetheless, the danger may seem serious enough to make it worth using power.

A nurse who forbids patients to smoke in the hospital grounds, a boss who orders employees not to listen to the radio while working, or a teacher who insists her students wear 'no more than one item of jewellery' are all achieving the behaviour they want without affecting the others' values in the slightest. The most predictable result is resentment.

What could they do if they really wanted to influence these people?

John Gottman found that 69% of all relationship conflicts were in this category, in both successful and unsuccessful relationships (Gottman and Silver, 1999, p 130). Gottman calls these conflicts "unsolvable problems", where the partners' basic dreams are in conflict. He doesn't mean that nothing can be done about such conflicts; simply that they cannot be resolved in a session of "problem-solving" talk. In fact, he notes that successful couples learn to respect and honour each other's differing values.

Consulting

A consultant is a person hired to offer their expert skills and knowledge. There are business consultants, educational consultants, health consultants (everyone from chemists to the Avon salesperson), and so on.

You can use the consultant model to influence others' values. Effective consultants:

1 get prepared - they are well-informed about their subject. Don't bother trying to convince your kids about the dangers of drugs if they know more than you.

2 don't start trying to influence until the other person has agreed to listen. (In other words, get yourself hired first.) The first statement of every good salesperson is a request to talk to you.

3 explain opinions using I messages in as brief a way as possible
4 listen to the other person's opinions using reflective listening
5 leave the other person to make their own decision.

For example, imagine a nurse trying to be a health consultant to a patient who smokes, and failing to use the above principles.

Nurse: 'Mr Smith, you shouldn't be smoking.'
Mr Smith: 'Why not: what's it to you?'
Nurse: '*You* know very well why not; don't be silly.'
Mr Smith: '*I* don't see why I should stop now. It's one of the few pleasures I have.'
Nurse: 'I'm only telling you this for your own good Mr Smith. Do you want to be in here forever?'
Mr Smith: 'No, I don't. just leave me alone.'
Nurse: '*You'll* be sorry. Mark my words. I know a lot more about this than *you.'*
Mr Smith: (Stony silence)

In this brief exchange, the Nurse has been 'fired' as a consultant. By trying to use increasing force, she has lost any ability to influence. Mr Smith begins to experience her as using her power over him, and his anger will prevent him cooperating in other areas of their relationship.

It's by 'consulting' like this that many parents get fired by their teenagers,

many teachers get fired by their students, and many managers get fired by their team members. Here's how it could have been handled more effectively:

Nurse: 'Mr Smith, I'm really concerned about your smoking. Do you mind if we talk about it briefly?'
Mr Smith: '*I* suppose not. What does it matter?'
Nurse: 'We find that men who quit smoking at your stage of coronary disease have a much lower rate of recurrence than those who carry on. I believe it's one of the most important things you could do to give yourself a long and enjoyable life.'
Mr Smith: 'But smoking is one of the few pleasures I have, especially if I have to be on this damn diet.'
Nurse: '*I* guess it does seem like a lot of restrictions happening all at once. I think of this as a time when people need to discover a new range of things to enjoy. Everyone needs treats, that's for sure.'
Mr Smith: 'Hmm. Well, I'm going to finish this one anyway. I'll think about it, OK?'

Nurse: 'OK. See you inside later.'
Mr Smith: *(smiles)* 'Right'.

This time, the result is quite different. Most important of all, the relationship between the nurse and Mr Smith is still intact. You can only influence someone who is willing to relate with you. Also, Mr Smith may well be about to change his value and stop smoking. Very few people change their values as you talk to them. Mostly, they need time to go away and think about it, imagine what the new value would be like, check how it feels and talk it over with themselves. If you leave them while they still feel good about you, they have a head start to feeling good about what you said.

Modelling

The second powerful skill for influencing someone's values is modelling. Modelling simply means demonstrating, by your own actions, that what you value works. 'Practise what you preach' may be a well-known saying, but it's fascinating how many people ignore this truth in their daily life. Teachers who routinely smoke in their staff room give out detentions to students caught smoking in the school toilets. Parents who make a practice of lying about their motives ('I'd like to give you a donation, but I have to go to the bank,' 'Sorry we can't come over to visit this Saturday, we have relatives coming,' and so on) tell their kids not to lie. The very country which has defied United Nations resolutions and invaded Grenada (1984), Panama (1989) and Nicaragua (1981-1990) was most eager a year later to punish another country for invading Kuwait (1991). A man who ends family arguments by punching his wife tells his kids to control their tempers.

If your values really work for you, others will adopt them. This is particularly true if you have a good relationship with those people. People tend to copy the values of those they admire. Notice how often a husband and wife end up with similar opinions, or a group of friends all wear the same-style clothes. When a collection of much-admired rock musicians runs a concert to aid famine victims, hundreds of thousands of their fans donate money. If you remember a teacher you really admired from earlier in your life, you can probably recall right now some of the ways you used that teacher as a model.

Metaphor

A third skill for influencing values is a combination of consulting and modelling. People do not usually change as a result of rational arguments in consulting – in fact rational argument often convinces people that their old view was correct. Values or priorities (and thus values-laden behaviours) change when people have profound experiences where they model the new value from someone they can identify with. When they have that experience they need to believe that the change in behaviour will feel good to them (ie it will be valuable), and to believe that it will be possible for them to achieve. It is not always possible to give people a direct modelled experience of the value being expressed and so you need to create vicarious experiences. That means using metaphorical stories, just as teachers like Jesus and Buddha did. David Poindexter runs a business using metaphor via television and radio programs to change people's attitudes.

Starting in 1993, for example, he ran a radio drama in Tanzania, which had one of the highest AIDS rates in the world. Polling showed that the main male character in his program, Mkwaju, was initially an attractive macho role model to male listeners. He was abusive to his wife, drank excessively, and had sex with prostitutes regularly. However, opinions shifted over the course of the program. As Mkwaju died of AIDS, his wife, Tenu, made the decision to leave him, and set up her own successful business. By 1997 listenership of this program increased to 66% of Tanzanian adults. 82% of listeners said they adopted a method of HIV/AIDS prevention as a direct result of listening to the programme. The Dodoma area of Tanzania was excluded from radio transmission for this program in the years 1993-1995, as an experimental control. The ongoing high AIDS rate there resulted in this controlled part of the experiment being ended after two years in order to share the benefits the rest of the country received.

Challenging The Environmental Values Of Business Leaders

A good example of values conflict over the last fifty years has been the struggle by environmental groups to influence the values of business leaders around the world. Sometimes, their approach has been directly coercive. For example, Weiss, a Hamburg oil refinery, had poured illegal discharge into the harbour for years when Greenpeace activists took the matter into their own hands. They plugged up the pipe and told Weiss they had two hours to work out how to clean up before its tanks started overflowing. The plant shut down for six months during which time it redesigned its processes to produce zero discharge since then (Hawken, Lovins and Lovins, 1999, p 65).

However some environmental activists have taken a completely different approach. Amory Lovins is an example. The Wall Street Journal named him one of 28 people world-wide "most likely to change the course of business". Car Magazine ranked him as one of the 22 most powerful people in the global automotive industry, despite his avowed total opposition to the internal combustion engine. He works with a quarter of the world's top 50 brand names, corporations that he says "are bringing us, at their highest levels, business strategies so radical that you'd think they were written by Greenpeace activists, only more so."

How does Lovins achieve this? He explains "I think this work is attracting more and more adherents across the whole political spectrum and especially in the private sector because it makes sense and makes money. It is quite trans-ideological, and we are of course non-partisan and work with everybody. We are also non-adversarial. We try not to tell people they are wrong; we honor their beliefs as we would our own, even if we disagree with them. This is an art that might be called aikido politics, where you don't fight with an opponent, you dance with a partner. You are committed to process, not outcome, in the belief that from a good process will emerge a better outcome than anyone had in mind in the first place. And then, of course, if that good outcome emerges, as it generally does, your job is to make sure that whoever needs to take credit for it will do so, whether deservedly or not. In the Tao Te Ching there is a remark about water: "That the thing which is of all things most yielding can overcome that which is most hard is a fact known by all but used by none. Being substanceless, it can enter in even where there are no cracks." We need to use the same subtly effective approach in dealing with conflict and diverse ideas about what ought to be done." (Witt, 1999)

Why influence ?

The main reason people try to influence others' values is to help those people. That is, they are motivated by love. Consulting and modelling give you ways to share your values with love, instead of creating conflict with the very person you care for. If, after time, your attempts to influence someone are not working, you might ask yourself: 'Is that so terrible? Can I not live my values and allow them to live theirs?'

In some cases, you may decide that the best and most achievable solution is to change your relationship to allow for your different values. For a non-smoker and a smoker, this might mean agreeing on a separate area where the smoker can continue their habit. For two people with strongly opposed political beliefs, it may mean agreeing not to discuss certain topics. For a wife who cannot accept her husband's active alcoholism, it may mean living separately.

In other cases, you may discover that it is possible to continue your relationship exactly as it is and, simply by adopting a different attitude to your difference, come to feel more accepting of it. Is any of us so absolutely certain of our map of the world that we can insist all others follow?

Metaprograms; the basis of personality

Similar issues occur between people as a result of their personality styles (metaprograms). Being introverted (preferring to be alone more, especially when you 'recharge your batteries') or extroverted (preferring to be with people more, especially to 'recharge batteries') is a good example. Two people may love each other very much, and find out on their first holiday together that they have totally different ideas about how to relax.

Another important metaprogram is the variation between what Jungian psychotherapist Isobel Briggs Myers calls judgers and perceivers (see James and Woodsmall, 1988). Judgers like to make decisions, finish things, get a sense of closure, plan their future. Perceivers like to go with the flow, put off decisions, delay finishing and just live in the 'now'. If an extreme judger goes on holiday with an extreme perceiver, the judger will be trying to timetable their day while the perceiver just does whatever happens. Give them both a work assignment, and the judger tries to get it finished and out of the way as soon as possible. The perceiver leaves it until the last minute, to keep their options open.

A third example is our approach to similarities and differences. Some people notice the differences in life more, while some people notice the similarities. People who notice the differences are called mismatchers. If you tell a mismatcher it's likely to be sunny today, they'll tell you it will probably rain later (or if you say it's raining, they'll tell you it will clear up soon!). The matcher tends to agree with anything you say. Jobs where people need to notice the differences (like lawyers, accountants and proof readers) will be easier for mismatchers. Jobs where people need to create similarity (like selling, counselling and the military) will be easier for matchers.

A fourth example is the way we motivate ourselves, which can be by focusing on what we want to move towards (our goals, described positively) or what we want to move away from (our problems and potential risks). In this book, at times I have advocated paying attention to goals rather than to problems, and unless there is some real danger, this is generally more enjoyable. It is also important to know that perhaps half the people you encounter will not understand the focus on goals, and will consider someone who just talks about goals as living in a dream-orld and not paying attention to the very real dangers and problems we face. Some career paths focus especially on such dangers, and so medical practitioners and lawyers, for example, are likely to be more "away from" motivated than say real estate salespeople, who need to see the potential of things rather than the problems.

Chunking up or down

Thinking about details (sensory specifics, small pieces) or thinking about the big picture, is a fourth metaprogram. Imagine two people living together where one prefers to pay attention to detail and one prefers to get the overall impressions. 'How was your day?' says the overview person. 'Well,' replies the details person, ,at 8 30 am I tidied the main room - there were a lot of books to put back on the shelf. By 9 am I was finished and I got a phone call from Freda. She says ......

'No, no!', interrupts the overview person, in *general* how was your day?' Giving up, the details person asks: 'Well, how was your day?'

'Fine', explains the overviewer. The details person waits for more specific information, but as far as the overview person is concerned, they have already said it all.

In time, the overview person will possibly think of the details person as bogged down in trivia, nit-picking and so on. The details person may consider the overview person as vague, head in the clouds, hard to pin down. In fact, they just sort their experiences differently. To use NLP terms, one is good at chunking up (getting the overview, the big chunks) while one is good at chunking down (getting the specific details of what actually happened). Both processes are useful. Flexibility is an advantage - being able to chunk up by asking 'what's this an example of?' and being able to chunk down by asking 'what's an example of this?' (You can find a further explanation of chunking up and chunking down on pages 216-220.)

This is one of the reasons to learn about metaprograms: being able to have the flexibility to choose how you behave increases life satisfaction. Another reason is that, like it or not, we share the world with people who have different metaprograms from us. Understanding metaprograms helps us to understand others better, and to communicate with them in ways that make sense to them. The final reason you'll find this useful is that you can never be sure which metaprogram will be most useful to you in a particular situation....

Are you sure?

Philosopher Robert Fulghum tells of a friend of his who has some very alternative beliefs:

"'It's all crap," says he, "all lies. Your senses lie to you, the president lies to you, the more you search the less you find, the more you try the worse it gets. Ignorance is bliss. just be, man. Don't think or do -just be. The world is coming to an end!"

'The day before he left, he jumped off a lakeside dock with his clothes on, to help a child who appeared to be in danger of drowning in the deep water. And he confessed to being in town for the National Lawyers Guild Convention, since he's a member of its social justice committee.

"' So, if it's all lies and crap - and ignorance is the ultimate trip - then how come... I say

"'Well," says he, "I might be wrong.

To recap

Our values are those things we consider important, right and good. Part of building rapport is identifying and working with the values that we share.

In a conflict of values, using your power over others can possibly change their behaviour (if you have enough power), but this will not change their values. If you would like to change someone's values, it's important to keep a relationship of mutual respect. This maximises the possibility that you can then influence them, using modelling, consulting, and metaphor. Good consultants:

- get prepared
- get hired
- use I messages
- use reflective listening, and
- leave the other person to make their decision.

When you are unable to influence someone's values, you may choose to simply accept the differences between you, or to change your relationship so that your differing values have less impact on each other.

Similar issues occur with differences in metaprograms. Metaprograms are personality differences - differences in the way people pay attention to what's happening. They include differences between introverts and extroverts, people who chunk up and those who chunk down, judgers and perceivers, matchers and mismatchers.

Activity 9.1

AIM: to find shared values for your group

1 Identify the main subject being studied by your group (for example communication, nursing, relationships, systems analysis).

2 Each person should individually list six values important to them when considering this subject, and rank them from most to least important.

3 Collect all the values group members have listed on a central list (for example on the whiteboard or a large sheet of paper).

4 Clear a floor space in the room and declare one end 'important' and the other end 'not important'. For each of the values on your central list, get group members to stand along this 'continuum' space. You are searching for the most strongly shared value.

5 When you have identified this most strongly shared value, brainstorm ways in which the group could more fully express this quality in their interaction.

Activity 9.2

AIM: to discover the qualities of good influencers

1 Use a relaxation process such as in activity 2.3 (see page 27).

2 Think back through your adult life to a time when someone else influenced you (that is, when you changed the way you behaved or your opinions as a result of someone else's actions) and when you accepted and welcomed that influence. The person may have been a relative, a teacher, a friend - even someone you read about or saw in a film. See that person in front of you, hear the kind of thing that person would usually say in their tone of voice, and feel what it would be like to have that person beside you now. Once you can recall this person fully, find words for the qualities this person had which enabled them to influence people. What was it about this person: what did they do that caused others to accept their influence? Having done this, thank the person in your mind, because they were probably someone very special to you. You may not have realised how much this person meant to you until now. Now gently put them out of your mind, remembering the qualities they had.

3 Repeat step (2) with a person who influenced you earlier in your life.

4 Share your experiences in pairs. Then, as a group, collect the list of qualities these influencers had, and discuss:

- do we have these qualities?
- are these the qualities we usually call upon when trying to influence others?

Activity 9.3

AIM: to practise consulting about a values issue, with a partner who has different values about that issue

1 Clear a space on the floor and declare one end 'yes', the middle 'don't know', and the other end 'no'. Read out each of the statements listed (a) to (p) below, and each place yourselves according to your own response. (You will need to alter some statements if you're using the book outside New Zealand.) Ask people to use their own interpretation of the statements. Do not clarify or discuss the statements at this stage. As soon as you have people on opposite sides for any issue, pair those people up: one 'yes' with one 'no'. These pairs should move out of the floor space, and not participate in the rest of the yes-no voting.

2 Each pair should sit next to each other, and elect one person A and the other person B. The sequence of their discussion should strictly follow the procedure below (to prevent a loss of safety):

- Person A describes their opinion about the statement, using an I message.
- Person B listens reflectively to this, until person A agrees that their main point has been understood.
- Person B describes their opinion with an I message.
- Person A listens reflectively to person B's satisfaction. Repeat the process at least twice.

3 Collect the group together again and check how it went. Did people discover they actually agreed? Did people shift their positions? Did people become more accepting of their differences?

Statements

- Marijuana use should be legal.
- Genetically modified foods are safe and should be accepted

- Immunisation of children is the best choice for their safety
- In cases of terminal illness, euthanasia is an individual's right
- Corporal punishment should be used in schools.
- Capital punishment should be used for some cases of murder.
- It should be against the law for parents to hit children.
- If people don't arrange their own insurance, they should not get government handouts for health care.
- The business of business is business, and not "social responsibility".
- Abortion should be each individual woman's right to decide.

Activity 9.4

AIM: to clarify values-based decisions

Obtain the game'A Question of Scruples' (Milton Bradley Co. (1986)). Each group member should select a question card from this game for discussion. (Alternatively, the group leader could select a few cards she or he considers relevant for that group.) For each card chosen:

- read out the card
- discuss what you expect the group members' responses to this card will be, and
- disclose your own response to the card and invite others to share theirs. (Remember to use I messages.)

the cards, if you are unable to obtain a pack, have questions such as:

1. The taxi driver offers to leave the amount of the fare blank on your receipt. You can claim expenses. Do you accept the offer?
2. Your teenage children ask if you ever smoked marijuana. You did. Do you admit it?
3. A friend who needs a job applies at your business. Someone who is better qualified also applies. Do you hire your friend?
4. During lunch, a valued client makes some offensive racist remarks. Do you express your true feelings and risk offending the client?
5. You need work. An employer whose workers are on strike offers you a job. Do you take it?
6. A colleague at a large company is stealing from petty cash. Do you warn him/her to stop?
7. You are offered $10,000 to appear nude as a centerfold in a national magazine. Do you accept?
8. You want to landscape your property but find that trees cost too much. Do you drive into the woods and take some to transplant?

9. You're on a romantic get-away weekend. Your lover wants you to "play hooky" from your job on Monday. Do you call in sick?
10. When withdrawing money from an electronic banking machine, you mistakenly receive an extra $100. Your account, however, still displays your accurate balance. Do you keep the money?
11. A good friend has just bought an expensive painting and asks you if you like it. You think it is awful. Do you say so?
12. Your mate has had an affair. Do you leave him or her?

Activity 9.5

AIM: to begin identifying your own metaprograms

Answer the following questions by rating yourself on a continuum between one answer and the other:

Answer (a) both/either/depends Answer (b)

1 2 3 4 5 6 7

1. When it's time to recharge your batteries, do you prefer to be:
   a . alone (introvert)
   b. with people (extrovert)

2. If you were going to study a certain subject, would you be more interested in:
   a. the facts and how to use them in a specific situation (chunk down)
   b. the relationship between the facts and the overview of the concepts (chunk up)

3. If we were going to do a project together, would you prefer:
   a. that it was outlined, planned and orderly (judger)
   b. that we be more flexible about how we do it (perceiver)

4. Think of your friends. As you compare them, are you aware more of the:
   a. differences (mismatcher)
   b. similarities (matcher)

5. When you think about what's important to you in life (your values) are you more aware of:
   a. what you want to avoid, or protect yourself from (away from)
   b. what you want to achieve, create and discover (towards)

Summary

In part, this short chapter continues the discussion of conflict discussed in Chapter 8. In a conflict of values, the use of power will at best change the behaviour of the other person, but not their values. Better ways to influence their values include modelling your values and consulting. A good consultant:

- gets prepared
- gets hired
- uses I messages
- listens reflectively, and
- leaves the other to decide.

However, this chapter not only discusses conflict situations, it is also an encouragement to clarify your own values (what's important to you) and metaprograms (what you pay attention to), and to find out what values and metaprograms you share with the others in your life. When you know these you can use the other skills in this book to create a truly fulfilling lifestyle.

Chapter 10: Group communication

KEY CONCEPTS

- Group development
- Task and maintenance needs
- Group facilitation
- Meeting structuring
- Consensus

What happens in groups

AIM: to be able to list three main group functions related to the task dimension, and three related to the maintenance dimension; and to describe the three stages of group development according to William Schutz.

What is a group?

In the world of communication, two's company and three is usually a group. You probably belong to several groups: family, friends, workplaces, neighbourhoods, clubs, and classes of students are among the common examples.

Human beings spend a lot of their time in groups. Not every collection of three or more people is a group, though: the people waiting at the bus stop aren't really a group, even though they happen to be near each other. To be a group, people need to have some recognition of who does and does not belong, as well as what needs are met by the group's existence.

When groups are so important in our lives, what's fascinating is how little thought we give them. In this chapter we'll explain how to use communication skills in a group setting, but first I want to mention two very important facts about groups themselves:

* groups have a series of stages they go through, and
* the interaction between people in a group happens on two levels (task and process).

Cohesive groups

The morning before I wrote this section was the first day for 160 new nursing students at Christchurch Polytechnic. They filed uncertainly into the lecture theatre, not quite sure what to expect. By and large they were a quiet group, speaking - when they did - mainly in response to questions from staff or secondyear students. No one person stood out, or expressed any strong opinions.

In contrast, the group of second-year students who welcomed these newcomers was talkative and relaxed. People spoke loudly and confidently, chatting and laughing amongst themselves. Several second-year students described their closeness to the others in their own classes and to their tutors. They spoke of the friendships that the first-year students could expect in the coming year. Looking at them, I had the impression of people who had known each other for a long time. They discussed their different experiences of nursing in an easy manner, joking about the dissimilarities within their own group (for example who was old, who was young, who had more children than the national average, etc.).

Next year, of course, the scene will repeat itself. The quiet, reserved, homogenous group of first-year students will have become a vocal, outgoing, affection-expressing and differencefilled group of second-year students. A group like these second years can be described as cohesive (meaning they' stick together') although it's interesting that people in a cohesive group are more able to express their differences as well as their similarities.

Stages of group life

A cohesive group doesn't just' happen'. It develops, and that development occurs in fairly predictable steps. Group theorist William Schutz divides the development of group cohesion into three stages:

* the inclusion phase (called in some models "forming" and "norming")
* the control phase, and (called in some models "storming")
* the intimacy phase (called in some models "performing")

The new students described above were experiencing the inclusion stage of their group's life. At this stage, the main types of question people are asking themselves are whether they 'belong' here, whether they are included by others, and so on. Therefore members may make a lot of statements about what a good group it is, but they don't refer to any particular people they like or dislike, or any particular issues they agree or disagree on. At this stage people tend to 'go with the flow' to show they belong. If you're planning activities for a group in the inclusion phase, you'll get better results by giving them opportunities to introduce themselves to each other, and to feel a part of the activity.

For our nursing students, the control phase is usually in full swing about halfway through their first year. Having assured themselves they belong (or having left), people now start thinking about how much control they have, whether they can get their needs and values respected, and so on. There may be conflicts with the person / s who 'run / s' the group, and disagreements over who has more say. Some members will react to these conflicts with a fear that the group is breaking up' (because they are still not sure about their inclusion). Indeed, some groups don't survive this challenge. Exercises and activities which increase people's active participation, as well as opportunities to renegotiate ground rules, are helpful at this time.

The second-year students I described above are in the intimacy stage of their group. Knowing that their needs will be respected, group members are now able to express their different feelings towards other members, and face the risks of both closeness and rejection. Although this is sometimes painful, it also brings some extraordinary moments of real human contact. Free to be different, people meet each other as they really are, instead of as the carefully presented image offered earlier on. Such a group will respond to a wide variety of different activities, especially enjoying those where affection can be shared.

Group and individual development

According to several group theorists, the stages a group goes through (development) are very similar to the stages an individual person grows through. For example, Eric Erikson (1968) suggests that people pass through eight life stages as they grow: his model of 'psychosocial' development. Each stage has its own central issue. If a person does not resolve that issue successfully, later stages will cause difficulty. It's as if the stages were building blocks piled one on top of the other if an early block is faulty, later blocks may fall down.

Erikson's stages, with the qualities which he says are the result of completing each stage successfully or not, can be compared to Schutz's stages of group development on the right.

Erikson's stages of psychosocial development		**Schutz's stages of group life**
Birth - 18 months (Infancy)	Trust or mistrust	Inclusion phase
18 months - 3 years (Early childhood)	Autonomy or shame & doubt	
3 years - 5 years (Middle childhood)	Initiative or guilt	
6 years - 12 years (Schoolage)	Industry or inferiority	Control phase
12 years -18 years (Adolescence)	Identity or role confusion	
18 years - 30 years (Young adulthood)	Intimacy or isolation	Intimacy phase
30 years - 60 years (Middle adulthood)	Generativity or stagnation	
60 years - death (Old age)	Integrity or despair	

It's as if the group has its own infancy (inclusion phase), childhood (control phase) and adulthood (intimacy phase).

Task & maintenance

When people think about groups, they usually think about the task the group has to achieve. As we said, to qualify as a 'group', a collection of people needs to have a common purpose (for example, learning about communication, raising children, making money or playing tennis), and this is the group task.

But a group is much more than just a machine doing a task. It is a collection of human beings. How these people get on together, and how they get their own needs met, make up the other side of what a group does. This other side is often called the 'group process', and you could think of it as the ways in which the group looks after or maintains itself.

The task is the stuff that gets written down in the minutes, if you keep minutes. When someone brings in a cup of tea it probably isn't worth writing in the minutes - but it sure is worth doing! Sharing a cup of tea maintains the group.

When people only pay attention to the task, the group will eventually break up, because the needs of individual members and of their relationships are being ignored. An example would be a very boring lecture. There may be lots of important content in such a lecture, but this is wasted if people are asleep. Several members being asleep is part of the group process.

On the other hand, when people only pay attention to group maintenance, the group fails to get its job done, and again it tends to collapse. Think of a student 'study evening' which turns into an all-night party. Everyone's individual needs are cared for, people cooperate really well, and no one remembers what the task was.

A successful group is one which balances task and maintenance needs. Keeping yourself aware of the balance is the single most important contribution you can make to any group to which you belong.

Task and maintenance functions

What do you do in a group to help keep this balance between getting the task done and supporting the group of people who do the task? Comments group members make which support the task are called task functions, and they include:

1 giving information or opinions about the task discussed, for example: 'I think we should have our next meeting on Monday 15th'

2 asking others for information or opinions about the task being discussed, for example: 'Who else is available on that Monday?'

3 using the problem-solving model (see Chapter 4) to discuss the task (i.e. starting the discussion, summarising information collected, defining the challenge, suggesting a method of finding solutions, checking solutions, and evaluating decisions), for example: 'OK, so far we have two possible dates. Shall we just take the one which most people can come to?'.

Other comments focus on the group itself, and are known as maintenance functions. They include:

1 expressing your own needs and feelings, using I messages, humour, and so on, for example: 'I'm starting to feel overwhelmed with information. Let's take a five-minute break'

2 encouraging others to express their own needs and feelings, using reflective listening skills, for example: 'You're still frowning. Are you unhappy about us making a decision in this way?'

3 using the problem-solving model to discuss the group (i.e. saying what you've observed of the group process, acknowledging interpersonal challenges, suggesting solutions to better meet everyone's needs in the group, and evaluating how the group 'contract' is working), for example: 'I'm aware that in the last ten minutes only the men have been talking. I think it would be good if we listened to some of the women's responses'.

These are the six key functions which any group needs to succeed. Together they make up what has in the past been called 'leadership'. In this way of understanding it, leadership is a set of functions which someone in the group needs to perform. You could let one person do them all, but in a well-developed group (one that has worked through the control phase), these functions are shared by the whole group.

The more members who contribute to these functions, the more your group is using its full talent, and the better decisions you'll make.

All these functions can be learned - in fact, they are all described in other chapters of this book.

To recap

A group is a collection of people who have a sense of belonging and purpose together. As groups develop they tend to go through an inclusion phase, a control phase and an intimacy phase, which are analogous to the infancy, childhood and adulthood of a person's life.

A group has a content which is being discussed, and a process by which the discussion occurs. 'Leadership' can be thought of as the set of functions which keep a balance between the group task and group maintenance. These are:

* Task functions:

- giving information or opinions
- receiving information or opinions, and
- problem solving the task.

* Maintenance functions:
  - expressing needs or feelings
  - encouraging others to express needs or feelings, and
  - problem solving the group process.

Activity 10.1

AIM: to develop skills in group observation

Assign each group member a session of the group for them to observe, and get them to take notes using the headings below. At the end of the session, or at a later date, the observer should report back to the group and enable the group to discuss their comments.

Group observation

1 Posture

a How close are people sitting?
b Who leans towards the group and who leans away?
c Who has an open body position and who has a closed position?
d Who seems physically tense, and who is relaxed?
e Who sits still and who moves? How, exactly, do they move?

2 Facial expression

a Who looks away from the group and who looks towards others?
b Who smiles or laughs?
c Who frowns?
d Who yawns?
e What other body language are you aware of?

3 Speech

a Who speaks and who is silent?
b Who is able to finish what they say? Who interrupts?
c Who changes the subject?
d Who makes jokes or uses humour?
e Who criticises, blames, judges or insults others?

4 Leadership functions

a Who offers information or opinions?
b Who asks for information or opinions from others?
c Who suggests moving to the next step of problem-solving /working on the group task?
d Who expresses their feelings or needs in an I message?
e Who uses reflective listening skills?
f Who invites the group to discuss or problem solve their process?

5 Summary

a What was the task of this group in this particular session?
b How would you generally describe the group process, based on all the previous questions? (For example is the group friendly, withdrawn, tired, energetic, tense, relaxed, cooperative, resistant?)
c Did you think a good balance was kept between task and maintenance needs in the group? If so, what helped? If not, what would have helped?

Activity 10.2

AIM: to explore levels of intimacy in the group

1 Using a copy of the circular diagram below, write in the names of all the other members of your group, showing by where you place them who are:

* best friends you talk to or spend time with a lot
* close friends you talk to or spend time with fairly often
* friends/ acquaintances you spend time with less frequently.

2 Get into pairs and discuss:

* What it was like to fill in this form, and
* anything of what you wrote down you feel comfortable sharing.

3 If the group is sufficiently trusting, each person could be invited to set out their diagram using the actual people in the room, and an imaginary large-size diagram on the floor.

Helping a group to reach agreement

AIM: to be able to help a group create consensus decisions, by using the skills of:

- meeting structuring, and
- win-win conflict resolution.

Facilitation

Psychotherapist Milton Erickson told a simple story which clarifies his method of helping. He explained that, when he was a child, he found a horse wandering aimlessly down a country lane. Realising it had escaped from some nearby farm, he climbed on and rode it five miles up the road. At this point the horse turned off the road and walked up a drive, where they met its astonished owner. 'How did you know he should come here?' the farmer asked. Erickson explained: 'I didn't know. The horse knew. All I did was keep his attention on the road.' (Quoted in Gordon & Meyers-Andeson 1981, p 6)

Helping a group make decisions (or an individual for that matter) is like that. Every time the group 'wanders off the road to eat the grass' you lead them back, and eventually they will find their own way. This model of running a group is often called facilitation.

Chairperson v facilitator

The facilitator's job is to make it easy (from the Latin word facilis meaning 'easy') for the group to find solutions. Being a facilitator can be contrasted with being a chairperson in a more traditional 'meeting'. The role of the chairperson includes making decisions for the group at times. People are expected to speak 'to the chairperson' rather than directly to each other. On the other hand, the job of the facilitator is to ensure that people speak as directly as possible to each other. The chairperson is expected to know and perform the key group functions, whereas the facilitator encourages others to perform these functions.

Does this mean that facilitating is easier than chairing a meeting? I don't think so. Being an effective facilitator requires an ability to use all the communication skills we have studied in this book. It takes an awareness of body language and an ability to help people alter their state of mind (for example relaxing them if they are too tense, or energising them if they are tired). It is first and foremost a helping role, in that the facilitator's aim is to help others sort out what they want, rather than to persuade them to choose the facilitator's solutions.

And yet the facilitator needs to be able to explain her or his own intentions in clear I messages, and to use the skills of modelling clear communication and consulting - skills aimed at offering group members new values. Most of all, the facilitator needs to have a very clear idea of who owns which challenges, and of how to use the problem-solving, win-win process. She or he needs to know this process well enough to teach and assist others to use it, too. And finally, the facilitator needs to know how to structure the group time, so as to provide a beginning (warm-up) and an ending (closure).

Power use in groups

Resolving conflicts in a group is similar to resolving conflicts between two people. There are several methods of making decisions in a group, whereby one or more people use their power over others to win at the others' expense. These include the following:

- autocratic: one person makes decisions for the group
- minority rule: a few people make decisions for the group
- autocratic or minority rule with consultation: as above, but before making the decision, the decision-makers check what other people think and may (or may not) take their views into consideration
- majority rule: everyone in the group discusses the decision, and the decision is made by whoever has the largest number of people supporting their proposal.

Challenges with power

In all of these methods, some people's needs are not met. This is more obvious in the first two cases, where people's needs are not even listened to (the situation in most workplaces, in many schools and in political dictatorships). In the last two cases, people can explain their concerns. However, there is an incentive for people to argue against each other rather than cooperate, because whoever is the least persuasive could lose totally. Often in a majority rule system, one party of likeminded people always votes together, therefore minorities end up having next to no influence on group decisions (the situation in the USA government: only the party in government can make decisions). Adolf Hitler's Nazi party was voted in by majority, and was able to 'democratically' override the needs of such minorities as psychiatric patients, Gypsies, and Jews.

As with conflicts between two people, the use of power may be worth the resentment it can create in certain circumstances, for example when there is no time for discussion (see Chapter 8, page 163). Also, many groups accept that minor decisions will be made by one of these methods, but major decisions are sorted out using the win-win method.

Consensus

Consensus is the name given to the use of win-win conflict resolution in a group. The goal of consensus is a decision consented to by all group members. This doesn't have to mean that everyone thinks this is the very best solution (a unanimous decision). It just means that everyone can live with the decision and will agree to support the group in choosing it. This goal encourages people to work together to find solutions acceptable for everyone, instead of competing.

As with all win-win decision making, the big advantages of consensus are that:

- everyone's creativity is used to generate good solutions, and
- people tend to be very committed to making decisions work.

The disadvantages are that

- it takes time (remember, though, that time enforcing unwanted solutions will be saved), and
- at least some people in the group need good communication skills to make it work (hence the advantage of having one person designated 'facilitator').

Amongst groups who use consensus are the Religious Society of Friends (Quakers), a large number of Maori Marae, cooperatives such as Women's Refuges, and many workplace groups (including our company).

A great deal of research has been done by such groups into how to best create consensus (see for example *Building United Judgement: A Handbook for Consensus Decision making,* by M. Avrey, B. Auvine, B. Streibel and L. Weiss). The suggestions which follow come out of this experience.

Making a start

Henare, a community worker, was invited to help sort out a disagreement between the four workers at a community creche. He arranged a two-hour time slot (from 5-7 pm one Thursday) and suggested they begin by sitting in a circle so they could all see and hear clearly. Henare began by telling them that he was pleased to be with them and that he planned to help them find solutions they could all live with. He emphasised that he wasn't there to tell them the rules, but he had a couple of ideas about how they could find their own agreements. He invited them to take three minutes of silence to collect their thoughts and relax into the meeting.

After this Henare suggested each person briefly introduce themselves and say how their day had been. He started: 'I had a hectic day today, and it's actually nice to be concentrating on one task for these two hours'.

A woman to his left continued: 'My name is Miriam; I'm the person who phoned you, and I'm just hoping we can sort this out soon and have a better year. I suppose I'm feeling quite anxious.'

'Me too,' agreed the man beside her, 'I'm Roy. I wasn't working today so I've just come in for this meeting. I'd rather be sleeping.'

'My name is Lesley,' the woman next to Roy put in, 'I've been working here two years now, and I'm not really sure if I plan to carry on. I feel quite tense.'

'Moana is my name,' the fourth person finished, 'I've only been here a few weeks and I feel like I've sort of walked into all this conflict. I had a good day, no problems.'

Henare continued by checking that the 7 pm ending time was OK for everyone. 'What things led to the decision to invite me here this evening?' he prompted.

Roy began. 'Well, last year we had a couple of really unpleasant situations here, where conflicts happened between staff. There was a lot of backbiting, and eventually one person got so upset she left. I want to make sure it doesn't get to that again, so I suggested we have an agreement about not talking behind people's backs.'

'Yeah,' Miriam nodded, 'I agree with Roy. People have got to be honest with each other for it to work. I think, last year, we all ended up grizzling about things to the wrong people.'

'Well, there was a lot of aggro...' Lesley paused. 'But it's just not as simple as you make it sound, Miriam. *Sometimes people* get upset about something and they don't really know what it is until they've talked to someone else. Sandy that's the woman who left, Henare -she... it just took her a long time to be able to...'

'Yeah. And in the meantime she started telling all the parents who came here that I was some sort of ogre!' interrupted Miriam.

Lesley was about to reply, but Henare intervened: 'I know this is important to both of you, and I want to make sure you each get a chance to say your bit. I think it will help if we wait for each person to finish their comment. Is that agreeable?' There were nods.

'That was all, anyway,' Lesley concluded, 'I don't think it's that simple.'

'I suppose,' contributed Moana,' that I'd have to go along with Roy and Miriam. But one thing I find is that they're really used to all this communication stuff. And I can see that I'd find it intimidating to be in that situation. So I don't know...'

'OK.' Henare checked everyone was ready to go on. 'So the main thing you'd all like to sort out is what happens when someone is unhappy with a situation. It sounds like Miriam and Roy both want an understanding about not talking behind people's backs. You'd go along with that Moana, but you can also understand what Lesley says, which is that in real life it seems less simple. Is that right?' General nods. 'And that's the main thing we need to sort out?' Again, nods.

Meeting structuring

Already, Henare has structured this meeting to make sure that several important group processes occur, in a useful order. These include:

1 Starting on time and clarifying the arrangements about ending

It may be that the meeting will carry on until things are resolved, or it may be that people have other commitments (for example needing to get back for babysitters) and will appreciate an agreed-on ending time.

2 Sitting in a circle

Seating arrangements set the tone of any get-together. Ensuring everyone sits in a circle gives a sense of equal power: no one is 'in front' of anyone else.

3 Checking how people are

Providing an opportunity to say briefly how everyone is, helps people learn who is here. It creates a sense of group cohesion.

4 Working out what the task is and how we will achieve it

This really creates a sense of contract. Henare has requested agreement about two processes already. One is that his role as a facilitator will be to assist them to reach consensus. The other is that people will allow each speaker to finish their statement. He has also checked the agenda, which in this case has only one item. A more formal process might include: a collecting people's suggestions for group guidelines (such as no interrupting, confidentiality) and listing those agreed to on a large sheet of paper b listing agenda items, estimating how much time each item will take, and deciding in which order to discuss the items. If there are too many items for your time, some will need to be put off until the next meeting.

5 Leaving time for evaluation

Someone needs to keep track of time if there is a set agenda and an agreed ending. The facilitator may do this, or a separate timekeeper could be appointed. At the end, a space for people to each say how they found the meeting will help give a sense of closure to the meeting. (Cohesion and contract, the two key elements in the warm-up to the beginning of a meeting, are discussed in more detail in Chapter 1. Closure is commented on in Chapter 11.)

The facilitator's comments

If you look back at what Henare actually said in the first few minutes of this meeting, you'll realise that he uses all the communication skills described in Chapters 5-9. Particularly important is his use of:

1 I messages
(for example: 'I want to make sure you each get a chance to say your bit. I think it will help if we wait for each person to finish their comment'). These are used to share his feelings, and to offer his opinions as a consultant.

2 Reflective listening
(for example: '... this is important to both of you. So the main thing you'd all like to sort out is what happens when someone is unhappy with a situation.'). Notice that Henare not only reflects what individuals say, but also restates what is happening to the group or to couples in the group. This might be called 'summarising' or 'sorting issues'.

3 Reframing

At the same time, Henare skilfully reframes the significance of what is occurring. His reflections draw attention to similarities and areas of agreement between those in the conflict (even when the only similarity is that both people are angry or upset, or that both people want a solution!) As a facilitator he asks himself: 'Which are the areas of disagreement here, and where are the areas of agreement?', and: 'Can the conflict be narrowed down by agreeing about part of it, and then considering the remaining area of disagreement?'

Finding agreement

Henare realised, near the start of the meeting, that in a majority vote Miriam, Roy and Moana would all vote for Roy's proposal. Both Moana and Lesley would probably end up unhappy with the result. He understood Miriam's need to avoid having people talking behind her back. She gave a more detailed account of what had happened when Sandy had done this the previous year, and everyone (including Lesley) agreed that this wasn't acceptable. But he wasn't quite clear about Lesley's concern.

'Could you tell me some more about what your concern is Lesley? Maybe: "what would an agreement need to do, for it to work for you?"'

'Well, I don't know.' She frowned. 'I just know that some people find it really hard to do what Roy's asking. Because they don't exactly know what they're upset about.'

Henare nodded: 'And you think in that case, they can't go and tell the person they're annoyed with until they've worked that out.'

Miriam sighed: 'But that's just being unassertive.'

'Maybe it is,' Henare accepted, 'but it's also a genuine difficulty which you, Lesley, are acknowledging someone might have. Are there any ways to support people with that difficulty, which don't involve talking behind people's back either?'

'Getting assertiveness training,' urged Miriam.

'Or having a person like you available to help them work it out', suggested Moana. 'I mean, what you're doing with us is, like, listening so we can sort this out. You could do that with someone who is annoyed, instead of them talking to the parents or anyone off the street who wants to hear.'

'Why can't we do that for each other?' Lesley asked.

'Because that's talking behind each other's back.'

Lesley nodded: 'Yes, but if it was only once to sort out the thing you wanted to say...'

Roy considered. 'Well, I suppose I could live with that if it was very clear how it happened.'

Henare wrote quickly on a sheet of paper. 'OK. We've got three ideas here. Assertiveness training; use a facilitator; talking once with someone to clarify ideas. Any other ideas?'

As they explored further, a solution which combined the first and third suggestion developed. Ideally, people would discuss any unhappiness with the person they had concerns about. If they couldn't work out what to say, though, they could talk it over once only with another person on the staff. That person's job would be to help them go back to the person they were unhappy with, and discuss the challenge in an assertive way.

Henare checked a couple of times to see how well the solution was meeting each person's need or goal. 'Let's just find out how we're going here. On a continuum where this...' he held his arms wide apart, palms facing each other '... represents a perfect solution which meets all your needs, and this...' he held his hands with palms together'... represents a disaster; how would you rate the agreement we've got written down here?' People held their arms with palms at varying distances apart, and had a look around to see the result.

Can we reach consensus?

You'll recognise, from Chapter 8, the win-win conflict resolution method Henare used here. Working with a group, he also needed to find a way to test for 'consensus' which didn't take several minutes of talking. One example is the 'sociometric' method he used above. Another technique would be a 'straw vote', where a vote is taken purely to check how close to total agreement the group is (rather than to find a majority for a win-lose decision). With a long list of possible solutions, one of these methods could be used to assess the initial feeling about each solution.

What about when it just doesn't seem to be possible? Groups that use consensus have evolved many different answers to this question. They include:

- voting on whether to revert to majority rule. If the vote is 'yes', then a second vote decides the issue. If the vote is 'no', the issue is postponed until the next meeting
- representatives of each main 'faction' within the group hold a smaller meeting where they seek a consensus
- a break in the discussion is called. People may use this time to play group building games, to release their feelings about the issue, to relax, or to imagine this situation from the other points of view, and think up new solutions.

Attitude

A facilitator's attitude is as important as her or his skills. Science-fiction writer Theodore Sturgeon tells a story about this attitude (much as I like Sturgeon's fiction, this story happens to be true).

One time during Sturgeon's youth, he was at a family gathering with his grandparents and his uncle. His grandfather was a retired English church rector whose 'brains were beginning to melt just a little', while his grandmother was still very much present and 'in charge'. During the gathering, a ferocious argument erupted between Uncle Ernest and the grandmother, about her attempts to make the decisions for the family. The uncle stormed off in a huff, and took an overdose of the adrenaline which he used to counter his asthma. When he came back, he had pinpoint pupils, his cheeks were fiery red, and he held a.38 automatic pistol in his hand. In fury he screamed that he was going to kill himself and burn down the house.

Frantically working out how best to leap into the fray, and simultaneously wondering how his uncle could burn the house down after killing himself, Sturgeon sat on the edge of his chair. Then suddenly, '... my grandfather came back from Out There, set his tea cup down on the low table, got up and stood nose to nose with the wild man. "I say, Ernest", he said in that soft oboe voice of his, "Why can't we all be chums?"'

Why can't we?

The effect was dramatic. Uncle Ernest burst into laughter, started coughing, and collapsed into a chair, dropping his gun in the process. The humour in this story is, of course, based on the fact that we all recognise the grandfather's out-of-touch naivety. But Sturgeon offers a dramatic reframe. Who, he asks, is really out of touch with reality? The old man with his simple question: 'Why can't we all be chums?' or those of us who sit powerlessly by as a man plans murder? It is a question which Sturgeon says haunts him every time he watches a couple of cats fighting... or a flight of

B52 bombers taking off for some middle eastern village. He concludes: 'So really - why can't we all be chums? Why can't we? Why?

It is precisely this question which the group facilitator asks at each moment, to create consensus.

To recap

The process of helping a group develop win-win solutions that all can live with, is called facilitating consensus. A facilitator's skills must combine meeting structuring and conflict resolution. Meeting structuring includes:

- keeping to arranged start and finish times
- sitting in a circle
- checking how people are, and enabling them to meet as people (building cohesion)
- clarifying the task: (building contract)
  - defining group guidelines
  - listing, timing, and prioritising an agenda
- evaluating at the end (building closure).

To assist the creation of consensus, facilitators use:

- 'I' messages
- reflective listening, both individuals and group
- reframing to find similarities and agreement
- testing for consensus, and
- using alternative strategies such as representative consensus, voting, and time out, when consensus is not achieved.

Activity 10.3

AIM: to develop group members' consensus-building skills

The following tasks require the group to reach consensus. It is best if the group leader explains the task and then sits back, leaving the group to their own devices. Another option is to divide the group in half: one half undertakes the task while the other half observes (one observer sitting behind each person in the task group). The observers can each use a form listing the six group functions, placing a tick beside one of the functions each time the task group member they are observing speaks. These functions are:

a giving information/ opinions
b seeking information/ opinions
c problem-solving the task
d expressing needs/feelings
e encouraging others to express needs/feelings, and
f problem-solving the group process.

Tasks

1 Design an advertising campaign, with a slogan, a poster and a TV ad, to attract people into your group.
2 Rank the following occupations, from those which have the highest percentage of women employed in them, to those which have the lowest percentage.

Builder
Carpenter
Cleaner
Farm worker
Member of parliament
Primary school teacher
Registered nurse
Retail manager
Sales assistant
Secretary
Truck driver

(Answers for New Zealand from Else and Bishop, 2003)

3 New Zealanders were asked: 'What attracted you to your spouse?' in a survey which collected separate results for men and for women. Below are the results (in random order) of the ten most valued qualities listed by each sex. Rank them as you would expect the actual results, from I (most highly rated) to 10 (least highly rated).

(A class could work on one list (men or women), with half undertaking the task and the other half observing, then the two halves could swap to look at the second list.)

Women value	Men value
entertaining ability	entertaining ability
erotic ability	erotic ability
social ability	social ability
looks, physical attraction	looks, physical attraction
general personality	general personality
the way he relates to me	the way she relates to me
good communication	good communication
affection	intelligence
sense of humour	similar interests/activities
quiet and shy	purely sexual attraction

(From Colgan, Dr A. and McGregor, J. *Sexual Secrets,*

Summary

Working successfully with a group draws on the skills discussed throughout this book. In this chapter you have learned two models for understanding groups. The first was a simple model which showed group development as having an inclusion phase, a control phase and an intimacy phase. The second was our division of group needs into two areas: task needs and maintenance needs. Being aware of the balance between these two areas is crucial for any group's success.

This chapter also explained the specific skills of a group facilitator (the person assisting a group to make its decisions). These skills include structuring the meeting so it has a beginning and an end, and including time to meet both task and maintenance needs. They also include such previously explained skills as I messages, reflective listening, refraining and conflict resolution. The creation of win-win solutions in a group is called consensus.

Chapter 11: Conclusions

KEY CONCEPTS
- Stages of grief
- Tangihanga
- Closure, in groups and helping
- Chunking: from specifics to concepts

Saying goodbye

AIM: to be able to discuss closure in human relationships as including grieving, evaluation, referral, and futurepacing.

Ending a relationship

At some time in our life, most of us have had the experience of an important relationship coming to an end. It may have been a marriage ending in divorce, a love affair ending in separation, a friendship terminated by conflict or distance apart, or the death of a close relative.

As you will no doubt remember, these situations bring up powerful feelings - feelings such as sadness and grief, but also, at times, feelings like regret, guilt, confusion, fear, loneliness, relief, depression or anger. It's not always easy to understand where these emotions come from.

Confusing feelings

The most important goodbye in my childhood was the death of my grandmother. Throughout my childhood she had played with me, told me stories, indulged my interest in comics and provided me with a home away from home. It was she who first suggested - when I was four years old - that, because of 'the way I talk', I should be a teacher.

On the day she died, it shocked me to realise that I could not cry for her. Even more mysteriously, on the day of her funeral I completely forgot the situation and went to a friend's place to play. When I arrived home late, my parents were furious. I couldn't understand the incredible anger they unleashed.

It's not just when someone dies that people react in such unpredictable ways. In some -perhaps smaller - ways, any 'goodbye' brings up the range of feelings we describe as grief. Here we'll identify the main 'ingredients' of grief, and think about how to assist people to deal with the ending of a relationship.

Grieving stages?

One well-known model of the grieving process was developed by Swiss doctor Elisabeth Kubler-Ross. Kubler-Ross spent much of her life with those most of us prefer not to think about: the dying. She suggests that those who face a loss tend to work their way through a simple five-step process. Here are the stages as she observed them:

1 Denial and isolation: 'It can't be true... no, not me'
2 Anger and blaming: 'Why me?'
3 Bargaining: 'If I live, I'll give my life to God'
4 Depression: A temporary 'shutdown'
5 Acceptance: 'It's OK'

In research on those who are grieving, however, there is no clear evidence at all for Kubler-Ross' stages. Researchers such as Robert Neimeyer (2002) urge that we face the fact that there is no guaranteed set of stages that people go through in grief, and no required set of emotions that proves they are grieving “correctly”. Neimeyer suggests that grief can best be thought of as the creation of new meanings which support a person making sense of their life in a changing context. Researchers quoted in his book are finding that those who pass through grief frequently report an increased sense of independence, and a sense of clearer values.

There is also no evidence that people have to cry a certain amount in order to have grieved “correctly”. Certainly, it is normal to weep when someone close to you dies. However, the more someone cries after the death of a spouse, the more likely they are to experience prolonged and pathological grief reactions (Znoj, 1997). Furthermore, if people do not become overly tearful early on after bereavement, then they are not likely to become overly tearful or depressed later either. There is no truth to the theory that those who don't cry early on will suffer some "delayed grief reaction". Research now reveals this to be a myth promoted by those who needed a validation of traditional models of grief. In grief, those who cope well early on will also tend to cope well later (Bonanno and Field, 2001).

The NLP grief process

In this context, the developers of NLP have proposed a radically new approach to resolving grief. Steve and Connirae Andreas, in their book *Heart of the Mind,* note that the length of time people take to recover from grief depends almost entirely on their beliefs about what is appropriate timing. This varies between cultures and between individuals. Whenever the time seems right, whether that is hours or years after a significant loss, people make certain predictable changes to the way they think of the object of their grief. That is, they change the submodalities they use when they think of that person or thing (see Chapter 2).

NLP trainers set out to model exactly how people who have successfully resolved grief, undertook the process. They found that these people tended to have experienced successful recovery from loss before. From this discovery, they developed a way of transferring these already existing processes of recovery, into the situation where grief has not yet been resolved.

The following is an example of a client who resolved a long-term grief challenge, in a session with NLP trainer Margot Hamblett. Margot was my life partner and co-trainer until her death in 2001, and the very process which she describes here is one I also used to help respond resourcefully to my own loss after her death.

'When Gail came to see me, her husband had been dead for 15 years. Gail had successfully brought up three children on her own, and was a successful businessperson. But she was constantly struggling with depression, and was distressed by her frequent angry outbursts at her teenage children. After all this time, she felt a deep sense of rage at being abandoned. Whenever someone asked if she had a husband, tears would instantly spring to her eyes, and she would experience an agonising sense of pain and absence. She found this distressing and embarrassing. Although Gail wanted a new relationship, and Often met men she liked, she felt there was a part of her that was "still waiting" for her husband to come back.

'I asked Gail to think of someone she used to be close to, perhaps when she was much younger, who she no longer had contact with. Someone she could think of now with a really good feeling. She smiled with pleasure as she talked about a friend, Linda, who was a student with her 20 years ago. Linda had since moved overseas, and Gail had lost touch with her, but she still enjoyed remembering her.

'I asked Gail to notice the visual image of Linda that she could see when she thought of her, Then I asked questions about the submodalities of the image. We discovered that Gail was making a large, clear, brightly coloured picture of Linda. The picture seemed to be about one foot in front of her, a little to her left. In the image, Linda was laughing happily.

'When I asked Gail how she pictured her husband, she saw him in the hospital bed where he had died. This time, the picture was small, dark, and shadowy. It was a little further away, about two feet in front, to her right. She tensed up again as she thought of him.

'I checked with her that it would be OK to have the same kind of good feelings she had when she thought about Linda, when she thought about her husband. She said that would be amazing, and just what she wanted.

'"OK, " I said, "now just imagine that picture of your husband moving rapidly away from you, out in front of you, until it disappears as a tiny dot off the horizon. Now I'd like you to bring back from the horizon a new picture, and bring it to this place where the picture of Linda was. The new picture is an image of your husband at a time he was well and happy, a time you can enjoy remembering. Bring it right here now, (gesturing the position) and make it big, bright, and really clear. How does that look now?"

'She let out a long breath, and relaxed. "That looks really good," she said, with a smile. Then she frowned. "But it doesn't seem like this picture will stay there."

'"That's right, " I said. "Let's just repeat that until it stays. Get back that old picture of him over there, make it go way out to the horizon, then bring back the new picture over here, big, bright and clear. Now repeat that as quickly as you can until you can't get back the old picture any more. "

'She concentrated for a few minutes, then relaxed and smiled again. "It's gone. I can only get the new one now. "

'"So how is that different now?"

'"It's amazing. I feel really calm... I feel at peace. It's strange in a way, because I feel as if now I really know that he's dead, but at the same time, I feel much closer to him. I have a sense that he will always be with me."

Following this session, Gail's mood lifted, and she reported enjoying her life again. She said she did not think of her husband very often now, but when she did, she enjoyed recalling the good times they had shared. She had stopped 'snapping' at her kids, and was aware of positive experiences she was enjoying in her life. In our experience, these results are typical of the NLP grief process.

Take a moment now, to think of someone you used to enjoy being close to, someone who is no longer part of your life. Someone it feels <u>good</u> to think about. For example, many people have old school friends who they think of in this way. The person may have died, or moved away, or simply lost contact with you. It is important to choose someone who you can think of now without any sense of pain or loss. When you remember them, you feel only pleasant feelings, as you think of the good experience of being with them.

As you think of that person now, notice the picture that you have of them. Check the submodalities of the picture: the closeness or distance, and the exact location of the picture (for example, is it in front or behind, to left or right). Also notice the size, brightness and clarity, and whether the image is still, like a photograph, or moving, like a film. It is common for the image of this person you feel good about to be close up, bright, and moving. Whatever <u>your</u> image is like, these submodalities are your brain's way of coding <u>resolved grief.</u> This means that if there is ever a time in your life when you want to move through the natural grieving process more quickly, (for example, if you felt stuck or unable to move on), you can do it easily. You simply need to change the submodalities of the image of the person you have lost, into the submodalities of resolved <u>grief</u> that you have just identified. You will then experience the good feelings and different perspective that goes with this state.

It is also important to check that, when you think of the person you have lost, the image is a positive one. For example think of them at a time when they were well, rather than sick or hurt. If the circumstances of the loss were traumatic, it is useful to do the NLP trauma process (see Chapter 4).

In addition to this submodality change, it can be very helpful to spend a few minutes reviewing all the positive experiences you had with the person in the past, and all the positive qualities of your relationship. Realise that all these experiences and qualities are an important and precious part of you, which you now carry into all your future experiences.

It is important to remember that using this process to heal grief should be a matter of choice -it should only be used when a person chooses to use it. We have helped many people with this short process, even when they have been distressed by grief for years. It generally allows them to resolve any pain that was there, and to recover an appropriate sense of appreciation and closeness to their memory of the person.

The tangihanga

Each culture finds its own way to say goodbye. The Maori tangihanga, or funeral, acknowledges a grief cycle which involves all of the five stages suggested by Elisabeth Kubler-Ross. Throughout these stages, a fundamental belief in another form of life is expressed. The dead have passed on to the next plane of existence, referred to as Hawaiki nui Hawaiki roa, Hawaiki pamamao.

At the tangihanga, unfinished business is dealt with: time is given for people to openly vent anger, frustration, excitement, happy memories and so on. The event also provides a platform that allows and welcomes people sharing other sources of grief and anger (apart from that of the death of the person for whom the tangi is being held).

The processes of haakari and whakangaahau (celebration with food and entertainment) coupled with 'takahi o te whare' (tramping the house to ensure the dead person's soul or spirit has departed and has no need to delay its journey back to Hawaiki) allows mourners time (generally three days and nights after the burial - sometimes shorter, but never longer) to refocus on real life again. Closure occurs through a group process (i.e. whanaungatanga, relationship).

The poroporoaki (farewell) allows people time to detach from the gathering and refocus their attention on departing for home.

Closure in a group

In a group, the goodbye could be called 'closure'. The whole group may weave its way through stages which are the reverse of Schutz's group development model.

Schutz says that towards the end of its life, the issues of inclusion, control and intimacy reemerge in a group in reverse order, thus:

* Intimacy: People daydream, arrive late and/or forget to come more often,

and withdraw from closeness.

* Control: People may bring up old issues and re-evaluate the group leader. They may also attempt to bargain for the group to continue.

* Inclusion: People begin to look forward to a life without the group, no longer thinking of themselves as group members. This may not occur until some time after the actual separation.

Closure in helping

It's important for helpers to be aware that the same process occurs for both them and their clients. When I was nursing, the very first patient under my individual care was an elderly man. The day before I left his ward, I explained that the next day would be my last on his ward.

'I suppose I won't see you again then', he said sadly.

'Oh no', I reassured him, overwhelmed by my own sadness. 'I'll be able to come back in and check how you are, on my way to the next ward.'

A week later I realised, with a little maths, that within six months I might be 'checking in' on about 24 people a day: it was important that I begin to acknowledge closure.

Helpers can set aside time to assist the closure process, whether they are working with individuals or with groups. During this time, their tasks include evaluation, referral and futurepacing.

Evaluation

Evaluation means checking:

* how the process of the relationship was for each person, and
* Whether any specific goals were achieved.

At the end of a group session, time could be provided for people to say one thing they liked and one thing they'd change about the session. A counsellor might use one or more sessions to review the story of their counselling, check achievement of the original goals, and discuss what the person's next step will be.

Referral

This next step may well include referring the person on to another helper or group. If you want your referral to work, there are three important factors to consider:

1. The person you are referring

It is crucial to discuss the suggestion fully with them, and to explain the advantages you believe referral will have. After all, it is their feelings that will determine whether referral works. They deserve to know what, if any, information you intend to give their new helper.

2. The person/s you are referring them to

Ensuring you understand what service they offer, and how they like people to be referred, will enable them to feel more positive about their new client. There may be special information they need from you, or other help they'd like to be able to get from you.

3. The linking process

This includes ensuring the person you refer knows when and where they will meet up with their next helper. It may even involve you assisting at this meeting.

Futurepacing

'Futurepacing' means referral back to real life. It is the process of ensuring that personal changes don't stay 'anchored' to the relationship with the helper, but are anchored to the real-life situations where they are needed.

My friend Annette and I shared an office. Each time Annette came to work and saw my biscuits, she remembered that it was nice to have a snack available for morning tea. She was committed to buying some to share, but in the meantime she shared mine. After some weeks, we realised that this was a challenge of futurepacing. Annette's good intentions (of buying biscuits) were anchored to the office (where they were utterly useless - our office did not have a biscuitvending machine).

I got Annette to imagine herself coming into her local dairy. I told her to see the things that she would see as she came in the door, and to look over to the shelf where the biscuits were. I told her to imagine herself walking over to the shelf and picking up a packet. In this way, her good intention would be likely to be anchored to the naturally occurring sights and feelings of Annette's real life, the exact moment before they were needed. Sure enough, the next time Annette came into the office, she reported success. She had walked into the dairy to buy milk, seen the biscuit shelf, walked over to it ... and realised she had no money in her pocket to buy biscuits!

Using futurepacing

Anyway, you get the hang of it from my story If you want people to do the things they learn in their real life, simply get them to roleplay, or to imagine themselves in the situations, doing the things they have learned. This is the natural way people use to remember things. If you decide you are going to compliment your friends more, you imagine seeing your friend in front of you, you hear her or his voice, you feel your mouth forming the words, and you listen to the sound as it will sound in real life. People who rehearse new skills in this way are likely to use them. That's futurepacing.

At the end of a course, a group session or a counselling process, futurepacing is the natural link to a new way of life. Imagine how your memory will improve when you use it. See yourself in your mind's eye, right now, as you rehearse your way through all those things that in the past you've forgotten. Hear the words you'd say if you were futurepacing, and be aware of the self-assured feeling that a good memory will give you...

Life and death

Once we are more aware of closure, we actually value our time together. Elisabeth KublerRoss says that she considers our western culture has lost immeasurably by hiding death from view. When parents realise that their children may die, they tend to put a lot more energy into saying how they love them and a lot less into yelling at them. When a person knows they are going to die, they are far less likely to waste their life 'waiting for something to happen' or brooding over a past argument that they never bother to resolve. Their lives, Kubler-Ross suggests, often become richer, more real, more loving.

NLP developer Richard Bandler says that the thing that struck him when he began working as a therapist, was that people spend a lot of their time waiting. Waiting to relax, waiting to have fun, waiting to do the things they need to do. Their lives have no closure (Bandler & Grinder 1979, p193).

If you knew that today was the last day of your life, what things would you want to do? Who would you spend time with? What things would you want to say to those people? Now.. what stops you from actually doing those things? Whatever it is, is it really so important that it's worth waiting for all of your life, day after day? Every moment that passes will never return. The sky above you will never again look just like it does at this moment. The sound of the birds outside, or the laughter of the children, or the rise and fall of the wind is for this second only. And the actual feeling of your body, of life flowing through your lungs and your heart, can only be experienced now. The memory is not the same.

Death is real - utterly, undeniably real. But only as real as the fact that you are alive right now. If all my wishes for you were one wish, it would be that you live each moment with the understanding that this truth can bring.

To recap

Grieving tends to involve the five processes of:

1. denial and isolation
2. anger
3. bargaining
4. depression, and
5. acceptance.

If you are bringing closure to a relationship, be aware that these feelings may occur. However focusing on what has been positive in the relationship is an important part of the creation of new meaning after a goodbye.

You could also plan opportunities to:

- evaluate how the relationship went
- assist linking up others to a new relationship, in referral, and
- help the person anchor new learnings to the sensory experiences of real life, a process called futurepacing. Being more aware of closure means living each moment more fully.

Activity 11. 1

AIM: to futurepace the learnings from your course

I Use the relaxation activity (activity 2.3, see page 27) or a similar process.

2 The group leader should then read out the following instructions, using the same relaxed voice as in (1), pausing briefly at each'...'

'Now I'd like you to remember how it was when you first began this course...

the things you saw as you first came into this group and heard my voice and the voices of the others in the group... and the feeling of sitting in the chairs for the first time... and really wondering... what the course is going to be like... and whether you will learn new things... because there are many ways to learn new things... not only by listening to the things I explained and reading about communication skills... but also by really meeting the people in the group... and particularly those people in this group who have had special importance for you... at those specific times when you really enjoyed the fact that they were there... or learned from the things they said... and what you did together... as the course went on... learning new skills... and trying out the ways of talking that you discussed here... to see which were most useful for you personally... realising that some of the skills just clicked into place... and you could see right away what use you wanted to make... or feel the way that skill would fit for you... and thinking through the various topics we studied, all the way up to today..

'It's impressive how many things you did learn ... not always what you expected... or even what the course planned ... but what you needed... and now I'd like you to feel all that wisdom inside you... as you remember the place where, above all else you want to use these skills in your life... because if you could use these skills in that most important relationship... even enough to recognise that you are behaving differently now... and you have changed subtly... then you would know that you can use these skills in any situation you need them... at home... with friends... in your job... in this group... and with those people who are most challenging for you... or most precious to you... so let's take a situation where it's most important to use communication skills... and look at that situation... and see the place... and the person or people there... clearly enough so you can see the particular expression they have at the time you can use your new skills... and hear the very tone of voice which reminds you that now is the time to find the words you need ... which is the very best time to anchor that feeling of relaxation again ... and imagine yourself actually using the skills you have learned' [pause]

'listening as you surprise yourself with a new way of responding to whatever they say... and always knowing that in your collection of skills you can find the right solutions... now or in the future... so that you may be beginning to be aware of the sense of confidence that this will bring... and how these new skills can create whole new ways to meet your needs and the needs of those you love... which is a good understanding to bring back to the room... as you become aware of your surroundings here in the room... returning in your own time to being fully aware and awake and ready to talk again.'

Activity 11.2

AIM: to create a sense of closure in life

Imagine that this is the last day of your life. You take a pen and paper to write some final comments on your life to leave for those you love.

1 You have 20 minutes to write answers to the following questions:
   a. What have you valued most of all in your life?
   b. What are the most important insights you have gained from life?
   c. Who or what had the most influence on your life?
   d. What has challenged you most in this life?
   e. What are your life's most important achievements?
   f. What are your biggest unfulfilled dreams or desires?
   g. What would you do differently if you had the chance?
   h. Who do you need to speak to today? What will you say?
   i. What do you most want to do today?
   j. What advice do you have for others in a similar life to yours?

2 Share in pairs:
   a. What did you learn writing this?
   b. Which questions were most difficult to answer?
   c. Which questions were most useful to consider?

Putting the pieces together

AIM: to be able to use the process of chunking to assist learning.

The shrine

Once upon a time, a brave explorer travelled into the centre of a harsh, lifeless desert. There she discovered a mysterious group of people. In the only oasis in the desert wastes, these people were facing hard times. There was barely enough food for them to survive from one year to the next, and in the cold winter nights the weaker of the people died from lack of adequate nourishment and covering.

For many years they had braved this terrible environment, but it did not seem likely that even those courageous souls who were left would last much longer... for the high priest of this people, a man named Ler-Na, had taken to demanding an ever-increasing share of their food as offerings to his sacred shrine.

The explorer was puzzled. Crossing the desert had been risky, but there was a way. Surely these people could have left their tiny oasis and found their way to the green pastures beyond the desert's end. Why had they never sent out scouts to search for the passage? Did their ancestors not know the way?

Eventually, she confronted Ler-Na and asked him these questions. He smiled tolerantly, and beckoned her to follow him.

'I know you are puzzled,' he answered reassuringly, 'but our deliverance is at hand. We have the answer to all our problems right here in this oasis, and it was indeed passed on to us by those same ancestors who brought us here. If only we treat it with the reverence it deserves, it will end all the difficulties we face here. It can also help you and your people.'

He led her into a deep cave beside the village. At first she could not see in the darkness, but as the priest lit a lantern the explorer recognised what must surely be the sacred shrine itself. Around it she could see the ashes of the food offerings. And perched on top of a huge stone slab was the magical focus of this people's religion.

'You may touch it,' the priest encouraged, 'it is for the benefit of all humanity. We are merely the caretakers of this powerful magic.'

Slowly, she opened it. Perfect in every detail, it was a map of the region, clearly marking the way out to green pastures.

Maps and actualities

The people of the oasis are starving because of a confusion about the purpose of maps. Every one of us moves around in the world by the use of our maps - our internal models of reality. But maps are only of use if you are willing to put them aside once you have studied them, and actually live.

This book gives you many new maps to understand communication: maps such as ' challenge ownership', 'problem solving', 'helping' and 'assertiveness'. Once you have learned these maps you will know' where you are' in a relationship, and 'which road to take' to get to the places you want to be.

Like the explorer, you will understand that these maps are not sacred. It is life itself which is sacred. Where the map doesn't fit with your life, you will have the wisdom to redesign the map so it suits you. Maps are only useful when they help you get around in the world.

Six main maps

There are six main maps in this book. They are:

1. States: With this map you can recognise what state of mind you and others are in, change your own state, and assist others to change theirs.
2. From problems to solutions: This map enables you to recognise who owns a challenge, and to find useful solutions.
3. Helping: When someone else owns a challenge, this map gives you specific skills to assist them in finding solutions that will work for them.
4. Assertion: This map provides specific skills to express your own feelings or opinions, and explain your own challenges in relation to others, without putting others down.
5. Resolving conflict: Combining the maps for problem-solving - helping and assertion - this map helps you to prevent, recognise and resolve the three types of conflict.
6. Group work: With this last map, the skills of the other five maps can be used in the more complex environment of a group.

Each of these six main maps has several sub-maps, as shown below. Helping and assertiveness have a special relationship: a relationship of balance. Assertion is more active, ensuring my needs are met, whereas helping is more passive, simply enabling the other person to meet their needs.

The diagram on the next page is used in China and Japan to express the way active and passive intertwine. As the diagram shows, in the middle of active (assertive) times, there is also a place for being passive. In the middle of passive (helping) times, there is an area where being active is useful. In conflict resolution and group work, this balance between assertion and helping is emphasised even more.

Chunking down

The final skill which I want to explain to you is the skill of creating your own maps.

Try saying the alphabet to yourself for a moment... The alphabet has 26 bits of information (letters) in it, and to remember it you almost certainly said it in sections rather than in a continuous stream. These sections are called 'chunks', and the process of dividing something up into little bits is called chunking down. To learn a complex subject you need to chunk it down. You probably remember people's telephone numbers the same way: in two chunks.

7 ± 2

Communications theorist George Miller, from Harvard University, (reported in *Accelerated Learning* by C. Rose 1985), published a remarkable paper about chunking down. He showed that people can hold only between five and nine (or 'seven plus or minus two' to use Miller's words) bits of information at one time. So if you want to remember something, break it into chunks that have around seven facts each. Using lists of 10 or 20 things makes them difficult to remember. Incidentally, this principle is also used in this book. All 'unchunked' lists have seven or less items. For example, look at the diagram on page 326: there are six main maps: states, challenge management, helping, assertion, conflict management and group work. Each of these is then chunked into five or less sections.

Balancing Assertion and Helping

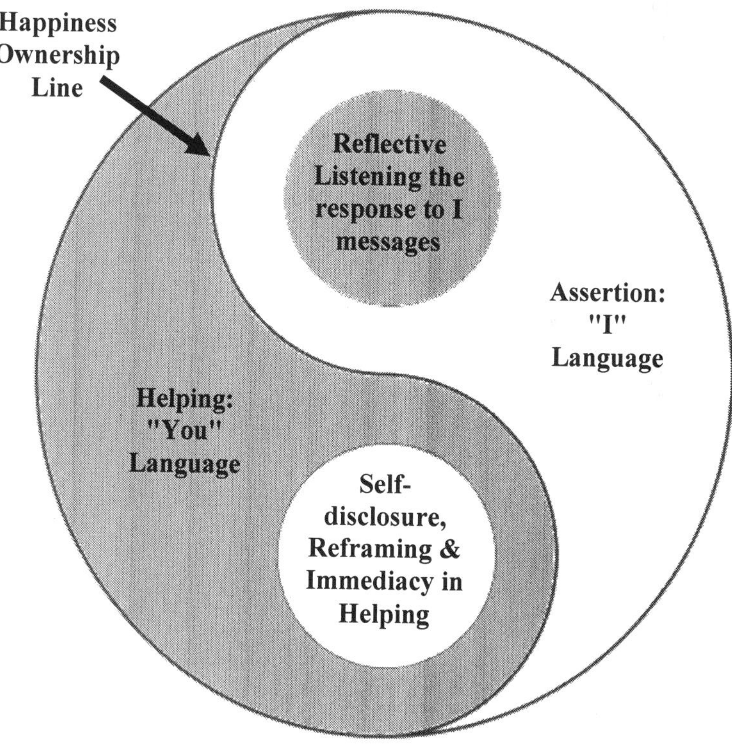

The Transforming Communication Model

It is also possible to understand the book as an algorithm for assessing the situation in a relationship from moment to moment and taking the most effective action to create rapport. In this decision-making flowchart, notice that there are two pivotal points: checking whether anyone owns a challenge, and, in the case of a disagreement, using the "Two step" process to check what type of conflict is involved.

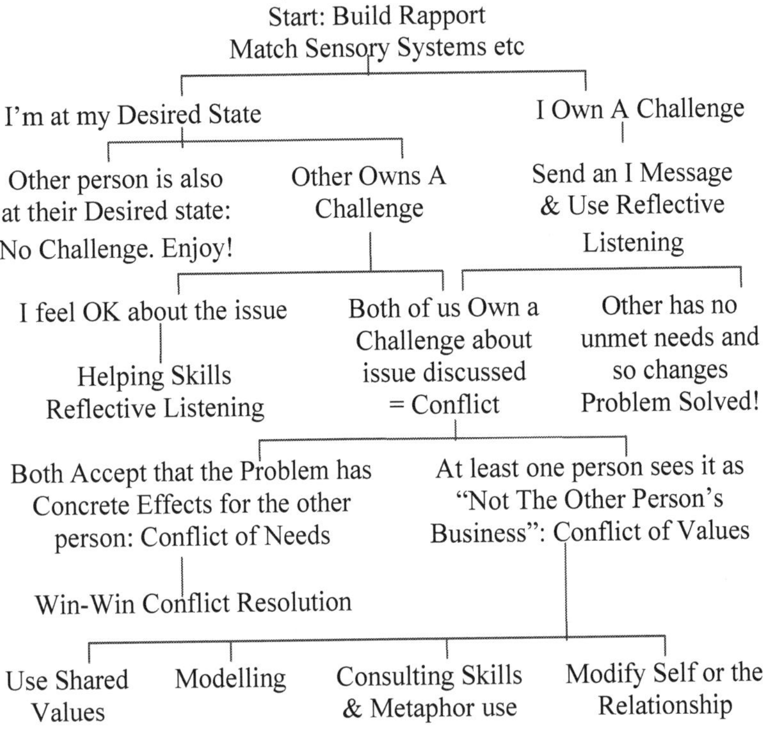

Sections of this book grouped in six main maps

States: Create states, Rapport, Incongruity, Non-verbals, Sensory language.

Challenges to Solutions: Happiness ownership. Goalsetting.

Helping: Avoiding Rescue. Listening. Advanced helping Helping models.

Assertion: Assertiveness model. I messages. Introductions.

Conflict: Power use. Prevention. Needs Conflict. Values Conflict. Metaprograms.

Group-work: Grp development. Facilitation. Warmup. Closure. Leadership skills.

Chunking up or down

Knowing when to chunk down (get more detailed) and when to chunk up (get more general) is extremely important in communication. It's the secret behind many of the skills taught in this book. Whenever you are defining a challenge (for example, telling someone in an I message what upsets you, or helping a person clarify what upsets them), it's important to chunk down to details.

This means talking in a' sensory specific' way - saying what you can see, hear, smell, taste and touch. Most people (including most counsellors and therapists) tend to forget this. They talk about people being 'nice', or 'aggressive', or 'unsupportive'; 'coping', 'not coping'; 'in such and such a role', 'neurotic', 'psychotic', 'negative', and so on, without clarifying exactly what they saw or heard. As a result, others who are listening have to guess what actually happened - to 'hallucinate' the meaning. Usually, they hallucinate differently from the speaker. Defining a challenge as: 'I felt really resentful when you started speaking halfway through my sentence' will need less hallucination than: 'Your aggressive manner bothers me'.

On the other hand, when you are seeking new solutions to challenges, it can help to chunk up -to get more general. Reframing is an example of chunking up. It involves making new and more useful generalisations about what is happening. When someone says: 'I hate you', to say: 'Thank you for being honest' is reframing; it makes a new generalisation ('being honest') about the three specific words 'I hate you'. To chunk up, ask yourself, 'What is this specifically an example of?'

Conflict resolution involves chunking up. When you define your basic goals or needs instead of your solution, you are describing things in a more general, less specific way. Instead of saying, ' I want the car this Saturday night ' (a specific solution) you say 'I need to get to my meeting on Saturday' (a more general goal which could have several specific solutions).

Learning as chunking

All the models, the maps, the 'communication skills' in this book are generalisations from specific things that people said and did. Thomas Gordon (1970), for example, developed the six step process of win-win conflict resolution. When he taught it to parents, several came back to his classes saying it didn't work for their specific situations. These situations included a teenage daughter wanting to wear a miniskirt, an adolescent who preferred a group of friends his parent didn't like, an a youngster who refused to go to church.

From these specific situations, Gordon recognised a general principle: there were two different types of conflict (conflicts of needs and values collisions) and the win-win method was not the most effective skill for values conflicts. Here is the process Gordon used:

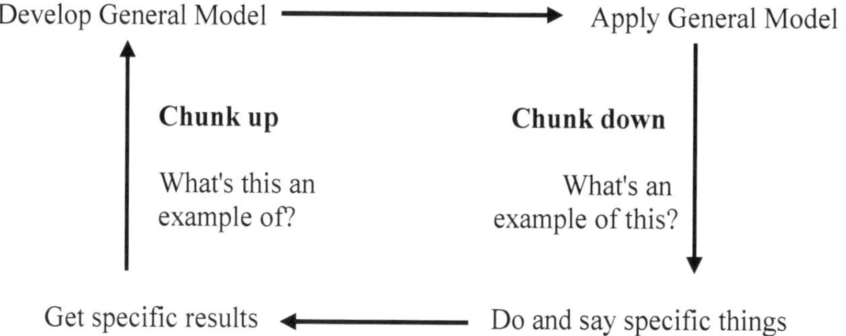

If you've been doing the exercises in this book, you've already been using this learning process. As you use communication skills in more and more specific situations, you're able to create generalisations which work for you (your own maps). In summary:

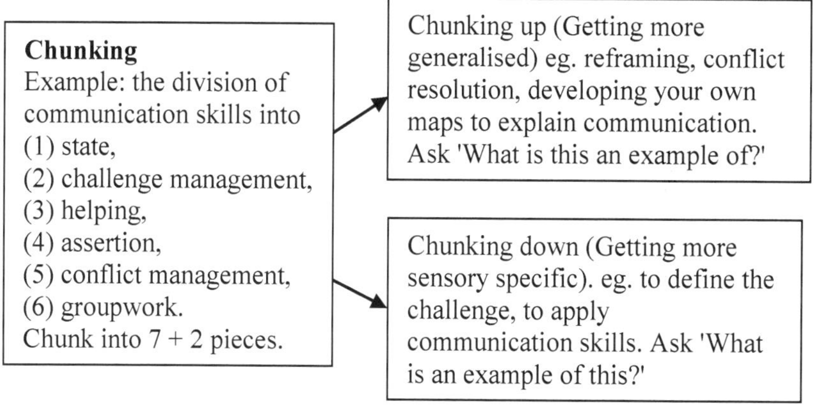

Chunking
Example: the division of communication skills into
(1) state,
(2) challenge management,
(3) helping,
(4) assertion,
(5) conflict management,
(6) groupwork.
Chunk into 7 + 2 pieces.
Chunking up (Getting more generalised) eg. reframing, conflict resolution, developing your own maps to explain communication. Ask 'What is this an example of?'
Chunking down (Getting more sensory specific). eg. to define the challenge, to apply communication skills. Ask 'What is an example of this?'

Love.

The most useful generalisation I've been able to make about communication is that good communication is based in love. From the beginning, when my very survival depended on my mother and father's love, life has repeated this message again and again.

I thank those who have taught me personally (people like John Grinder, Tad James, John Overdurf, Julie Silverthorn, Steve Andreas, Connirae Andreas, George Sweet, Fred Grosse and Vimala Thakar) for so clearly demonstrating and re-emphasising the importance of love. It seems to me that the writings of the great explorers in communication (I think of Carl Rogers, Thomas Gordon, Virginia Satir and Milton Erickson) are also most of all about love. And love improves when you share it.

Whatever you've learned in this book will become clearer when you let it flow on to others. In Alcoholics Anonymous this is called 'The Twelfth Step'. When one alcoholic reaches sobriety, he or she finds another to help. I don't know whether you will teach, whether you will be a parent, a counsellor, a caregiver or an artist, but I know you will find a time and place to reinforce your own learning by helping another learn whatever was precious here.

Gifts

No gift is too small that it cannot make a difference. You may be surprised where your assistance to another ends up. For example, when I was four years old, my mother bought me a young children's version of the *Bambi* story She must have read it to me a hundred times -so many times that by the end I finally understood that the first five chunks of letters on page one were the first five words of the story. I had learned to read. Would I be writing a book now if not for that gift? Probably not.

When I was nine, my father told me how, during his own childhood, he used to spend hours lying on a tree branch overlooking a river. And there he dreamt of the future, and asked himself what life was. I could see the light in his eyes as he remembered this. Would I be writing here about the importance of love if I never had that childhood permission to wonder about the meaning of it all? I doubt it.

Anthony Robbins (1988, p 326) tells the following story about passing on what you receive:

'When I was a kid, our parents worked extremely hard to take good care of us. For various reasons we found ourselves in extremely tight financial situations. I remember one Thanksgiving when we had no money. Things were looking dim until someone arrived at thefront door with a box full of canned goods and a turkey. The man who delivered it said it was from someone who knew we would not ask for anything and loved us and wanted us to have a great Thanksgiving. I never forgot that day. So every Thanksgiving, I do what someone did for me that day: Igo out and buy about a week's worth of food and deliver it to a family in need. I deliver the food as the worker or delivery boy, never as the person actually providing the gift. I always leave a note that says: "This is from someone who cares about you, and hopes some day you will take good enough care of yourself that you'll go out and return the favour for someone else in need. '"

That's the note I'd like to leave with this book, too. I have no illusions about the world. The world can be a very brutal place, and good communication is rare. But you and I both know that it can change. Live long and prosper. And as you discover the secrets of living your life fully, may you pass them on to someone else in need.

Activity 11.3

AIM: to practise the use of chunking, and teaching communication skills

1 Reach a group consensus as to which are the five most important communication skills for a particular population (for example: high school students, healthcare workers, parents, a particular work group).

2 Plan five two-hour sessions at which you will teach these five skills to a group of these people. Take 30 minutes. Decide:

- how well you expect the students to learn these skills
- what handouts with information, or worksheets, you'll need, and
- what activities you will use to practise the skills.

Summary

Mostly this chapter has been about endings. We examined Kubler-Ross' grief process (denialanger-bargaining-depression-acceptance), and considered various situations where grief is expressed, including the Maori process of tangihanga. For those times when the ending of a relationship is planned, we can assist the process of closure by allowing for evaluation, referral, and futurepacing.

As part of the ending of this book, this chapter not only presents an overview of the concepts taught, but also an explanation of chunking. Chunking is the actual process of making generalisations from the details of our experience. With it you can design your own map of this book, and create your own concepts.

A farewell

The first book I read about communication changed my life. I was 12 years old, and the book (it happened to be *Between Parent and Child* by Dr Haim Ginott) explained I messages and reflective listening. Right away I felt incredibly excited. I realised that these simple ideas would enable people to relate in an entirely different way.

If you've read this far, you have shared in that excitement. You will have learned some new ways of understanding what goes on in your life; you may have discovered some new skills, or looked at some old skills in a new light; and you may notice, even now, some changes in the way you're thinking about your relationships. And that's good, because it means that your experience has already begun to shift at a deeper level, hasn't it? You are moving towards the kind of choices you've wanted to make.

But you've done much more than read a book, because this book is a journey through many of the things that are precious to me personally. In that very real sense, I believe you will have met me, and those who wrote this book with me. And so you'll understand that I wish you well, as your conscious mind considers and makes sense of all these things, and as your unconscious mind creates opportunities for you to put into practice those things that will work for you.

If I could make one final suggestion, it would be that you put this book somewhere easy for you to find when you want to read it again.

Best wishes as you return to your present and to your journey.

Index to activities

Answers to activities

Activity 4.4

There are an infinite number of solutions. Any solution where the cake is cut in half first and then the halves are divided into an even half, will also work. Any solution where two lines cross the centre at right angles will work. Solutions can be found by complex division of the square, or by using curved lines to vary any other solution.

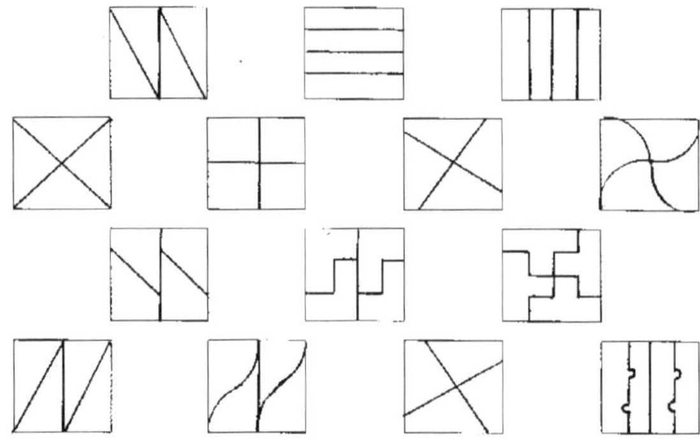

Activity 10.3

Percentage of Women Employed in NZ 2001

97% Secretary
94% Registered nurse
84% Primary school teacher
69% Cleaner
62% Sales assistant
47% Retail manager
32% Farm worker
28% Member of parliament
03% Truck driver
01% Carpenter
01% Builder

Most preferred characteristics in a spouse:

	Women		**Men**
1	Looks, physical attraction	1	Looks, physical attraction
2	Way he relates to me	2	General personality
3	General personality	3	Way she relates to me
4	Good communication	4	Erotic ability
5	Sense of humour	5	Intelligence
6	Social ability	6	Similar interests/attitudes
7	Affection	7	Good communication
8	Erotic ability	8	Entertaining ability
9	Entertaining ability	9	Social ability
10	Quiet and shy	10	Purely sexual attraction

Further reading

Chapter 1

Fine, D. *(2005) The Power of Meeting New People, Start Conversations, Keep Them Going, Build Rapport, Develop Friendships, and Expand Business*, Possibility Press, Austin, Texas

Cotton, G. *(2013) Say anything to anyone, anywhere!: 5 Keys to Successful Cross-Cultural Communication*, Wiley, New York

Metge, J. and Kinloch, P. *(1984) Talking Past Each Other,* Victoria University Press, Wellington

Chapter 2

Andreas, S. and Faulkner, C. (Ed) *(1994) NLP: The New Technology Of Achievement,* William Morrow and Company, New York

Andreas, C. and Andreas, S. *(1989) Heart Of The Mind,* Real People Press, Moab, Utah

Wake, L., Gray, R.M. and Bourke, F.S. eds *(2013) The Clinical Effectiveness of Neurolinguistic Programming* Routledge, London

Chapter 3

Pease, A. *(1990) Body Language,* Camel Publishing, Avalon Beach, New South Wales, Australia

Robbins, A. *(1988) Unlimited Power,* Simon & Shuster, London

Gottman, J.M. and Silver, N. *(1999) The Seven Principles For Making Marriage Work* Three Rivers Press, New York

Chapter 4

Gordon, Dr *1 (1974) T.E.T. Teacher Effectiveness Training,* Peter H. Wyden, New York

Robbins, A. *(1988) Unlimited Power,* Simon & Schuster, London

Wiseman, R. *(2009) 59 Seconds: Think A Little, Change A Lot.* Macmillan, London

Chapter 5

Egan, G. *(1975) The Skilled Helper,* Brooks/Cole Publishing, Monterey, California

Gordon, Dr *T. (1974) TE.T Teacher Effectiveness Training,* Peter H. Wyden, New York

Chapter 6

Bolstad, R. *(2002) RESOLVE: A New Model of Therapy* Crown House, Bancyfelin, Wales

Bolstad, R. and Kurusheva, J. *(2013) Out-frames* Transformations, Auckland

Chia, M. and Chia, M. *(1993) Awaken Healing Light Of The Tao* Healing

Tao Books, Huntington, New York
Wake, L. *(2008) Neurolinguistic Psychotherapy: A Postmodern Perspective (Advancing Theory in Therapy*, Routledge, London

Chapter 7

Lange, A. J. and Jakubowski, *P. (1978) Responsible Assertive Behaviour,* Research Press, Champaign, Illinois

Chapter 8

Adams, L. *(1989) Be Your Best,* Perigee, New York
Coleman, P.T. , Deutsch, M. and Marcus, E.C. eds *(2014) The Handbook of Conflict Resolution* Jossey-Bass, Brisbane

Chapter 9

James, T. and Woodsmall, *W. (1988) Time Line Therapy and The Basis of Personality,* Meta Publications, Cupertino, California
Charvet, S.R. *(1997) Words That Change Minds* Kendall/Hunt, Dubuque, Iowa

Chapter 10

Johnson. D.W. and Johnson, *F. (1975) Joining Together: Group Theory and Group Skills,* Prentice-Hall, Englewood Cliffs, New Jersey
Kantor, D. *(2012) Reading the Room: Group Dynamics for Coaches and Leaders* Jossey-Bass, Brisbane

Chapter I I

Rose, C. *(1985) Accelerated Learning,* Accelerated Learning Systems Ltd, Aylesbury, Buckinghamshire, England
O'Connor, J. and Seymour, J. *(1990) Introducing Neuro Linguistic Programming,* Mandala, London

Bibliography

Adams, L. *(1979) Effectiveness Training for Women,* G.P. Putnams Sons, New York

Adams, L. *(1989) Be Your Best,* Perigee, New York

Adamson, G. *(1986) My Pride and Joy,* Collins Harvill, London

Alder, H. *(1995) Think Like A Leader* Piatkus, London

Anderson, C. *(2006) "The Simple Choice"*, p 53 in Newsweek Special Edition on *The Knowledge Revolution*, December 2005 – February 2006.

Anderson, R.C. *(1998) Mid-Course Correction* Peregrinzilla, Atlanta, Georgia, 1998

Andreas, C. and Andreas, S. *(1989) Heart Of The Mind,* Real People Press, Moab, Utah

Andreas, C., and Andreas, T., *(1994) Core Transformation,* Real People Press, Moab, Utah,

Andreas, S. *(1999)* "*What Makes A Good NLPer*?" p 3-6 in *Anchor Point*, Vol 13, No. 10, October 1999

Andreas, S. and Andreas, C. *(1987) Change Your Mind and Keep The Change,* Real People Press, Moab, Utah

Andreas, S. and Faulkner, C, (Ed) *(1994) NLP: The New Technology Of Achievement,* William Morrow and Company, New York

Andrillon, T., Nir, Y., Cirelli, C., Tononi, G., and Fried, I. *(2015) "Single-neuron activity and eye movements during human REM sleep and awake vision"*, Nature Communications, Volume: 6, Article number: 7884, doi:10.1038/ncomms8884, 11 August 2015

Ash, M.K. *The Mary Kay Way: Timeless Principles from America's Greatest Woman Entrepreneur* Wiley, New York, 2008

Ash, M.K. *(2008) The Mary Kay Way: Timeless Principles from America's Greatest Woman Entrepreneur* Wiley, New York, 2008

Avrey, M., Auvine, B., Streibel, B., Weiss, L. *(1981) Building United Judgement,* Centre for Conflict Resolution, Madison, Wisconsin

Bach, G.R. and Deutsch, R.M. *(1970) Pairing,* Avon Books, New York

Baird, J.E. *(1976) Sex Differences in Group Communication: A Review of Relevant Research,* in *Quarterly Journal of Speech* 62, no.1, (April), pp 179-192

Balcetis, E. and Dunning, D. *(2013) "Wishful Seeing: How Preferences Shape Visual Perception"* Current Directions in Psychological Science February 1, 2013 22: 33-37

Bandler, R. and Grinder, J. *(1979) Frogs Into Princes,* Real People Press, Moab, Utah,

Bandler, R. and Grinder, J. *(1981) Reframing,* Real People Press, Moab, Utah

Bandler, R. and Grinder, J. *(1975) The Structure of Magic I* Science and Behavior Books, Palo Alto, California, 1975

Bandler, R. and La Valle, J. *(1996) Persuasion Engineering*™ Meta Publications, Capitola, California, 1996

Bandler, R. *(1984) Magic In Action*, Meta Publications, Cupertino

Bandler, R., Grinder, J., Satir, V. *(1976) Changing With Families,* Science and Behaviour Books, Palo Alto, California

Batson, C. D., and Coke, J. S. *(1981) "Empathy: A source of altruistic motivation for helping?"* p 167-187 In Rushton, J.P. and Sorrentino, R.M. (Eds.), *Altruism and Helping Behavior* Erlbaum, Hillsdale, New Jersey, 1981

Bennis, W. *(1997) Organising Genius* Nicholas Brealey, London

Berg, I.S. *(1994) Family Based Services, A Solution Focused Approach, W. W.* Norton & Co., New York

Bergin, A. and Garfield, S. *(1994) Handbook of Psychotherapy and Behaviour Change*, Wiley & Sons, New York

Birch, B. *(1988) Marie Curie,* Exley, Watford, Herts

Birdwhistell, R.L. *(1952) Introduction to Kinesics,* University of Louisville Press, Louisville, Kentucky

Block, P. *(1981) Flawless Consulting:A Guide To Getting Your Expertise Used* Pfeiffer & Co., San Diego

Bolstad, R. *(2001) "Co-operative Business",* in *Anchor Point* p 31-41 in Vol 15, No 5 (May 2001); and p 4-11 in Vol 15, No 6 (June 2001)

Bolstad, R. *(1989) Breaking the Ice,* in *Tutor* 37, January 1989, Tutor Education Centre, Wellington

Bolstad, R. *(2002) RESOLVE: A New Model of Therapy* Crown House, Bancyfelin, Wales

Bolstad, R. and Hamblett, M. *(2000) "Preventing Violence In Schools: An NLP Solution"* p 3-14 in *Anchor Point*, Vol 14, No. 9, September 2000

Bolstad, R. and Hamblett, M. *(1995) A New Perspective on Phobia and Trauma,* in *The New Zealand Journal of Counselling, Vol* 17, No. 2

Bolton, K. *(1979) People Skills,* Prentice-Hall, Englewood Cliffs, New Jersey

Bonanno, G.A., and Field, N.P. *(2001) "Evaluating the delayed grief hypothesis across 5 years of bereavement"* p 798-816 in American Behavioral Scientist, No. 44

Bond, J.T., Galinsky, E. and Swanberg, J.E. *(1998) The 1997 National Study of the Changing Workforce* Families and Work Institute, New York, 1998

Booth, P. *(1992) Edmund Hillary: The Life of a Legend*, Moa Beckett, Auckland

Bowman, G. *(1996) "Helping The Blind To See With NLP"* p 44-47 in *Anchor Point*, Vol 10, No. 11, November 1996

Boyett, J. And Boyett, J. *(1998) The Guru Guide* John Wiley & Sons, New York

Brandenburger, A.M. and Nalebuff, B.J. *(1996) Co-opetition* Doubleday, New York

Brockman, W.P. *(1980) "Empathy revisited: the effects of representational system matching on certain counselling process and outcome variables"*, Dissertation Abstracts International 41(8), 3421A, College of William and Mary, 167pp., 1980

Brown, J. *(1992) "Corporation As Community: A New Image For a New Era"* p 122-139 in Renesch, J. ed *New Traditions In Business* Berrett-Koehler, San Francisco, 1992

Brown, L. et alia, Starke, L. ed *(2000) State of the World 2000*, W.W. Norton & Co., London, 2000

Brown, L., Renner, M. and Halweil, B. *(1999) Vital Signs*, W.W. Norton & Co., London

Brummer, A. *(2008) The Crunch* Random House, Croydon, England, 2008

Bush, A. and Geist, C. *(1992) "Geophysical Variables and Behavior: Testing Electromagnetic Explanations for a Possible Psychokinetic Effect of Therapeutic Touch on Germinating Corn Seed".* Psychological Reports, 70

Cameron-Bandler, L. *(1985) Solutions,* Futurepace Books, San Rafael, California

Carkhuff, R.R. *(1973) The Art Of Helping*, Human Resource Development, Amherst, Massachusetts

Carkhuff, R.R. and Berenson, B.G. *(1977) Beyond Counselling and Therapy*, Holt, Rinehart and Winston, New York

Carter, R. *(1998) Mapping The Mind Phoenix*, London

Cedar, R. *(1985) "A Meta-analysis of the Parent Effectiveness Training Outcome Research Literature",* Ed D. Dissertations, Boston University

Chapman, M. and Skinner, E.A. *(1985) "Action in Development – Development in Action"* in Frese, M. and Sabini, J. eds Goal Directed Behaviour LEA, Hillsdale, New Jersey

Charvet, S.R. *(1997) Words That Change Minds* Kendall/Hunt, Dubuque, Iowa, 1997

Chevalier, A.J., *(1995) On The Client's Path*, New Harbinger, Oakland, California

Chia, M. and Chia, M. *(1993) Awaken Healing Light Of The* Tho, Healing Tao Books, Huntington, New York

Chomsky, N. *(1957) Syntactic Structures* Mounton, The Hague

Clanchy, M. *(1986) Sometimes It's Difficult to Say 'Hello',* Hyland House, Melbourne

Cohen, A.R. and Bradford, D.L. *(1991) Influence Without Authority* John Wiley & Sons, New York

Colgan, A. and McGregor, J. *(1981) Sexual Secrets* Alister Taylor, Martinborough, New Zealand

Collins, J.C. and Poros, J.I. *(1996) "Building Your Company's Vision"* in *Harvard Business Review, p 74 in September-October, 1996*

Condon, W. S. *(1982) "Cultural Microrhythms"* p 53-76 in Davis, M. (ed*)* Interactional Rhythms:Periodicity in Communicative Behaviour Human Sciences Press, New York,

Cornelius, R.R. *(2001) "Crying and Catharsis"* p 199-211 in Vingerhoets, Ad J.J.M. and Cornelius, R.R. Adult Crying: A Biopsychosocial Approach Brunner-Routledge, Hove, East Sussex

Coutu, D. *"(2007) Making Relationships Work"* Harvard Business Review, Harvard Business School Publishing, Cambridge, USA, December 2007

Covey, S.R. *(1991) Principle-Centred Leadership* Simon & Schuster, New York, 1991

Craldell, J.S. *(1989) "Brief treatment for adult children of alcoholics: Accessing resources for self care"*p 510-513 in *Psychotherapy*, Volume 26, No 4, Winter, 1989

Craldell, J.S. *(1989) "Brief treatment for adult children of alcoholics: Accessing resources for self care"*p 510-513 in Psychotherapy, Volume 26, No 4, Winter

Csikszentmihalyi, M. *(1990) Flow* Harper Collins, New York

Daviss, B. *(2005) "Tell Laura I Love Her"* p 42-46 in *New Scientist*, Vol 118, No 2528, 3 December 2005

De Bono, E. *(1992) Sur/Petition: Going Beyond Competition* Fontana, London,

Deci, E.L. and Ryan, R.M. *(1985) Intrinsic Motivation and Self-Determination in Human Behaviour* Plenum, New York

Deming, W.E. *(1986) Out Of The Crisis* MIT Centre For Advanced Engineering Study, Cambridge

Derks, L., *(1998) The Social Panorama Model*, Son Repro Service BV, Eindhoven, 1998

Devaliant, J. *(1992) Kate Sheppard* Penguin, Auckland

Dilts, R. and Epstein, T., *(1995) Dynamic Learning,* Meta, Capitola, California

Dilts, R. and McDonald, R. *(1997) Tools Of The Spirit* Meta, Capitola, California, 1997

Dilts, R. *(1998) Modelling With NLP* Meta Publications, Capitola, California, 1998

Dilts, R. *(1996) Visionary Leadership Skills* Meta, Capitola, California, 1996

Dilts, R., Grinder, J., Bandler, R. and DeLozier, J. *(1980) Neuro-Linguistic Programming: Volume 1: The Study of Subjective Experience*, Meta, Cupertino, California

Dilts, R.B. and DeLozier, J.A. *(2000) Encyclopedia of Systemic Neuro-Linguistic Programming and NLP New Coding* NLP University Press, Scotts Valley, California page 125-127

Dilts, R.B., Epstein, T. and Dilts, R.W. *(1991) Tools for Dreamers*, Meta Publications, Capitola, California

Dolan, Y.M. *(1985) A Path With A Heart*, Brunner/Mazel, New York

Dreyfus, Stuart *(1981) "Formal Models vs Human Situational Understanding: Inherent Limitations on the Modeling of Business Expertise*". University of California, Berkeley.

Dreyfus, Stuart and Dreyfus, Hubert. *(1980) "A five Stage Model of the Mental Activities Involved in Directed Skill Acquisition*".

Dunning, D., Heath, C. and Suls, J.M. *(2004) "Flawed Self-Assessment: Implications For Health, Education and the Workplace"* p 69-106 in Psychological Science In The Public Interest Volume 5, 2004

Durie, M. *(1992) Maori Mental Health,* Video, Mental Health Foundation, Auckland

Durie, M. H., & Kingi, T. K. *(1997). A Framework for Measuring Mäori Mental Health Outcomes, A Report to the Ministry of Health.* Palmerston North: Department of Mäori Studies, Massey University.

Egan, G. *(1975) The Skilled Helper,* Brooks/Cole Publishing, Monterey, California

Einspruch, E. *(1988) Neurolinguistic Programming in the Treatment of Phobias,* in *Psychotherapy in Private Practice,* 6(l): 91-100

Elders, F. ed *(1974) Reflexive Water: The Basic Concerns of Mankind* Souvenir Press

Else, A. and Bishop, B. *(2003) Occupational Patterns For Employed New Zealand Women* Ministry of Womens Affairs, Wellington

Emerson, R.W. *(1983) Essays and Lectures* Library of America, New York, 1983

Erickson, M.H. and Rossi, E.L. *(1979) Hypnotherapy: An Exploratory Casebook*, Irvington, New York

Erikson, E. *(1968) Childhood and Society, W.W.* Norton, New York

Eysenck, H. *(1992) The outcome problem in psychotherapy,* in Dryden, W. and Feltham, C. (Ed) in *Psychotherapy and its Discontents,* Open University, Buckingham, pp 100-123

Fadiga, L., Fogassi, G., Pavesi, G. and Rizzolatti, G. *(1995) "Motor Facilitation during action observation: a magnetic stimulation study"* p 2608-2611 in Journal of Neurophysiology, No. 73

Fadiga, L., Fogassi, G., Pavesi, G. and Rizzolatti, G. *(1995) "Motor Facilitation during action observation: a magnetic stimulation study*" p 2608-2611 in *Journal of Neurophysiology*, No. 73, 1995

Feather, N.T. *(1990) "Bridging the gap between values and actions: Implications of the expectancy-value model"* p151-192 in Higgins, E.T. and Sorrentino, R.M. eds, Handbook of Motivation and Cognition Volume 2, Gulford Press, New York, 1990

Fiedler, F.E. *(1951) "Factor analysis of psychoanalytic, non-directive and Adlerian therapeutic relationships*" p 32-38 in *Journal of Consulting Psychology*, No. 15, 1951

Finney, J.W. and Moos, R.H. *(1998) "Psychosocial Treatments for Alcohol Use Disorders"* p 156-1666 in Nathan, P.E. and Gorman, J.M. *A Guide To*

Treatments That Work, Oxford University, New York

Fisher, R. and Ury, W. *(1981) Getting to Yes,* Hutchinson Business, London

Foster, D. *(2000) The Global Etiquette Guide to Asia,* John Wiley & Sons, New York

Franken, A. *(1992) I'm Good Enough, I'm Smart Enough, and Doggone It, People Like Me!* Dell Trade Paperbacks, New York

Frankl, V. *(1969) Man's Search For Meaning: An Introduction to Logotherapy,* Simon & Schuster, New York

Freeman, M. and Bolstad, R. *(2003) "Maybe We Should Ask For Directions, Dear?"* p 3-12 in Anchor Point magazine, Vol 17, No 4

Frey, W.H. *(1985) Crying: The Mystery of Tears,* Winston Press, Minneapolis, Minnesota

Frey, W.H., Hoffman-Ahern, C., Johnson, R.A., Lykken, D.T. and Tuason, V.B., *(1983) "Crying behaviour in the human adult"* p 94-98 in Integrative Psychiatry, Vol 3

Fulghum, R. *(1990) All I Really Need To Know I Learned In Kindergarten,* Grafton Books London

Gaulke, E.H. *(1975) You Can Have A Family Where Everyone Wins,* Lutheran Publishing House, Adelaide

Genser-Medlitsch, M. and Schütz, P., *(1997) "Does Neuro-Linguistic psychotherapy have effect? New Results shown in the extramural section."* Martina Genser-Medlitsch and Peter Schütz, ÖTZ-NLP, Vienna

Ginott, H. *(1965) Between Parent And Child* Avon, New York

Goldratt, E.M. *(1985) The Goal* North River Press, Great Barrington, Massachusetts

Goldratt, E.M. *(1990) Theory Of Constraints* North River Press, Great Barrington, Massachusetts, 1990

Gordon, Dr T. *(1988) Dr Thomas Gordon's Youth Effectiveness Training Instructor Guide* Effectiveness Training, Solana Beach, California

Gordon, T. *(1970) Parent Effectiveness Training*, Peter H. Wyden, New York

Gordon, T. *(1974) TE.T. Teacher Effectiveness Training, Peter H.* Wyden, New York

Gordon, T. *(1978) Leader Effectiveness Training (L.E.T.),* G. P. Putnam's Sons, New York

Gordon, T. *(1989) Teaching Children Self Discipline* Random House, New York

Gordon, T. *(1995) "Teaching People To Create Therapeutic Environments"* in Suhd, M. M. ed Positive Regard, Science and Behaviour Books, Palo Alto California, pp 301-336

Gottman, J.M. and Silver, N. *(1999) The Seven Principles For Making Marriage Work* Three Rivers Press, New York, 1999

Gottman, J.M. *(1999) The Marriage Clinic* W.W. Norton and Co., New York,

Gray, J. *(1992) Men Are From Mars, Women Are From Venus,* Thorsons, London

Gray, R. and Liotta, R. *(2012) "PTSD: Extinction, Reconsolidation and the Visual-Kinesthetic Dissociation Protocol"* http://home.comcast.net/~richardmgray/PTSDnVKDprepub.pdf

Green, L. and Campbell, J. *(2004) The Kiwi Effect* Avocado Press, Wellington, New Zealand, 2004

Greenberg, J. and Greenberg, H. *(1991) "Money Isn't Everything*" p 10-14 in *Sales And Marketing Management*, May 1991

Greenspan, M. *(1983) A New Approach to Women and Therapy,* McGraw-Hill, New York

Gross, ,J.J., Fredrickson, B.L. and Levenson, R.W. *(1994) "The psychophysiology of crying"* p 460-468 in Psychophysiology, Vol 31

Gross, D. *(1996) Forbes Greatest Business Stories Of All Time* John Wiley & Sons, New York,

Gross, J.J. *(1989) "Emotional expression in cancer onset and progression"* p 1239-1248 in Social Science and Medicine, Vol 12

Gurney, S. *(2003) "When The Flag Drops, It's Time To Rock"* p 27 in Symmetry: The Magazine For Subaru Enthusiasts, No. 15, Winter

Gurney, S. *(2003) "Gurney's Gossip*" Online Edition 31 March 2003 (http://www.gurneygears.com/gossip.htm)

Guzzo, R.A., and Katzell, R.A. *(1987) "Effects of Economic Incentives on Productivity: A Psychological View*" in Nalbantian, H.R. ed *Incentives, Co-operation and Risk Sharing: Economic and Psychological Perspectives on Employment Contracts* Rowman & Littlefield, Totowa, New Jersey

Haigh, L. *(1994) "Empowering Employees: Makes Dollars and Sense*" p 7-13 in *People and Performance*, Vol. 2 No. 2, June 1994

Haley. J. *(1973) Uncommon Therapy: The Psychiatric Techniques of Milton H. Erickson,* W.W. Norton, New York

Hall, E.T. *(1959) Silent Language,* Doubleday, New York

Hall, L.M. *(2000) "A Few Secrets About Wealth Building*" p 25-31 in *Anchor Point* journal, Vol 14, No. 4, April 2000

Hall, L.M., Bodenhammer, B., Bolstad, R.D. and Hamblett, M.H. *(1997) The Structure of Personality* Anglo American Book Company, Bancyfelin, Wales

Halliwell, E.M. and Ratey, J.J. *(1994) Driven To Distraction* Touchstone, New York, 1994

Handy, C. *(1996) Beyond Certainty* Arrow Books, London, 1996

Hansen, M.V. and Allen, R.G. *(2002) The One Minute Millionaire* Harmony, New York

Hatfield, E., Cacioppo, J. and Rapson, R. *(1994) Emotional Contagion* Cambridge University Press, Cambridge

Herzberg, F. *(1987) "Workers' Needs: The Same Around The World*" p 30 in

Industry Week, 21 September, 1987

Hess, E. *(1975) The Tell-Tale Eye,* Van Nostrand Reinhold, New York

Hinze, M., PhD, and Louise, M., PhD. *(1988) "The Effects of Therapeutic Touch and Acupressure on Experimentally-Induced Pain".* Thesis, University of Texas at Austin, UMI #8901377

Hischke, D. " *A definitional and structural investigation of matching perceptual predicates, mismatching perceptual predicates, and Milton-model matching."* In Dissertation Abstracts International 49(9) p 4005

Hoekelman, R.A. *(1975) Nurse-Physician Relationships,* in *American Journal ofNursing* (July), page 1151

Hornstein, H. A. *(1976) Cruelty and Kindness: A new look at aggression and altruism.* Prentice-Hall, Englewood Cliffs, New Jersey, 1976

Hutchinson, M.G. *(1985) Transforming Body Image,* The Crossing Press, Trumansburg, New York

Ivey, A. *(1972) Microcounselling: Interviewing Skills Manual,* Thomas, Springfield, Illinois

Ivey, A.E., Bradford Ivey, M., and Simek-Morgan, L. *(1996) Counseling And Psychotherapy* Allyn and Bacon, Boston

Jablensky, A., Sartorius, N., Ernberg, G., Anker, M., Korten, A., Cooper, J.E., Day, R., and Bertelsen, A., *(1992) "Schizophrenia: manifestations, incidence and course in different cultures. A World Health Organisation ten country study."* In Psychological Medicine, Suppliment 20, p 1-97

James, M. and Jongeward, D. *(1971) Born To Win,* Addison-Wesley Publishing, Reading

James, T. *(1995) "General Model For Behavioural Intervention"* in *Time Line Therapy® Practitioner Training* (manual. Version 3.1), Time Line Therapy™ Association, Honolulu, 1995

James, T. and Woodsmall, W. *(1988) Time Line Therapy and the Basis of Personality,* Meta Publications, Cupertino, California

Johnson, D.W. *(1972) Reaching Out,* Prentice Hall, Englewood Cliffs, New Jersey

Johnson, D.W. and Johnson, F. *(1975) Joining Together: Group Theory and Group Skills,* Prentice-Hall, Englewood Cliffs, New Jersey

Johnson, K. *(1994) Selling With NLP* Nicholas Brealey, London

Jones, E. *(1961) The Life And Work Of Sigmund Freud,* Basic Books, New York

Kasl, C.D. *(1990) Women, Sex and Addiction,* Mandarin, London

Kasl, C.D. *(1994) Many Roads, One Journey: Moving Beyond The Twelve Steps,* Harper and Row, San Francisco

Kasser, T. and Ryan, R.M. *(1993) "A Dark Side Of The American Dream: Correlates Of Financial Success As A Central Life Aspiration"* p 410-422 in *Journal of Personality and Social Psychology*, Vol 65, No. 2, 1993

Kasser, T. and Ryan, R.M. *(1996) "Further Examining The American Dream: Differential Correlates Of Intrinsic And Extrinsic Goals"* p 280-

287 in *Personality and Social Psychology Bulletin*, Vol 22, No. 3, 1996

Katz, J.H. *(1984) No Fairy Godmothers, No Magic Wands: The Healing Process After Rape,* R & E Publishers, Saratoga, California

Kaufman, R. *(1976) Identifying and Solving Problems. A Systems Approach,* University Associates, La Jolla, California

Kawasaki, G. *(1991) Selling The Dream*, Harper Collins, New York

Kelly, K. *(1999) New Rules For The New Economy* Fourth Estate, London

Kennedy, H. *(1984) Food Secrets of The Aborigines,* in *Omega Science Digest,* (July/August), pp. 86-89

King, M. *(1991) Whina*, Penguin, Auckland

Knight, S. *(1995) NLP At Work* Nicholas Brealey, London

Kohn, A. *(1998) "Challenging Behaviourist Dogma: Myths About Money and Motivation*" March/April 1998

Kohn, A. *(1993) Punished By Rewards* Houghton Mifflin, New York

Kohn, A., *(1986) No Contest*, Houghton Mifflin, Boston

Kopelowicz, A. and Liberman, R.P. *(1998) "Psychosocial Treatments for Schizophrenia"*, p 190-211 in Nathan, P.E. and Gorman, J.M. *A Guide to Treatments That Work,* Oxford University Press, New York

Korzybski, A. *(1994) Science and Sanity*, Institute of General Semantics, Englewood, New Jersey

Kotter, J.P. *(1996) Leading Change*, Harvard Business School, Boston

Koziey, R, and McLeod, G.*(1987) Visual Kinesthetic Dissociation in Treatment of Victims of Rape* in *Professional Psychology; Research and Practice,* 18(3); 276-282

Kubler-Ross, Dr E. *(1980) On Death and Dying,* MacMillan, New York

Kuhl, J., Goschke, T., and Kazén-Saad, M. A Theory of Self-Regulation. Personality, Assessment and Experimental Analysis Volume 1: Theory, Universität Osnabrück, Osnabrück, Germany, 1991

Kuhl, J., Goschke, T., and Kazén-Saad, M. *(1991) A Theory of Self-Regulation. Personality, Assessment and Experimental Analysis* Volume 1: Theory, Universität Osnabrück, Osnabrück, Germany, 1991

Laborde, G. *(1987) Influencing With Integrity* Syntony Publishing, Mountain View, California

Labott, S.M. and Martin, R.B. *(1987) "The stress moderating effects of weeping and humour"* p 159-164 in Journal of Human Stress, Vol 13

Labott, S.M., Ahleman, S., Wolever, M.E. and Martin, R.B. *(1990) "The physiological and psychological effects of the expression and inhibition of emotion"* p 182-189 in Behavioural Medicine, Vol 16

Lader, M. *(1975) The Psychophysiology ofMental Illness,* Routledge and Kegan Paul, London

Lambert, M. and Bergin, A. *(1994) "The Effectiveness of Psychotherapy"* in Bergin, A. and and Garfield, S. *Handbook of Psychotherapy and Behaviour Change* Wiley, New York

Lange, A. J. and Jakubowski, P. *(1978) Responsible Assertive Behaviour,*

Research Press, Champaign, Illinois
Legge, J. *(1990) Chaos Theory and Business Planning* Schwartz & Wilkinson, Melbourne
Leibrich, J; Paulin, J & Ransom, R *(1995). Hitting home. Men speak about abuse of women partners.* New Zealand Department of Justice, Wellington.
Lepore, D. and Cohen, O. *(1999) Deming And Goldratt: The Theory Of Constraints And The System Of Profound Knowledge* North River Press, Great Barrington, Massachusetts
Lerner, H.G. *(1985) The Dance of Anger,* Harper & Row, New York
Leshan Li, *(1999) Action Theory and Cognitive Psychology in Industrial Design* published on the Internet
Levinson, J.C. and Hanley, P.R.J. *(2005) The Guerrilla Marketing Revolution, Piatkus, London,*
Locke, E.A. and Latham, G.P. *(1990) "Work Motivation and Satisfaction: Light At The End Of The Tunnel*" in *Psychological Science* 1, p 240-246
Loiselle, F. *(1985) The effect of eye placement on orthographic memorization* Faculté des sciences sociales, Université de Moncton
Ludbrook, R. *(2003) Counselling and the Law*, New Zealand Association of Counsellors, Hamilton
Luria, A.R. *(1969) The Mind of a Mneumonist,* Penguin, Harmondsworth, Middlesex
Luthans, F. *(1988) Real Managers*, Ballinger Publishing Company, Pensacola, Florida
Lynch, D. and Kordis, P. *(1988) Strategy of the Dolphin*, Fawcett Columbine, New York
Macrae, J. *(1988) Therapeutic Touch: A Practical Guide,* Alfred A. Knopf, New York
Macroy, T.D. *(1978) "Linguistic surface structures in family interaction"* in Dissertation Abstracts International, 40 (2) 926-B, Utah State University, 133 pp, Order = 7917967, 1978
Makower, J. *(1994) Beyond The Bottom Line* Simon and Schuster, New York
Malloy, T. E.; Mitchell, C., Gordon, O. E. *(1987) "Training cognitive strategies underlying intelligent problem solving"*. In Journal of Perceptual and Motor Skills, No. 64, p. 1039-1046
Malloy, T.E., *(1989) Cognitive strategies and a classroom procedure for teaching spelling. Dept. of Psychology*, University of Utah
Mandela, N. *(1994) Long Walk To Freedom,* Abacus, London
Mann, L., Beswick, G., Allouache, P. and Ivey, M. *(1989) "Decision workshops for the improvement of decisionmaking: Skills and confidence"* in Journal of Counselling and Development, 67, p 478-481
Manthei, M. *(1981) Positively Me,* Methuen, Auckland
Manz, C.C. and Sims, H.P. *(1995) Business Without Bosses* John Wiley &

Sons, New York, 1995
Marcia, J.E. *(1980) "Identity in Adolescence"* in Adelson, J. ed Handbook of Adolescent Psychology Wiley, New York, 1980
Marlatt,G. and Gordon, J. *(1985) Relapse Prevention: Maintenance Strategies in the Treatment of Addictive Behaviours* Guilford, New York
Marsh, A. *(1984) "Smoking; Habit or Choice?"* in Population Trends, 37: 20
Maslow, A. *(1971) The Farther Reaches of Human Nature* Viking, New York.
Maturana, H.R. and Varela, F.J. *(1992) The Tree Of Knowledge* Shambhala, Boston
Mayer, J.E. and Timms, N. *(1970) The Client Speaks - Working Class Impressions of Casework* Routledge and Kegan Paul, London
McClintock, C. G. *(1974) "Development of social motives in Anglo-American and Mexican-American children*" p 348-354 in *Journal of Personality and Social Psychology*, No. 29, 1974
McCracken, J. *(2000) "Creating Cooperative Classrooms"* p 48-51 in Trancescript, No. 20, June, 2000, Transformations, Christchurch
McDermott, I. And O'Connor, J. *(1996) NLP And Health* Thorsons, London
McFarlane, G. *(1984) Alexander Fleming: The Man and the Myth.* Oxford: Oxford University Press
McKay, M. and Fanning, F. *(1987) Self Esteem,* New Harbinger Publications, Oakland, California
McKenna, C. *(1998) Powerful Communication Skills*, Career Press, Franklin Lakes, New Jersey
McMaster, K. and Swain, F. *(1989) A Private Affair? Stopping Men's Violence to Women,* G.P. Books, Wellington
McMaster, M. and Grinder, J. *(1993) Precision, A New Approach To Communication,* Grinder, Delozier and Associates, Scotts Valley, California
McMaster, M.D. *(1986) Performance Management* Metamorphous, Portland, Oregon,
Meece, J.L., Wigfield, A. and Eccles, J.S. *(1990) "Predictors of Math Anxiety and its Influence on Young Adolescents' Course Enrollment Intentions and Performance in Mathmatics*" in *Journal of Educational Psychology* 82, p 60-70
Mehrabian, A. *(1971). Silent messages.* Wadsworth, Belmont, California
Menikheim, M. *(1979) Communication Patterns of Women and Nurses,* in Jervik, D.K. and Martinson, I.M. (eds) *Women in Stress - A Nursing Perspective,* Appleton-Century-Crofts, New York
Menzies Lyth, I. *(1988) Containing Anxiety in Institutions,* Free Associations, London, 1988. pp 43-85.
Metge, J. *(1986) In and Out of Touch,* Victoria University Press, Wellington
Metge, J. and Kinloch, P. *(1984) Talking Past Each Other,* Victoria

University Press, Wellington
Meyer, J.E. *(1970) Client Speaks: Working Class Impressions Of Casework* Intervale Publishing, Intervale, New Hampshire
Milgram, S. *(1974) Obedience To Authority,* Harper and Row, New York
Miller, G., Galanter, E. and Pribram, K. *(1960) Plans And The Structure Of Behaviour*, Henry Holt & Co., New York
Miller, K., Zener, A., Burch, N., and Gordon, Dr T. *(1988) Dr Thomas Gordon's Teacher Effectiveness Training Instructor Guide* Effectiveness Training, Solana Beach, California
Miller, W. *(1985) "Motivation for treatment: a review with special emphasis on alcoholism."* In Psychological Bulletin, Vol 98 (1), p 84-107
Ministerial Committee of Inquiry Into Violence *(1987), 'Report of Ministerial Committee of Inquiry Into Violence'* (The Roper Report) Wellington: Department of Justice
Ministry of Health *(2012) Suicide Facts: Deaths and intentional self-harm hospitalisations 2010* New Zealand Government, Wellington
Ministry of Women's Affairs *(2002) "Towards an Action Plan for New Zealand Women"*, New Zealand Government, Wellington
Moine, D. *(1981) "A psycholinguistic study of the patterns of persuasion used by successful salespeople"* in Dissertation Abstracts International, 42 (5), 2135-B, University of Oregon, 271pp, Order = 8123499
Molden, D. *(1996) Managing With The Power Of NLP* Pitman, London
Montagu, A. *(1971) Touching,* Harper & Row, New York
Moreno, J. *(1977) Psychodrama: First Volume* Beacon House, New York
Morgan, J.M. and Liker, J.K. *(2006) The Toyota Product development System: Integrating People, Process and Technology*, Productivity Press, New York, 2006
Morris, D. *(1977) Manwatching,* Abrams, New York
Mosley, L. *(1986) The Real Walt Disney*, Grafton, London
Munro, A., Manthei, B. and Small, J. *(1988) Counselling: The Skills of Problem Solving,* Longman Paul, Auckland
Muss, D. *(1991) "A New Technique For Treating Post-Traumatic Stress Disorder"* in *British Journal of Clinical Psychology*, 30, p 91-92
Muss, Dr D. *(1991) The Trauma Trap,* Doubleday, London
Myers, D. *(1983) Social Psychology,* McGraw-Hill, Auckland
Nairn, M. and Nairn, R. *(1981) The Racism of Economics and the Economics of Racism,* in Davis, P. (ed), *New Zealand Labour Perspectives: The Challenge of the Third Depression,* Ross, Wellington
Neimeyer, R.A. ed *(2002) Meaning Reconstruction & The Experience Of Loss* American Psychological Association, Washington
Newbold, G. *(1985) The Big Huey* William Collins, Auckland
Nuttin, J. *(1984) Motivation, Planning and Action* LEA, Hillsdale, New Jersey
O'Connor, J. and Prior, R. *(1995) Successful Selling With NLP* Thorsons,

London
O'Connor, J. and Seymour, J. *(1990) Introducing Neuro Linguistic Programming,* Mandala, London
O'Donohue W, Buchanan JA, and Fisher JE. *(2000) Characteristics of empirically supported treatments"* p 69-74 in the Journal of Psychotherapy Practice and Research 2000 Spring; 9(2)
Palubeckas, A.J. *"Rapport in the therapeutic relationship and its relationship to pacing"* Dissertation Abstracts International 42(6), 2543-B 2544-B, Boston University School of Education, 127pp, Order = 8126743
Patterson, K., Grenny, J., Maxfield, D., McMillan, R. and Switzler, A. *(2008) "Influencer",* McGraw-Hill, New York, 2008
Pavlov, I.P. *(1927) Conditioned Reflexes: An Account Of The Physiological Activities Of The Cerebral Cortex* Oxford University Press, London
Pease, A. *(1990) Body Language,* Camel Publishing, Avalon Beach, New South Wales
Peck, S., RN, PHD. *(1998) "The Efficacy of Therapeutic Touch for Improving Functional Ability in Elders With Degenerative Arthritis".* Nursing Science Quarterly, 11:3
Perls, F.S. *(1969) Gestalt Therapy Verbatim,* Real People Press, Moab, Utah
Peters, T.J. and Waterman, R.H. *(1982) In Search of Excellence* Harper & Row, New York
Pomerantz, E. *(2001) "Parent & Child Socialization: Implications for development of depressive syndromes"* p 510-525 in Journal of family Psychology, Number 15
Porras, J., Emery, S. and Thompson, M. *(2007) Success Built To Last* Wharton School Publishing, Upper Saddle River, New Jersey, 2007
Powers, E. and Witmer, H *(1951) An Experiment in the Prevention of Delinquency - The Cambridge-Somerville Youth Study* Columbia University Press, New York
Prochaska, J.O., Norcross, J.C. and Diclemente, C.C. *(1994) Changing For Good,* William Morrow and Company, New York
Ragge, K. *(1998) The Real AA: Behind the Myth of 12 Step Recovery,* See Sharp Press, Tucson
Reckert, H.W. *(1994) "Test anxiety... removed by anchoring in just one session?"* in *Multimind,* NLP Aktuell, No 6, November/December 1994
Bandler, R. and Grinder, J *(1979) Frogs Into Princes* Real People Press, Moab, Utah
Renesch, J. ed *(1992) New Traditions In Business* Berrett-Koehler, San Francisco
Richardson, A.J. and Montgomery, P. *(2005) "The Oxford-Durham Study: A Randomized, Controlled Trial of Dietary Supplementation With Fatty Acids in Children With Developmental Coordination Disorder"* page 1360-1366 in Vol. 115 No. 5, Pediatrics, May 2005
Rindfleisch, A., Burroughs, J. and Denton, F. *(1997) "Family Structure,*

Materialism and Compulsive Consumption," p 312-325 in the *Journal of Consumer Research*, Vol 23, No. 4, March 1997

Ritchie, J. and Ritchie, J. *(1981) Spare the Rod,* Allen and Unwin, Sydney

Rizzolatti, G., Fadiga, L., Gallese, V. and Fogassi, L. *(1996) "Premotor cortex and the recognition of motor actions"* p 131-141 in Cognitive Brain Research, No. 3

Rizzolatti,G. and Arbib, M.A. *(1998) "Language within our grasp"* p 188-194 in Trends in Neuroscience, No. 21

Robbins, A. *(1988) Unlimited Power,* Simon & Schuster, London

Robinson, D.Gaines and Robinson, J.C. *(1995) Performance Consulting: Moving Beyond Training* Berret-Koehler, San Francisco

Roddick, A. *(2008) Business As Unusual* Anita Roddick Publications, Chichester, England

Rogers, C. *(1965)* in Shostrum, E. (ed), *Three Approaches to Psychotherapy* (film number 1), Psychological Films, Orange, California

Rogers, C.R. *(1980) A Way of Being,* Houghton Mifflin, Boston, page 150

Roos, T. *(2002) Mental Coaching*, Trafford Publishing, Victoria, Canada

Rosa, L., Rosa, E., Sarner, L., Barrett, S *(1998) "A Close Look at Therapeutic Touch". Journal of the American Medical Association*, April 1, 1998; 279(13):1005–1010.

Rose, C. *(1985) Accelerated Learning,* Accelerated Learning Systems Ltd, Aylesbury, Buckinghamshire, England

Rosen, R.H. *(1992) "The Anatomy of a Healthy Company"* p 108-120 in Renesch, J. ed *New Traditions In Business* Berrett-Koehler, San Francisco, 1992

Rosenberg, M. *(1999) Nonviolent Communication: A Language of Compassion* Puddle dancer, Del Mar, California

Rossi, E.L. *(1986) The Psychobiology of Mind-Body Healing, W.W.* Norton & Co, New York

Rossi, E.L. ed *(1980) The Collected Papers of Milton H. Erickson on Hypnosis: Volume IV, Innovative Hypnotherapy*, Irvington, New York, 1980

Rowland, Diana *(1993) Japanese Business Etiquette,* Warner Books, London

Sandhu, D.S., Reeves, T.G. and Portes, P.R. *(1993) "Cross-cultural counseling and neurolinguistic mirroring with Native American adolescents"* p 106-118 in Journal of Multicultural Counselling and Development, Vol 21, No. 2, April

Sanford, L. and Donovan, M.E. *(1994) Women and Self Esteem,* Anchor Press/Doubleday, Garden City, New York

Satir, V. *(1993) "Everybody Has A Dream"* p 204-206 in Canfield, J. and Hansen, M.V. *Chicken Soup For The Soul* Health Communications Inc, Deerfield Beach, Florida

Satir, V. and Baldwin, M. *(1983) Satir Step By Step,* Science and Behaviour Books, Palo Alto, California
Schachter, S. *(1982) "Recidivism and self-cure of smoking and obesity"* in American Psychologist 37: P 436-444
Schaef, A.W. *(1985) Women's Reality,* Harper & Row, San Francisco
Schaef, A.W. *(1988) When Society Becomes An Addict,* Harper and Row, San Francisco
Schutz, W. *(1975) Elements of Encounter,* Bantam, New York
Semler, R. *(1993) Maverick!* Century, London, 1993
Shaffer. J.B.P. and Galinsky. M.D. *(1974) Models of Group Therapy and Sensitivity Training,* Prentice-Hall, Englewood Cliffs, New Jersey
Shaw, G.B. *(1980) Man And Superman* Penguin, Harmondsworth, 1980
Shostrom, E. (Ed). *(1965) Three Approaches to Psychotherapy* Film No I (1965). Psychological Films, Orange, California
Siegal, B.S. *(1988) Love, Medicine and Miracles,* Arrow Books, London
Simons, D.J. and Levin, D.T. *(1998) "Failure to detect changes to people during real-world interaction"* p 644 in Psychonomic Bulletin And Review, Vol. 4
Slavik, D.J. *(2003) "Keeping your eyes on the prize : outcome versus process focused social comparisons and counterfactual thinking"* Thesis (Ph. D.), University of Arkansas, Fayetteville
Freeman, M. as Snell, M. *(1992) New Mens Magazines* Dissertation for M.Sc Econ, Media Studies, University of Wales, Cardiff
Snitow, A., Stansell, C. and Thompson, S. *(1984)* (eds) *Desire. The Politics of Sexuality,* Virago, London
Solter, A.J. *(1990) The Aware Baby,* Shining Star, Goleta, California
Spender, D. *(1982) Invisible Women: The Schooling Scandal.* Writers and Readers, London
Spoonley, P. *(1988) Racism and Ethnicity,* Oxford University, Auckland
Steiner, C.M. *(1974) Scripts People Live,* Bantam, New York
Stevens, J.0. *(1971) Awareness: Exploring Experimenting Experiencing,* Real People Press, Moab, Utah
Stewart, 1. and Joines, V. *(1987)* TA. *Today,* Lifespan Publishing, Nottingham, England
Stirling, R *(1990) The Dangers of Dieting,* in the *Listener,* October 1-7, pp. 10-18.
Sturgeon, T. *(1989) The Golden Helix,* Carroll & Graf Publishers, New York
Swack, J.A., *(1992) "A Study of Initial Response and Reversion Rates of Subjects Treated With The Allergy technique"*, in *Anchor Point*, Vol 6, No2, Feb 1992
Sweet, G. *(1989) The Advantage of Being Useless,* Dunmore Press, Palmerston North
Tanner Pascale, R. *(1990) Managing On The Edge* Simon & Schuster, New York

Tauroa, H. and Tauroa, P. *(1986) Te Marae,* Reed Methuen, Auckland
Thalgott, M.R. *(1986) "Anchoring: A "Cure" For Epy"* p 347-352 in *Academic Therapy*, Volume 21, No 3, January 1986
Thayer, R.E. *(1996) The Origin of Everyday Moods*, Oxford University Press, New York, 1996
The Holy Bible: Revised Standard Version (1973) Collins, New York
Gordon, D. and Meyers-Anderson, M. *(1981) Phoenix: Therapeutic Patterns of Milton H. Erickson* Meta Publications, Capitola, California
Thomas, K. *(1987) "General practice consultations: is there any point in being positive?"* in British Medical Journal Vol 294, p 1200-1202
Thomas, K.B. *(1994) "The placebo in general practice"* p 1066-1067 in Lancet, Vol 344 (8929) October 15
Thomas, K.W. and Schmidt, W.H. *(1976) "A Survey of Managerial Interests with Respect to Conflict"* in *Academy of Management Journal*, June 1976
Tichy, N. and Charan, R. *(1989) "Speed, Simplicity, Self-Confidence: An Interview with Jack Welch."* P 112-121 in Harvard Business Review, Number 5, September-October 1989
Timpany, L. *(2005) "Building Outcome Bridges"* p 3-4 in Trance Script 36, October 2005, Transformations, Christchurch, 2005
Tracy, B. *(2004) Time Power: A Proven System for Getting More Done in Less Time Than You Ever Thought Possible* Amacom, New York
Trimpey, J. *(1996) Rational Recovery,* Simon & Schuster, New York
Ury, W. *(1991) Getting Past No,* Century Business, London
Van Lawick-Goodall, J. *(1967) My Friends the Wild Chimpanzees.* Washington D.C.: National Geographic Society
Vingerhoets, A.J.J.M. and Scheirs, J.G.M. *(2001) "Crying and Health"*, p 227-247 in Vingerhoets, A.J.J.M. and Cornelius, R.R. *Adult Crying: A Biopsychosocial Approach* Brunner-Routledge, Hove, East Sussex
Wager, S. MD and Kunz, D. *(1996) A Doctor's Guide to Therapeutic Touch*, Perigee, New York
Waldegrave, C. and Coventry, R. *(1987) Poor New Zealand,* Platform Publishing, Wellington
Wainwright, M. *(2005) "E-mails Pose Threat to IQ"* The Guardian, 22/04/2005
Walker, R. *(1989) Maori Identity,* in Novitz. D. and Willmott, B. eds. *Culture and Identity in New Zealand,* Government Printing Office, Wellington, pp. 35-52
Wall, B. Solum, R. and Sobol, M., *(1992) The Visionary Leader* Prima, Rockman, California, 1992
Watkins, M. and Rosegrant, S. *(2001) Breakthrough International Negotiation* Jossey-Bass, San Francisco
Watson, C. and Hoffman, R. *(1996) "Managers as Negotiat*ors" in *Leadership Quarterly*, 7(1), 1996

Weeks, D., *(1994) The Eight Essential Steps To Conflict Resolution,* G.P. Putnam's Sons, New York

Weisbord, M.R. and Janoff, S., *(1995) Future Search*, Berrett-Koehler, San Francisco, 1995

Weisbord, M.R. ed, *(1992) Discovering Common Ground,* Berret-Koehler, San Francisco

Wheatley, M.J. *(1994) Leadership and the New Science* Berrett-Koehler, San Francisco

Weaver, W. and Shannon, C.E. (1963). The Mathematical Theory of Communication. Univ. of Illinois Press.

Whyte, W.F. and Whyte, K.K. (1991) Making *Mondragon* ILR Press, New York

Williams, H.W. *(1985) A Dictionary of the Maori Language* PD Hasselberg, Wellington

Williams, J.H.G., Whiten, A., Suddendorf, T. and Perrett,D.I. *(2001) "Imitation, mirror neurons and autism"* p 287-295 in Neuroscience and Biobehavioural Review, No 25

Williams, J.H.G., Whiten, A., Suddendorf, T. and Perrett,D.I. *(2001) "Imitation, mirror neurons and autism*" p 287-295 in *Neuroscience and Biobehavioural Review*, No 25, 2001

Williams, P. and Williams, R. *(2003) How To Be Like Women Of Influence* Health Communications Inc., Deerfield Beach, Florida

Williams, T. and McMaster, K.*(1984) Anger Management: A Course For Aggressive Men,* in *New Zealand Social Work journal, vol.* 9, no. 2, pp. 2-7

Wilson, G.D., and McLaughlin, C. *(2001) The Science of Love* Fusion Press, London

Wirth, D. MS, JD. *(1990) "The Effect of Non-Contact Therapeutic Touch on the Healing Rate of Full Thickness Dermal Wounds".* Subtle Energies, Vol 1, No 1

Wirth, D., MS, JD, and Cram, J., PhD. *(1993) "Multi-Site Electromyographic Analysis of Non-Contact Therapeutic Touch*". International Journal of Psychosomatics, Vol 40,

Wiseman, R. *(2009) 59 Seconds: Think A Little, Change A Lot*. London: Macmillan,

Wood, J., Perunovic, E. W., & Lee, J. *(2009). Positive Self-Statements: Power for Some, Peril for Others.* Psychological Science (DOI: 10.1111/j.1467-9280.2009.02370.x)

Wyckoff, H. ed *(1976) Love, Therapy & Politics* Grove Press, New York

Yapko, M.,*(1981) The Effects of Matching Primary Representational System Predicates on Hypnotic Relaxation,* in the *American Journal of Clinical Hypnosis,* 23, pp. 169-175

Yapko, M.D. *(1992) Hypnosis and the Treatment of Depressions*, Brunner/Mazel, New York

Yapko. M., *(1981) "The Effects of Matching Primary Representational System Predicates on Hypnotic Relaxation."* in the *American Journal of Clinical Hypnosis*, 23, p169-175

Yunupingu, M. *(1994) 'Yothu Yindi - Finding the Balance'* p 1-11 in H. Semmler, ed. *Voices from the Land: 1993 Boyer Lectures*, Sydney: ABC Books

Zaiss, C. and Gordon, T. *(1993) Sales Effectiveness Training* Penguin, New York

Zilbergeld, B. *(1983) The Shrinking of America,* Little Brown & Co,Boston

Zimbardo, F. *(1981) Shyness,* Pan Books, London

Znoj, H.J.*(1997) "When remembering the lost spouse hurts too much: First results with a newly developed observer measure for tears and crying related coping behaviour"* p 337-152 in Vingerhoets, A.J.J.M., Van Bussel, F.J., and Boelhouwer, A.J.W. eds *The (Non)Expression Of Emotions In Health And Disease* Tilburg University Press, Tilberg, Netherlands,

Important
Owners of this book can download it in PDF form from

www.transformations.net.nz/tcbook.html

Transforming Communication: Index

More Information?

The Rapport Based Family, The Rapport Based Organisation, Creating a Cooperative World, and Transforming Communication are all texts based on the same model, taught in Transforming Communication . Creating a Cooperative World is published in German as Für eine kooperative Welt and is available at http://www.bod.de/index.php?id=1132&objk_id=91773
The Rapport Based Family is also published and used with permission by the New Zealand Peace Foundation. It is available in Russian from Института НЛП, Москва (http://www.institutnlp.ru/) and in Japanese as "NLP Coaching For Parents", from Shunjusha Publishing (www.shunjusha.co.jp/)NLP子育てコーチング—親の信頼がこどもを伸ばす [単行本] and in Chinese as **默契之家：為孩子的幸福投資** (http://www.ebookdynasty.net/Authors/RichardBolstad/indexEN.html). from eBook Dynasty. Transforming Communication is available in Polish from Metamorfoza http://relaksacyjna.pl/komunikacja-transformujaca

Would You Like To Be An Instructor Of Transforming Communication?

- ✓ **Train your colleagues so they understand the skills you're using.**
- ✓ **Become a leader in your organisation or community.**
- ✓ **Deepen your communication skills, and get more results you want.**
- ✓ **Open up new career options as a trainer.**

There are three steps to become a Transforming Communication Instructor

1. **Transforming Communication Basic Training**
2. **NLP Practitioner Certification**
3. **Transforming Communication Instructor Training**

At The 18 Day International NLP Practitioner Certification You Will Learn How To:

- Deepen your rapport skills and your ability to match sensory systems.
- SPECIFY and help others SPECIFY goals, and place them in the future so that they are guaranteed to happen.
- Identify and predict the decisionmaking and thinking processes that others use, by observing precise body language changes. Make the perfect next move to match both your style and others' styles.
- Become powerfully persuasive, convincing and inspiring others on both a conscious and unconscious level.
- Use others objections and disagreements as useful information to develop solutions which work for both of you, using skilful reframing techniques.
- Work with another's style of thinking, using precision questions and statements to help them clarify what they actually want and plan action successfully.
- Develop your anchoring skills so as to enter, or help someone else enter, a state of high motivation and confidence, or a state of deep relaxation, at will in any situation.
- Use and teach others more of the skills of memory and accelerated learning.
- Eliminate stressful feelings, guilt, fears, depression, procrastination and other internal problems that have held you back from ultimate success.
- Take charge of the direction of your life, using effective, permanent personal empowerment processes.

At The 9 Day Transforming Communication Instructor Training, You will Learn How To:

- ♦successfully market seminars to people you want to teach; in business, education, parenting or open groups.
- ♦teach in ways that inspire others to dramatically improve their professional and personal relationships.
- ♦create a co-operative group environment that makes teaching and learning easy.
- ♦use NLP language patterns to resolve barriers to learning before they arise.
- ♦easily respond to teaching challenges such as handling questions, and giving feedback.
- ♦apply the skills from your NLP training (anchoring, metaphor, rapport skills etc) to teach with charisma.
- ♦become a model of the co-operative relationship skills from the Transforming Communication Basic Seminar.

Can I be a Trainer?

At the end of her Instructor Training, Dr Brenda Kaye wrote; *"In one week I've gone from being unable to imagine myself instructing comfortably, to being completely relaxed and at ease in front of a small group."* And only three months later, Brenda was getting written feedback from her first course participants saying that her course... *"completely changed my life!", "gave a whole new insight into how we treat others", "is an essential aid to relationships", and "is a definite must"*

.

Contact us at +64-9-478-4895 learn@transformations.net.nz for seminar information now!

www.transformations.net.nz

Made in the USA
San Bernardino, CA
17 February 2018